DATE DUE

			PRINTED IN U.S.A.

SOMETHING ABOUT THE AUTHOR

ISSN 0276-816X

SOMETHING ABOUT THE AUTHOR

**Facts and Pictures about Authors
and Illustrators of Books for Young People**

EDITED BY
ANNE COMMIRE

VOLUME 56

Gale Research Inc.
Book Tower • Detroit, Michigan 48226

Editor: Anne Commire

Associate Editors: Agnes Garrett, Helga P. McCue

Senior Assistant Editor: Dianne H. Anderson

Assistant Editors: Elisa Ann Ferraro, Eunice L. Petrini, Linda Shedd

Sketchwriters: Marguerite Feitlowitz, Mimi H. Hutson, Dieter Miller

Researcher: Catherine Ruello

Editorial Assistants: Catherine Coray, Joanne J. Ferraro, Marja T. Hiltunen,
Deborah Klezmer, June Lee, Karen Walker

Permissions Assistant: Susan Pfanner

Production Manager: Mary Beth Trimper

External Production Associate: Laura McKay

External Production Assistant: Anthony J. Scolaro

Internal Production Supervisor: Laura Bryant

Internal Production Associate: Louise Gagné

Internal Production Assistants: Shelly Andrews, Sharana Wier

Art Director: Arthur Chartow

Special acknowledgment is due to the members of the *Something about the Author Autobiography Series* staff
who assisted in the preparation of this volume.

Contents

Introduction

As the only ongoing reference series that deals with the lives and works of authors and illustrators of children's books, *Something about the Author (SATA)* is a unique source of information. The *SATA* series includes not only well-known authors and illustrators whose books are most widely read, but also those less prominent people whose works are just coming to be recognized. *SATA* is often the only readily available information source for less well-known writers or artists. You'll find *SATA* informative and entertaining whether you are:

— a student in junior high school (or perhaps one to two grades higher or lower) who needs information for a book report or some other assignment for an English class;

— a children's librarian who is searching for the answer to yet another question from a young reader or collecting background material to use for a story hour;

— an English teacher who is drawing up an assignment for your students or gathering information for a book talk;

— a student in a college of education or library science who is studying children's literature and reference sources in the field;

— a parent who is looking for a new way to interest your child in reading something more than the school curriculum prescribes;

— an adult who enjoys children's literature for its own sake, knowing that a good children's book has no age limits.

Scope

In *SATA* you will find detailed information about authors and illustrators who span the full time range of children's literature, from early figures like John Newbery and L. Frank Baum to contemporary figures like Judy Blume and Richard Peck. Authors in the series represent primarily English-speaking countries, particularly the United States, Canada, and the United Kingdom. Also included, however, are authors from around the world whose works are available in English translation, for example: from France, Jean and Laurent De Brunhoff; from Italy, Emanuele Luzzati; from the Netherlands, Jaap ter Haar; from Germany, James Krüss; from Norway, Babbis Friis-Baastad; from Japan, Toshiko Kanzawa; from the Soviet Union, Kornei Chukovsky; from Switzerland, Alois Carigiet, to name only a few. Also appearing in *SATA* are Newbery medalists from Hendrik Van Loon (1922) to Paul Fleischman (1989). The writings represented in *SATA* include those created intentionally for children and young adults as well as those written for a general audience and known to interest younger readers. These writings cover the spectrum from picture books, humor, folk and fairy tales, animal stories, mystery and adventure, science fiction and fantasy, historical fiction, poetry and nonsense verse, to drama, biography, and nonfiction.

Information Features

In *SATA* you will find full-length entries that are being presented in the series for the first time. This volume, for example, marks the first full-length appearance of Judy Taylor Hough, Andrew Lloyd Webber, George Lucas, Barry Moser, Michael C. Thaler, Laurel Trivelpiece, and Elie Wiesel.

Obituaries have been included in *SATA* since Volume 20. An Obituary is intended not only as a death notice but also as a concise view of a person's life and work. Obituaries may appear for persons who have entries in earlier *SATA* volumes, as well as for people who have not yet appeared in the series. In this volume Obituaries mark the recent deaths of Richard Chase, Adele DeLeeuw, Eleanor Estes, Harlow Rockwell, Robert J. Unstead, and others.

Revised Entries

Since Volume 25, each *SATA* volume also includes newly revised and updated entries for a selection of *SATA* listees (usually four to six) who remain of interest to today's readers and who have been active enough to require extensive revision of their earlier biographies. For example, when Beverly Cleary first appeared in *SATA* Volume 2, she was the author of twenty-one books for children and young adults and the recipient of numerous awards. By the time her updated sketch appeared in Volume 43 (a span of fifteen years), this creator of the indefatigable Ramona Quimby and other memorable characters had produced a dozen new titles and garnered nearly fifty additional awards, including the 1984 Newbery Medal.

The entry for a given biographee may be revised as often as there is substantial new information to provide. In this volume, look for revised entries on Bianca Bradbury, Elizabeth Coatsworth, Virginia Hamilton, and Alvin Schwartz.

Illustrations

While the textual information in *SATA* is its primary reason for existing, photographs and illustrations not only enliven the text but are an integral part of the information that *SATA* provides. Illustrations and text are wedded in such a special way in children's literature that artists and their works naturally occupy a prominent place among *SATA*'s listees. The illustrators that you'll find in the series include such past masters of children's book illustration as Randolph Caldecott, Walter Crane, Arthur Rackham, and Ernest H. Shepard, as well as such noted contemporary artists as Maurice Sendak, Edward Gorey, Tomie de Paola, and Margot Zemach. There are Caldecott medalists from Dorothy Lathrop (the first recipient in 1938) to Stephen Gammell (the latest winner in 1989); cartoonists like Charles Schulz ("Peanuts"), Walt Kelly ("Pogo"), Hank Ketcham ("Dennis the Menace"), and Georges Rémi ("Tintin"); photographers like Jill Krementz, Tana Hoban, Bruce McMillan, and Bruce Curtis; and filmmakers like Walt Disney, Alfred Hitchcock, and Steven Spielberg.

In more than a dozen years of recording the metamorphosis of children's literature from the printed page to other media, *SATA* has become something of a repository of photographs that are unique in themselves and exist nowhere else as a group, particularly many of the classics of motion picture and stage history and photographs that have been specially loaned to us from private collections.

Indexes

Each *SATA* volume provides a cumulative index in two parts: first, the Illustrations Index, arranged by the name of the illustrator, gives the number of the volume and page where the illustrator's work appears in the current volume as well as all preceding volumes in the series; second, the Author Index gives the number of the volume in which a person's biographical sketch, Brief Entry, or Obituary appears in the current volume as well as all preceding volumes in the series. These indexes also include references to authors and illustrators who appear in *Yesterday's Authors of Books for Children* (described in detail below). Beginning with Volume 36, the *SATA* Author Index provides cross-references to authors who are included in *Children's Literature Review*.

Starting with Volume 42, you will also find cross-references to authors who are included in the *Something about the Author Autobiography Series* (described in detail below).

Character Index

If you're like many readers, the names of fictional characters may pop more easily into your mind than the names of the authors or illustrators who created them: Snow White, Charlotte the Spider, the Cat in the Hat, Peter Pan, Mary Poppins, Winnie-the-Pooh, Brer Rabbit, Little Toot, Charlie Bucket, Lassie, Rip Van Winkle, Bartholomew Cubbins—the list could go on and on. But who invented them? Now these characters, and several thousand others, can lead you to the *SATA* and *YABC* entries on the lives and works of their creators.

First published in Volume 50, the Character Index provides a broad selection of characters from books and other media—movies, plays, comic strips, cartoons, etc.—created by listees who have appeared in all the published volumes of *SATA* and *YABC*. This index gives the character name, followed by a *"See"* reference indicating the name of the creator and the number of the *SATA* or *YABC* volume in which the creator's bio-bibliographical entry can be found. As new *SATA* volumes are prepared, additional characters are included in the cumulative Character Index and published annually in *SATA*. (The cumulative Illustrations and Author Indexes still appear in each *SATA* volume.)

It would be impossible for the Character Index to include every important character created by *SATA* and *YABC* listees. (Several hundred important characters might be taken from Dickens alone, for example.) Therefore, the *SATA* editors have selected those characters that are best known and thus most likely to interest *SATA* users. Realizing that some of your favorite characters may not appear in this index, the editors invite you to suggest additional names. With your help, the editors hope to make the Character Index a uniquely useful reference tool for you.

What a *SATA* Entry Provides

Whether you're already familiar with the *SATA* series or just getting acquainted, you will want to be aware of the kind of information that an entry provides. In every *SATA* entry the editors attempt to give as complete a picture of the person's life and work as possible. In some cases that full range of information may simply be unavailable, or a biographee may choose not to reveal complete personal details. The information that the editors attempt to provide in every entry is arranged in the following categories:

1. The "head" of the entry gives

   —the most complete form of the name,
   —any part of the name not commonly used, included in parentheses,
   —birth and death dates, if known; a (?) indicates a discrepancy in published sources,
   —pseudonyms or name variants under which the person has had books published or is publicly known, in parentheses in the second line.

2. "Personal" section gives

   —date and place of birth and death,
   —parents' names and occupations,
   —name of spouse, date of marriage, and names of children,
   —educational institutions attended, degrees received, and dates,
   —religious and political affiliations,
   —agent's name and address,
   —home and/or office address.

3. "Career" section gives

   —name of employer, position, and dates for each career post,
   —military service,
   —memberships,
   —awards and honors.

4. "Writings" section gives

   —title, first publisher and date of publication, and illustration information for each book written; revised editions and other significant editions for books with particularly long publishing histories; genre, when known.

5. "Adaptations" section gives

   —title, major performers, producer, and date of all known reworkings of an author's material in another medium, like movies, filmstrips, television, recordings, plays, etc.

6. "Sidelights" section gives

> —commentary on the life or work of the biographee either directly from the person (and often written specifically for the *SATA* entry), or gathered from biographies, diaries, letters, interviews, or other published sources.

7. "For More Information See" section gives

> —books, feature articles, films, plays, and reviews in which the biographee's life or work has been treated.

How a *SATA* Entry Is Compiled

A *SATA* entry progresses through a series of steps. If the biographee is living, the *SATA* editors try to secure information directly from him or her through a questionnaire. From the information that the biographee supplies, the editors prepare an entry, filling in any essential missing details with research. The author or illustrator is then sent a copy of the entry to check for accuracy and completeness.

If the biographee is deceased or cannot be reached by questionnaire, the *SATA* editors examine a wide variety of published sources to gather information for an entry. Biographical sources are searched with the aid of Gale's *Biography and Genealogy Master Index*. Bibliographic sources like the *National Union Catalog*, the *Cumulative Book Index, American Book Publishing Record*, and the *British Museum Catalogue* are consulted, as are book reviews, feature articles, published interviews, and material sometimes obtained from the biographee's family, publishers, agent, or other associates.

For each entry presented in *SATA*, the editors also attempt to locate a photograph of the biographee as well as representative illustrations from his or her books. After surveying the available books which the biographee has written and/or illustrated, and then making a selection of appropriate photographs and illustrations, the editors request permission of the current copyright holders to reprint the material. In the case of older books for which the copyright may have passed through several hands, even locating the current copyright holder is often a long and involved process.

We invite you to examine the entire *SATA* series, starting with this volume. Described below are some of the people in Volume 56 that you may find particularly interesting.

Highlights of This Volume

ELIZABETH COATSWORTH......was born in Buffalo, New York, and travelled widely with her family. "Most of my fifth year was spent abroad. I scarcely remember England, but I have definite memories of the spa to which we went in Germany, and of how nasty the waters tasted, and of Switzerland and of Italy." Besides travel, she was always interested in writing, especially poetry. This interest remained constant for the rest of her life. "Writing was an intoxication," she said. "[It] was for me an addiction like drink, which I kept as much as possible out of sight." During a writing career that spanned a half century, Coatsworth produced award-winning prose and poetry books for children and adults. Her fourth children's book, *The Cat Who Went to Heaven*, won the 1931 Newbery Medal.

VIRGINIA HAMILTON......spent her childhood in Yellow Springs, Ohio, where her family had lived for generations. "I am a teller of tales, in part, because of the informal way I learned from Mother and her relatives of passing the time....They could appreciate a good story in the companionship of one another." Hamilton's one major ambition was to become a writer, although she has worked at "every source of occupation imaginable, from singer to bookkeeper." Since the successful publication of her first children's book, *Zeely*, in 1967, Hamilton has consistently produced critically acclaimed books for young adults and for children. She was the first Black writer to receive the Newbery Medal. "What personal self I have is in my books," says Hamilton. "Everything that might become neurotic or personally problematic I put into a narrative. My stories are little pieces of me."

GEORGE LUCAS......wanted "to be a race car driver—sports cars, Formula One. That was it. My whole life." A near fatal car accident the day before his high school graduation changed his perspective, however, and made him aware of other possibilities. At the University of Southern California, Lucas studied filmmaking, despite objections from his hot-rodder friends. "All my friends laughed at me, and warned, 'You're crazy, you're going to become a ticket-taker at Disneyland.' " When his first film, "American Graffiti," was released, Lucas never expected to produce another film as successful. But then came "Star Wars." The financial returns from "Star Wars" allowed Lucas the freedom to build his own film production company, his own research and special effects division, and Skywalker Ranch—an environment in which he and his friends can work to expand the art of filmmaking. Subsequent films—"The Empire Strikes Back," "Raiders of the Lost Ark," "Return of the Jedi," "Indiana Jones and the Temple of Doom," and "Willow"—have also been box-office sensations.

BARRY MOSER......was "a constant source of disapproval" to his Southern family who were bent on quashing his dreams of being an artist. After military school, he studied mechanical engineering (that's about building cars, so it was acceptable). Once his family's money "ran out," Moser was able to study painting at the University of Chattanooga. "This time I was footing the bills so the family had nothing to say about what I did." His art education included studying everything he could about printmaking, engraving, and drawing. Moser eventually settled in Northhampton, Massachusetts, where he established Pennyroyal Press. Today he is considered one of the finest graphic artists in the United States. He has illustrated over eighty books, including *Moby Dick, Alice's Adventures in Wonderland, Through the Looking Glass and What Alice Found There, Frankenstein, Huckleberry Finn,* and *The Wonderful Wizard of Oz.*

ALVIN SCHWARTZ......first became interested in folklore "when most of us do, in childhood." But he had no idea that the games, riddles, songs, and jokes that he knew were all part of a popular literary genre. Schwartz studied journalism in high school, college, and graduate school before he accepted a job on a newspaper in upstate New York. In 1963 he turned to free-lance writing, producing his first children's books about the "kinds of things that interested me as a journalist—social issues and American institutions and things of that sort." He began collecting folklore after his successful book *A Twister of Twists, A Tangler of Tongues: Tongue Twisters* appeared. "I am frequently asked where I obtain the folklore I include in my books," he said. "Whenever it is feasible, I collect material from the folk—particularly from children, our strongest, most cohesive folk group, and from the elderly, who in many respects are as important."

ELIE WIESEL.......spent his earliest years as a devout student of the Talmud and the mystical teachings of Hasidism and the Kabala. His bucolic life in Sighet, Transylvania ended abruptly in 1944, however, when the Nazis shipped the entire Jewish community to Auschwitz. Fortunately for mankind, Wiesel survived his incarceration. At the age of sixteen, he was liberated and sent to France, where he studied and worked as a tutor, translator, and choir director before becoming a journalist and author. Today he is known as a writer whose subjects include not only the victims of the Holocaust, but all victims of prejudice. When he was awarded the 1986 Nobel Peace Prize, Wiesel urged mankind to work for universal peace. "None of us is in a position to eliminate war," said Wiesel. "But it is our obligation to denounce it and expose it in all its hideousness. War leaves no victors, only victims."

These are only a few of the authors and illustrators that you'll find in this volume. We hope you find all the entries in *SATA* both interesting and useful.

Yesterday's Authors of Books for Children

In a two-volume companion set to *SATA, Yesterday's Authors of Books for Children (YABC)* focuses on early authors and illustrators, from the beginnings of children's literature through 1960, whose books are still being read by children today. Here you will find "old favorites" like Hans Christian Andersen, J. M. Barrie, Kenneth Grahame, Betty MacDonald, A. A. Milne, Beatrix Potter, Samuel Clemens, Kate Greenaway, Rudyard Kipling, Robert Louis Stevenson, and many more.

Similar in format to *SATA, YABC* features bio-bibliographical entries that are divided into information categories such as Personal, Career, Writings, and Sidelights. The entries are further enhanced by book illustrations, author photos, movie stills, and many rare old photographs.

In Volume 2 you will find cumulative indexes to the authors and to the illustrations that appear in *YABC*. These listings can also be located in the *SATA* cumulative indexes.

By exploring both volumes of *YABC*, you will discover a special group of more than seventy authors and illustrators who represent some of the best in children's literature—individuals whose timeless works continue to delight children and adults of all ages. Other authors and illustrators from early children's literature are listed in *SATA*, starting with Volume 15.

Something about the Author Autobiography Series

You can complement the information in *SATA* with the *Something about the Author Autobiography Series (SAAS)*, which provides autobiographical essays written by important current authors and illustrators of books for children and young adults. In every volume of *SAAS* you will find about twenty specially commissioned autobiographies, each accompanied by a selection of personal photographs supplied by the authors. The wide range of contemporary writers and artists who describe their lives and interests in the *Autobiography Series* includes Joan Aiken, Betsy Byars, Leonard Everett Fisher, Milton Meltzer, Maia Wojciechowska, and Jane Yolen, among others. Though the information presented in the autobiographies is as varied and unique as the authors, you can learn about the people and events that influenced these writers' early lives, how they began their careers, what problems they faced in becoming established in their professions, what prompted them to write or illustrate particular books, what they now find most challenging or rewarding in their lives, and what advice they may have for young people interested in following in their footsteps, among many other subjects.

Autobiographies included in the *SATA Autobiography Series* can be located through both the *SATA* cumulative index and the *SAAS* cumulative index, which lists not only the authors' names but also the subjects mentioned in their essays, such as titles of works and geographical and personal names.

The *SATA Autobiography Series* gives you the opportunity to view "close up" some of the fascinating people who are included in the *SATA* parent series. The combined *SATA* series makes available to you an unequaled range of comprehensive and in-depth information about the authors and illustrators of young people's literature.

Please write and tell us if we can make *SATA* even more helpful to you.

Acknowledgments

Grateful acknowledgment is made to the following publishers, authors, and artists for their kind permission to reproduce copyrighted material.

ADDISON-WESLEY PUBLISHING CO., INC. Illustration by Jean Charlot from *A Hero by Mistake* by Anita Brenner. Copyright 1953 by Anita Brenner. Reprinted by permission of Addison-Wesley Publishing Co., Inc.

ATHENEUM PUBLISHERS. Jacket illustration by Troy Howell from *Mind-Call* by Wilanne Schneider Belden. Copyright © 1981 by Wilanne Schneider Belden./ Illustration by Ian Wallace from *Very Last First Time* by Jan Andrews. Text copyright © 1985 by Jan Andrews. Illustrations copyright © 1985 by Ian Wallace./ Illustration by Ian Wallace from *Chin Chiang and the Dragon's Dance* by Ian Wallace. Copyright © 1984 by Ian Wallace. All reprinted by permission of Atheneum Publishers, an imprint of Macmillan Publishing Co.

BALLANTINE/DEL REY/FAWCETT BOOKS. Illustration from *The Art of Star Wars*, edited by Carol Titelman. Copyright © 1979 by Star Wars Corporation./ Illustration by Michael Whelan from *Michael Whelan's Works of Wonder* by Michael Whelan. Copyright © 1987 by Michael Whelan. Both reprinted by permission of Ballantine/Del Rey/Fawcett Books.

BANTAM BOOKS. Cover illustration from *Night* by Elie Wiesel. Copyright © 1960 by MacGibbon & Kee. Reprinted by permission of Bantam Books.

BOHEM PRESS. Illustration by Josef Palecek from *Das Lied vom Apfelbaum* by Jaroslav Seifert. Copyright © 1985 by Bohem Press. Reprinted by permission of Bohem Press.

CRC PRESS, INC. Illustration by Rich Bishop from *All Nature Sings* by Joanne E. DeJonge. Copyright © 1985 by CRC Publications. Reprinted by permission of CRC Press, Inc.

CAROLRHODA BOOKS, INC. Illustration by Nancy Carlson from *Loudmouth George and the Big Race* by Nancy Carlson. Copyright © 1983 by Nancy Carlson. Reprinted by permission of Carolrhoda Books, Inc.

COWARD-McCANN. Jacket illustration by Edwin Earle from *Here I Stay* by Elizabeth Coatsworth. Copyright © 1938 by Elizabeth Coatsworth Beston. Reprinted by permission of Coward-McCann.

CROWN PUBLISHERS, INC. Illustration by David Cox from *Bossyboots* by David Cox. Copyright © 1985 by David Cox./ Sidelight excerpts from *Skywalking: The Life and Films of George Lucas* by Dale Pollack. Copyright © 1983 by Dale Pollack. Both reprinted by permission of Crown Publishers, Inc.

ANDRE DEUTSCH. Illustration by Helen Ganly from *Jyoti's Journey* by Helen Ganly. Copyright © 1986 by Helen Ganly. Reprinted by permission of Andre Deutsch.

DODD, MEAD & CO., INC. Photograph by Galen Burrell from *Headgear* by Ron Hirschi. Text copyright © 1986 by Ron Hirschi. Photograph copyright © 1986 by Galen Burrell. Reprinted by permission of Dodd, Mead & Co., Inc.

FARRAR, STRAUS & GIROUX, INC. Jacket illustration by Michele Chessare from *Invincible Summer* by Jean Ferris. Text copyright © 1987 by Jean Ferris. Illustrations copyright © 1987 by Michele Chessare./ Illustration by Margot Zemach from *The Cat's Elbow and Other Secret Languages*, collected by Alvin Schwartz. Text copyright © 1982 by Alvin Schwartz. Illustrations copyright © 1982 by Margot Zemach. Both reprinted by permission of Farrar, Straus & Giroux, Inc.

FOUR WINDS PRESS. Illustration by Arlene Dubanevich from *Pigs in Hiding* by Arlene Dubanevich. Copyright © 1983 by Arlene Dubanevich./ Illustration by Judy Glasser from *The S.S. Valentine* by Terry Wolfe Phelan. Text copyright © 1979 by Terry Phelan. Illustrations copyright © 1979 by Judy Glasser. Both reprinted by permission of Four Winds Press, an imprint of Macmillan Publishing Co.

GREENWILLOW BOOKS. Illustration by Krystyna Turska from *Marra's World* by Elizabeth Coatsworth. Copyright © 1975 by Elizabeth Coatsworth Beston./ Illustration by Ted Harrison from *The Cremation of Sam McGee* by Robert W. Service. Text copyright 1907 by The Estate of Robert Service. Illustrations copyright © 1986 by Ted Harrison. Both reprinted by permission of Greenwillow Books.

G.K. HALL & CO. Sidelight excerpts from *A Personal Geography: Almost an Autobiography* by Elizabeth Coatsworth. Reprinted by permission of G.K. Hall & Co.

HARCOURT BRACE JOVANOVICH, INC. Illustration by Stewart Daniels from *Frankie!* by Wilanne Schneider Belden. Text copyright © 1987 by Wilanne Schneider Belden. Illustrations copyright © 1987 by Stewart Daniels./ Illustration by Barry Moser from *In the Beginning: Creation Stories from Around the World* by Virginia Hamilton. Text copyright © 1988 by Virginia Hamilton. Illustrations copyright © 1988 by Pennyroyal Press, Inc./ Illustration by Barry Moser from *Jump Again! More Adventures of Brer Rabbit* by Joel Chandler Harris. Adapted by Van Dyke Parks. Text copyright © 1987 by Van Dyke Parks. Illustrations copyright © 1987 by Pennyroyal Press, Inc./ Illustration by Barry Moser from *Two Tales: Rip Van Winkle and The Legend of Sleepy Hollow* by Washington Irving. Copyright © 1984 by Pennyroyal Press, Inc./ Illustration by Barry Moser from *The Scarlet Letter* by Nathaniel Hawthorne. Copyright © 1984 by Pennyroyal Press, Inc. All reprinted by permission of Harcourt Brace Jovanovich, Inc.

HARPER & ROW, PUBLISHERS, INC. Illustration by Wayne Anderson from *The Flight of Dragons* by Peter Dickinson. Text copyright © 1979 by Peter Dickinson. Illustrations copyright © 1979 by Wayne Anderson./ Illustration by Margot Tomes from *The Shadowmaker* by Ron Hansen. Text copyright © 1987 by Ron Hansen. Illustrations copyright © 1987 by Margot Tomes./ Illustration by Ned Delaney from *Will You Cross Me?* by Marilyn Kaye. Text copyright © 1985 by Marilyn Kaye. Illustrations copyright © 1985 by T. N. Delaney III./ Illustration by Dirk Zimmer from *In a Dark, Dark Room and Other Scary Stories*, retold by Alvin Schwartz. Text copyright © 1984 by Alvin Schwartz. Illustrations copyright © 1984 by Dirk Zimmer./ Illustration by Bruce Degen from *In The Middle of the Puddle* by Mike Thaler. Text copyright © 1988 by Mike Thaler. Illustrations copyright © 1988 by Bruce Degen./ Illustration by Maxie Chambliss from *It's Me, Hippo!* by Mike Thaler. Text copyright © 1983 by Mike Thaler. Illustrations copyright © 1983 by Maxie Chambliss. All reprinted by permission of Harper & Row, Publishers, Inc.

HILL & WANG. Sidelight excerpts from *Night* by Elie Wiesel./ Cover illustration from *The Accident* by Elie Wiesel. Copyright © 1961 by Editions du Seuil. Translation copyright © 1962 by Elie Wiesel. Both reprinted by permission of Hill & Wang.

HENRY HOLT & CO., INC. Illustration by Tony Ross from *Jenna and the Troublemaker* by Hiawyn Oram. Text copyright © 1986 by Hiawyn Oram. Illustrations copyright © 1986 by Tony Ross. Reprinted by permission of Henry Holt & Co., Inc.

HOUGHTON MIFFLIN CO. Illustration by Charles Robinson from *My Pretty Girl* by Bianca Bradbury. Copyright © 1974 by Bianca Bradbury./ Jacket illustration by Marvin Friedman from *A New Penny* by Bianca Bradbury. Copyright © 1971 by Bianca Bradbury./ Illustration by John Gretzer from *The Loner* by Bianca Bradbury. Copyright © 1970 by Bianca Bradbury./ Illustration by Richard Cuffari from *In Her Father's Footsteps*. Copyright © 1976 by Bianca Bradbury./ Jacket illustration by Ted Levin from *Reasons to Stay* by Margaret Walden Froehlich. Copyright © 1986 by Margaret Walden Froehlich. All reprinted by permission of Houghton Mifflin Co.

INDIANA UNIVERSITY PRESS. Sidelight excerpts from *Folklorist's Progress* by Stith Thompson. Reprinted by permission of Indiana University Press.

KIDS CAN PRESS. Illustration by Ted Harrison from *The Cremation of Sam McGee* by Robert W. Service. Text copyright 1907 by The Estate of Robert Service. Illustrations copyright © 1986 by Ted Harrison. Reprinted by permission of Kids Can Press (in Canada).

ALFRED A. KNOPF, INC. Illustration by Leo and Diane Dillon from *The People Could Fly: American Black Folktales*, told by Virginia Hamilton. Text copyright © 1985 by Virginia Hamilton. Illustrations copyright © 1985 by Leo and Diane Dillon./ Illustration by Joseph Schindelman from *The Staff* by Mike Thaler. Text copyright © 1971 by Mike Thaler. Illustrations copyright © 1971 by Joseph Schindelman. Both reprinted by permission of Alfred A. Knopf, Inc.

LERNER PUBLICATIONS CO. Jacket illustration by Kirsten Jensinius from *Hi, Daddy, Here I Am* by Grete Janus Hertz. Translated by Margaret Young Gracza. Copyright © 1964 by Lerner Publications Co. Reprinted by permission of Lerner Publications Co.

J. B. LIPPINCOTT CO. Illustrations by Stephen Gammell from *Scary Stories to Tell in the Dark: Collected from American Folklore* by Alvin Schwartz. Text copyright © 1981 by Alvin Schwartz. Illustrations copyright © 1981 by Stephen Gammell./ Illustration by Glen Rounds from a *Twister of Twists, A Tangler of Tongues* by Alvin Schwartz./ Illustration by Stephen

Gammell from *More Scary Stories to Tell in the Dark: Collected from Folklore,* retold by Alvin Schwartz. Text copyright © 1984 by Alvin Schwartz. Illustrations copyright © 1984 by Stephen Gammell./ Jacket illustration by Kenneth Dewey from *During Water Peaches* by Laurel Trivelpiece. Text copyright © 1979 by Laurel Trivelpiece. Illustrations copyright © 1979 by Kenneth Dewey. All reprinted by permission of J.B. Lippincott Co., a division of Harper & Row, Publishers, Inc.

MACMILLAN PUBLISHING CO. Illustration by Stefan Martin from *Bonnie and the Chief's Son* by Elizabeth Coatsworth. Copyright © 1962 by Macmillan Publishing Co./ Illustration by Janet Doyle from *The Lucky Ones: Five Journeys Toward a Home* by Elizabeth Coatsworth. Copyright © 1968 by Macmillan Publishing Co./ Illustration by Ingrid Fetz from *The Werefox* (originally published as *Pure Magic*) by Elizabeth Coatsworth. Text copyright © 1973 by Elizabeth Coatsworth Beston. Copyright © 1973 by Macmillan Publishing Co./ Illustration by Lynd Ward from *The Cat Who Went to Heaven* by Elizabeth Coatsworth. Copyright 1930, renewed © 1958 by Macmillan Publishing Co. Copyright © 1958 by Elizabeth Coatsworth Beston./ Cover illustration by Jerry Pinkney from *M. C. Higgins, the Great* by Virginia Hamilton. Text copyright © 1974 by Virginia Hamilton. Cover illustration copyright © 1987 by Macmillan Publishing Co./ Illustrations by Eros Keith from *The House of Dies Drear* by Virginia Hamilton. Text copyright © 1968 by Virginia Hamilton. Copyright © 1968 by Macmillan Publishing Co./ Illustration by Symeon Shimin from *Zeely* by Virginia Hamilton. Text copyright © 1967 by Virginia Hamilton. Copyright © 1967 by Macmillan Publishing Co./ Jacket illustration from *Zeely* by Virginia Hamilton. Copyright © 1967 by Virginia Hamilton. Copyright © 1967 by Macmillan Publishing Co./ Cover illustration by Jerry Pinkney from *The Planet of Junior Brown* by Virginia Hamilton. Text copyright © 1971 by Virginia Hamilton. Cover illustration copyright © 1986 by Jerry Pinkney. Copyright © 1986 by Macmillan Publishing Co. All reprinted by permission of Macmillan Publishing Co.

WILLIAM MORROW & CO., INC. Illustration by Barry Moser from *Around the World in Eighty Days* by Jules Verne. Copyright © 1988 by Pennyroyal Press. Reprinted by permission of William Morrow & Co., Inc.

NORD-SUD VERLAG. Illustration by Binette Schroeder from *Crocodile Crocodile* by Peter Nickl. Copyright © 1975 by Nord-Sud Verlag. Copyright © 1976 by Ebbitt Cutler. Reprinted by permission of Nord-Sud Verlag.

THE OVERLOOK PRESS. Jacket illustration by Juan Suarez from *A Prayer for Katerina Horovitzova* by Arnost Lustig. Copyright © 1973 by Arnost Lustig. Reprinted by permission of The Overlook Press.

PANTHEON BOOKS, INC. Illustration by Evaline Ness from *The Princess and the Lion* by Elizabeth Coatsworth. Text copyright © 1963 by Elizabeth Coatsworth. Illustrations copyright © 1963 by Evaline Ness. Reprinted by permission of Pantheon Books, Inc.

CLARKSON N. POTTER. Illustration by Binette Schroeder from *Beauty and the Beast,* translated by Ann Carter. Reprinted by permission of Clarkson N. Potter.

THE PUTNAM BERKLEY GROUP, INC. Illustration by Heiderose and Andreas Fischer-Nagel from *A Kitten Is Born* by Heiderose and Andreas Fischer-Nagel. Copyright © 1983 by Heiderose and Andreas Fischer-Nagel./ Illustration by Peter Cross from *Dudley in a Jam* by Judy Taylor. Text copyright © 1986 by Judy Taylor. Illustrations copyright © 1986 by Peter Cross. Both reprinted by permission of The Putnam Berkley Group, Inc.

RADUGA PUBLISHERS. Illustration by Pyotr Ivashchenko from *The Cranes Fly Early* by Chinghiz Aitmatov. Translation into English by Eve Manning. English translation copyright © 1983 by Raduga Publishers. Reprinted by permission of Raduga Publishers.

RANDOM HOUSE, INC. Sidelight excerpts from *One Generation After* by Elie Wiesel. Copyright © 1965, 1967, 1970 by Elie Wiesel./ Jacket illustration from *A Beggar in Jerusalem* by Elie Wiesel./ Illustration by Joe Mathieu from *The Book of the Unknown* by Harold and Geraldine Woods. Text copyright © 1982 by Harold and Geraldine Woods. Illustrations copyright © 1982 by Joe Mathieu. All reprinted by permission of Random House, Inc.

SCHOLASTIC, INC. Illustration by Michael Racz from *Midnight at Monster Mansion* by Steven Otfinoski. Copyright © 1984 by Steven Otfinoski. Reprinted by permission of Scholastic, Inc.

SIMON & SCHUSTER, INC. Cover photograph by Edmund Shea from *The Abortion: An Historical Romance 1966* by Richard Brautigan. Copyright © 1970, 1971 by Richard Brautigan./ Cover illustration by Paul Bacon from *The Testament* by Elie Wiesel. Copyright ©

1981 by Elirion Associates, Inc./ Illustrations by Mark Podwal from *The Golem: The Story of a Legend as Told by Elie Wiesel,* translated by A. Borchandt. Copyright © 1983 by Mark Podwal and Elirion Associates, Inc. All reprinted by permission of Simon & Schuster, Inc.

STEMMER HOUSE PUBLISHERS, INC. Frontispiece by Paul Brittenham from *Dooley's Lion* by Gudrun Alcock. Copyright © 1986 by Paul N. Brittenham. Reprinted by permission of Stemmer House Publishers, Inc.

TUNDRA BOOKS OF NORTHERN NEW YORK. Illustration by Warabe Aska from *Who Hides in the Park* by Warabe Aska. Copyright © 1986 by Warabe Aska. Reprinted by permission of Tundra Books of Northern New York.

WALKER BOOKS. Illustration by Binette Schroeder from *Beauty and the Beast*, translated by Ann Carter. Reprinted by permission of Walker Books (in Canada).

WARNER BOOKS, INC. Cover illustration by Wendell Minor from *The Fifth Son* by Elie Wiesel. Translated from the French by Marion Wiesel. Copyright © 1986 by Warner Books, Inc. Translation copyright © 1985 by Elirion Associates, Inc. Reprinted by permission of Warner Books, Inc.

Sidelight excerpts from an article "Being Banned" by Norma Klein, spring, 1985 in *Top of the News*. Reprinted by permission of American Library Association./ Sidelight excerpts from an article "More Realism for Children," by Norma Klein, April, 1975 in *Top of the News*. Reprinted by permission of American Library Association./ Illustration by Dennis Hockerman from *The Innkeeper's Daughter* by Jill Briscoe. Copyright © 1984 by Ideals Publishing Corp. Reprinted by permission of Jill Briscoe./ Sidelight excerpts from *Books Are by People* by Lee Bennett Hopkins. Copyright © 1969 by Lee Bennett Hopkins. Reprinted by permission of Curtis Brown Ltd./ Sidelight excerpts from an article "Who Goes to the Park," by Warabe Aska, 1985/1986 in *Our Choice/Your Choice*. Reprinted by permission of The Children's Book Centre./ Illustration by Glo Coalson from *On Mother's Lap* by Ann Herbert Scott. Copyright © 1972 by Glo Coalson. Reprinted by permission of Glo Coalson./ Illustrations by Barry Moser from *Alice's Adventures in Wonderland* by Lewis Carroll. Copyright © 1982 by The Pennyroyal Press. Reprinted by permission of Richard Curtis Associates, Inc./ Illustration by Barry Moser from *The Adventures of Huckleberry Finn* by Mark Twain. Copyright © 1985 by The Pennyroyal Press. Reprinted by permission of Richard Curtis Associates, Inc./ Illustration by Barry Moser from *The Wonderful Wizard of Oz* by L. Frank Baum. Copyright © 1986 by The Pennyroyal Press. Repinted by permission of Richard Curtis Associates, Inc./ Illustration by Barry Moser from *I Remember Grandpa* by Truman Capote. Copyright © 1987 by The Pennyroyal Press. Reprinted by permission of Richard Curtis Associates, Inc./ Illustration by Judy Hierstein of Becky Daniel's son on which Daniel based her character Maximillian. Reprinted by permission of Becky Daniel./ Sidelight excerpts from an article "The Stinky Kid Hits Big Time," by Stephen Farber, spring, 1974 in *Film Quarterly*. Reprinted by permission of Stephen Farber./ Photograph courtesy of *Focus on Sports* from *Lynette Woodard* by Matthew Newman. Copyright © 1986 by Crestwood House, Inc. Reprinted by permission of *Focus on Sports*./ Sidelight excerpts from an article in *Horn Book*, June, 1979. Reprinted by permission of The Horn Book, Inc./ Photograph by Kit Houghton from *Horses and Riding* by Georgie Henschel. Copyright © 1986 by Piper Books Ltd. Reprinted by permission of Kit Houghton.

Sidelight excerpts from an article "Profile: Alvin Schwartz," April, 1987 in *Language Arts*. Copyright © 1987 by The National Council of Teachers of English. Reprinted by permission of *Language Arts*./ Jacket illustration by Rufus Wells III from *Night and Hope* by Arnost Lustig. Copyright © 1976 by Arnost Lustig./ Cover illustration from *Diamonds of the Night* by Arnost Lustig. Copyright © 1978 by Arnost Lustig./ Jacket illustration by Rufus Wells III from *Darkness Casts No Shadow* by Arnost Lustig. Copyright © 1976 by Arnost Lustig./ Illustration by Dennis B. Meehan from *Wilderness Plots: Tales about the Settlement of the American Land* by Scott R. Saunders. Copyright © 1983 by Dennis B. Meehan. Reprinted by permission of Dennis B. Meehan./ Illustration by Krystyna Turska from *Marra's World* by Elizabeth Coatsworth. Copyright © 1975 by Elizabeth Coatsworth Beston. Reprinted by permission of Paterson & Associates./ Sidelight excerpts from an article "Who Makes Children Feel Riddle-culous?," by Deena Mirow, March 17, 1985 in *Plain Dealer*. Reprinted by permission of *Plain Dealer*./ Sidelight excerpts from an article "Illustrator at Work: Barry Moser," July 6, 1984 in *Publishers Weekly*. Reprinted by permission of *Publishers Weekly*./ Sidelight excerpts from an article "The Force Behind George Lucas," August 25, 1987 in *Rolling Stone*. Reprinted by permission of *Rolling Stone*./ Sidelight excerpts from an article "The Empire Strikes Back," by Jean Vallely, June 12, 1980 in *Rolling Stone*. Reprinted by permission of *Rolling Stone*./ Sidelight excerpts from an article "George Lucas Wants to Play

Guitar,"by Paul Scanlon, August 4, 1983 in *Rolling Stone*. Reprinted by permission of *Rolling Stone*.

Jacket photograph by Naomi Savage from *The Gates of the Forest* by Elie Wiesel. Reprinted by permission of Naomi Savage./ Sidelight excerpts from an article "Profile: Alvin Schwartz," April, 1987 in *Language Arts*. Copyright © 1987 by The National Council of Teachers of English. Reprinted by permission of Alvin Schwartz./ Sidelight excerpts from an article "Children, Humor and Folklore," by Alvin Schwartz, August, 1977 in *Horn Book*. Copyright © 1977 by Alvin Schwartz. Reprinted by permission of Alvin Schwartz./ Illustration by Symeon Shimin from *Sam* by Ann Herbert Scott. Copyright © 1967 by Ann Herbert Scott and Symeon Shimin. Reprinted by permission of Symeon Shimin./ Sidelight excerpts from an article "The George Lucas Saga—Chapter One: A New View," by Kerry O'Quinn, July, 1981 in *Starlog*. Reprinted by permission of *Starlog*./ Sidelight excerpts from an article "The George Lucas Saga—Chapter Two: The Cold Fish Strikes Back," by Kerry O'Quinn, August, 1981 in *Starlog*. Reprinted by permission of *Starlog*./ Sidelight excerpts from an article "George Lucas, an Interview," by Audie Bock, May, 1979 in *Take One*, Volume 17, number 6. Reprinted by permission of *Take One*./ Photograph of Andrew Lloyd Webber, January 18, 1988 on the cover of *Time* magazine. Reprinted by permission of *Time*./ Cover photograph by Erik Weber from *Loading Mercury with a Pitchfork* by Richard Brautigan. Copyright © by Erik Weber. Reprinted by permission of Erik Weber./ Cover photograph by Erik Weber from *Trout Fishing in America* by Richard Brautigan. Copyright © by Erik Weber. Reprinted by permission of Erik Weber./ Photograph of Elie Wiesel, 1945 by AP/Wide World Photos. Reprinted by permission of AP/Wide World Photos./ Photograph by AP/Wide World Photos from *Cocaine* by Geraldine and Harold Woods. Copyright © 1985 by Geraldine and Harold Woods. Reprinted by permission of AP/Wide World Photos./ Photograph by Wayne Harman Enterprises from *Formula One* by Sylvia Wilkinson. Copyright © 1981 by Regensteiner Publishing Enterprises, Inc. Reprinted by permission of Sylvia Wilkinson.

PHOTOGRAPH CREDITS

Nancy Carlson: Mark LaFavor; Elizabeth Coatsworth: Robert C. Frampton; Carolyn Croll: Stan Lilly, 1988; Gloria Rand Dank: Bert Corman; Charlotte Graeber: Richard Chapman, *Elgin Daily Courier News*; Virginia Hamilton: Cox Studios; Edward Hardy Harrison: Parks Canada; Ron Hirschi: *The Bremerton Sun*; Andrew Lloyd Webber (Phantom of the Opera): Clive Barda; George Lucas: (Willow) Keith Hamshere, (American Graffiti) Albert Clarke; Barry Moser: T. Elder; Barbara Nickl: © by Barbara Gass; Josef Palecek: Stanislav Tuma; Ruth Yaffe Radin: Shelden Radin; Scott Russell Sanders: Roger Pfingston; Alvin Schwartz: Pryde Brown; Elie Wiesel: Boston University Photo Service; Sylvia Wilkinson: Jan Bigelow.

SOMETHING ABOUT THE AUTHOR

AINSWORTH, Catherine Harris 1910-
(Catherine Harris)

PERSONAL: Born October 5, 1910, in Elkin, N.C.; daughter of Edwin Ephraim (a canning factory owner) and Catherine Elizabeth (a housewife; maiden name, Alexander) Harris; married Clyde David Eller, February 18, 1931 (died, September 9, 1942); married Walter Ainsworth (a retired professor), March 29, 1956; children: (first marriage) Elizabeth Eller Swanson, Clyde Harris Eller (daughter). *Education:* University of North Carolina, Greensboro and Chapel Hill, A.B., 1931; attended University of Florida, 1947; University of Michigan, M.A., 1950; graduate work at University of Buffalo, 1962-64. *Politics:* Independent. *Religion:* Episcopalian. *Home:* 174 Depew Ave., Buffalo, N.Y., 14214. *Office:* The Clyde Press, 373 Lincoln Parkway, Buffalo, N.Y. 14216.

CAREER: Teacher in high schools in Elkin and Booneville, N.C., 1932-46, and Jonesville, N.C., 1946-47; Disston Junior High School, St. Petersburg, Fla., mathematics teacher, 1951-61; Holly High School, Pontiac, Mich., English teacher, 1962; University of Buffalo, Buffalo, N.Y., teaching fellow, 1964, Millard Fillmore College, instructor, 1964; Niagara County Community College, Niagara Falls, and Sanborn, N.Y., associate professor, 1964-78. Camp Fire Girls Camp Wathana, Detroit, Mich., assistant director, 1952; Camp Greilick, Traverse City, Mich. director, 1954; Camp Tilting Acres, Zanesville, Ohio, director, 1955; Camp Sherwood, Pontiac, Mich., director, 1959. *Member:* American Folklore Society, New York Folklore Society (member of executive committee), North Carolina Folklore Society, Faculty Association of Niagara County Community College, Daughters of the American Revolution, United Daughters of the Confederacy, Buffalo and Erie County Historical Society, Landmarks Society of Niagara Frontier, Twentieth Century Club of Buffalo, Northern New York College English Teachers Association. *Awards, honors:*

CATHERINE HARRIS AINSWORTH

Plaque from the Buffalo and Erie County Historical Society, 1971, for published books; Award from the National Endow-

1

ment for the Arts, 1985, for *Games and Lore of Young Americans*.

WRITINGS:

JUVENILE

Superstitions from Seven Towns of the United States, Buffalo University Press, 1973.
Black and White and Said All Over: Riddles, Clyde Press, 1976.
Jump Rope Verses around the United States, Clyde Press, 1976.
Games and Lore of Young Americans, Clyde Press, 1983.

OTHER

Eclectic Essays, Kendall-Hunt, 1974.
Italian-American Folktales, Clyde Press, 1976.
Polish-American Folktales, Clyde Press, 1977.
Niagara Falls and Nearby Buffalo, Clyde Press, 1977.
Legends of New York State, Clyde Press, 1978, 2nd edition, 1983.
American Calendar Customs, Volume I, Clyde Press, 1979.
American Calendar Customs, Volume II, Clyde Press, 1980.
Folktales of America, Volume I, Clyde Press, 1980.
Folktales of America, Volume II, Clyde Press, 1982.
American Folk Foods, Clyde Press, 1984.
Family Life of Young Americans, Clyde Press, 1986.
Folktales of America, Volume III, Clyde Press, 1988.
Sirrah (three-act play), Clyde Press, 1988.

Contributor of numerous articles to *New York Folklore, Western Folklore, North Carolina Education, Southern Folklore Quarterly*, and *Buffalo Courier Express*.

WORK IN PROGRESS: A personal biography, *South to North*.

SIDELIGHTS: "My growing-up was a very happy time in my life. I wish I could repeat my childhood. I had wonderful parents, a successful father and capable mother. My father was in the canning business with satellite canneries over three counties in North Carolina. Blackberries were a specialty, and he canned cherries, beans, tomatoes, peaches, apples and other produce. He was very interested in getting new and better varieties for the farmers to grow.

"I loved the social structure of the small town I lived in and my parents' discussion of its development. I loved the nearness to the woods, creeks, and rivers; and I learned the names of many plants, trees, and animals. I was very aware of the garden my parents tended together and of the foods we had on our table.

"At public school, I absorbed many things besides my lessons. Although I could put every one in his proper nitch, I early became aware of the injustices in the systems of things. I absorbed the tales and songs of my parents.

"I was married when I was twenty years old and my first daughter was born about two and a half years later. My second and last child, a daughter, was born seven and a half months after her father died of a coronary occlusion. My work began even while I was pregnant and has continued, with some interruptions, ever since. I have been collecting folklore since about 1950, folklore of all kinds, although folktales are my specialty. The strength of my collection lies, I believe, in the fact that I have left them, unembellished and unprettified, in the words of the writers of the lore, usually young college students.

HOBBIES AND OTHER INTERESTS: Bridge, gardening.

AITMATOV, Chinghiz 1928-

PERSONAL: Born December 12, 1928, in Sheker Village, Kirghizia, U.S.S.R.; son of Torekul and Nahima Aitmatov; married wife, Keres (a physician); children: two sons. *Education:* Received degree in animal husbandry from Kirghiz Agricultural Institute; attended Moscow Literary Institute of the Union of Soviet Writers. *Home:* 43 Dzerzhinsky, Flat 1, Frunze, Kirghiz, U.S.S.R. *Office:* c/o Kirghiz Branch of the Union of Writers of the U.S.S.R., Ulitsa Pushkina 52, Frunze, U.S.S.R.

CAREER: Writer, 1952—. Communist Party of the Soviet Union, assistant to the secretary of Sheker Village Soviet, c. 1943, member, 1959—; People's Writer of Kirghiz Soviet Socialist Republic, 1968. Candidate member of Central Committee of Kirghiz Soviet Socialist Republic; vice-chairman of committee of Solidarity with Peoples of Asian and African Countries; deputy of U.S.S.R. Supreme Soviet. Cinema Union of Kirghiz Soviet Socialist Republic, first secretary, 1964-69, chairman, 1969. *Awards, honors:* Lenin Prize for literature and the fine arts, 1963, for *Povesti gor i stepei;* Order of the Red Banner of Labor (twice); U.S.S.R. State Prize, 1968, for *Proschai, Gul'sary!;* Hero of Socialist Labor, 1978.

WRITINGS:

IN ENGLISH TRANSLATION

Dzhamilia (novel), Pravda, 1959, translation published as *Jamila*, Foreign Languages Publishing House (Moscow).
Povesti gor i stepei, Sovetskii Pisatel, 1963, translation published as *Tales of the Mountains and Steppes*, Progress Publishers, 1969.

CHINGHIZ AITMATOV

Proschai, Gul'sary! (novella), Molodia Guardiia, 1967, translation by John French published as *Farewell, Gulsary!*, Hodder & Stoughton, 1970.

Posle skazki, Belyj parokhod (novel), 1970, translation by Mirra Ginsburg published as *The White Ship* (*Horn Book* honor list), Crown, 1972 (translation by Tatyana Feifer and George Feifer, published in England as *The White Steamship*, Hodder & Stoughton, 1972).

(With Kaltai Mukhamedzhanov) *Voskhozhdenie na Fudzhiamu* (play; first produced in Moscow, U.S.S.R., 1973; produced as "The Ascent of Mount Fuji" in Washington, D.C., at Kreeger Theatre, 1975), translation by Nicholas Bethell published as *The Ascent of Mount Fuji*, Farrar, Straus, 1975.

The Cranes Fly Early, translation by Eve Manning, Imported Publications, 1983.

The Day Lasts More Than a Hundred Years, translation by John French, Indiana University Press, 1983.

(With others) *You Have to Treat Your Heart*, Imported Publications, 1986.

A Time to Speak, International Publications, 1988.

The Scaffold, translation by Natasha Ward, Grove, 1989.

OTHER WRITINGS

Rasskazy (title means "Stories"), Sovetskii Pisatel, 1958.

Verbliuzhii glaz (short stories and novellas; title means "The Camel's Eye"), Sovetskii Pisatel, 1962.

Materinskoe Pole (novel; title means "The Field of Mothers"), Pravda, 1963.

Samanchy zholu (short stories and novellas), Basmasy, 1963.

Povesti (title means "Novellas"), Izvestia, 1967.

Pervyi uchitel (novel; title means "The First Master"), Detskaia Literatura, 1967.

Atadan kalgan tuiak, Mektep, 1970.

Povesti i rasskazy (title means "Novellas and Stories"), Molodaia Guardiia, 1970.

Pegil pes, begushchij kraem moria, Sovetskii Pisatel, 1977.

V soavtostve s zemleiu i vodoiu (essays and lectures), Kyrgyzstan, 1978.

Also author of *Tri povesti*, translation published as *Short Novels*, Progress Publishers.

SIDELIGHTS: Unlike such dissident Soviet writers as Solzhenitsyn and Tsabour, Aitmatov has managed to remain in the U.S.S.R. and write of life in the republic of his birth, Kirghizia. A member of one of the Soviet Union's central Asian minorities, he is the first Kirghiz author to become known throughout the world. His books have been widely translated, with several appearing in French, German, Polish, English, and Arabic editions. His work has also been the focus of several Soviet films.

Aitmatov is an active and prominent member of the Communist party. Nevertheless, as *Newsweek's* Jay Axelbank noted, he "tries to steer clear of political ideology and concentrate on psychological portraits" in his writing. He incorporates aspects of the Kirghiz oral tradition into the reality of Soviet society and culture. Aitmatov believes that "the logic of a work of art follows its own rules, and these rules are not subject to the author's will."

Underlying Aitmatov's support of the Soviet system is a strong determination to uphold this freedom of artistic expression. These aspects of Aitmatov's character have led him, occasionally, to violate certain literary taboos of the Soviet state.

Drowsily he thought again: how good it was that he had father. ■ (From *The Cranes Fly Early* by Chinghiz Aitmatov. Translated by Eve Manning. Illustrated by Pyotr Ivashchenko.)

In *The White Ship*, for example, Aitmatov depicts the suicide of a seven-year-old boy who becomes despondent after witnessing the brutal slaying and consumption of a rare deer.

Some Soviet readers were offended by the pessimism of the story, and the outcry against it prompted the author to defend his artistic integrity in the *Literaturnaya Gazeta*. Countering suggested changes in the tale, Aitmatov was quoted in the *New York Times:* "I had a choice, either to write or not to write the story. And if to write it, then only as I did." The author also asserted that evil is inexorable and, lacking the capacity to overcome the adult evil surrounding him, the boy had to sacrifice his life or his childhood ideals. "In showing the death of the boy in *The White Ship* I by no means show evil triumphing over good but pursue a life-asserting aim, through the rejection of evil in its most [u]ncompromising form, through the death of the hero. . . . Yes, the boy dies but spiritual and moral victory remains his."

FOR MORE INFORMATION SEE:

New York Times, July 30, 1970.
Times Literary Supplement, May 28, 1971.
UNESCO Courier, October, 1972.
Horn Book, December, 1972, February, 1974.
Newsweek, June 24, 1974, June 30, 1975.
Books Abroad, summer, 1975.
Commonweal, July 18, 1975.
Nation, August 30, 1975.
Journal of Reading, February, 1982.
Observer (London), August 21, 1983.
New Yorker, April 23, 1984.
Soviet Life, January, 1984, January, 1986.

COLLECTIONS

Kerlan Collection, University of Minnesota.

ALCOCK, Gudrun 1908-

PERSONAL: Born April 18, 1908, in Stockholm, Sweden; came to the U.S.; daughter of Gunnar Otto (a pressman) and Maria (a typesetter; maiden name, Blomdahl) Holmquist; married Thomas Hoban Alcock (an attorney), May 18, 1935 (died, November, 1986). *Education:* Northwestern University, B.S., 1928. *Home:* 1300 North Lake Shore Dr., Apt. 30D, Chicago, Ill. 60610.

CAREER: Marshall Field & Company, Chicago, Ill., assistant art director, became art director, 1934-41; *Chicago Sun* (now *Sun-Times*), Chicago, woman's editor, 1941-42; author 1941—. Has worked as an artist for *Redbook,* as a teacher in layout at the Commerce School of Northwestern University, and as a layout artist in an advertising agency until 1934. *Awards, honors: Turn the Next Corner* was selected one of Child Study Association of America's Children's Books of the Year, 1969.

WRITINGS:

Run, Westy, Run (illustrated by W. T. Mars), Lothrop, 1966.
Turn the Next Corner, Lothrop, 1969.
Duffy (illustrated by Robert Clayton), Lothrop, 1972.
Dooley's Lion: A Junior Novel (illustrated by Paul Brittenham), Stemmer House, 1986.

Turn the Next Corner has been published in Sweden.

WORK IN PROGRESS: Short stories based on her travels.

SIDELIGHTS: "As a child who was transported from Sweden, I was prone to the illnesses of children here, so I was an

GUDRUN ALCOCK

undersized, often sick youngster. I loved to read, but because of my small size, I wasn't admitted to grammar school until I was seven. I remember being the one who made up most of the plays that my playmates and I liked to act out.

"I managed to graduate at the age of twelve and became a Girl Scout which started my love of the outdoors. I was exposed to piano lessons (wouldn't practice) and art lessons. Showing some aptitude for art, I went to Saturday classes at the Art Institute from the age of twelve.

"Finishing high school when I was sixteen, I entered college. Looking back, that was too young. My main subjects were art, English and advertising, all subjects which readied me for my first job.

"That job was to make layouts and finished drawings for *Redbook.* From there I worked as a layout artist in an advertising agency. After two years I took time out, having saved enough money to go to Europe for two months with a friend. I returned to the agency but left about 1934 to join the advertising department of Marshall Field & Company, Chicago's leading retail store. After being an assistant art director for several years, I became art director of all the advertising. I was also teaching an evening class in layout at the Commerce School of Northwestern University.

"After eight years I left Marshall Field in 1941 to become the first woman's editor of the new *Chicago Sun,* now the *Sun-Times. This is when I began to write* and traded my drawing board for a typewriter. I also started to take evening classes in writing at Northwestern University.

"Due to World War II, I resigned from the newspaper to join my husband who was a major in the U.S. Air Force and stationed in San Angelo, Texas. While there I did volunteer work in one of the hospitals as a Red Cross nurse's aide. I continued to write, however, and would get critiques by mail from my university professor.

"After the war, upon our return to Chicago in 1946, I decided to free-lance in order to have time to write and enjoy my other interests. I gathered my share of rejection slips but gradually began to sell short stories and articles to magazines and newspapers. I volunteered at a children's guidance center and that is where I became interested in writing for children.

"I learned a great deal at this center and moved on to do volunteer work as a tutor in a children's home for dependent children. I tutored one boy who kept saying he would run away, so I decided to try to write a book that showed what could happen to a runaway. This meant research in the juvenile courts and in detention centers. The result was my first book, *Run, Westy, Run.*

"I next tutored a boy who would never talk about his father who was in prison. This resulted in my second book, *Turn the Next Corner,* about a boy whose lawyer father went to prison for embezzlement. Here I did much research, especially in prisons.

"My third book, *Duffy,* was not motivated by a specific youngster, but by my observations of children who had to live in a home because of some tragedy, such as the automobile accident in *Duffy.*

"*Dooley's Lion* was written after my husband and I went on a camera safari in Kenya. I loved the beauty of Kenya and the wild animals, and wanted to share this with children. Sadly, my husband died a month before the book was published in

Everything was quiet. All Dooley could hear was his own breathing. ■ (From *Dooley's Lion* by Gudrun Alcock. Illustrated by Paul R. Brittenham.)

November of 1986, and he never saw the book that was dedicated to him.

"We had begun to travel and made numerous trips throughout Europe, then the Orient, Australia, New Zealand, and Africa, as well as in the United States. We had always had a farm near Lake Geneva, Wisconsin, and spent many weekends up there. I still do.

Also, while still writing articles on assignment, plus some short stories, plus the research and writing of a book that 'just missed,' I had various hobbies during these years. Studied the guitar, then the piano, but found they cut into writing time. A current hobby is to try to retain my knowledge of the Swedish language I spoke as a child. I manage to keep it active through a Swedish friend. I'm now working on a short story that seems to be turning into another novel, and I still love to travel.

"Yet the writing of books has been my happiest accomplishment in all these years. To have held a new book in my hands and realize that I created it was to feel deep satisfaction, even surprise—'Did I really write this?'"

FOR MORE INFORMATION SEE:

COLLECTIONS

Kerlan Collection at the University of Minnesota.

ALLEN, Kenneth S(ydney) 1913-
(Avis Murton Carter, Alastair Scott)

PERSONAL: Born September 18, 1913, in Southend, Essex, England; son of George Thomas (a builder) and Hannah Daisy (Sellar) Allen; married Avis Murton Carter, June 3, 1950; children: David Stuart, Alastair Scott, Fiona Margaret. *Education:* Attended Southend College of Art, and St. Martin's School of Art. *Politics:* "Minimal." *Religion:* "Minimal."

Home and office: 74 Eastbury Rd., Northwood, Middlesex HA6 3AR, England.

CAREER: Worked for advertising agencies in London, England, 1931-39; Gaumont British Films Co., London, various positions, 1945-49; Associated British Picture Corp., London, in public relations and publicity, 1954-72; full-time writer, 1972—. Escorted many international stars around the world. *Military service:* British Merchant Navy, 1939-45. *Member:* Film Publicity Guild, Association of Film and Television Technicians, Poetry Club (London), Variety Club.

WRITINGS:

Wings of Sail: The Story of British Ships in the Glorious Days of Sail (self-illustrated), John Crowther, 1944.
Mistress of the Seas: The Story of Britain's Steamships (self-illustrated), John Crowther, 1945.
The A.B.C. of Stagecraft for Amateurs (self-illustrated), Stacy, 1948.
The Silver Screen, John Gifford (London), 1948.
In the Beginning, Warne, 1948.
Sea Captains and Their Ships (illustrated by Peter M. Woods), Odhams, 1965.
(Editor) *Radiology in World War II,* Office of the Surgeon General, Department of the Army, 1966.
Crimson Harvest: The Story of the Bloodiest Massacre Britain Has Ever Known, R. Hale, 1966.
Sailors in Battle (juvenile; illustrated by Martha Hart), Odhams, 1966.
Soldiers in Battle (juvenile; illustrated by James McIntyre), Odhams, 1966.
Exploring the Cinema (juvenile; illustrated by Jane Michaelis), Odhams, 1966.
Exploring the Sea (illustrated by Wilfred Hardy), Odhams, 1966.
The Story of London Town (juvenile; illustrated by Janet Duchesne), Odhams, 1967.
The World's Greatest Sea Disasters, Odhams, 1968.
Ships of Long Ago, Macdonald Educational, 1970.
Knights and Castles, Macdonald Educational, 1970.
Fighting Ships (juvenile; illustrated by George Tuckwell), Purnell, 1971.
Pirates and Buccaneers, Macdonald Educational, 1971.
Fighting Men and Their Uniforms (juvenile; illustrated by John Berry), Hamlyn, 1971.
Mighty Men of Valour: The Great Warriors and Battles of Biblical Times, Smythe, 1972.
(Contributor) *What Do You Know? An Illustrated History of Aircraft,* Hamlyn, 1972.
The Vikings, Purnell, 1973.
Record Breakers, Purnell, 1973.
One Day in Tutankhamen's Egypt (juvenile), Tyndall, 1973, Abelard, 1974.
(Under pseudonym Avis Murton Carter) *One Day with the Vikings* (juvenile), Tyndall, 1973, Abelard, 1974.
The Story of Gunpowder (juvenile), Wayland, 1973.
The Wars of the Roses (juvenile), Wayland, 1973.
Spotlight on the Wild West (juvenile; illustrated by G. J. Galsworthy, Michael McGuinness and Michael Shoebridge), Hamlyn, 1973.
A First Look at Transporting Goods (illustrated by G. Tuckwell), F. Watts (England), 1973.
(Under pseudonym Avis Murton Carter) *One Day in Shakespeare's England* (juvenile), Tyndall, 1973, Abelard, 1974.
A First Look at Transporting People (illustrated by G. Tuckwell), F. Watts (England), 1973.
One Day in Roman Britain (juvenile), Tyndall, 1973.
Battle of the Atlantic (juvenile), Wayland, 1973.

(Under pseudonym Alastair Scott) *One Day in Regency England* (juvenile), Tyndall, 1974.

(Under pseudonym Alastair Scott) *One Day in Victorian England*, Tyndall, 1974.

One Day in Ancient Greece (juvenile), Tyndall, 1974.

One Day in Ancient Rome (juvenile), Tyndall, 1974.

Ships and Boats (juvenile; illustrated by Jack Pelling), Collins, 1975.

"That Bounty Bastard": The True Story of Captain William Bligh, R. Hale, 1976, St. Martin's, 1977.

Big Guns of the Twentieth Century and Their Part in Great Battles, Firefly Books, 1976.

The Children's Book of Cars, Trains, Boats, and Planes, Mayflower Books, 1978.

(Editor) *Spy and Mystery Stories* (juvenile), Octopus Books, 1978.

Lawrence of Arabia (juvenile; illustrated by Roy Schofield), Macdonald Educational, 1978.

What Animal Is That? (juvenile), Octopus Books, 1978.

Great Warriors (juvenile), MacDonald Educational, 1979.

Also author of *The History of the Ship*, 1968; *Cowboys*, 1973; *The London Experience*, 1977; *Earthquakes and Volcanoes; One Day in Inca Peru; One Thousand Great Events.* Author of radio series "Personal Appearance"; editor of cassette series "The Historymakers." Contributor to *International Encyclopedia of Aviation, Question and Answer Book, Magpie Story Book, Great Disasters, One Hundred Great Adventures,* and *Fifty Great Journeys.*

WORK IN PROGRESS: A novel with a film background.

ANDERSON, Wayne 1946-

PERSONAL: Born November 10, 1946, in Leicester, England; son of David (a stock control manager) and Joan (a knitwear designer; maiden name, Swann) Anderson; married wife, Jennifer (a laboratory assistant), February 24, 1968; children: Nick, Rosy, Lizzie, Faye. *Education:* Leicester College of Art, B.A., 1966. *Home:* 1 Melbourne Close, Kibworth Beauchamp, Leicestershire, England.

CAREER: Illustrator in London, England, 1968; free-lance author and illustrator in Leicestershire, England, 1970—. *Awards, honors:* Gold Medal for the Best Illustrated Children's Book from the American Society of Illustrators, 1976, for *Ratsmagic; The Flight of Dragons* was selected one of the American Library Association's Best Books for Young Adults, 1979.

WRITINGS:

JUVENILE; ALL SELF-ILLUSTRATED

(With Christopher Logue) *Ratsmagic*, Pantheon, 1976.
(With Peter Dickinson) *The Flight of Dragons*, Harper, 1979.
(With C. Logue) *The Magic Circus*, Viking, 1979.
(With Leonard Price; retold by Naomi Lewis) *A Mouse's Tale*, Harper, 1984.

ILLUSTRATOR

Heinrich Seidel, *The Magic Inkstand*, translated by Elizabeth W. Taylor, Salem House, 1982.

Contributor of illustrations to Time-Life's "Enchanted World" series.

WORK IN PROGRESS: "*Everyone a Winner,* a book about a race with split pages in which children can manipulate and alter the image from page to page. In this book animals and

WAYNE ANDERSON

birds are racing towards the back page of the book traveling on all types of crazy home-made vehicles. By changing the head and body and means of transport the child (reader) can choose who wins!"

SIDELIGHTS: "I had a conventional upbringing and childhood, and for as long as I can remember I have been drawing and painting. Leaving school at fifteen I was lucky to be offered a place at art school in a three-year vocational course studying design and advertising. The offer of the course was based on my obvious passion for the subject as at fifteen I did not have the qualifications necessary to enter art school. After three years I was offered a postgraduate year and left at the age of nineteen.

"At this time I was unaware that I could make a living at illustration and while looking for jobs in advertising agencies and design groups, one of the people who interviewed me recognised the overwhelming influence of drawings in my portfolio and suggested the possibility of illustration.

"This I decided to do, and I gradually established myself as an illustrator working on posters, magazines, greeting cards, record sleeves, packaging, advertising, and eventually, a full-length animated film based on my book *The Flight of Dragons.*

"As a result of my illustrations, I was approached by the owner of an advertising agency in Paris who liked my work, and he asked what ambition I had that had not been fulfilled. I told him that I had always yearned to do a children's book, and he said that if I could produce a good story he would supply the money. That is how I began *Ratsmagic,* my first children's book, and things have developed from there.

"I am now working on a book in a completely different way. Normally I am commissioned by a publisher, but this time I am half way through a book and hope to find a publisher interested in it.

It had outgrown the size of the well, and came forth full-grown. ■ (From *The Flight of Dragons* by Peter Dickinson. Illustrated by Wayne Anderson.)

URSULA ARNDT

"As you may deduce, my life/career has been a combination of luck, accident, and hard work."

About illustrating children's books, Anderson comments: "I like to have as much time as possible and a free hand, which is not always possible. But I find, for me, that's the way to get the best results."[1]

Anderson's other interests include designing three-dimensional illustrated puzzles, football and relaxing with friends.

FOOTNOTE SOURCES

[1]Lee Kingman and others, editors, *Illustrators of Children's Books: 1967-1976*, Horn Book, 1978.

ARNDT, Ursula (Martha H.)

PERSONAL: Born in Duesseldorf, Germany; daughter of Ernst and Helene (Plate) Arndt. *Education:* Attended the Academy of Arts, Duesseldorf, 1942-47.

CAREER: Free-lance artist and illustrator, 1961—; H. G. Caspari, Inc., New York, N.Y., Christmas card designer, beginning 1963.

ILLUSTRATOR:

ALL JUVENILE, EXCEPT AS INDICATED

Alfred Slote, *The Princess Who Wouldn't Talk* (fiction), Bobbs-Merrill, 1964.

Mike Thaler, *The Prince and the Seven Moons* (fiction), Macmillan, 1966.

Blanche J. Thompson, compiler, *All the Silver Pennies: Combining "Silver Pennies" and "More Silver Pennies"* (anthology of poems), Macmillan, 1967.

Mary Cantwell, *St. Patrick's Day,* Crowell, 1967.

Elizabeth Coatsworth, *Troll Weather* (fiction), Macmillan, 1967.

Phyllis Purscell, *Old Boy's Tree House and Other Deep Forest Tales,* Weybright & Talley, 1968.

Stephen Seskin, *The Stone in the Road* (fiction), Van Nostrand, 1968.

Edna Barth, *Lilies, Rabbits and Painted Eggs: The Story of the Easter Symbols,* Seabury, 1970.

E. Barth, *Holly, Reindeer, and Colored Lights: The Story of the Christmas Symbols,* Seabury, 1971.

E. Barth, *Witches, Pumpkins, and Grinning Ghosts: The Story of the Halloween Symbols,* Seabury, 1972.

E. Barth, *Hearts, Cupids, and Red Roses: The Story of the Valentine Symbols,* Seabury, 1974.

E. Barth, *Turkeys, Pilgrims, and Indian Corn: The Story of the Thanksgiving Symbols* (Junior Literary Guild selection), Clarion Books, 1975.

Klaus F. Wellmann, *Muzzinabikon: Indianische Felsbilder Nordamerikas aus fuenf Jahrtausenden* (adult; also illustrated with photographs by K. F. Wellmann), Akademische Druck- u. Verlagsanstalt, 1976, published as *A Survey of North American Indian Rock Art,* 1979.

E. Barth, *Shamrocks, Harps, and Shillelaghs: The Story of the St. Patrick's Day Symbols,* Clarion Books, 1977.

E. Barth, compiler, *A Christmas Feast: Poems, Sayings, Greetings, and Wishes,* Clarion Books, 1979.

James C. Giblin, *Fireworks, Picnics, and Flags: The Story of the Fourth of July Symbols,* Clarion Books, 1983.

Also contributor of illustrations to periodicals.

ASKA, Warabe 1944-
(Takeshi Masuda)

PERSONAL: Born Takeshi Masuda, February 3, 1944, in Kagawa, Japan; immigrated to Canada, 1979; son of Satoru (an office worker) and Miyoko (a dressmaker; maiden name, Fujimoto) Masuda; married Keiko Inouye (a housewife), October 17, 1979; children: Yohyoh, Mari, Kohta. *Education:* Attended Takamatsu Technological School. *Religion:* Buddhist. *Home and office:* 1019 Lorne Park Rd., Mississauga, Ontario, Canada L5H 2Z9.

CAREER: Ad House (design studio), Tokyo, Japan, founder and president, 1965-78; artist and writer, 1979—. *Exhibitions*—One-man shows: Konohana Gallery, Tokyo, Japan, 1972; Mitsukoshi Gallery, Takamatsu, Japan, 1973; Madden Galleries, London, 1975, 1982; Tokai Gallery, Nagoya, Japan, 1978; Gustafsson Galleries, Toronto, Canada, 1982; Market Gallery, Toronto, 1983; Shayne Gallery, Montreal, Canada, 1984; Colborne Lodge, Toronto, 1984; Art Emporium, Vancouver, Canada, 1986. Group shows: "Discovering High Park," Market Gallery, Toronto, Canada, 1983; Biennale of Graphic Design, Brno, Czechoslovakia, 1984, 1988; International Youth Year Poster Competition, Bologna, Italy, and Otani Memorial Art Museum, Nishinomiya, Japan, both 1985; Biennale of Illustration, Bratislava, Czechoslovakia, 1985, 1987; Biennale of Illustration, Barcelona, Spain, 1986; Illustrators' Exhibition, Bologna, Italy, 1986; "Once upon a Time," Vancouver Art Gallery, Canada, 1988. Collections: Hino Motors Co.,

Ltd., Tokyo, Japan; Corporation of the Collection of the City of Toronto, Canada; Osborn Collection, Toronto Public Library, Canada.

AWARDS, HONORS: UNESCO Exhibition Prize from Japan's minister of Education, 1966; City of Toronto Book Award, Choice Book from the Children's Book Centre (Toronto), and selected one of the Society of Graphic Designers of Canada Best Books of the Eighties, all 1985, and Honorable Mention as one of the Best Designed Books from All over the World at the International Leipzig Book Fair, East Germany, 1986, all for *Who Goes to the Park;* work selected for UNICEF greeting card, London, England, 1985; Special Mention from the International Youth Year Poster Competition, 1985.

WRITINGS:

JUVENILE; ALL SELF-ILLUSTRATED

Discovering Japan in Eighty Days, Maki Shoten, 1973.
A Midsummer Night's Dream, Alice Kan, 1976.
Ma Vlast, Alice Kan, 1977.
Harry Janos, Alice Kan, 1977.
Dandelion Puffs, Liblio Publishing (Tokyo), 1981.
P-yororo O-yororo, Liblio Publishing, 1982.
Who Goes to the Park, Tundra Books, 1984.
Who Hides in the Park, Tundra Books, 1986.

ADAPTATIONS:

"Who Goes to the Park" (filmstrip; also available in French), Prisma.

WORK IN PROGRESS: Fairies in the Garden, tentative title.

SIDELIGHTS: Aska (born Takeshi Masuda) immigrated to Canada in 1979 after extensive travel and numerous exhibi-

WARABE ASKA

The sea and sky are full of mysteries. ■ (From *Who Hides in the Park* by Warabe Aska. Illustrated by the author.)

tions of his work in England, France, Italy, Spain, and West Germany. His books have received international acclaim. *Who Goes to the Park,* a collection of paintings and poems about Toronto's High Park, has been recommended by critics as a delightful and refreshing tribute that should appeal equally to adults and young people. Aska's next book, *Who Hides in the Park,* is a similar tribute to Stanley Park in Vancouver. Critics have praised the work, which is trilingual in English, French, and Japanese, as imaginative, breathtaking, and unique.

"In my childhood I became interested in reading, writing, and painting when in junior high school, a friend invited me to the activities of an art club. At the age of twenty-eight I had my first exhibit at a gallery in Tokyo. After traveling around Japan I had the chance to write and illustrate for various monthly magazines, and a year later I wrote and illustrated my first book, *Discovering Japan in Eighty Days.* It was a turning point in my career, as I began to focus on the book world instead of on commercial artwork.

"I have traveled extensively in western and eastern Europe, a world I've found very different from the Japan I know, and I have developed many new ideas from my discoveries there. My next five picture books for children are based on my ex-

periences in countries as varied as England, Czechoslovakia, Spain, and Canada.

"Many of my ideas come to me during my time spent in airplanes, trains, buses, boats, and cars. I also find that sitting out in the open air inspires me. Natural objects like trees, flowers, birds, animals, the sun and the moon, clouds, water, and cheerful children trigger my ideas. My imagination has been expanding greatly since I immigrated to Canada in 1979 because of the many interesting subjects that motivate me here, such as the people, Canada's multicultural aspect, and its nature.

"The readers of my books are gradually beginning to include adults. I never think of a particular age group while creating a book."

Aska describes the beginnings of his book *Who Goes to the Park.* "A huge pond had been on my mind since I came to Toronto. It is called Grenadier Pond, in the southwest corner of High Park. It has been the scene of a thousand lovers' trysts and has inspired fantasies of high adventure for generations of children. The water of the pond was always reflecting the changing of seasons. In winter the water froze over the pond and turned the ice rink into a white carpet. In spring the ice melted away and turned into a cradle for the waterfowl. In summer the water was moved in waves by the fishes, boats and yachts and turned into an ocean. In fall the water took up the colour of autumn and turned into a mirror.

"Thus the water of the pond was changing vividly just like magic. I felt as if someone had conjured up the pond. Since then I have been fascinated by its magical scenes and I started work for the book at once.

"One day in winter I stood on the ice in the pond then tried to hop and stamp along on it. But nothing happened at all. The ice was so thick, hard as concrete pavement. I couldn't believe that because I was raised in a warm country. I was. . .thrilled. . .it was my first chance to stand and enjoy walking on the pond. Afterwards these experiences brought many ideas to me. Then my interest expanded into the whole park.

"There are many activities,. . .and facilities there such as skating, cross-country skiing, bird watching, fishing, picnicing, boating, summer concerts, swimming, tennis, lawn bowling, a little zoo, nature trails, playgrounds and so on. All ages from babies to old folks were having good times. An epitome of life and society existed there.

"Who goes to the park? Why do they go for a walk? What do they do? How does nature grow, how does it breathe? Where do they touch and fit in with. . .nature?. . .etc. I usually kept these questions in my mind while observing. This is because impression, discovery and learning by experience are very important for me to write about and to paint. Therefore I spent time in getting these answers for more than two years."[1]

FOOTNOTE SOURCES:

[1]Warabe Aska, "Who Goes to the Park," *Our Choice/Your Choice,* 1985/86.

FOR MORE INFORMATION SEE:

Toronto Star, March 1, 1985.
Canadian Bookseller, April, 1985 (p. 16).
Gazette (Montreal), April 13, 1985 (p. C-2).

BEARDEN, Romare (Howard)   1914(?)-1988

OBITUARY NOTICE—See sketch in *SATA* Volume 22: Born September 2, 1914 (some sources say 1912) in Charlotte, N.C.; died following a stroke (some sources say cancer), March 11 (some sources say March 12), 1988, in New York, N.Y. Artist, social worker, semi-professional athlete, composer, and author. Bearden will be best remembered for his highly acclaimed artwork, particularly his collages featuring themes from black life. One of the first critically and financially successful black artists in the United States, Bearden nevertheless periodically served as a social worker in New York to supplement his painting income. While in college he played for a time with the Boston Tigers, an all-black baseball team. Bearden also composed songs, including the jazz classic "Seabreeze." Music, especially jazz, greatly influenced his art. He once told an interviewer that "abstract expressionism is very close to the aesthetics of jazz. That's the feeling you get from it—involvement, personality, improvisation, rhythm, color."

Bearden exhibited his art in many one-man shows at locations such as New York City's Museum of Modern Art and the Albert Loeb Gallery in Paris, France. Credited with doing a great deal to promote black art, Bearden and some of his associates founded the Cinque Gallery in the 1960s to feature the work of minority artists. He also was a founding member of the Spiral Group whose purpose was to help black artists. In 1987, he was awarded the National Medal of Arts by President Reagan. "Art," defined Bearden, "is a process that renders the things of the world about us into a style—which is a humanizing process."

Throughout his distinguished art career, Bearden illustrated such books as Samuel Allen's *Poems from Africa,* penned the foreword to Elton Clay Fox's *Black Artists of the New Generation,* and co-authored *The Painter's Mind: A Study of the Relations of Structure and Space in Painting,* and *Six Black Masters of American Art.*

FOR MORE INFORMATION SEE:

School Arts, September, 1977.
New Yorker, November 28, 1977.
Horizon, August, 1979.
Smithsonian, March, 1981.
Contemporary Authors, Volume 102, Gale, 1981.
Who's Who in American Art, 17th edition, Bowker, 1986.
Current Biography, H. W. Wilson, 1988.

OBITUARIES

New York Times, March 13, 1988.
Los Angeles Times, March 14, 1988.
Washington Post, March 14, 1988.
Chicago Tribune, March 15, 1988.

BELDEN, Wilanne Schneider   1925-

PERSONAL: Born October 14, 1925, in Pittsburgh, Pa.; daughter of W. J. (a salesman) and Ida Mary (a teacher; maiden name, Hood) Schneider; married Robert Adams Belden (a business consultant and college lecturer), August 14, 1948; children: Leigh Schneider (son). *Education:* State University of Iowa, B.F.A., 1946; San Diego State College (now San Diego State University), Teacher's Certificate, 1958; California Western University (now United States International University), M.A., 1963; further graduate study at various universities. *Politics:* Republican. *Religion:* Episcopalian. *Home and office:* 1029 Santa Barbara St., San Diego, Calif. 92107.

CAREER: Erie Playhouse, Erie, Pa., founding director of children's theatre, and writer and director of Children's Theatre Radio Program, 1948; San Diego Chamber of Commerce, San Diego, Calif., corresponding secretary, 1955-58; San Diego Unified School District, San Diego, teacher, 1958-86; University of California Extension, San Diego, teacher of animated filmmaking, 1973; La Jolla Museum of Contemporary Art, La Jolla, Calif., staff teacher in filmmaking, 1973-74; author, 1979—. Lecturer. Founding member and performer, Old Globe Consort, 1955; founding director of San Diego Gilbert and Sullivan Repertory Company, 1970. Consultant to San Diego Unified School District GATE program. Member, Friends of the San Diego Public Library for Children's Services. *Member:* Authors League of America, Authors Guild, California Association for the Gifted, Association of San Diego Educators for the Gifted, Sunset View Elementary School Parent-Teachers Association (life member).

WRITINGS:

JUVENILE FANTASY

Frankie! (illustrated by Stewart Daniels), Harcourt, 1987.

I just barely didn't snicker at the change in the men's expressions. ■ (From *Frankie!* by Wilanne Schneider Belden. Illustrated by Stewart Daniels.)

YOUNG ADULT FANTASY

Mind-Call, Atheneum, 1981.
The Rescue of Ranor, Atheneum, 1983.
Mind-Hold, Harcourt, 1987.
Mind-Find, Harcourt, 1988.

CONTRIBUTOR

Andre Norton, editor, *Tales of the Witch World,* Pinnacle Books, 1987.
A. Norton and Martin H. Greenberg, editors, *Cat Fantastic,* DAW, 1989.

WORK IN PROGRESS: *Shanna and the Piper; Martin and the Wrizzle; Jerith;* a sequel to *Frankie!;* three titles in the *Mind* series; a variety of other works for adults and young readers.

SIDELIGHTS: "I grew up in a suburb of Cleveland, Ohio, so long ago that I could go off to Nine Mile Creek with only my big white collie for company, spend the day there safely and happily, and trudge home in semi-darkness or stumble up the steep slope when my mother came to get me in the car. An only child with few friends—sick too much, too imaginative, too 'apart from' for reasons I did not understand—I cherished those friends I made and have several of them still. We 'played pretend' for hours. How I wish I had those plots and characters to use now!

"I wrote from the time I could hold a crayon and still remember writing down stories for which I had to make up my own symbols in order to record them. I participated in ballet from the age of five and planned to be a prima ballerina. I might have been one, had I not grown too tall and developed a foot ailment which meant I could never wear toe shoes. This hurt, but I had, to some degree, outgrown the intent, and I switched to tap, square, round, folk, and still dance whenever I can. At six, I joined the Cleveland Playhouse Children's Theatre, where I was in one production after another during elementary school. In high school my primary extra-curricular activities were playing the clarinet in concert, marching, and pep bands and participating in occasional dramatic productions.

"Being a member of the drama department at the University of Iowa didn't do much for my isolation. Drama majors were (and, I suspect, still are) looked on as being peculiar—even if they're as square as I was. During my four years I was in the cast or crew of every University Theatre production. I also had a children's radio program on which I took three items suggested by listeners and told a story about them—ad lib and live. (It went very well indeed, to my delight!) My intent was to become a director of a community theatre. But I graduated, got a job on a radio station giving household hints (ye gods!), and hoped for better.

"The following year I spent as the founding director of the Children's Playhouse in Erie, Pennsylvania, and writing and directing radio productions for a local station using my students as actors. Looking back, I know I did the latter far better than the former and have nothing but gratitude for Newell Tarrant, Playhouse Director, who kept me on, gave me the freedom to find out my strengths, and let me go at the end of the year with nothing but kind thoughts.

"I married, moved to San Diego, tried to get into the drama field—no luck as a director, though I did some acting—and produced a son. Five years later I found myself answering twenty to twenty-five hundred letters a year at the Chamber of Commerce and answering hundreds of questions at the Information Desk.

"At last, I got into teaching as an intern. I, who'd said I'd scrub other people's floors before I'd teach kids, found that I'd been shoved (kicking and screaming) into the best possible profession for me. I admit to being so non-standard that the powers-that-be did everything they could to discourage me, but 'my kids' *learned*. I kept at it for nearly thirty years—and I'm proud of the job I did. The oddball creative kids deserve at least one oddball creative teacher along their way.

"Those kids forced me to try to publish. They'd read everything! And what was being produced so infrequently was of the character I knew they needed. As other people play violins or backgammon, follow football teams or movie stars, I write—and always have. Writing was *my* thing, and I had no personal need to see the work in print. But what I write is what they want/need to read. I hope I get another five out in the next five years, though writers' block does interfere, and so does redecorating, gardening, travel, and over a hundred lectures a year—most of them in GATE classes, at Authors' Fairs, etc.

"I tell the students I talk with, that I hope they'll be as lucky as I've been. The two most important things in my professional life are kids and writing, so I have the best of both worlds—and time to enjoy them."

The writings of Belden form an integral part of her larger concern, the nurturing and guidance of highly intelligent children. "Somehow, to be different in this way is to be other-

MIND-CALL

Every moment she had spent in dream replayed itself in her memory. ■ (From *Mind-Call* by Wilanne Schneider Belden. Illustrated by Troy Howell.)

than-human. The kids I teach have to face this. And they aren't nonhuman. They are the best the human race has yet developed. I want other children to meet such young people, to accept that having intellectual gifts makes a person only as different from others as all others are from each other.''

Belden's *Mind* group of books were written in response to the shortage she perceived in literature that "faced squarely and without equivocation the almost insurmountable problem of being very highly intelligent. I write what my editor calls science fiction and what I call modern fantasy because I read it and always have. The most interesting, exciting, mind-stretching books I read as a child and young person were in those categories." Belden named MacDonald, Tolkien, Lang, Norton, Bradbury, Burroughs, and Le Guin among those who influenced her writing.

Underlying Belden's personal philosophy is a belief that every child is gifted in some way. She summed up her views on the writer's craft by saying: ''While a story is written with a specific target audience in mind, the book is enjoyed by people of all ages who retain the attributes of childhood—the ability to wonder, to explore, to greet each new thing with delight.''

HOBBIES AND OTHER INTERESTS: Drama, dance, photography, music, gardening, reading, cooking, basketmaking, handcrafts, and travel (England, Europe, India, Mexico).

BRADBURY, Bianca   1908-1982
(Jane Wyatt, Molly Wyatt)

PERSONAL: Born December 4, 1908, in Mystic, Conn.; died May 29, 1982, in New Milford, Conn.; daughter of Thomas Wheeler (a purchasing agent) and Blanche (Keigwin) Ryley; married Harry Burdette Bradbury (an attorney), August 14, 1930 (died, December 3, 1977); children: William Wyatt, Michael Ryley. *Education:* Connecticut College for Women (now Connecticut College), B.A., 1930. *Politics:* Democrat. *Home:* New Milford, Conn. *Agent:* McIntosh & Otis., 475 Fifth Ave., New York, N.Y. 10017.

CAREER: Author, writing primarily for children and young adults. Member, New Milford (Conn.) Board of Education, 1953-63. New Milford Library, trustee, 1965-82, member of the board, 1965-77. Co-founder of New Milford Animal Welfare Society. *Member:* Poetry Society of America, American Literary Guild, Authors League of America, New Milford Historical Society. *Awards, honors:* German Children's Book Prize Honor List, 1968, for the German edition of *Two on an Island; Dogs and More Dogs* was selected one of Child Study Association of America's Children's Books of the Year, 1968, *Andy's Mountain*, 1969, and *Nancy and Her Johnny-O*, 1970.

WRITINGS:

JUVENILE

Muggins, Houghton, 1943.
Five Baby Chicks, Houghton, 1944.
The Antique Cat (Junior Literary Guild selection), Winston, 1946.
(Under name Jane Wyatt) *Rowdy,* Tell-A-Tale-Books, 1946.
Amos Learns to Talk, Rand McNally, 1951.
Brave Fireman, Grosset, 1951.
The Brave Fireman and the Firehouse Cat, Wonder Book, 1951.
One Kitten Too Many (illustrated by M. Nichols), Houghton, 1952.
Tough Guy, Houghton, 1953.
Mutt, Houghton, 1956.
Mike's Island, Putnam, 1958.
Jim and His Monkey (illustrated by V. Guthrie), Houghton, 1958.
Happy Acres, Steck, 1958.
A Flood in Still River, Dial, 1960.
The Circus Punk, Macrae, 1963.
Two on an Island (ALA Notable Book; illustrated by Robert MacLean), Houghton, 1965.
Sam and the Colonels, Macrae, 1966.
The Three Keys (illustrated by R. MacLean), Houghton, 1967.
Dogs and More Dogs (illustrated by R. MacLean), Houghton, 1968.
Andy's Mountain (illustrated by R. MacLean), Houghton, 1969.
The Loner (illustrated by John Gretzer), Houghton, 1970.

YOUNG ADULT NOVELS

Say Hello, Candy, Coward, 1960.
The Amethyst Summer (Junior Literary Guild selection), Ives Washburn, 1962.
Goodness and Mercy Jenkins, Ives Washburn, 1963.

BIANCA BRADBURY

Shoes in September, Ives Washburn, 1963.
Laughter in Our House (Junior Literary Guild selection), Ives Washburn, 1963.
Flight into Spring (Junior Literary Guild selection), Ives Washburn, 1965.
Laurie, Ives Washburn, 1965.
Lots of Love, Lucinda, Ives Washburn, 1966 (published in England as *Lucinda,* MacDonald, 1969).
The Undergrounders (illustrated by Jon Nielsen), Ives Washburn, 1966.
The Blue Year, Ives Washburn, 1967.
Red Sky at Night, Ives Washburn, 1968.
To a Different Tune, Ives Washburn, 1968.
Girl in the Middle, Ives Washburn, 1969.
Nancy and Her Johnny-O, Ives Washburn, 1970.
A New Penny, Houghton, 1971.
Those Traver Kids (illustrated by Marvin Friedman), Houghton, 1972.
My Pretty Girl (illustrated by Charles Robinson), Houghton, 1973.
Boy on the Run, Seabury, 1974.
In Her Father's Footsteps (illustrated by Richard Cuffari), Houghton, 1976.
I'm Vinnie, I'm Me (illustrated by R. Cuffari), Houghton, 1976.
Where's Jim Now?, Houghton, 1978.
Mixed-Up Summer, Houghton, 1979.
The Dogwalker, Warne, 1979.
The Girl Who Wanted Out, Scholastic Book Services, 1981.
The Loving Year, Scholastic Book Services, 1982.
(Under name Molly Wyatt) *Kim's Wonder,* New American Library, 1982.

OTHER

Half the Music (poetry), Fine Editions, 1944.
The Curious Wine (novel), Beechhurst, 1948.

Contributor to periodicals, including *Saturday Evening Post, Woman's Day, Colliers, Yankee Magazine, Family Circle, Saturday Review of Literature,* and *New York Herald Tribune.*

SIDELIGHTS: Bradbury died on May 29, 1982, in New Milford, Conn. Her son, Michael Bradbury kindly provided *Something about the Author* with an insight into her life: "My mother was the youngest of three children. She was a Ryley, which is an English not an Irish family. Her mother's family was Keigwin. They go all the way back to George Denison, who came over on the Mayflower and settled in the southwestern part of Connecticut. My great uncle who researched the Keigwin family traced it quite far back to some distant royal family in England. Unfortunately, he died before he could finish his research.

"Mystic, where my mother spent her early childhood, is a beautiful town overlooking a river by the same name. When she was nine, the family moved to New Haven overlooking the harbor. The sea held an important place in her life as is evidenced in her writings. It represented something romantic to her. After all, her grandfather ran away to sea when he was twelve, later to become a ship captain, and her father carried on tradition by going to sea as a sailor. And, when my mother turned sixty, she and my father bought a thirty-foot cabin cruiser, which they kept anchored in Mystic and sailed every weekend from late April until late September.

"After attending public schools in New Haven, my mother went to Connecticut College for Women in New London. She worked as a waitress and other odd jobs to put herself through school. Her brother, Roger, went to Wesleyan University as a pre-med student, and through him she met my father. They married in 1930 and moved to New Milford where my father set up his law practice. In 1937 they bought the old house in which I was born. My brother was already around, having

The horse took off, racing around her meadow, snorting, muscles moving like silk, free. ■ (From *My Pretty Girl* by Bianca Bradbury. Illustrated by Charles Robinson.)

been born in 1936. The house, it turned out, was haunted. My mother was very much into parapsychology and firmly believed that she was visited by a ghost.''[1]

The ghost, it was discovered, was Oliver. The story went like this: ''The family—mother, father, child—who owned the house previously ran it as a farm with handyman Oliver as caretaker of barn and cattle. When Oliver took sick, the child prevailed upon his parents to allow Oliver the use of his room until he recuperated. Oliver did not get better and died in the child's room, the same room that later became my mother's bedroom. My mother wrote a paper about Oliver's presence and sent it to a group of parapsychologists at Duke University. Years after we moved out, the house burned down and her first thought was, 'Poor Oliver, I wonder what happened to him?'

''In 1942, my father joined the army, the house was sold, my brother, mother and I moved to Stonington into yet another haunted house. It was during the fall of that year that my brother suffered severe asthma attacks and was deathly allergic to the house. He couldn't breathe and spent most of his time outside wrapped up in a blanket. We lived in the house long enough to find out about the ghosts, however. The two brothers who previously owned the house had a falling out and divided their quarters in half, boarding up all the doors between them. One brother committed suicide by throwing himself down the other's well. Theoretically his ghost is still float-

ing around in the well, but my mother did not feel comfortable with him. He was not a 'nice Oliver.' So, we moved into a modern house in Mystic.''[1] The family returned to New Milford when their father returned from the war in 1946.

''Before my brother and I were born, my mother was already submitting poetry, short stories and articles to *Family Circle, Women's Day* and other magazines. I don't know exactly when she started writing. I grew up thinking that writing was her 'job,' so I always saw it as a normal thing for a mother to do. She would say, 'I got another book published,' but she never made a big deal out of it. It wasn't until much later that I realized she had gained a certain degree of fame. She was very prolific, publishing, at one point, two books a year. She started with small children's books. A source of frustration for her was that publishers did not like controversial issues. Publishers looked for set formats—mommy and daddy and a stereotypic life and no deviation from that; no divorce, no sex, no death, etc. My mother did not see life as a perfect bubble and felt that children should be made aware of that. So, she turned more and more to teenage novels where she was able to get into some meatier subjects, like the death of a parent, the drug problems or the sexual situations teenagers go through.

''After my brother and I were grown up, she wrote about teenage girls' problems. Through her activities at the Animal Welfare, the Library and the Board of Education, she had met quite a few teenage girls. She witnessed a lot of situations and

Carey scooped him up and held him to her skinny shoulder. He cooed and then he belched. ■ (From *A New Penny* by Bianca Bradbury.)

problems girls have to deal with at that age, enough to inspire her to write several books.''[1]

Many readers wrote to her and felt comfortable relating some of their personal difficulties. ''I always wanted to do a story about a girl growing up with a family of boys,'' Bianca Bradbury wrote. ''I grew up in such a house. I hasten to say that brothers are wonderful and give a girl good practical training, but I can sympathize with Bayley's trials in this story. I started [*The Amethyst Summer*] and almost immediately Bayley and her brothers, parents, neighbors, boy friends, great-aunt, and even her dog took over and the story wrote itself. It seems to me that every girl goes through what Bayley did—comes to a time when she has to stop being harum-scarum and start taking responsibility.

''Maybe that's the best thing about being a writer—you meet such nice people. Ever since I finished *The Amethyst Summer,* I've wondered what Bayley and the others are up to. One character in the book I don't wonder about is Bayley's dog Happy. Happy is also our own large, long-eared basset hound and I *know* what he's doing. He is slopping around the house dragging his rope, trying to talk me into a walk on the hill. It seems a good idea.''[2]

Flight into Spring is about Bianca Bradbury's grandmother, affectionately known to her as 'Mom.' It was a book she ''most enjoyed doing. . . .[My grandmother, a Southerner,] met my grandfather [a Northerner] at the beginning of the Civil War and they fell in love. Grandpa fought through the Shenandoah campaigns and was imprisoned three times after capture. It's true that 'Mom' went to Lincoln's funeral. She and my grandfather worshipped Abraham Lincoln. When I was a little girl, I wasn't taught 'Twinkle, Twinkle' and other childish poems. Grandpa saw to it that I memorized Lincoln's Gettysburg Address and I was reciting it when I was six.

''Mom lived in Connecticut all her [married] life, a long life, for she died in her hundredth year. But she remained in many ways a southern woman. She was a tiny little thing, pretty as a picture right to the end. She never had a sick day. In her nineties, she used to walk to the beauty parlor in Mystic once a week to have her pure white hair 'crimped' and she wore it tied back with a black velvet ribbon.

''I have many of her things which I treasure: the little tin in which she used to make cupcakes when she was a bride, her silk wedding slippers, the gold brooch given her by her cousin who fought with Lee's army. I also keep hanging by our fireplace the. . .skillet my grandfather carried fastened to his belt through three years of war.

''When Mom was very old, I wrote down the stories she told me of her girlhood which have gone into *Flight into Spring.* I guess its fairly obvious that I adored that lovely, gallant, little old lady.''[3]

Bradbury's mother was a rigid woman. She was a member of the Women's Temperance Society, and, needless to say, when she came to visit, the liquor bottles were hidden with care. Nobody ever offered her a drink stronger than ice tea. She also never understood how her daughter could earn a living writing books.''[1]

Bianca Bradbury's working habits ''were very regular,'' recalls Michael. ''She usually got up around five in the morning when it was quiet in the house. She made herself a cup of coffee, fed her animals, and then sat down at the kitchen counter with her notebook. She did that every day. She wrote down thoughts, new ideas for stories, feelings about the books she

He stared at the boat and a great longing swelled in him. ■ (From *The Loner* by Bianca Bradbury. Illustrated by John Gretzer.)

was reading, and any topic that struck her fancy. She also kept a pad next to her bed, and if she woke up in the middle of the night with an idea in her head, she would jot it down. When she actually started to write a book, she looked through her notes and typed directly from them. By 11 a.m., she would call it quits. When my brother and I were still young, she would be interrupted by the daily routine of getting us off to school and getting my father off to work. Then she would go back to her writing for a while. But after we left home, she just plugged away at it.

''She wrote mostly from experience, sometimes using bits and pieces of her children's experiences. When I served in the Peace Corps in tropical Africa as a generalist in rural development, I met Lucinda who was working for the education department. She was sent to the United States on a sabbatical, and I suggested that if she happened to go through Connecticut, to give my folks a call. She did, in fact, get to Connecticut and spent a very long weekend with my parents. My mother took her to meet a couple of very straight-laced old Polish farmers who had never been off their farm. They were quite fascinated by Lucinda with her head all wrapped up in a turban and her long piece of cloth wrapped around her body. The farmer's wife asked Lucinda how she put her dress on. Well, right there in the front yard, Lucinda unwrapped herself and stood completely naked before demonstrating how she wrapped herself in the cloth. *Lots of Love, Lucinda* was the result of the weekend visit.

''In 1955, the East Coast was hit by a hurricane, devastating whole towns and injuring many people. During the time of the flood my mother and father were involved in the food and clothing bank for people who had lost everything. It was interesting because there was a huge regional effort at organizing and helping. My father was the regional director of Civil Defense. He and mother organized the massive food and clothing bank. *A Flood in Still River* was based on that experience.

"*The Curious Wine* was the only adult novel she wrote. She wrote it shortly after World War II, in 1948. It is the story of a Jewish man marrying a Christian woman in a small New England town. It was not well received at all. The town people of Mystic, it seemed, identified too closely with the story, and were very offended to be considered bigots. During those years people didn't want discussion of controversial issues. But my mother did, and in many ways was ahead of her time. She was a very straightforward woman. You always knew where she stood.

"She sometimes suffered dry spells and was very frustrated when things didn't seem to jell. About three years before she died, she felt that her writing days were over. She sold one book that year, and couldn't get on with a second. But then, inspiration came back. She was so relieved. I only remember those very serious dry spells happening twice. Usually when she was stuck with her writing, she would put it out of her mind for a while, and let the inspiration come back to her in a natural way. She occupied herself with other hobbies like vegetable and flower gardening. She also kept animals over the years—rabbits, dogs and cats, a goat, and a pig named by

my father after a colonel in the army he didn't like. Dogs and cats were her favorite and her desire to help unwanted animals caused her and a few friends to organize the New Milford Animal Welfare Society which arranged placement of animals, inoculation, and spaying fees.

"She was quite a character, my mother. She loved life and was very spirited. I remember when she was sixty, she was looking for a new car. She looked at Volvos and Pontiacs, but then she saw this Alpha Romeo sport car and had to have it. It's ridiculous, a little sixty-year-old lady doesn't drive a bright red convertible Alpha Romeo. But, she did. She loved shifting and going fast. She was caught one time drag racing some of the kids downtown after one of her Board of Education meetings.

"The last six months of her life were pretty tough. She had been a smoker all her life and as a result suffered from emphysema. She didn't like it much when she got sick—too much of a bother. She was in and out of the hospital, but kept up with her writing. In the middle of May, it was a great relief for her to send the finished manuscript to her agent. Unfortunately, it was never published. She wasn't able to do the rewrites. The week she died, she was very upset because she had not been able to respond to some of the fan letters that were on her desk. That's when I started doing it, so that she would know the letters would be answered. She received mail from all over, Canada, England, etc. and made it a point to answer every one. She felt that was part of her responsibilities. She would give her opinions when anyone asked for advice.

The fire was eating through the roof. ■ (From *In Her Father's Footsteps* by Bianca Bradbury. Illustrated by Richard Cuffari.)

And if they asked her how to get into the business of writing, she always encouraged them to keep reading and keep writing."[1]

FOOTNOTE SOURCES

[1]Based on an interview by Catherine Ruello for *Something about the Author.*
[2]*Junior Literary Guild,* February, 1963.
[3]*Junior Literary Guild,* February, 1965.

FOR MORE INFORMATION SEE:

Horn Book, October, 1969.
Library Journal, June 15, 1970.
Martha E. Ward and Dorothy A. Marquardt, *Authors of Books for Young People,* 2nd edition, Scarecrow, 1971.
Doris de Montreville and Elizabeth D. Crawford, editors, *Fourth Book of Junior Authors and Illustrators,* H. W. Wilson, 1978.

OBITUARIES

New Milford Times (Conn.), June 3, 1982.
Litchfield County Times (Conn.), June 4, 1982.

BRADFORD, Ann (Liddell)   1917-

PERSONAL: Born November 9, 1917, in San Leandro, Calif.; daughter of Charles Andrew and Emma Beauvard (De Camp) Liddell; married Gene Waukenas Bradford; children: Charles Churchill O'Neil, Margaret Ann O'Neil Gale. *Education:* California State University, Fresno, B.A., 1952, M.A., 1957; University of Maryland, College Park, Ed.D., 1964. *Home:* 686 Riverlake Way, Sacramento, Calif. 95831. *Office:* California State University School of Education, 6000 Jay St., Sacramento, Calif. 95819.

CAREER: Fresno County Schools, Calif., teacher, 1946-52; Kern County Schools, Calif., speech therapist, 1952-54, elementary consultant, 1954-64; Fresno State College, assistant professor, 1957-64; University of California, Santa Barbara, assistant professor, 1964-66; Santa Maria School District, Calif., supervisor, 1964-66; University of California, Davis, assistant professor, 1966; San Francisco State College, Calif., associate professor of elementary education, 1966-69; California State University, Sacramento, professor, 1969—, chairman, department of teacher education, 1982-83. Consultant to Siskiyou County, El Dorado County, San Joaquin County, Sacramento County, Berkeley County City Schools, Sacramento City Schools, Desert Sands City Schools, Riverside City Schools, Episcopalian Church, Marin County, State Department of Education, Calif., and Migrant Education, North Calif., 1966—. President and member of board of directors for Community Child Care Programs, 1971-81; member of Network for Citizens Participation in Education, 1982.

MEMBER: California Teachers Association, California Professors of Early Childhood Education (newsletter editor, publisher, 1973-80, vice-president, 1979-82, president, 1982—), Association of California School Administrators (task force chairman, 1972-74), National Science Foundation (fellow, 1973-74), National Association for Education of Young Children, Pi Lambda Theta.

WRITINGS:

Working with Primaries through the Sunday School, Convention Press (Nashville), 1961.
(With Kal Gezi) *Beebi, the Little Blue Bell: A Story to Finish* (illustrated by Dan Siculan), Child's World, 1976.

(With K. Gezi) *One Little White Shoe: A Story to Finish* (illustrated by D. Siculan), Child's World, 1976.

"MAPLE STREET FIVE" SERIES; ALL WITH KAL GEZI; JUVENILE; ALL ILLUSTRATED BY MINA G. McLEAN

The Mystery of the Live Ghosts, Child's World, 1978.
The Mystery of the Missing Raccoon, Child's World, 1978.
The Mystery in the Secret Club House, Child's World, 1978.
The Mystery of the Blind Writer, Child's World, 1980.
The Mystery of the Missing Dogs, Child's World, 1980.
The Mystery at Misty Falls, Child's World, 1980.
The Mystery at the Tree House, Child's World, 1980.
The Mystery of the Square Footprints, Child's World, 1980.
The Mystery of the Midget Clown, Child's World, 1980.

Also author of *The Teaching of Spelling,* 1959; *Home Visitations,* 1960; *How to Write Anecdotes and Analyze Data,* 1960; *Developmental Tasks for Children,* 1960; and (with Harold Murai) *Supplementary Reader.*

BRAUTIGAN, Richard (Gary)   1935-1984

PERSONAL: Born January 30, 1935, in Spokane, Wash; died of an apparently self-inflicted gunshot wound, c. September, 1984, in Bolinas, Calif.; son of Bernard F. (a laborer) and Lula Mary (Keho) Brautigan; married Virginia Dionne Adler, June 8, 1957 (divorced, July 28, 1970); married second wife, Akiko (divorced); children: (first marriage) Ianthe. *Home:* San Francisco, Calif. *Agent:* Helen Brann, 14 Sutton Place S., New York, N.Y. 10022.

CAREER: Poet and author. Poet-in-residence, California Institute of Technology, 1967. *Awards, honors:* National Endowment for the Arts grant, 1968-69.

WRITINGS:

NOVELS

A Confederate General from Big Sur, Grove Press, 1965.
Trout Fishing in America, Four Seasons Foundation, 1967.
In Watermelon Sugar, Four Seasons Foundation, 1967.
Revenge of the Lawn: Stories 1962-1970, Simon & Schuster, 1971.
The Abortion: An Historical Romance, 1966, Simon & Schuster, 1971.
The Hawkline Monster, Simon & Schuster, 1974.
Willard and His Bowling Trophies: A Perverse Mystery, Simon & Schuster, 1975.
Sombrero Fallout, Simon & Schuster, 1976.
Dreaming of Babylon: A Private Eye Novel 1942, Delacorte/Seymour Lawrence, 1977.
The Tokyo-Montana Express, Delacorte, 1980.
So the Wind Won't Blow It All Away, Delacorte, 1982.

POETRY

The Return of the Rivers, Inferno Press, c. 1957.
The Galilee Hitch-Hiker, White Rabbit Press, 1958, reissued, Or Press, 1968.
Lay the Marble Tea: Twenty-Four Poems, Carp Press, 1959.
The Octopus Frontier, Carp Press, 1960.
All Watched Over by Machines of Loving Grace, Communications Company, 1967.
The Pill Versus the Springhill Mine Disaster, Four Seasons Foundation, 1968.

When I first met Vida she had been born inside the wrong body. ■ (Cover photograph by Edmund Shea from *The Abortion: An Historical Romance, 1966* by Richard Brautigan.)

Please Plant This Book (eight poems printed on separate seed packet envelopes), Graham Mackintosh, 1968.
Rommel Drives on Deep into Egypt, Delacorte, 1970.
Loading Mercury with a Pitchfork, Simon & Schuster, 1976.
June 30th, June 30th, Delacorte/Seymour Lawrence, 1978.

COLLECTIONS

Trout Fishing in America, The Pill Versus the Springhill Mine Disaster, and In Watermelon Sugar, Delacorte, 1969.

Co-editor, *Change* (single issue magazine), 1963.

SIDELIGHTS: Known in literary circles during the 1960s as one of the San Francisco Poets, Brautigan became a cult hero with the 1967 publication of his novel *Trout Fishing in America*. The novel sold over two million copies world wide and captured the spirit and sounds of the hippie generation. Sometimes referred to as Brautigan's "Hemingway book," it told the story of a man and his family in search of the perfect trout stream, in search of a pastoral myth, but discovers instead that the great American outdoors has been spoiled by commercialism.

His other novels depicted a world populated by social misfits: born losers, ineffectual rebels, solitary old people, and loners.

His poems in *The Pill Verses the Springhill Mine Disaster* and *Rommel Drives on Deep into Egypt* fell into three general categories: personal poems, poems of fantasy, and poems of social comment.

Brautigan was born in Spokane, Washington in 1935 and grew up in poverty in the Pacific Northwest. He had an early and thorough education in fishing and hunting. He began writing as a teenager and would stay up all night learning his craft. "I wrote poetry for seven years to learn how to write a sentence because I really wanted to write novels and I figured that I couldn't write a novel until I could write a sentence. I used poetry as a lover but I never made her my old lady."[1]

Brautigan moved to San Francisco from his native Oregon in 1958, the year of the "Beat" movement. "One day when I was twenty-five years old, I looked down and realized that I could write a sentence. Let's try one of those classic good-bye lines, 'I don't think we should see so much of each other any more because I think we're getting a little too serious,' which really meant that I wrote my first novel *Trout Fishing in America* and followed it with three other novels.

"I pretty much stopped seeing poetry for the next six years until I was thirty-one or the autumn of 1966. Then I started going out with poetry again, but this time I knew how to write

(Cover photograph by Erik Weber from *Trout Fishing in America* by Richard Brautigan.)

a sentence, so everything was different and poetry became my old lady. God, what a beautiful feeling that was!

"I tried to write poetry that would get at some of the hard things in my life that needed talking about but those things that you can only tell your old lady."[1]

Brautigan's writing method was to "get it down as fast as possible and on an electric typewriter, 100 words per minute. I can't spend time on character delineation and situation. I just let it come out. And when it doesn't want to come, I don't sit around and stare at the typewriter or anything. I just go down and see about two or three movies—the worse they are the better. And for some reason that loosens me up and gets things going again. That's what I do when I'm stuck."[2]

In *The Beat Generation,* author Bruce Cook likened Brautigan to Mark Twain. "The two have in common an approach to humor that is founded on the old frontier tradition of the tall story. In Brautigan's work, however, events are given an extra twist so that they come out in respectable literary shape, looking like surrealism. *A Confederate General from Big Sur* is a kind of Huck Finn-Tom Sawyer adventure played out in those beautiful boondocks of coastal California where Jack Kerouac flipped out in the summer of 1960. But it is with *Trout Fishing in America* that Brautigan manages to remind us of Mark Twain and at the same time seem most himself. . . .In the book—call it a novel if you will—whopper is piled on dream vision with such relentless repetition that the ultimate effect is a little like science fiction. The narrator's visit to the Cleveland Wrecking Yard, for instance, is at once quite funny and a sadly serious comment on the awful junkyard America is fast becoming. This one, like every other episode in the book, is delivered in Brautigan's distinctively oblique, understated, and offhand manner."[2]

Cook described Brautigan as "quiet and somewhat withdrawn" without ambition "to be a Beat writer."[2]

Trout Fishing in America catapulted Brautigan into the mainstream of publisher interest. There were readings on campuses all over the country (Brautigan himself had never attended college), and a few weeks as poet-in-residence at the California Institute of Technology. "I can't explain it. Maybe they brought me there thinking of me as some kind of exotic influence or something."[2]

Although he continued to write novels, interest in Brautigan's work began to decline in the 1970s. His close friend, novelist Tom McGuane, summarized the collapse of Brautigan's literary career, saying, "When the 1960s ended, he was the baby thrown out with the bathwater."

In the last year of his life friends noted that Brautigan had become increasingly despondent over his fading career. "The fact that his readership was diminishing was what was breaking his heart," his former agent noted. His last book, *So the Wind Won't Blow It All Away* sold only about 15,000 copies.

Brautigan apparently died of a self-inflicted gunshot wound in September, 1984, but his body was not discovered until October 25th of that year. He died at the age of forty-nine at his secluded house in Bolinas, California.

Brautigan's works have been translated into twelve languages and some of his works have been recorded by Columbia Records.

FOOTNOTE SOURCES

[1] Richard Brautigan, "Old Lady," *The San Francisco Poets,* edited by David Meltzer, Ballantine, 1971.

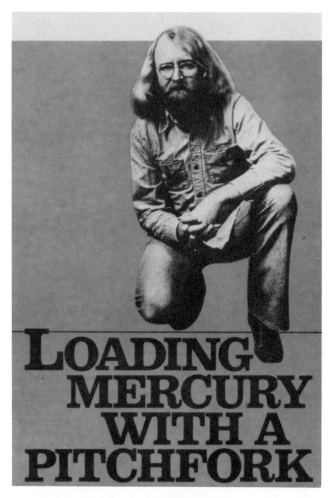

(From *Loading Mercury with a Pitchfork* by Richard Brautigan. Photograph by Erik Weber.)

[2] Bruce Cook, *The Beat Generation,* Scribner, 1971.

FOR MORE INFORMATION SEE:

Poetry, June, 1968, March, 1970.
New York Times Book Review, February 15, 1970, January 16, 1972.
John Stickney, "Gentle Poet of the Young, *Life,* August 14, 1970.
Robert Adams, "Brautigan Was Here," *New York Review of Books,* April 22, 1971.
Tony Tanner, *City of Words,* Harper, 1971.
Terence Malley, *Richard Brautigan: Writers for the Seventies,* Warner, 1972.
Carolyn Riley, editor, *Contemporary Literary Criticism,* Gale, Volume I, 1973, Volume III, 1974.
Dictionary of Literary Biography, Volume 2: *American Novelists Since World War II,* Gale, 1978.
People Weekly, June 8, 1981, June 8, 1984.
New Yorker, December 3, 1984.
Rolling Stone, April 11, 1985.

OBITUARIES

Chicago Tribune, October 27, 1984.
Los Angeles Times, October 27, 1984.
New York Times, October 27, 1984.
Washington Post, October 27, 1984.
Detroit Free Press, October 27, 1984, October 29, 1984.
Time, November 5, 1984.

BRENNER, Anita   1905-1974

PERSONAL: Born August 13, 1905, in Aguascalientes, Mexico; died December 1, 1974; daughter of Isidore and Paula (Duchan) Brenner; married David Glusker, June 18, 1929; children: Peter, Susannah (Mrs. John Page). *Education:* Attended Our Lady of the Lake, San Antonio, University of Texas, and National University of Mexico; Columbia University, Ph.D., 1929. *Religion:* Jewish. *Residence:* Rancho la Barranca, Aguascalientes, Mexico.

CAREER: Writer, rancher, editor. Free-lance correspondent for *New York Times Magazine* and for North American Newspaper Alliance (NANA), during 1930s, 40s, and 50s; art editor, *Brooklyn Daily Eagle,* 1935-36; special correspondent in Mexico for *Fortune* magazine, 1937; editor and publisher of *Mexico This Month,* published by Grafica de Mexico, 1955-71. *Member:* Foreign Correspondents Club of Mexico City (founding member). *Awards, honors:* Guggenheim fellowship, 1930-32; *New York Herald Tribune*'s Spring Book Festival Award Honor Book, 1942, for *The Boy Who Could Do Anything and Other Mexican Folktales,* and 1953, for *A Hero by Mistake;* Gold Medal from the Boys Club of America, 1966, for *The Timid Ghost; A Hero by Mistake* was selected one of *New York Times* Best Illustrated Children's Books of the Year, 1953; cited in the *Junior Encyclopaedia Britannica* list of authors of classic children's books; decorated by the National Tourist Council of the Mexican Government for pioneer work in tourist development; received parchment from

The more he ran the more afraid he was. ■ (From *A Hero by Mistake* by Anita Brenner. Illustrated by Jean Charlot.)

the University of Florida for contributions to the resolution of inter-American problems.

WRITINGS:

JUVENILE

The Boy Who Could Do Anything and Other Mexican Folk Tales (illustrated by Jean Charlot), W. R. Scott, 1942.
I Want to Fly, W. R. Scott, 1943, reissued with *The Little Fireman,* by Margaret Wise Brown, E. M. Hale, 1956.
A Hero by Mistake (illustrated by J. Charlot), W. R. Scott, 1953.
Dumb Juan and the Bandits, W. R. Scott, 1957.
The Timid Ghost; or, What Would You Do with a Sackful of Gold? (illustrated by J. Charlot), W. R. Scott, 1966.

OTHER

Idols behind Altars, Payson & Clarke (New York), 1929, reissued, Beacon Press, 1970.
The Influence of Technique on the Decorative Style in the Domestic Pottery of Culhuacan, Columbia University Press, 1931, reissued, AMS Press, 1969.
Your Mexican Holiday: A Modern Guide, Putnam, 1932, 4th revised edition, 1947.
The Wind That Swept Mexico: The History of the Mexican Revolution, 1910-1942, Harper & Brothers, 1943, new edition, University of Texas Press, 1971.

TRANSLATOR FROM THE SPANISH

Waldo D. Frank, *Tales from the Argentine,* Books for Libraries, 1930.
Mauricio Magdaleno, *Sunburst,* Viking, 1944.
Gregorio Lopez y Fuentes, *El Indio,* Ungar, 1961.

Columnist for *Mademoiselle* during the 1930s; regular contributor to *Nation, New York Times, New York Post, Holiday,* and *Menorah Journal.*

WORK IN PROGRESS: At the time of her death, Brenner was working on two books, one of them possibly a juvenile.

SIDELIGHTS: "Due to having been born in Mexico, I have tended to side with the underdog and be sympathetic to rebellion and revolution whose deepest psychological, economic and social roots have always intrigued me. This is also due to the fact that I am Jewish, and although I was not an underdog on this account in Mexico, the minute we hit Texas as refugees from the Mexican Revolution (my father having been a landowner), the problem hit me full in the face when I was too small to know what it was that was hitting me.

"I have therefore devoted a great deal of time and research to Jewish preoccupations, history, traditions and basic commitments, which has definitely healed the scars inflicted by the roughing up when I hit Texas, and has deepened and fortified my sense of identity."

Brenner was involved with the John Dewey Committee in the 1930s, and reported that the group was among the first to attempt "to uncover and make public the 'Lie' which makes things run so brutally in the Soviet Union and which then was picked up by Hitler as a modus operandi and did the entire world an immense amount of harm. We have by now become accustomed to it as a commercial gadget and as a political way of life and it has made a climate that is as poisonous to the mind and spirit as the junk that gets dumped into the sea is to the fishes." As a result of her activities with the Committee, she earned "the honor of being attacked in *Pravda* along with many of the other members of this group which included the most vigorous writers of the time.'' Brenner was the only correspondent to have interviewed Trotsky when he was in hiding outside of Paris; this interview appeared in the *New York Times.*

FOR MORE INFORMATION SEE:

OBITUARIES

New York Times, December 3, l974.
AB Bookman's Weekly, December 16, l974.

BRISCOE, Jill (Pauline) 1935-

PERSONAL: Born June 29, 1935, in Liverpool, England; came to the United States in 1970; daughter of William A. (a motor trader) and Peggy (Pont) Ryder; married Stuart Briscoe (a clergyman), July 26, 1958; children: David, Judith, Peter. *Education:* Homerton College, Cambridge, teacher's diploma, 1958. *Religion:* Christian. *Home:* Brookfield, Wis. *Office:* Elmbrook Church, 777 South Barker Rd., Waukesha, Wis. 53186.

CAREER: Grade school teacher in Liverpool, England, 1958-60; Capernwray Missionary Fellowship of Torch Bearers, Lancaster, England, missionary with youth mission, 1960-70, superintendent of youth club and nursery school, 1965-70; presently director of Briscoe Ministries, Waukesha, Wis., and writer. Lecturer; women's Bible study leader.

WRITINGS:

JUVENILE

(Reteller) *Jonah and the Worm* (illustrated by Tom Armstrong and Florence Davis), T. Nelson, 1983.

JILL BRISCOE

The Innkeeper's Daughter (illustrated by Dennis Hockerman), Children's Press, 1984.
Harrow Sparrow, T. Nelson, 1985.

ADULT

There's a Snake in My Garden, Zondervan, 1975.
Prime Rib and Apple, Zondervan, 1979.
Here Am I, Send Aaron, Victor Books, 1979.
Hush, Hush, Zondervan, 1979.
A Time for Giving, Ideals Publishing, 1979.
A Time for Living, Ideals Publishing, 1980.
Thank You for Being a Friend, Doubleday, 1981.
Fight for the Family, Zondervan, 1981.
How to Fail Successfully, Revell, 1982.
Queen of Hearts: The Role of Today's Woman Based on Proverbs 31, Revell, 1984.
How to Follow the Shepherd When You're Being Pushed around by the Sheep, Revell, 1984.
Wings, T. Nelson, 1984.
(With daughter, Judy Golz) *Space to Breathe, Room to Grow: The Hows and Whys of Loving, Intimate Relationships,* Oliver-Nelson, 1985.
Women in the Life of Jesus, Victor Books, 1986.
Evergrowing, Evergreen, Victor Books, 1986.
Faith Enough to Finish, Victor Books, 1987.
Body Language, Victor Books, 1987.
By Hook or by Crook: The Life of Peter, Word Books, 1987.
Starlight, Victor Books, 1988.

ALL WITH HUSBAND, STUART BRISCOE

Mountain Songs: Selections from the Psalms, T. Nelson, 1982.
Songs from Green Pastures: Selections from the Psalms, T. Nelson, 1982.
River Songs: Selections from the Psalms, T. Nelson, 1984.
Songs from Deep Waters: Selections from the Psalms, T. Nelson, 1984.
Songs from Heaven and Earth: Selections from the Psalms with Prayer Meditations, T. Nelson, 1985.
Songs of Light, T. Nelson, 1985.
Desert Songs, T. Nelson, 1985.
What It Means to Be a Christian, Cook, 1987.
Our Favorite Verse, Accent Books, 1987.
Journey of a Disciple, Regal, 1988.

CASSETTE

''Waiting for a Song to Sing,'' Word Books.

Also author of study guides, greeting cards and of taped lectures.

ADAPTATIONS:

''Space to Breathe, Room to Grow'' (cassette), Nelson.

WORK IN PROGRESS: Caleb's Colt, a children's book; *Running on Empty.*

SIDELIGHTS: ''After twelve years working full time with European youth...my heart is with those who will live in the somewhat frightening but challenging future. I want to challenge them to a philosophy of Christian discipleship I believe is the answer to the world's problems.

''I'm an overachiever. I tend to take on too much. But now I know people are more important than things, including deadlines and pressures to accomplish. If the kids or my husband, Stuart, suddenly appear in the midst of my achieving, I've learned to stop and attend to them. Now I make it a priority to work in quality time with my family. It takes flexibility and

Keturah was unhappy. ■ (From *The Innkeeper's Daughter* by Jill Briscoe. Illustrated by Dennis Hockerman.)

adapting, but I'm learning to constantly reorganize and take stock.

"In fact, now the entire family is working on giving each other time, not things. For Christmas last year we all decided we had all the 'things' we wanted. Or needed. So we decided to give 'time.' One of the children gave Stuart and I a reservation at a restaurant and picked up the check, so the two of us could spend time together. David gave Peter two tickets to a ball game, and they went together. David sent Judy money for her to spend on a phone call to him at college. It's really neat to see.

"Sometimes people ask me if I feel guilty about all the time my traveling and speaking takes away from the kids, but really, by making a conscientious effort, my speaking engagements have actually encouraged time together. When Judy was still in high school I purposely took speaking engagements geared toward mother/daughter functions, so Judy and I could go together. She and her best girlfriend would often come along and sing to the groups. It was a terrific opportunity for Judy to see her mother in action. And it helped her to understand what I did when I was away. Now I deliberately take meetings in the Minneapolis and Chicago areas, so I can visit my kids in college. I probably see more of them than most parents do in the same situation, and my ministry is what allows this. And my kids are seeing a model of self sacrifice and service first hand.

"When it comes to my ministry, I don't go out and look for speaking opportunities or books to write. The needs come to me. Of course, I know the need isn't the call, it's just part of it.

"When Stuart accepted his position as Pastor of Elmbrook Church, people just tended to assume his wife was a teacher, too. I soon was given more and more opportunities to teach. At first I felt extremely threatened. I didn't know if I could do it. . .or should do it. But if you're never on risk's edge, you never grow, you never find out what gifts you have. That's why I never said 'no' if I knew I had the gift to do something asked of me. After all, you have to stretch. You're not trusting God if you're just doing what you know you can do through past experience. First, it was mother/daughter functions. Then invitations to speak on college campuses. Now it's the challenge of speaking to mixed audiences. . .women *and* men.

"I'm always nervous before I speak. I know I have the technical gifts, because I've been professionally trained through secular education and the ministry. But when you're dealing with the Word of God, it's not like teaching arithmetic. You're God's spokesperson. It's not a matter of preparing a message, it's a matter of preparing yourself. It's not a technique I concentrate on, but the power of God. Am I in touch with the Spirit? Am I clean? Am I a willing vessel? Then you must depend on the Spirit of God to do the work in people. It's an awesome responsibility to think someone may be affected spiritually by what I say to them in God's authority.

"I'm still growing and learning, and sometimes I feel the opportunities are outstripping my growth. I struggle with my inadequacies. And pride. It takes a proper balance. After all, if you feel too inadequate, you can't communicate properly. So I've learned to be God confident, *not* self confident."

HOBBIES AND OTHER INTERESTS: "Travelling round the world talking to kids and parents wherever they are and wherever I can"; racquetball, jogging, going to the theater.

CARLSON, Nancy L(ee) 1953-

PERSONAL: Born October 10, 1953, in Minneapolis, Minn.; daughter of Walter J. (a contractor) and Louise (a homemaker; maiden name, Carlson) Carlson; married John Barry McCool (a graphic designer), June 30, 1979; children: Kelly Louise, John Patrick. *Education:* Attended University of Minnesota, Duluth, 1972-73, and Santa Fe Workshop of Contemporary Art, 1975; Minneapolis College of Art and Design, B.F.A., 1976. *Home and office:* 9240 Yukon Ave. S., Bloomington, Minn. 55438.

CAREER: Artist and illustrator, 1975—; author and illustrator of children's books, 1979—. Visiting artist at schools, including Bemidji State University, 1983; Minnetonka Schools, Minn., 1985; and Minneapolis College of Art and Design, 1986. Lecturer; public speaker. Card buyer for Center Book Shop, Walter Art Center, 1977-80; arts and crafts specialist for city of South St. Paul, Minn., 1978; illustrator of greeting cards for Recycled Paper Products, 1982, and of posters.

EXHIBITIONS—One-woman shows: Minneapolis College of Art and Design Print Gallery, Minn., 1975, 1976; "Nancy Carlson: Drawing and Books," Northland Gallery, Minneapolis, 1983. Group shows: "Commencement Exhibition," Minneapolis College of Art and Design, 1976; "New Works by Three Artists," Honeywell Plaza, Minneapolis, 1980; Dolly Fiterman Gallery, Minneapolis, 1980, 1982; Art Center of Minnesota, Minnetonka, 1981, 1983; "Minnesota Women," WARM Gallery, Minneapolis, 1981, 1982; Minnesota State Fair Art Exhibition, 1981; "American Art: The Challenge of the Land," Pillsbury World Headquarters, 1981; "Illustrator's Art," Inland Gallery, Minneapolis, 1982; "Young Minnesota Artists," University Gallery, University of Minnesota, 1982; Minneapolis College of Art and Design, 1982, 1985; Master Eagle Gallery, New York, N.Y., 1983, 1985; Talley Gallery, Bemidji State University, Bemidji, Minn., 1983; Edgewood

Nancy Carlson with children, Kelly and John Patrick.

Orchard Gallery, Door County, Wis., 1984, 1985; St. Olaf College, Northfield, Minn., 1985.

AWARDS, HONORS: Printmaking Awards from Northshore Arts Festival, 1975; Award from the Minnesota State Fair Art Exhibition, 1981, for drawings of fish; Purchase Award from Young Minnesota Artists, University of Minnesota, 1982; Award from Women in International Design Competition, 1983; Parents' Choice Award from the Parents' Choice Foundation, 1985, for *Louanne Pig in the Talent Show;* Award from the Minnesota Graphic Design Association, 1985.

WRITINGS:

ALL SELF-ILLUSTRATED CHILDREN'S BOOKS

Harriet and Walt, Carolrhoda, 1982.
Harriet and the Roller Coaster, Carolrhoda, 1982.
Harriet and the Garden, Carolrhoda, 1982.
Harriet's Recital, Carolrhoda, 1982.
Harriet's Halloween Candy, Carolrhoda, 1982.
Loudmouth George and the Cornet, Carolrhoda, 1983.
Loudmouth George and the New Neighbors, Carolrhoda, 1983.
Loudmouth George and the Fishing Trip, Carolrhoda, 1983.
Loudmouth George and the Sixth-Grade Bully, Carolrhoda, 1983.
Loudmouth George and the Big Race, Carolrhoda, 1983.
Bunnies and Their Hobbies, Carolrhoda, 1984.
Louanne Pig in Making the Team, Carolrhoda, 1985.
Louanne Pig in the Mysterious Valentine, Carolrhoda, 1985.
Louanne Pig in the Perfect Family, Carolrhoda, 1985.
Louanne Pig in the Talent Show, Carolrhoda, 1985.
Louanne Pig in Witch Lady, Carolrhoda, 1985.
Bunnies and Their Sports, Viking, 1987.
Arnie and the Stolen Markers, Viking, 1987.
Arnie Goes to Camp, Viking, 1988.
I Like Me, Viking, 1988.
Poor Carl, Viking, 1988.

ILLUSTRATOR

Joyce Kessel, *Halloween*, Carolrhoda, 1980.
Geoffrey Scott, *Egyptian Boats*, Carolrhoda, 1981.
(With Trina Schart Hyman, Hilary Knight and Peter E. Hanson) Pamela Espeland and Marilyn Waniek, *The Cat Walked through the Casserole and Other Poems for Children*, Carolrhoda, 1984.
Susan Pearson, *The Baby and the Bear*, Viking, 1987.
S. Pearson, *When the Baby Went to Bed*, Viking, 1987.

ADAPTATIONS:

CASSETTES, EXCEPT AS NOTED

"Harriet and Walt," Live Oak Media, 1984.
"Harriet and the Roller Coaster," Live Oak Media, 1985.
"Harriet and the Garden," Live Oak Media, 1985.
"Harriet's Halloween Candy," Live Oak Media, 1985.
"Harriet's Recital," Live Oak Media, 1985, (filmstrip with cassette), Random House.
"Loudmouth George and the Cornet," Live Oak Media, 1986.
"Loudmouth George and the Fishing Trip," Live Oak Media, 1986.
"Loudmouth George and the Sixth-Grade Bully," Live Oak Media, 1986.
"Loudmouth George and the Big Race," Live Oak Media, 1986.
"Loudmouth George and the New Neighbors," Live Oak Media, 1987.
"Louanne Pig in the Talent Show," Live Oak Media, 1987.
"Louanne Pig in Witch Lady," Live Oak Media, 1987.
"Louanne Pig in the Perfect Family," Live Oak Media, 1987.

I'll start training tomorrow. ■ (From *Loudmouth George and the Big Race* by Nancy Carlson. Illustrated by the author.)

"Louanne Pig in Making the Team," Live Oak Media, 1987.

WORK IN PROGRESS: Books about Arnie, and Louanne the Pig.

SIDELIGHTS: "Harriet is a character created with a little of myself (and girls I grew up with) in her. Walt is modeled after my brother David, and Loudmouth George represents all the loud, bragging kids I went to school with. All the stories are based on things that happened to me as a kid, and each has a simple moral. For example, *Harriet's Halloween Candy* teaches children to share; *Harriet and the Roller Coaster* encourages children to try new things, to be brave.

"I am an artist who enjoys making up stories for children. When I'm not writing for kids, I'm drawing pictures for shows and galleries."

HOBBIES AND OTHER INTERESTS: "I love sports. Running, swimming, biking, and hiking. Spend summers in Northern Wisconsin. Also compete in marathons and triathlons."

FOR MORE INFORMATION SEE:

"When You Create, You Want the World to See," *Austin Herald*, April 30, 1982.
Gene Lyons, "A Christmas Grab Bag," *Newsweek*, December 6, 1982.
Mickey Murphy, "Local Author Delights the Young with Harriet," *Sun News Paper*, December 22, 1982.
Jeff Strickler, "Authors of Children's Books Fight Kidstuff Label," *Minneapolis Star and Tribune*, January 16, 1983.

COLLECTIONS

Kerlan Collection at the University of Minnesota.

CHASE, Richard   1904-1988

OBITUARY NOTICE: Born February 15, 1904, near Huntsville, Ala.; died February 2, 1988, in Huntsville, Ala. Folklorist, editor, and author. A renowned storyteller of Appalachian folktales based on Celtic and English stories, Chase traveled to many educational institutions throughout the United States lecturing on Appalachian folklore and telling stories during his lifetime. He was a founder of an Appalachian craft industry and conducted folk art workshops and festivals. In addition, he edited several books of folktales, including *Old Songs and Singing Games; The Jack Tales: Told by R. M. Ward and his Kindred in the Beech Mountain Section of Western North Carolina and by Other Descendants of Council Harmon (1803-1896) Elsewhere in the Southern Mountains: With Three Tales from Wise County, Virginia; Grandfather Tales: American-English Folk Tales;* and *American Folk Tales and Songs, and Other Examples of English-American Tradition as Preserved in the Appalachian Mountains and Elsewhere in the United States.* Chase's own works include *Jack and the Three Sillies* and *Wicked John and the Devil.*

FOR MORE INFORMATION SEE:

Contemporary Authors, Volumes 61-64, Gale, 1976.
Who's Who in America, 41st edition, Marquis, 1980.

OBITUARIES

School Library Journal, June/July, 1988.

COATSWORTH, Elizabeth (Jane) 1893-1986

PERSONAL: Born May 31, 1893, in Buffalo, N.Y.; died August 31 (one source cites September 2), 1986, in Nobleboro, Me.; daughter of William T. and Ida (Reid) Coatsworth; mar-

ELIZABETH COATSWORTH

ried Henry Beston (an author and naturalist), June 18, 1929 (died, April 15, 1968); children: Margaret (Mrs. Dorik Mechau), Catherine (Mrs. Richard Barnes). *Education:* Vassar College, B.A., 1915; Columbia University, M.A., 1916; also attended Radcliffe College. *Residence:* Chimney Farm, Nobleboro, Me.

CAREER: Author and poet. *Member:* P.E.N., North East Poetry Society, Phi Beta Kappa. *Awards, honors:* Newbery Medal from the American Library Association, 1931, for *The Cat Who Went to Heaven;* Children's Spring Book Festival Honor Award, 1940, for *The Littlest House,* and 1971, for *Under the Green Willow;* Litt.D., University of Maine, 1955; L.H.D., New England College, 1958; New England Poetry Club Golden Rose, 1967; Child Study Association of America Children's Books of the Year for *Bob Bodden and the Good Ship Rover* and *The Lucky Ones: Five Journeys toward a Home,* both 1968, *The Snow Parlor and Other Bedtime Stories,* 1971, *Good Night,* 1972, *The Wanderers,* 1973, *All-of-a-Sudden Susan,* 1974, and *Marra's World,* 1975; Hans Christian Andersen Award Highly Commended Author (U.S.), 1968; Kerlan Award from the University of Minnesota, 1975, for "recognition of singular attainments in the creation of children's literature."

WRITINGS:

JUVENILE

The Cat and the Captain (illustrated by Gertrude Kaye), Macmillan, 1927, revised edition (illustrated by Berniece Loewenstein), 1974.
Toutou in Bondage (illustrated by Thomas Handforth), Macmillan, 1929.
The Boy with the Parrot: A Story of Guatemala (illustrated by Wilfred Bronson), Macmillan, 1930, reissued, 1964.
The Cat Who Went to Heaven (illustrated by Lynd Ward), Macmillan, 1930, reissued, 1972.
Knock at the Door (illustrated by Francis D. Bedford), Macmillan, 1931.
Cricket and the Emperor's Son (illustrated by Weda Yap), Macmillan, 1932 (British edition illustrated by Juliette Palmer, World's Work, 1962).
Away Goes Sally (illustrated by Helen Sewell), Macmillan, 1934 (British edition illustrated by Caroline Sharpe, Blackie, 1970).
The Golden Horseshoe (illustrated by Robert Lawson), Macmillan, 1935, new edition, 1968 (published in England as *Tamar's Wager* [illustrated by R. Payne], Blackie, 1971).
Sword of the Wilderness (illustrated by Harve Stein), Macmillan, 1936, reissued, 1966.
Alice-All-by-Herself (illustrated by Marguerite de Angeli), Macmillan, 1937, reissued, 1966.
Dancing Tom (illustrated by Grace Paull), Macmillan, 1938, reissued, 1967.
Five Bushel Farm (illustrated by H. Sewell), Macmillan, 1939 (British edition illustrated by C. Sharpe, Blackie, 1970).
The Fair American (illustrated by H. Sewell), Macmillan, 1940, reissued, 1968 (British edition illustrated by C. Sharpe, Blackie, 1970).
The Littlest House (illustrated by Marguerite Davis), Macmillan, 1940, reissued, 1967.
A Toast to the King (illustrated by Forrest Orr), Coward, 1940.
(With Mabel O'Donnell) *Alice and Jerry Books: Sixth Reader,* Row, Peterson, 1960.
Tonio and the Stranger: A Mexican Adventure (illustrated by W. Bronson), Grosset, 1941.
You Shall Have a Carriage (illustrated by Henry Pitz), Macmillan, 1941.
Forgotten Island (illustrated by G. Paull), Grosset, 1942.
(With M. O'Donnell) *Runaway Home* (illustrated by Gustaf Tenggren), Row, Peterson, 1942.

Houseboat Summer (illustrated by M. Davis), Macmillan, 1942.

The White Horse (illustrated by H. Sewell), Macmillan, 1942 (published in England as *The White Horse of Morocco,* illustrated by C. Sharpe, Blackie, 1973).

Thief Island (illustrated by John Wonsetler), Macmillan, 1943.

Twelve Months Makes a Year (stories; illustrated by M. Davis), Macmillan, 1943.

The Big Green Umbrella (illustrated by H. Sewell), Grosset, 1944.

Trudy and the Tree House (illustrated by M. Davis), Macmillan, 1944.

The Kitten Stand (illustrated by Kathleen Keeler), Grosset, 1945.

The Wonderful Day (illustrated by H. Sewell), Macmillan, 1946 (British edition illustrated by C. Sharpe, Blackie, 1973).

Plum Daffy Adventure (illustrated by M. Davis), Macmillan, 1947.

Up Hill and Down: Stories (illustrated by James Davis), Knopf, 1947.

The House of the Swan (illustrated by Kathleen Voute), Macmillan, 1948.

The Little Haymakers (illustrated by G. Paull), Macmillan, 1949.

The Captain's Daughter (illustrated by Ralph Ray), Macmillan, 1950.

First Adventure (illustrated by R. Ray), Macmillan, 1950, reissued, 1966.

Door to the North: A Saga of Fourteenth Century America (*Horn Book* honor list; illustrated by Frederick T. Chapman), Winston, 1950.

Dollar for Luck (illustrated by George Hauman and Doris Hauman), Macmillan, 1951 (published in England as *The Sailing Hatrack,* illustrated by Gavin Rowe, Blackie, 1972).

The Wishing Pear (illustrated by R. Ray), Macmillan, 1951.

The Last Fort: A Story of the French Voyageurs (illustrated by Edward Shenton), Winston, 1952.

Boston Belles (illustrated by Manning Lee), Macmillan, 1952.

(With Kate Barnes) *The Giant Golden Book of Cat Stories* (illustrated by Feodor Rojankovsky; also see below), Simon & Schuster, 1953.

The Giant Golden Book of Dog Stories (illustrated by F. Rojankovsky; also see below), Simon & Schuster, 1953.

Old Whirlwind: A Story of Davy Crockett (illustrated by M. Lee), Macmillan, 1953.

Aunt Flora (illustrated by M. Lee), Macmillan, 1953.

(With Kate Barnes) *Horse Stories* (illustrated by F. Rojankovsky; also see below), Simon & Schuster, 1954.

The Sod House (illustrated by M. Lee), Macmillan, 1954.

Cherry Ann and the Dragon Horse (illustrated by M. Lee), Macmillan, 1955.

Hide and Seek (illustrated by Genevieve Vaughan-Jackson), Pantheon, 1956.

The Peddler's Cart (illustrated by Zhenya Gay), Macmillan, 1956 (published in England as *The Pedlar's Cart,* illustrated by Margery Gill, Blackie, 1971).

(With K. Barnes) *The Giant Golden Book of Dogs, Cats, and Horses* (contains *Horse Stories, The Giant Golden Book of Cat Stories,* and *The Giant Golden Book of Dog Stories*), Simon & Schuster, 1957.

The Dog from Nowhere (illustrated by Don Sibley), Row, Peterson, 1958.

Down Tumbledown Mountain (illustrated by Aldren Watson), Row, Peterson, 1958.

The Cave (illustrated by Allan Houser), Viking, 1958 (published in England as *Cave of Ghosts,* Hamish Hamilton, 1971).

You Say You Saw a Camel! (illustrated by Brinton Turkle), Row, Peterson, 1958.

(Jacket illustration by Edwin Earle from *Here I Stay* by Elizabeth Coatsworth. Illustrated by Edwin Earle.)

Pika and the Roses (illustrated by Kurt Wiese), Pantheon, 1959.

Desert Dan (illustrated by Harper Johnson), Viking, 1960.

Lonely Maria (illustrated by Evaline Ness), Pantheon, 1960.

(Compiler) *Indian Encounters: An Anthology of Stories and Poems* (illustrated by F. T. Chapman), Macmillan, 1960.

UNICEF Christmas Book, UNICEF, 1960.

The Noble Doll (illustrated by Leo Politi), Viking, 1961.

Ronnie and the Chief's Son (illustrated by Stefan Martin), Macmillan, 1962.

The Princess and the Lion (*Horn Book* honor list; illustrated by E. Ness), Pantheon, 1963 (British edition illustrated by Tessa Jordan, Hamilton, 1971).

Jock's Island (illustrated by Lilian Obligado), Viking, 1963.

Jon the Unlucky (illustrated by Esta Nesbitt), Holt, 1963.

The Secret (illustrated by Don Bolognese), Macmillan, 1965.

The Hand of Apollo (illustrated by Robin Jacques), Viking, 1965.

Reading Round Table, Blue Book: Stories by Elizabeth Coatsworth, edited by George Manolakes, American Book, 1965.

Reading Round Table, Green Book, American Book, 1965.

The Place (illustrated by Marjorie Auerbach), Holt, 1966.

The Fox Friend (illustrated by John Hamberger), Macmillan, 1966.

(With husband, Henry Beston) *Chimney Farm Bedtime Stories* (illustrated by Maurice Day), Holt, 1966.

Bess and the Sphinx (illustrated by B. Loewenstein), Macmillan, 1967.

Troll Weather (illustrated by Ursula Arndt), Macmillan, 1967.

The Ox-Team (illustrated by Peter Warner), Hamish Hamilton, 1967.

American Adventures, 1620-1945 (illustrated by Robert Frankenburg), Macmillan, 1968.

Lighthouse Island (illustrated by Symeon Shimin), Norton, 1968.

Bob Bodden and the Good Ship ''Rover'' (illustrated by Ted Schroeder), Garrard, 1968.

The Lucky Ones: Five Journeys toward a Home (illustrated by Janet Doyle), Macmillan, 1968.

They Walk in the Night (illustrated by Stefan Martin), Norton, 1969.

Indian Mound Farm (illustrated by Fermin Rocker), Macmillan, 1969.

George and Red (illustrated by Paul Giovanopoulos), Macmillan, 1969.

Grandmother Cat and the Hermit (illustrated by Irving Boker), Macmillan, 1970 (published in England as *Grandmother Cat,* Bodley Head, 1971).

Bob Bodden and the Seagoing Farm (illustrated by Frank Aloise), Garrard, 1970.

Daniel Webster's Horses (illustrated by Cary), Garrard, 1971.

Under the Green Willow (illustrated by Janina Domanska), Macmillan, 1971, large print edition, Greenwillow, 1984.

The Snow Parlor and Other Bedtime Stories (illustrated by Charles Robinson), Grosset, 1971.

Good Night (illustrated by Jose Aruego), Macmillan, 1972.

The Wanderers (illustrated by Trina Schart Hyman), Four Winds, 1972.

Daisy (illustrated by Judith Gwyn Brown), Macmillan, 1973.

Pure Magic (illustrated by Ingrid Fetz), Macmillan, 1973, new edition published as *The Werefox,* Collier, 1975 (published in England as *The Fox Boy,* Blackie, 1975).

All-of-a-Sudden Susan (illustrated by Richard Cuffari), Macmillan, 1974.

Marra's World (illustrated by Krystyna Truska), Greenwillow, 1975, large print edition, 1975.

JUVENILE POETRY

Night and the Cat (illustrated by Fougita), Macmillan, 1950.

Mouse Chorus (illustrated by G. Vaughan-Jackson), Pantheon, 1955.

The Peaceable Kingdom and Other Poems (illustrated by Fritz Eichenberg), Pantheon, 1958.

The Children Come Running (illustrated by Roger Duvoisin and others), Golden Press, 1960.

The Sparrow Bush: Rhymes (*Horn Book* honor list; illustrated by S. Martin), Norton, 1966.

Down Half the World (illustrated by Zena Bernstein), Macmillan, 1968.

ADULT POETRY

Fox Footprints, Knopf, 1923.

Atlas and Beyond: A Book of Poems (illustrated by Harry Cimino), Harper, 1924.

Compass Rose, Coward, 1929.

Country Poems, Macmillan, 1942.

Summer Green (illustrated by Nora S. Unwin), Macmillan, 1948.

The Creaking Stair (illustrated by William A. Dwiggins), Coward, 1949.

Poems (illustrated by Vee Guthrie), Macmillan, 1957.

OTHER

The Sun's Diary: A Book of Days for Any Year, Macmillan, 1929.

Here I Stay (adult novel; illustrated by Edwin Earle), Coward, 1938.

Mary's Song, Nash, 1938.

(From *The Cat Who Went to Heaven* by Elizabeth Coatsworth. Illustrated by Lynd Ward.)

Even in the deepest sleep, that sound could rouse him and call him back. ■ (From *The Werefox* by Elizabeth Coatsworth. Illustrated by Ingrid Fetz.)

The Trunk (adult novel), Macmillan, 1941.
Country Neighborhood (adult; illustrated by Hildegard Woodward), Macmillan, 1944.
(Compiler and editor) William Henry Hudson, *Tales of the Gauchos* (illustrated by Henry C. Pitz), Knopf, 1946.
Maine Ways (adult; illustrated by Mildred Coughlin), Macmillan, 1947.
South Shore Town (adult), Macmillan, 1948.
The Enchanted: An Incredible Tale (adult novel; illustrated by Robert Winthrop), Pantheon, 1951 (other editions illustrated by Mary Frank, Pantheon, 1968, and by Joan Kiddell-Monroe, Dent, 1952).
Silky: An Incredible Tale (adult novel; illustrated by John Carroll), Pantheon, 1953.
Mountain Bride: An Incredible Tale (adult novel), Pantheon, 1954.
The White Room (adult novel; illustrated by George W. Thompson), Pantheon, 1958.
Maine Memories (adult), Stephen Greene, 1968.
(Editor) H. Beston, *Especially Maine: The Natural World of Henry Beston from Cape Cod to the St. Lawrence* (adult), Stephen Green, 1970.
A Personal Geography: Almost an Autobiography (adult), Stephen Greene, 1976, large print edition, G. K. Hall, 1979.

Also author of "The Once-upon-a-Time-in-America Books" series, Macmillan, 1950-55, and *With Car and Trailer across the U.S.A.: The Harding Family Seeks a New Home*, 1949. Contributor of short stories and poetry to periodicals, including *Atlantic Monthly, New Yorker, Yale Review, Poetry,* and *Dial.*

Some of Coatsworth's books have been translated into Swedish, Norwegian, German, French, and Japanese.

ADAPTATIONS:

"The Cat Who Went to Heaven" (record or cassette), Newbery Award Records, 1969, (filmstrip with cassette), Miller/Brody, 1970.
"Bob Bodden and the Good Ship 'Rover'" (filmstrip with cassette), Taylor Associates, 1970.

Away Goes Sally, The Cat Who Went to Heaven, The Enchanted, Here I Stay, Lonely Maria, A Personal Geography, Princess and the Lion, Pure Magic, and *Ronnie and the Chief's Son* have been adapted into talking books; *The Cat Who Went to Heaven, Country Neighborhood, The Enchanted, Good Night, Houseboat Summer, Last Fort, Mountain Bride, Old Whirlwind, Poems, Ronnie and the Chief's Son, Silky, Toast to the King, White Room, Wishing Pear,* and *Trunk,* have been adapted into Braille books.

SIDELIGHTS: **May 31, 1893.** Coatsworth was born in Buffalo, New York, the daughter of William T. and Ida Reid Coatsworth. "I am I then, much as I am now; the kernel was the same although there must have been fewer husks. I am sitting, happy, on Mother's lap. Perhaps there is a vague memory of her pince-nez eyeglasses. . . .

"When I was a girl in Buffalo—. . .where we lived until 1912—little was ever told us about the past. If, as we drove old Dolly up Delaware Avenue, Father should remark, 'When I was a boy, most of this was farmland beyond North Street,' the muse of history had received as much of her due as she was likely to get.

"As I look back on my upbringing I can see that it was a little unusual even then. Our family came in three layers, instead of the usual two of parents and children. We lived with our Grandmother Coatsworth in a wide-shingled house, one of the three in Buffalo designed by Henry Hobson Richardson, but how we came to have it is a mystery I cannot now solve. When it was built, Richardson was already dead, and it is hard to know how the plans reached Electa Coatsworth's architect. But they did, and it was a beautiful house, with wide lawns on either side and in front the elm-tree-bordered Soldiers Place, the circle where three parkways met. In due time Grandmother sold one side of our land to her niece, who with her husband and four children lived in an unspeakably dreary red-brick house designed by Frank Lloyd Wright; and a very gloomy house it was, with so deep a verandah and such wide eaves that the sun never reached any of the rooms. . . .

"For a number of years we spent our summers at Bay Beach on the Canadian shore of Lake Erie not far from Buffalo. Here our family had four cottages on a sandy ridge covered with maple trees above a perfect crescent between the amusement park of Crystal Beach, to which steamers came from Buffalo several times a day, and Point Abino. . . .Otherwise we seem always to have done a good deal of traveling. Before I was a year old I had spent a winter in California."[1]

Travel was part of family life; at five Coatsworth visited the Alps and rode a donkey across the deserts of Egypt. "Most of my fifth year was spent abroad. I scarcely remember England, but I have definite memories of the spa to which we went in Germany, and of how nasty the waters tasted, and of Switzerland and of Italy. The most vivid memories are of Vesuvius and then of Egypt, so strange and so different that when I went there again twenty-five years later it was as if I had been away only a few weeks."[1]

Coatsworth's education was conservative, although she frequently missed school when she travelled with her family. "My first eight years of school at the Franklin were Spartan. We followed a modified British model, with Latin in the fifth grade and French in the seventh. We were drilled unremittingly and stayed almost daily after school learning poetry by heart for the smallest infringement of rules. Even a borrowed pencil set us to learning poetry after the school bell had rung at last. The training was thorough, but I am not thorough."[1]

1906-1909. After years in a structured school environment, Coatsworth spent her first two years of high school in Pasadena, California. "It was as a freshman in high school that I was again taken to Pasadena. Father rented an ugly Victorian house in an orange grove on the unspoiled Arroyo Seco that he loved (where the Rose Bowl is now). We lived there for two years and I went to a long-vanished private school so different from the school in Buffalo that I never respected its teaching, perhaps because it was essentially amateur. I did like the motto: *'Fais ce que doit, advienne que pourra,'* which I hope is right but don't know. My French has grown very shaky.

"Father really had a gift for choosing places to go to. One winter we spent four weeks—this time without Grandmother Coatsworth—in the old pre-revolutionary Mexico. It is surprising how many sites we explored, even Monte Alban, at that time not yet excavated except for one trench lined with

"It is too beautiful to be evil," Mariam said. Neither of the animals showed the slightest uneasiness. ■ (From *The Princess and the Lion* by Elizabeth Coatsworth. Illustrated by Evaline Ness.)

ugly figures which they now say were of dead captives. It was my first long horseback ride and I loved seeing the world from the saddle. Next summer we spent a month at Catalina Island with a good deal of fishing for Father. I became seasick at the first opportunity so I didn't go with him. Besides, after catching one very small sunfish when I was little, I never wanted to kill anything again. I remember being proud of that sunfish and not even sorry for it, yet something in me said, 'That will do,' and it has done me for the rest of my life. Next we camped in the uncrowded Yosemite Valley and I climbed many of the trails. It was when I was at the top of the Yosemite Falls that I asked myself if I enjoyed climbing and answered, 'No!' I never voluntarily climbed again."[1]

1909-1911. Family returned to Buffalo. "My last two years before college were spent at the big new building of the Buffalo Seminary just across the parkway from our house, and there we had merriment and serious work mixed and I went to Vassar well prepared. Perhaps too well prepared, for much of my first year repeated work I had already done, and I lost the eagerness of my will to study, and never wholly regained it."[1]

1912. Father died; family gave up home in Buffalo. "After the house in Buffalo was sold, my mother and I went to Pasadena alternate winters to visit my Grandmother Reid and Uncle Frank. There was nothing cut and dried about it. We might go abroad for two winters in succession, or to California, but roughly speaking it was a pattern."[1]

1914. "Mother and [older sister] Margaret and I...lived in apartments or traveled, though of course I had a four-year harbor at college. It was during the last summer before graduating from Vassar that I joined Mother and Margaret in London, where they had just arrived from Italy. The difference between Margaret's age and mine had always made for occasional friction, but in that summer of 1914 the three years were bridged. We spent most of it on walking trips, while Mother drove in some of the last horse-drawn coaches, complete with horns.

"Three important things happened that summer: Margaret and I became life-long friends; I began writing poetry from an inner urge which never left me...and less personally, but more importantly, the first World War began. We happened to be in Stratford the evening before war was declared. The company played Henry V and when the young prince says, 'Let us make alliance with the King of France,' the entire audience rose to its feet and shouted. Later we were to see the Scots Greys in their kilts marching down the streets of Edinburgh to the skirl of their pipes. People said that you could hear the guns across the Channel. I am not sure that I did but I thought so."[1]

1915. Graduated from Vassar, and lived "...alone in New York, taking a Master's degree at Columbia. I lived in two rooms (with 'bath and kitchen privileges') in an apartment belonging to a school teacher. She must have had very different hours from mine because I seldom remember meeting her even in the hallway, and the kitchen I used only for making an eggnog which I drank with my two rolls for breakfast, for I still had not learned to like tea or coffee. The pint of milk was left each morning at the door and the eggs and rolls I bought at a nearby grocery every few days. My sharpest remembrance of the place is the pleasure of feeling my independence and the mysterious passing of the lighted elevated cars along the roofs below me at night. I was so unsophisticated, or perhaps genuine, as to think that they were beautiful. Even their roar I accepted as a dragon's roar.

"I lived on an allowance which I never overspent, and sometimes I would be left with perhaps eighty-three cents for Sunday, and lunch and supper might cost only twenty or thirty cents each, which—heaven help us!—seemed adventurous in those days. I explored the city either alone or with a boy with whom I had grown up during the long lakeshore summers. He was an incipient scientist and was spending a year in New York. We walked in Van Cortland Park, we visited half a dozen historic mansions; we went to Fraunces Tavern, where Washington bade farewell to his officers; we saw the last horsecars in New York (this was in 1916), we stared at the city's skyline from the crown—or was it the torch?—of the Statue of Liberty; we took a ferry across the Hudson and walked along the Palisades: and all of these things gave me far more pleasure than did my four courses, which I often skipped to spend long weekends with a former roommate in Philadelphia.

"I remember only one thing from a lecture by that Robinson who wrote the then standard *European History and Reader* and who was giving a crowded course in the history of the intellectual classes in Europe. 'If you are naturally conservative,' he said, 'do not be ashamed of it. A civilization needs a heavy anchor to keep it steady in the winds of change.' Then there was the fervid arguments on religion with a tall young Episcopal rector after or before the course on Dante we were taking with Professor Fletcher (I wrote a play laid in Renaissance Florence as my thesis, which he accepted and which I suppose is still lying somewhere in the immense archives of Columbia). . . . The religions we studied were the Mediterranean ones; there was a rabbi in the course and perhaps only ten or eleven of us in all. There was something clandestine about it: that after-sessions journey past the furnace rooms, that small classroom, the only one occupied at so late an hour, yet the general air of a secret meeting in the catacombs gave a sauce to the excellent teaching and discussion. It is still something of a mystery to me why a class should have been held at that time, in that place.

"In the second semester my mother and sister came back from a trip to Alaska and took an apartment in New York, and I joined them. It was pleasant but less of an adventure. We saw more of relatives and the theatre, and I did less exploring. I no longer went down the menu of cheap restaurants picking out a twenty-five-cent meal. I still skipped classes, but visited in Philadelphia less often. I was taking a Master's degree for no especial reason, and that was about all there was to it."[1]

1916-1918. Travel took her to the Orient; thirteen months in Japan, China, the Philippines, Java, Siam, Korea and a final month in Hawaii. "Of all the countries through which we traveled during those marvelous thirteen months, I loved China the most. At that time it was half ruinous, with the especial sadness and poetry that hang like a mist over ruins; I doubt if I should care much for communist China, though it may be a better place to live in. There were many books on China and Chinese poetry which I got hold of, none of them very good translations from the Chinese—Arthur Waley's work was still to reach us—but I could transform the pedestrian translations in my mind.

"I think my whole preference for China could be epitomized by a flaking wall near a temple, on which someone had sketched a narcissus and a line of Chinese characters. In Japan that would soon have been tidied up. But not in China, the lovely decrepit China of those days."[1]

Besides China, Coatsworth, her mother, and sister "went on horseback through the Philippine head-hunting country, explored little known temples in Java. . .and slept in Buddhist monasteries of the Korean Diamond Mountains, where we were sometimes the first white women the people had ever seen."[2]

To Pierre watching, standing on one foot, peace had come at last. ■ (From "The Cattle" in *The Lucky Ones: Five Journeys toward a Home* by Elizabeth Coatsworth. Illustrated by Janet Doyle.)

1920-1928. After her sister's marriage, Coatsworth and her mother ". . .bought the eighteenth-century house called Shipcote in Hingham, Massachusetts, overlooking the harbor, about a mile from the house bought by Margaret and her husband, Morton Smith. At last we had a home, and one which we loved.

"But we still traveled, and I still wrote and wrote, and was beginning to publish—my first book of poetry, *Fox Footprints*, being the direct result of the year in the Orient."[1]

1927. Coatsworth's first children's book, *The Cat and the Captain*, resulted from a discussion with a college friend, Louise Seaman, who had started the country's first children's book department at Macmillan. Coatsworth, who was now in her mid-thirties, focused her life around her travels and her writing. "In 1929 came a break in my travel. Travel had been my greatest joy. It continued to have a place, but the focus of my life changed. Marriage was a deeper fulfillment, the birth of a child more exciting than any journey.

"Henry [Beston] and I became engaged one January day before I started for California. The next six months were very happy and busy times for us both. He went to England and saw *The Outermost House* through the press. I wrote *The Cat Who Went to Heaven*, which was later to be awarded a Newbery Medal, and with Margaret went to Copan, that wonderful and at that time rarely visited ruin in what was then British Honduras. We hired mules and were gone for three or four days, sleeping in the hammocks which we carried tied to our saddles. I remember as very strange that in those mountains we were warned to look out for alligators if we bathed in the stream which the trail crossed and recrossed. Margaret bathed anyway, while I stood nervously watching for alligators.

"Then came the return, first to California and then to Hingham, where Henry and I were married in Morton and Margaret's house. We spent two weeks at the Fo'castle, where he had written *The Outermost House,* and then sailed for a summer in England.

"Our first daughter was born at the end of June 1930, and the second nearly two years later, so that the nurse carried her to Chimney Farm, near the Maine coast, in a market basket padded and lined with rose-sprigged dimity. We had meanwhile bought the farm overlooking Damariscotta Pond. 'And when I buy a house there will be nothing between it and the view,' said Henry, nor has there ever been, unlike dear Shipcote with a road unseen but not unheard below its hedges as one looked out to Hingham Harbor and far-off Boston Light.

"I was thirty-six years old when I married and Henry was five years older, so that for both of us it was very much of an adventure and we embarked upon it gaily and warmly. At the same time, writing remained of great importance to us both."' [1]

1931. Won the Newbery Medal for her fourth children's book, *The Cat Who Went to Heaven.* With her husband, Coatsworth bought "Chimney Farm" in Nobleboro, Maine. The family, which consisted of two daughters, Margaret and Catherine, grew up in the Maine woodlands and in their house in Hingham, Massachusetts, south of Boston. "After Henry and I settled. . .at the farm in Maine we did a great deal of writing. He wrote long and beautifully balanced books. . .as well as two anthologies. . . .And then I mustn't forget *Henry Beston's Fairy Tales,* some of them taken from two earlier books of fairy tales, often much rewritten, with later stories added to them.

"Before he wrote any book he 'sat for a long time considering his navel,' as he used to say. When at last he felt ready, he always had a publisher's contract at hand, and a kitchen table.

"There were many kitchen tables, one in the kitchen, one in the so-called library, one in the herb attic above my bedroom where he had a stove too, and a spool-bed to lie on to listen to the rain on the slanting roof close overhead, and one in the little building which was also his study and one stood close to the barn where he could oversee the house when the children were little and might suddenly need him. . . .

"At all of those tables he wrote, always with pencils which he kept very sharp, always on large loose sheets of paper which were lucky if they didn't find themselves crunched up into a ball and thrown over his shoulder onto the floor. . . .He was a meticulous writer, using a thesaurus and dictionary when he needed them. Occasionally an entire morning's work would be spent on a single sentence.

"But as for me, it was a different matter. I never had a contract. Before we were married I had used a Corona portable, but Henry felt that the rattle of the keys destroyed all natural rhythms of the mind so I wrote with a pencil too, or in later days with a ballpoint pen. I never used loose leaves but always school composition books with lined paper so that I could keep track of where I was. The idea for some stories appeared complete in my brain; some lay fallow for years. In either case they were written at top speed. Often I recognized that a sentence or a paragraph might be shaky but I would go right on,

Marra flung herself on the ground and began to cry in great silent sobs. ■ (From *Marra's World* by Elizabeth Coatsworth. Illustrated by Krystyna Turska.)

planning to come back to it later when I could see the chapter as a whole. In many cases I never did go back. The shaky sentence remains shaky to the end. But I had had good training in writing poetry, where every word counts, and the wrong word cannot take the place of the right one. Even when writing at top speed I think I was selective. I began to create a style, on the very simple premise that the writing should be as clear as glass and allow the subject to show through, with as little emphasis on the writer as possible. To this end whenever I could I chose words with Anglo-Saxon rather than Latin derivations.

"Over the years my subconscious became more and more a factor, as it learned the rules. The time came—I cannot give a date for it—when my subconscious took most of the responsibility. I would find myself taking dictation from it. Writing was an intoxication.

"I never wrote—or write—except between breakfast and luncheon, and if Henry was not writing I was prepared to leave my work at the first suggestion of his wishing us to do something together.

"Writing was for me an addiction like drink, which I kept as much as possible out of sight.

"And how fast I worked! I counted on forty hours as enough for most of my small books. My *Cat Who Went to Heaven* was written the winter before marriage while Henry was in England 'seeing *The Outermost House* through the press,' and I was in a summer cottage by the Pacific with my mother's family about to join my sister Margaret on a trip to Guatemala, at that time almost unspoiled by the blight of tourism. I had a little extra time on my hands, so I remembered the temple of Borobudur in Java and a picture in a Kyoto temple and with a little added here and there, worked hard for a week and finished *The Cat,* typed it and illustrated it crudely with drawings which Lynd Ward used later as a basis for his beautiful work. And that week, besides writing the book, I did my share of the housework, not including cooking, about which I knew nothing.

"But already the habit of writing fast and accurately was fully developed. My real training was in poetry. In those days of rhyme, when even free verse was careful of its rhythms, that muse was a demanding one, if often dissatisfied. All these years I have relied upon it, although I know that now, along with my conscious mind, it grows slipshod. It is still a muse, even if only a small one.''[1]

Coatsworth's books were greatly influenced by her New England life and countryside: *Alice-All-by Herself* (1937), *Here I Stay* (1938), *Houseboat Summer* (1942), *Thief Island* (1943), and *Trudy and the Tree House* (1944), to name a few.

1933-1954. Wrote and travelled with her family: to the Gaspe in 1933, to Yucatan and Mexico, Arizona and California in 1936-1938, to Canada, to Denmark, Sweden, Norway in 1953, to Paris, Denmark, Sweden, and Iceland in 1954. But always she wrote—memoirs, poetry, and books for children. "Most writers find it difficult to start off on a book or even an article. Many smoke cigarettes or drink an extra cup of coffee or rearrange their papers.

"'Make a beginning,' says my good angel.

"'I thought I'd pay bills and write letters this morning,' I say hastily.

"'They can wait,' says my angel. 'Make a beginning. It need be only a sentence.'

"'But the first sentence is very important.'

"'Write it then. You need write nothing more this morning if you don't want to. It will only take a minute. . . .'

"I get out my notebook, a lined composition book from the five-and-ten-cent store. . . .

"Pen in hand I write a sentence, rather at random.

"In some part of the world, in Africa, I think, they have a proverb: 'One cloud is lonely.' It may or it may not be true of clouds, but it certainly is true of sentences. Out of pure pity I write a second sentence to be company to the first. And then I am done for. I write a third and a fourth and soon I am hard at work. My good angel stands apart and makes no suggestions even when I follow a dead end and have to cross out several pages.

"'Yes, that wasn't good,' she agrees, reading over my shoulder. But that day she makes no suggestions. She is not a bit of help.

"The next morning she is there to do a little urging to get me started. Then she goes off and stares out the window. The ground is bare of snow and khaki-colored, and all the birds and the possible chipmunks are on the other side of the house

They were of all colors, and the shapes of their horns were never alike, though all were enormous. Some rose up into the air, curved like lyres. Some spread sideways into a scimitar sweep like the horns of wild buffalo, and some grew forward in upturned spikes.

They were of all colors, and the shapes of their horns were never alike. ■ (From *Ronnie and the Chief's Son* by Elizabeth Coatsworth. Illustrated by Stefan Martin.)

under the century-and-a-half-old apple tree. I can't imagine what she finds to look at all morning.

"This may go on for a good many days, but sooner or later she becomes really interested in the story as it evolves on the lined paper. Her hand softly descends on mine—I could scarcely say at what moment of time it happens—but now she is writing, using my hand as I used my ballpoint pen. I am often surprised by the ideas and details she puts in. They had not occurred to me when I was sketching out the general scheme of the work in bed the night before.

"But at last, sometimes sooner, sometimes later, she lifts her hand from mine.

"'Now finish,' my good angel says.

"'But that's the hardest part,' I protest, dependent after so much assistance.

"There is nothing for me to do but to finish the story as best I may, knowing that the editors will probably not be satisfied with it.

"'Now go over the whole thing and correct it,' she says over her shoulder.

"'But the parts you wrote don't need correcting,' I say.

"My good angel turns briskly to face me. 'Nonsense! My writing is no better than yours. It is only easier for you, that is all.'

"'But you——' I begin.

"'But I,' she mocks me; and adds; 'You know perfectly well that by whatever name you call me, I am only your subconscious.'

"Then my good angel smiles. 'Call me whatever muse you like. It doesn't alter what I am.'

"This is the usual course of writing a book. . . ."[1]

1957-1967. "Our lives followed the usual pattern. Our children, Margaret and Catherine—Meg and Kate—grew up and married; each [had] four children. Henry and I began to avoid 'mud time' at the farm by going to California in March, for five or six weeks.

"As time went on, Henry became more and more crippled by hardening of the arteries and the last four years of his life saw us at the farm all the year round, with Henry at first using a wheelchair and later staying mostly in bed attended by nurses round the clock. Almost until the very end he would go driving for a change, and I remember that a week before he died he asked to go out in the wheelchair to be under the sky. Of all the natural things he had so loved, the love of the sky remained with him to the end."[1]

1976. "Since Henry's death eight years ago I have had no desire to travel. I used to visit my sister in Hingham three or four times a year for a few days at a time, but since her death three years ago I take only relatively short drives.

"The long urge to write poetry has died almost completely away. And I live one day at a time.

"I am an old woman now, fighting my own losing battle with age, but with time to enjoy life along the way, as Henry always did. Naturally I think of death. I don't want to die because

She nudged against the bow of the boat, turning it. ■ (From *Marra's World* by Elizabeth Jane Coatsworth. Illustrated by Krystyna Turska.)

even in this narrower radius there are so many people and things still to enjoy. I do not fear death itself I think, but I often do not like its approaches. Only the other day I first formulated for myself the truism: 'You cannot conquer death, but perhaps you can conquer the fear of it.'

"All these things and a thousand more are embodied in me, the good years and the bad, the wide rings of growth and the narrow. One's past is not something we leave behind, but something we incorporate. When I write a story for children I am a child, with perhaps a grownup person's powers of criticism (at least so I hope). When I lunch with a group of young middle-aged people, I feel no difference between us; when I walk in to my neighbor's, watching every step for fear I may trip on something (my sense of balance is irretrievably lost!), I greet her as an equal as she sits in a big chair tatting, with her walker in front of her. Outwardly I am eighty-three years old, but inwardly I am every age, with the emotions and experience of each period. The important thing is that at each age I am myself, just as you are yourself. During much of my life I was anxious to be what someone else wanted me to be. Now I have given up that struggle. I am what I am.

"I have a thousand memories. I could, I suppose, travel still, but so cautiously and in such a diminished world! I am content to remember larger times. The world in which I live is enough for me. After so many travels, I am home, and my happiness here is no less than it was in foreign lands and my sense of wonder has not dulled with all these years. I am as happy as an old dog stretched out in the sunlight. I remember other times, other places, but (in the sunlight) I am content with here and now."[1]

September 2, 1986. Died at her home in Maine at the age of ninety-three. "The candle has been blown out, darkness closes over the room, but the stories told. . .have not been blown out."[1]

FOOTNOTE SOURCES

[1]Elizabeth Coatsworth, *A Personal Geography: Almost an Autobiography,* G. K. Hall, 1979.
[2]Rebecca Lukens, "Elizabeth Coatsworth," *Dictionary of Literary Biography,* Volume 22: *American Writers for Children, 1900-1960,* Gale, 1983.

FOR MORE INFORMATION SEE:

BOOKS

Anne Thaxter Eaton, *Reading with Children,* Viking, 1940.
May Hill Arbuthnot and Zena Sutherland, *Children and Books,* Scott, Foresman, 1947, 4th edition, 1972.
Stanley J. Kunitz and Howard Haycraft, editors, *Junior Book of Authors,* second edition, H. W. Wilson, 1951.
Harry R. Warfel, *American Novelists of Today,* American Book, 1951.
Ruth Hill Viguers, Cornelia Meigs, Elizabeth Nesbitt, and A. T. Eaton, *A Criticial History of Children's Literature,* Macmillan, 1953, revised edition, 1969.
Bertha Mahoney Miller and Elinor Whitney Field, editors, *Newbery Medal Books: 1922-1955,* Horn Book, 1955.
Louise Bechtel, *Books in Search of Children,* Macmillan, 1968.
Elinor W. Field, *Horn Book Reflections,* Horn Book, 1969.
Haviland and Smith, *Children and Poetry,* Library of Congress, 1969.
Nora Smaridge, *Famous Modern Storytellers for Young People,* Dodd, 1969.
Constantine Georgiou, *Children and Their Literature,* Prentice-Hall, 1969.
Brian Doyle, *The Who's Who of Children's Literature,* Schocken, 1970.
Martha E. Ward and Dorothy A. Marquardt, *Authors of Books for Young People,* Scarecrow, 1971.
Miriam Hoffman and Eva Samuels, editors, *Authors and Illustrators of Children's Books: Writings on Their Lives and Works,* Bowker, 1972.
W. J. Burke and Will D. Howe, *American Authors and Books, 1640 to the Present Day,* 3rd revised edition, Crown, 1972.
Lee Bennett Hopkins, *More Books by More People,* Citation Press, 1974.
John Rowe Townsend, *Written for Children: An Outline of English-Language Children's Literature,* Lippincott, 1974.
Children's Literature Review, Volume II, Gale, 1976.
D. L. Kirkpatrick, *Twentieth-Century Children's Writers,* St. Martin's, 1978, 2nd edition, 1983.
Jim Roginski, compiler, *Newbery and Caldecott Medalists and Honor Book Winners,* Libraries Unlimited, 1982.

PERIODICALS

New York Times, July 6, 1930, November 9, 1930, January 4, 1959.
Horn Book, November, 1930, January, 1936 (p. 27), September, 1948, January, 1951 (p. 26), December, 1967 (p. 747), June, 1968 (p. 332), August, 1969 (p. 402, 408), June, 1971, August, 1974 (p. 395).
Nation, November 19, 1930.
New Republic, November 19, 1930.
Chicago Daily Tribune, November 22, 1930.
New York World, November 23, 1930.
Atlantic Bookshelf, December 30, 1930.
Scholastic, April 24, 1937.
Library Journal, August, 1951.

Elementary English, January, 1954, December, 1969 (p. 991).
Christian Science Monitor, November 3, 1960 (p. 5B), November 2, 1967, November 5, 1975, January 19, 1977.
Times Literary Supplement, November 25, 1960, November 3, 1972 (p. 1321), July 5, 1974 (p. 722).
L. Jacobs, "Elizabeth Coatsworth," *Instructor,* November, 1962.
Bulletin of the Center for Children's Books, April, 1964 (p. 123), February, 1969 (p. 91), April, 1973 (p. 122), April, 1975 (p. 128).
Junior Bookshelf, June, 1965, December, 1967, December, 1972, August, 1974 (p. 208).
Book Week, September 4, 1966 (p. 15).
Young Readers Review, April, 1967, October, 1969.
School Library Journal, October, 1967 (p. 162), May, 1968 (p. 85, 88), March, 1973 (p. 104), September, 1974 (p. 56), March, 1975 (p. 86).
Book World, October 22, 1967 (p. 14), May 9, 1971.
Punch, November 29, 1967.
Children's Book Review, December, 1972.
Booklist, November 15, 1975 (p. 450).
America, December 6, 1975.
Country Journal, December, 1976 (p. 68).
Progressive, August, 1977.
Language Arts, April, 1980.

OBITUARIES

Portland Press Herald, September 2, 1986.
New York Times, September 3, 1986.
Facts on File, September 5, 1986.
Publishers Weekly, September 19, 1986 (p. 66).

COLLECTIONS

Baker Library, Dartmouth College, Hanover, New Hampshire.
Bowdoin College Library, Brunswick, Maine.
De Grummond Collection at the University of Southern Mississippi, Hattiesburg.
Kerlan Collection at the University of Minnesota, Minneapolis.
Lockwood Memorial Library at the State University of New York at Buffalo.
Miller Library at Colby College, Waterville, Maine.
Rare Book and Manuscript Library at Columbia University, New York.
Rare Book Room, Buffalo and Erie County Public Library, Buffalo, N.Y.
Special Collections at the University Research Library at the University of California at Los Angeles.
Vassar College Library, Poughkeepsie, N.Y.

COX, David (Dundas) 1933-

PERSONAL: Born June 20, 1933, in Goondiwindi, Australia; son of Hunter Cay (a grazier) and Charlotte (a housewife; maiden name, Barmby) Cox; married Guillemette Masson, February 28, 1959 (divorced September, 1975); married Betty Beath Eardley (a composer and pianist), February 22, 1976; children: Bruno (deceased), Abigail, Emma. *Education:* Attended St. Martin's School of Art, London, England, 1954-55. *Home:* 8 St. James St., Highgate Hill, Queensland 4101, Australia. *Office: Courier Mail,* Campbell St., Bowen Hills, Queensland 4006, Australia.

CAREER: Ranchhand and cowboy in Queensland, Australia, 1949-54; waiter, laborer, furniture remover, and gravedigger in Europe, 1955-63; Queensland Newspapers Pty. Ltd., Brisbane, Australia, head artist, 1964—; author and illustrator. *Exhibitions:* "200 Years of Australian Children's Illustration"

DAVID COX

(traveling exhibition), Bologna, Italy, London, England, and Tokyo, Japan. *Member:* Australian Journalists Association, Australian Society of Authors, Opera for Youth (United States), Indonesian Study Group, Playlab of Queensland. *Awards, honors:* Walkely Award from the Australian Journalists Association, 1978, for newspaper illustration; Children's Book of the Year Award Commendation from the Australian Children's Book Council, 1983, for *Tin Lizzie and Little Nell,* and 1985, for *Ayu and the Perfect Moon;* Parents' Choice Award Citation from the Parents' Choice Foundation, 1987, for *Bossyboots.*

WRITINGS:

SELF-ILLUSTRATED CHILDREN'S BOOKS

Sometimes Sam, E. J. Arnold, 1968.
The Picnic, E. J. Arnold, 1969.
The Gymhana, E. J. Arnold, 1969.
Abigail and the Bushranger (musical play; music by wife, Betty Beath), J. Albert, 1976.
Abigail and the Rainmaker (musical play; music by B. Beath), J. Albert, 1976.
Marco Polo (musical play; music by B. Beath), J. Albert, 1977.
Miss Bunkle's Umbrella, Bodley Head, 1981.
Francis (musical play; music by B. Beath), Playlab Press, 1982.

Tin Lizzie and Little Nell, Bodley Head, 1982, Salem House, 1984.
(With B. Beath) *Reflections from Bali,* Addison-Wesley, 1982.
Ayu and the Perfect Moon, Merrimack, 1984.
Bossyboots, Bodley Head, 1985, Crown, 1987.
Rightway Jack, Bodley Head, 1987.

ADULT

(With B. Beath) *Spice and Magic* (self-illustrated travel book), Boolarong Press, 1983.

Also author of short stories; children's book critic, Brisbane's *Courier Mail,* 1974-86.

WORK IN PROGRESS: "I am at present researching material, for example, the Irish rebel General Holt, and St. Francis. I now want to put a lot of time and effort into one of these subjects (or perhaps something else) to produce a really beautiful book. I feel that I need to make a step forward in terms of quality and content, so, am allowing myself some time to think before I launch into new work. Perhaps this work will take the form of a play."

SIDELIGHTS: "I am living proof of the saying 'You can take the boy out of the bush, but you can't take the bush out of the boy.' I was brought up on sheep and cattle stations (ranches) in the Australian interior, and I still have many of the mannerisms of a country boy. I worked in the bush for some years after leaving school, and the money I made and saved in the outback allowed me to go to London to study. When I write children's books, I seem to stick to country and historical themes.

"*Tin Lizzie and Little Nell* is a story taken from my own childhood. In it I present two families, one that owned a motor car and one that owned a horse and cart. I am remembering my own family before and after my father had bought a motor car. Like 'The Hare and the Tortoise,' the story is about the dangers of complacency.

"I think that *Miss Bunkle's Umbrella* was my best picture book so far; but (although it received some good reviews) it was not a success in terms of sales. It's the story of a school teacher on holiday who becomes lost in Java. She learns a little about Javanese villagers, and they learn something about her.

"My main inspiration has been my wife, Betty Beath, who is a composer. In our musical plays, written in collaboration, the link is obvious, but in other work also, where her name is not mentioned, she figures very strongly. Apart from that, her music adds color to my life.

"I am very keen on travel and language. Betty and I have spent quite a lot of time in Indonesia, partly because the culture of the country fascinates us and partly because we feel that we Australians should learn to know and understand our near neighbors. We also feel that we should lean less heavily on European art.

"I am as much illustrator as writer. My first short story was written as a vehicle for illustration. In the United States that story was published in braille. My next half dozen stories became radio broadcasts, which was a little frustrating.

"Horses and horsemanship are a part of my life of which I do not completely approve (I am sorry for the horses) but which, nevertheless, is an important part. I was brought up as a horseman, and the interest still remains."

HOBBIES AND OTHER INTERESTS: Languages (French, Indonesian, Greek), photography, music.

She even bossed the driver. ■ (From *Bossyboots* by David Cox. Illustrated by the author.)

CAROLYN CROLL

CROLL, Carolyn 1945-

PERSONAL: Born May 20, 1945, in Sioux Falls, S.D.; daughter of Lionel and Evelyn A. (Rosen) Croll. *Education:* Philadelphia College of Art, B.F.A., 1967. *Home and office:* 1420 Locust St., No. 22H, Philadelphia, Pa. 19102.

CAREER: Free-lance illustrator, 1967—; Philadelphia College of Art, Pa., teacher of design and illustration 1968-84; has also worked in packaging, fashion illustration, and greeting card design. *Member:* Philadelphia Children's Reading Round Table. *Awards, honors: Ramshackle Roost* was selected one of Child Study Association of America's Children's Books of the Year, 1972; *The Big Balloon Race* was selected a Children's Choice by the International Reading Association and the Children's Book Council, 1982.

WRITINGS:

ALL SELF-ILLUSTRATED

Too Many Babas, Harper, 1979, large print edition, 1979.
The Little Snowgirl, Putnam, 1989.

ILLUSTRATOR

Jane Flory, *Ramshackle Roost,* Houghton, 1972.
J. Flory, *We'll Have a Friend for Lunch,* Houghton, 1974.
Peter Limburg, *What's in the Names of Stars and Constellations,* Coward, 1976.
J. Flory, *The Unexpected Grandchildren,* Houghton, 1977.
J. Flory, *The Bear on the Doorstep,* Houghton, 1980.
Eleanor Coerr, *The Big Balloon Race* ("Reading Rainbow" selection), Harper, 1981.
Nancy Smiler Levinson, *Clara and the Bookwagon,* Harper, 1988.
Melvin Berger, *Switch On, Switch Off,* Harper, in press.
Lynda DeWitt, *What Will the Weather Be,* Harper, in press.

ADAPTATIONS:

"The Big Balloon Race" (cassette), Listening Library, 1986.

SIDELIGHTS: "I consider myself an artist, rather than a writer. I have come to writing through illustration, because I have the desire to make books for children and sometimes lack good material from other sources. I am very interested in history, particularly English and Russian history, and I love to travel. I've been to England, Scotland, France, Italy, and Russia. I collect folk art, hand-crafted toys, and original book illustrations. There are creative people on both sides of my family, so I come by my interests quite naturally."

DANIEL, Becky 1947-
(Rebecca Daniel)

PERSONAL: Born September 5, 1947, in Ottumwa, Iowa; daughter of John Andrew (a barber and a dental lab technician) and Naomi (maiden name, Knight; a dental lab technician) Mier; married Charles Willard Daniel (a writer and teacher), July 31, 1972; children: Amy Rebecca, Sarah Ruth, Eric Justin. *Education:* Fullerton Junior College, A.A., 1968; University of California, B.A., 1971. *Home:* 4335 Bristol Ct., Orcutt, Calif. 93455. *Address:* Shining Star Publications, P.O. Box 2532, Orcutt, Calif. 93455.

CAREER: Oceanview School District, Huntington Beach, Calif., teacher, 1971-73; Atascadero Unified School District, Carissa Plains, Calif., teacher, 1973-76; Good Apple Publications, Eu-

gene, Oregon, writer, 1976-80; *Shining Star* (magazine), Orcutt, Calif., writer, editor, 1980-87.

WRITINGS:

JUVENILE

Paper Airplane Factory (self-illustrated with Susan Kropal), Good Apple, 1978.
(With husband, Charles Daniel) *My Very Own Dictionary,* Good Apple, 1978.
(With C. Daniel) *Teacher Time Savers,* Good Apple, 1978.
Thinker Sheets (self-illustrated), Good Apple, 1978.
(With C. Daniel) *Warm Smiles, Happy Faces,* Good Apple, 1978.
Writing about My Feelings, Good Apple, 1978.
(With C. Daniel) *Freaky Fractions,* Good Apple, 1978.
(With C. Daniel) *Going Bananas over Language,* Good Apple, 1978.
(With C. Daniel) *Super Spelling Fun,* Good Apple, 1978.
Comprehension Zoo, Good Apple, 1979.
I Wonder, Good Apple, 1979.
Big Addition Book, Good Apple, 1979.
Big Subtraction Book, Good Apple, 1979.
What's Next?, Good Apple, 1979.
Fun with Addition, Prentice-Hall, 1979.
Rhyming and Reading, Good Apple, 1979.
Ready, Set. . .Read!, Good Apple, 1979.
Addition Riddles, Prentice-Hall, 1979.
Fun with Subtraction, Prentice-Hall, 1979.
Subtraction Riddles, Prentice-Hall, 1979.
Fun with Multiplication, Prentice-Hall, 1979.
Multiplication Riddles, Prentice-Hall, 1979.
Fun with Division, Prentice-Hall, 1979.
Division Riddles, Prentice-Hall, 1979.

BECKY DANIEL

Nutrition, Prentice-Hall, 1979.
Beginning Reading, Prentice-Hall, 1979.
Gameboard Books, 30 books, Prentice-Hall, 1980-81.
Phonics Reading Series, ten books, Prentice-Hall, 1980.
Reading Drill Design Series, five books, Prentice-Hall, 1980.
Math Drill Design Series, four books, Prentice-Hall, 1980.
Strain Your Brain, Learning Works, 1980.
The Multiplication Book, Good Apple, 1980.
The Division Book, Good Apple, 1980.
(With husband, C. Daniel) *Arithmetrix,* Good Apple, 1980.
Oh, My Word!, Good Apple, 1980.
I Can Draw a Circus, Good Apple, 1981.
Rainbow Factory, Good Apple, 1981.
Super Duper School Scrapbook, Good Apple, 1981.
First Words, Prentice-Hall, 1981.
Helping Your Child Write, Prentice-Hall, 1981.
Basic Reading, Prentice-Hall, 1981.
Learning about Money, Prentice-Hall, 1981.
Beginning Reading, Prentice-Hall, 1981.
First Crossword Puzzles, Prentice-Hall, 1981.
Learning to Read, Prentice-Hall, 1981.
Puzzle Fun for Arithmetic, Prentice-Hall, 1981.
Puzzles for Addition and Subtraction, Prentice-Hall, 1981.
Good Apple and Teacher Helpers, Good Apple, 1982.
Word Thinkercises, Good Apple, 1987.
Math Thinkercises, Good Apple, 1987.
Spelling Thinkercises, Good Apple, 1987.
Bible Story Hidden Pictures: Jesus' Life, Shining Star, 1987.
Mother, I'm Mad, Trillum Press, 1988.
Mother, I'm Embarrassed, Trillum Press, 1988.
Mother, I'm Worried, Trillum Press, 1988.
Mother, I'm Disappointed, Trillum Press, 1988.
Logic Thinkercises, Good Apple, 1988.
Writing Thinkercises, Good Apple, 1988.
Reading Thinkercises, Good Apple, 1988.
Bible Story Hidden Pictures: Famous Biblical Women, Shining Star, 1988.
Spelling Thinkercises, Good Apple, 1988.
Word Thinkercises, Good Apple, 1988.
Hooray for Addition, Good Apple, 1989.
Hooray for Subtraction, Good Apple, 1989.
Hooray for Multiplication, Good Apple, 1989.
Hooray for Division, Good Apple, 1989.
Math Thinkercises, Good Apple, in press.

"LIFE OF JESUS" SERIES; ALL JUVENILE; ALL ILLUSTRATED BY NANCEE McCLURE

Jesus: His Birth, Shining Star, 1983.
Jesus: His Boyhood, Shining Star, 1983.
Jesus: Gathering His Disciples, Shining Star, 1983.
Jesus: The Teacher, Shining Star, 1983.
Jesus: The Healer, Shining Star, 1983.
Jesus: His Miracles, Shining Star, 1983.
Jesus: His Parables, Shining Star, 1983.
Jesus: More Parables, Shining Star, 1983.
Jesus: Prophecies Fulfilled, Shining Star, 1983.
Jesus: His Last Days, Shining Star, 1983.
Jesus: His Last Hours, Shining Star, 1983.
Jesus: His Resurrection, Shining Star, 1983.

UNDER NAME REBECCA DANIEL; "GREATEST HERITAGE" SERIES; JUVENILE; ALL ILLUSTRATED BY GARY MOHRMANN, EXCEPT AS NOTED

Adam and Eve, Shining Star, 1983.
Noah, Shining Star, 1983.
Moses, Shining Star, 1983.
Joshua, Shining Star, 1983.
Samson, Shining Star, 1983.
Jonah, Shining Star, 1983.

David, Shining Star, 1983.
Joseph, Shining Star, 1983.
Daniel, Shining Star, 1983.
Abraham, Shining Star, 1983.
Solomon, Shining Star, 1983.
Women of the Old Testament, Shining Star, 1983.
Bible Teacher Time-Savers, Shining Star, 1983.
Hallelujah! I Am Special (illustrated by N. McClure), Shining Star, 1983.

Also author of *Biblical Christmas Performances,* published by Good Apple. Editor of a Christian Education book series, 1982-88.

WORK IN PROGRESS: Children's Lunch Box Cookbook; four children's books all illustrated by Judy Hierstein: *Maximillian, He's Ruining My Life, Maximillian's and My Great Surprise, Maximillian's Brilliant Idea, Maximillian's Loose Tooth,* and *Maximillian, the Big Show-Off;* several books for Good Apple: *See Me Read Short Vowels, See Me Read Long Vowels,* and *See Me Read Initial Consonants.*

SIDELIGHTS: "Even before graduating from college, I started my teaching career as a teacher's aide and an intern teacher in California. I loved teaching but soon discovered the lack of good teaching materials. Five years later, when my first daughter, Amy, was born, my husband, Charlie, and I decided to move to Oregon and open a teacher supply store.

"For the second time, I was faced with the fact that there wasn't very many good teaching ideas on the market. I put in my time—two days a week—in our teacher supply store. I spent hours reading what was available and wondering why someone wasn't writing quality materials for youngsters. It was then that I decided to become a writer. I remember one night jumping out of bed and starting my first draft on a book called, *Thinker Sheets.* Now, twelve years and over one hundred books later, I know that writing is the only profession that could ever really make me happy. I love to write! Good Apple has published about half of the books I have written. The owners of the company, Don Mitchell and Gary Grimm, basically have the same philosophy that I have about children and learning, so it is great fun to work for them.

"Five years ago Good Apple asked me to be the editor of a newspaper they planned to publish. After three years of publication, the newspaper changed formats and is now an eighty-page magazine called, *Shining Star.* As editor of *Shining Star* magazine, I spend a lot of time helping new writers get started. That is a real pleasure too. But best of all I like to write.

"I have three children, Amy, Sarah, and Eric. My office is in our home, and I really appreciate a job that makes it possible to be near my family when I am working. We live in a small town called Orcutt (in Santa Barbara County), California. It is very quiet and the perfect environment for creativity. My husband and children are actively involved in my writing. The children help me write my children's picture books. (Most of the stories are based on them.) And my older daughter, Amy, just had her first book published (*Bible Rebus Puzzles*). My younger daughter, Sarah, wants to be a picture book illustrator when she grows up.

"I found a publisher for four children's books I wrote, *Mother, I'm Mad, Mother, I'm Embarrassed, Mother, I'm Disappointed,* and *Mother, I'm Worried.* Finding a publisher for

Becky Daniel's character Maximillian (above) is based on her son, Eric. Illustrated by Judy Hierstein and planned as a four-book series, the project was two years in the making.

children's books is really an experience! Finding just the right publisher, a person that understands what you are trying to say to children takes patience. But once you find the right publisher it's all worth it. It's truly a thrill to write and know that others are enjoying the fruits of my labor. Touching children—thousands, possibly millions—with my words makes me very glad that I am a writer.''

HOBBIES AND OTHER INTERESTS: ''My family and I enjoy winter trips to Hawaii. Last winter we lived on the garden isle Kauai for four months. Our three children love the ocean and all collect sea shells. One of the many benefits of being a writer is the opportunity of working anywhere I choose. (Or at least anywhere I can carry my Apple II.) The best thing about writing is that it IS my hobby! When I am not editing the magazine, *Shining Star,* or writing a Good Apple book, I'm working on my own children's books. When you can earn your living doing something you enjoy as much as I enjoy writing, you know you are truly blessed.''

DANK, Gloria Rand 1955-

PERSONAL: Born October 5, 1955, in Toledo, Ohio; daughter of Milton (a physicist and writer) and Naomi (a hospital administrator; maiden name, Rand) Dank. *Education:* Princeton University, B.A. (summa cum laude), 1977; graduate study at Cambridge University, 1977-79. *Home:* Philadelphia, Pa. *Office:* c/o Greenwillow Books, 105 Madison Ave., New York, N.Y. 10016; and c/o Delacorte Press, 1 Dag Hammarskjold Plaza, 245 East 47th St., New York, N.Y. 10017.

CAREER: Gellman Research Associates, Inc., Jenkintown, Pa., computer programmer and research analyst, 1979-81; free-lance writer, 1981—. Volunteer telephone counselor for Contact Philadelphia, Inc., 1982—. *Member:* Phi Beta Kappa. *Awards, honors:* George C. Marshall scholar in England, 1977-79; *The Forest of App* was a Book of the Month selection of the Philadelphia Children's Reading Round Table, 1984.

WRITINGS:

The Forest of App (young adult fantasy novel), Greenwillow, 1983.

''GALAXY GANG MYSTERY'' SERIES; FOR YOUNG ADULTS; ALL WITH FATHER, MILTON DANK

The Computer Caper, Delacorte, 1983.
A UFO Has Landed, Delacorte, 1983.
The 3-D Traitor, Delacorte, 1984.
The Treasure Code, Delacorte, 1985.
The Computer Game Murder, Delacorte, 1985.

WORK IN PROGRESS: A fantasy novel for young adults, tentatively titled *The Changeling.*

SIDELIGHTS: ''I left graduate school in England in 1979 and worked for a consulting company for a year or so before beginning to write in earnest. I find in my fantasy writing that I get an initial idea for a situation and characters, and the plot unfolds from there. I try to work on infusing a certain 'energy' or interest into each of my characters, and on creating situations and dialogue which appeal to my sense of humor. All in all, writing is a mysterious business!

''Both my fantasy novels, *The Forest of App* and *The Changeling,* are concerned with the fading of magic and the lives of those who are 'left behind' as it fades: the faeries, the bogles, the witches, the unicorns, and the Old Ones who are

GLORIA RAND DANK

left hanging on as the magic vanishes. Their power is fading and they themselves are becoming bent and withered and ugly. What can they do? Along with this, I am concerned with the junction of the human and faery worlds, the everyday and the magical: How do they blend? What kind of resolution can there be between them? How does one get there from here and back again?

"I like the idea of a world where magic is ordinary and strange creatures, monsters, naiads, stoorworms, and giants live in the forests and streams. This is what I write about: worlds, where magic is right there, but those who have it are not invincible, not special, not so very different from the human beings who also exist in the same place and time. I am drawn to this theme of magic and the resolution of the two worlds.

"There are no real heroes in my books—I don't like heroes—and there are no real villains either, I'm afraid. I stay away from the 'good versus evil' fantasy plot. But like most writers, I don't have much choice about what I write: It comes or it doesn't. On good days (high barometric pressure, mild prevailing winds, etc.) I can write perhaps three to seven pages. On bad days I write one sentence which I then revise obsessively.

"My favorite writer is T. H. White, author of *The Once and Future King*."

Dank collaborated with her writer-father, Milton Dank, on the "Galaxy Gang Mystery" series. "We began by strictly alternating chapters, but it quickly became much more fluid—we'll assign scenes based on who feels more comfortable with that bit of action. We are constantly reading and rereading the other person's work, discussing the plot twists, and building the characters. The plot often changes as one of the characters takes over and begins to dominate a scene, so of course we have to bend to accommodate our characters' individual needs and preferences. When the first draft is completed, we go over it carefully to make sure our styles mesh and show no gaps. Since we both have very different viewpoints, we also argue.

But, perhaps surprisingly for an intra-family collaboration, conflict has been kept to a minimum."[1]

These young adult mystery novels have a science twist, are set in Philadelphia, a city with a colonial background, and have a group "hero." "We. . .have a gang of kids who pool their talents to solve the mysteries, instead of one 'hero' or 'heroine' who does all the puzzle-solving. There is an informal leader to our group, but the teenagers are all equal and simply contribute their different strengths toward a common goal. The main goal is not just solving mysteries, after all—it is staying together as a social group, giving each other support and friendship. Their different backgrounds provide a larger network of knowledge for them to draw on in solving these puzzles, as well as a richer fabric for the stories.

"As for the research, we'll read anything that looks interesting or might vaguely apply to our novels. For the first three 'Galaxy Gang' books, we did some reading on computers and the law, looked up the name of a noxious luminous chemical, and went through a pile of books on Benedict Arnold and the colonial era in Philadelphia. For the fourth 'Galaxy Gang' book,. . .[I] spent a lot of time standing outside City Hall in Philadelphia, staring up at the statue of William Penn which is on the top. The stories are very different, and so of course, our research reflects that. We can get the facts we need from newspapers, from the library, or from just walking around Philadelphia."[1]

FOOTNOTE SOURCES

[1]"A Conversation with Milton and Gloria Dank," *Dell Carousel*, fall/winter, 1983-84.

HOBBIES AND OTHER INTERESTS: Tennis, walking, classical and modern music.

DEADMAN, Ronald   1919-1988(?)

OBITUARY NOTICE: Born in 1919 in Shoeburyness, Essex, England; died about 1988. Educator, editor and author. Deadman gained recognition for his dedication to bringing higher and more imaginative standards of education to the schools in which he taught. After serving in World War II in the air and sea rescue service, he attended teachers' training college. His years of teaching experience between 1950 and 1966 included a Fulbright scholarship in 1957 to the United States—where he was influenced by American methods of teaching and reading—and a lecturing position for two years at Brentwood College of Education. A teacher at both the secondary and college levels, Deadman also educated middle-aged black and Asian immigrants in the London area. He became features editor of *The Teacher* in 1966, and from 1968 to 1976 he was editor of *Teacher's World*. Resuming his teaching career, Deadman became a tutor in adult education beginning in 1985. His writings for young people include the multivolume *Enjoying English*, *The Happening*, *Wanderbodies*, and *The Pretenders*. He also edited the two-volume *Round the World Folk Tales and English Language Texts*.

FOR MORE INFORMATION SEE:

International Authors and Writers Who's Who, 7th edition, Melrose, 1976.
Who's Who, 140th edition, St. Martin's, 1988.

OBITUARIES

Times (London), May 10, 1988.

DeJONGE, Joanne E. 1943-

PERSONAL: Surname sounds like "young"; born May 18, 1943 in Paterson, N.J.; daughter of Andrew John (a salesman) and Johanna (a secretary; maiden name DeHaan) Haan; married R. Wayne DeJonge (a graphic artist), July 25, 1969. *Education:* University of Michigan, B. Mus., 1965; Calvin College, M.A.T., 1978. *Religion:* Christian (Protestant). *Home:* 670 56th Street S.E., Grand Rapids, Mich. 49508. *Office:* Grand Rapids Christian School Association, 1812 Sylvan Street S.E., Grand Rapids, Mich. 49506.

CAREER: Peace Corps, Sarawak, Malaysia, teacher, 1965-67; Grand Rapids Christian School Association, Grand Rapids, Mich., strings teacher, 1968—; writer 1975—. Red Cross volunteer; member, United Way. *Member:* American String Teachers Association; Michigan School Band and Orchestra Association.

WRITINGS:

God's Wonderful World, CRC Publications, 1978.
Anaku, the True Story of a Wolf, Baker Book House, 1979.
More about God's Wonderful World, Paideia Press, 1981.
Bats and Bugs and Snakes and Slugs, Baker Book House, 1981.
Skin and Bones, Baker Book House, 1985.
A Beautiful Gift, Baker Book House, 1985.
Object Lessons from Nature, Baker Book House, 1989.

"RAINBOW BOOKS" SERIES

Crooked Footprints, Baker Book House, 1978.
Dandelions and Jumping Beans, Baker Book House, 1978.
Turtles, Sharks and Penguins, Baker Book House, 1978.

JOANNE E. DeJONGE

Bears and Beavers, Baker Book House, 1978.
Hummingbirds and Roadrunners, Baker Book House, 1978.
Spiderwebs and Spittlebugs, Baker Book House, 1978.

"MY FATHER'S WORLD" SERIES; ALL ILLUSTRATED BY RICHARD BISHOP

The Rustling Grass, CRC Publications, 1985.
Of Skies and Seas, CRC Publications, 1985.
My Listening Ears, CRC Publications, 1985.
All Nature Sings, CRC Publications, 1985.

Writer for the *Banner* (a denominational periodical), 1975—.

WORK IN PROGRESS: A book for children about endangered species, entitled *When the Canary Sings;* "I have recently created *Sophie,* an imaginary angel and taken her through several adventures corresponding to important dates in the Christian calendar. She's currently looking for a publisher who can reach a wider audience than my other books have."

SIDELIGHTS: "Being city born and bred, I grew up deeply involved in cultural affairs and completely oblivious to the natural world. That oblivion persisted, even through a two-year stay in Borneo, home to some of the world's most exotic creatures.

"A few years after I returned to the United States, I was asked to write an article for the young readers of our denominational magazine about my experiences in Borneo. Figuring that I had been home too long to remember accurately, I decided to write, instead, an article about ants. Why I picked ants, I'll never know. I like to think it was Divine guidance. I knew absolutely nothing about ants, but I was determined to write the article. That article changed my life.

"I went to the library, plowed through tons of scientific literature and found a whole new world. I was flabbergasted by the complexity of the little creatures, and fascinated by the way every little living thing ties in with other living things. From ants I moved to spiders, then insects, then any creature that any scientist had studied. I couldn't figure out how I had missed this absolutely fascinating world while I was in school. Then I realized that I was reading 'dry' scientific articles and simply translating the jargon to everyday words in my head. No one had done that for me before, so I decided I would do that for others. Since then I've written between five- and six-hundred articles about little creatures.

"I went back to school to enter the scientific world a little more formally, and earned my Masters in the art of teaching science studies. Through it all, I resisted using scientific jargon when everyday words would do.

"Now I love to sit in the library and read all the scientific journals and books which most people wouldn't touch. I fill my brain with obscure facts, figures and tidbits, then spill them all out in a form that lay people can understand. I'm always excited about some creature—how well it fits into creation, how neat it is, etc.—and try to pass that excitement on to my readers.

"The more I've studied the natural world, the more thoroughly convinced I become that absolutely everything has a place and we are responsible for the fate of these creatures. But to rule them wisely, we should know all we can about them. I love to pass on any information I can in an easily readable form.

"I'm still teaching music (stringed instruments), the profession I first chose, and I still love that, too. But now I feel I

I stared into its unblinking eye, trying to make it blink or look away. However, snakes can't blink. ■ (From "Blue Racer" in *All Nature Sings* by Joanne E. DeJonge. Illustrated by Rich Bishop.)

have the best of two worlds. I live with music some days, and on alternate days I live with these delightful creatures.''

DeLEEUW, Adele (Louise) 1899-1988

OBITUARY NOTICE—See sketch in *SATA* Volume 30: Born August 12, 1899, in Hamilton, Ohio; died of cancer of the colon, June 12, 1988, in Plainfield, N.J. Librarian and author. DeLeeuw pioneered two forms of teenage literature—the career story and the problem novel. She will be best remembered for her many books for children and teenagers, some of which were illustrated or co-authored by her sister, Cateau DeLeeuw. She began writing after starting a children's story hour at the public library in Plainfield where she was employed as an assistant librarian, and by 1926 writing was her sole occupation. DeLeeuw penned over seventy-five volumes, including: *The Expandable Browns, Where Valor Lies* (a 1959 Catholic Youth Book Club selection), *Casey Jones Drives an Ice Cream Train, Maria Tallchief: American Ballerina, Carlos P. Romulo: The Barefoot Boy of Diplomacy,* and *Remembered with Love.*

Together with her sister Cateau, she received a citation from the Mary Kinney Cooper Ohioana Library Association for the quality of their work over a period of many years. DeLeeuw believed that a good story should have ''a good storyline, but more subtle values—courage, independence, a new way of looking at life, the satisfaction of work well done, the joy of reaching a goal—whatever it is that can open a window on the world.'' Her books were translated into several foreign languages, transcribed into Braille, used for Projected Books for hospital patients, and adapted into radio programs.

FOR MORE INFORMATION SEE:

Ann Evory, editor, *Contemporary Authors: New Revision Series,* Gale, 1981.
The Writers Directory: 1988-1990, St. James Press, 1988.

OBITUARIES

New York Times, June 14, 1988.

DUBANEVICH, Arlene 1950-

PERSONAL: Born December 6, 1950, in Springfield, Vt.; daughter of Frank J. and Sophie (Hayna) Dubanevich; married J. Seeley (a professor of fine arts and photographer), April, 1973. *Education:* Rhode Island School of Design, B.F.A., 1972. *Home and office:* R.F.D. #1, South Rd., Portland, Conn. 06480.

CAREER: Free-lance illustrator, 1971—; author and illustrator of children's books, 1983—. *Member:* Authors League of America, Authors Guild. *Awards, honors:* Certificate of Excellence from the American Institute of Graphic Arts, Parents' Choice Award for Illustration from the Parents' Choice Foundation, and named one of *School Library Journal*'s Best Books, all 1983, and included in the American Institute of Graphic Arts Book Show, 1984, all for *Pigs in Hiding; Pig William* was exhibited at the Bologna International Children's Book Fair, 1985.

WRITINGS:

JUVENILE; ALL SELF-ILLUSTRATED

Pigs in Hiding (Junior Literary Guild selection), Four Winds, 1983.

(From *Pigs in Hiding* by Arlene Dubanevich. Illustrated by the author.)

Pig William, Bradbury, 1985.
Pigs at Christmas, Bradbury, 1986.
The Piggest Show on Earth, Orchard Books, 1989.

OTHER

(With Thomas R. Nassisi) *Hearts* (humor; self-illustrated), Macmillan, 1981.

ILLUSTRATOR

Carl Sesar, translator, *Selected Poems of Catullus*, Mason Lipscomb, 1974.

WORK IN PROGRESS: A picture book about cows on the loose.

SIDELIGHTS: "In 1981, the thought of doing eighty clever drawings to illustrate the sayings in *Hearts* seemed overwhelming. To my surprise, the last ten drawings were as good as the first ten. Conversely, I have found the writing of a story for a picture book to be much more difficult than I first thought.

"My first children's book, *Pigs in Hiding*, is about a group of pigs playing hide-and-seek. The pig who is 'it' cannot find any of his buddies even though they have hidden in very ob-

vious places. Eventually he comes up with a clever way to lure them out of hiding.

"The wonderfully simple idea for this book came to me almost in a flash. The action and the characters fell into place so easily. I expected the next book to evolve the same way. After three more books, I know how difficult, discouraging, and frustrating writing a 'simple' picture book can be.

"My background is that of an illustrator, but with each successive book I've become more comfortable with the title of author. My growing confidence and pleasure in working with words is allowing me to see broader possibilities for new books. After six years, I'm more excited about my future as a children's picture book author than ever before."

HOBBIES AND OTHER INTERESTS: Gardening, cooking.

FOR MORE INFORMATION SEE:

Middleton Press, December 17, 1983.

EAGER, George B.   1921-

PERSONAL: Born April 4, 1921, in Valdosta, Ga.; son of William G. and Eugene (Johnston) Eager; married Laura

Laura and George Eager

Brownell (a housewife), May 19, 1942; children: George Bruce Jr. (deceased), James B., Katharine Sherman, David W., Mary Margaret Castro, John Mark. *Education:* Attended Emory Junior College, 1936-37; Georgia Institute of Technology, B.S., 1942. *Home:* Valdosta, Ga. *Office:* 404 Eager Road, Valdosta, Ga. 31602.

CAREER: Princeton University, Princeton, N.J., naval science assistant professor, 1945; Westinghouse Electric Manufacturing Co., Birmingham, Ala., sales engineer, 1945-46; Eager Hereford Farm, Valdosta, Ga., owner, 1946—; Mailbox Club, Inc., Valdosta, Ga., founder-director, 1965—; author, 1965—. *Military service:* United States Navy, anti-aircraft officer, became lieutenant, 1942-45; received thirteen Battle Stars.

WRITINGS:

How to Succeed in Winning Children to Christ, Mailbox Club, 1979.
Why Wait 'til Marriage?, Mailbox Club, 1979.
Love and Dating (young adult), Mailbox Club, 1980.
Wake up World! Jesus Is Coming Soon! (young adult), Mailbox Club, 1980.
Teen Talk (young adult), Mailbox Club, 1981.
The New Life in Christ, Mailbox Club, 1987.
Love, Dating and Marriage (young adult; illustrated by Diana Philbrook and others), Mailbox Club, 1987.
Teen Talk I, Mailbox Club, 1987.

Also author of six Bible correspondence lessons; and of *Love, Dating and Marriage*, a quarterly published by Mailbox Club, 1987. Editor of *Teen Talk* (quarterly paper), 1965-79.

WORK IN PROGRESS: What Teens Should Know about Love, Dating and Sex, practical information for teens on the important subjects of love, dating and sex.

SIDELIGHTS: "After World War II, I was working as a sales engineer for Westinghouse in Birmingham when my father died. I came back to our home place in Valdosta and began operating it as a cattle farm. I loved it! I was thoroughly engrossed in acquiring more land, a better herd of cattle, etc. when our oldest son, Bruce—age 7, was killed in an accident on the farm. As a result of this, I came to know Jesus Christ as my personal Savior. Several years later, I became interested in working with children and young people. In 1965 I began writing Bible correspondence lessons for children, teenagers and adults. The Mailbox Club lessons are now going into sixty-two countries and have been translated into over thirty languages. I still enjoy farming but it is now limited for the most part to a one-half acre garden!

"To young people, I would say, 'Don't be afraid to try something!' There is no limit to what you can do if you work at it. Winston Churchill, the great leader of England during World War II, said, 'Never, never, never, never, never, never, never GIVE UP!'"

EDLER, Tim(othy) 1948-

PERSONAL: Born April 6, 1948, in New Iberia, Louisiana; son of Eddie N. and Lavinia (maiden name, Courville) Edler; married Rebecca Richard (a division sales manager), August 29, 1970; children: Spaine, Shanie, Brooke, Blake, Dustin. *Education:* University of S.W. Louisiana, B.S., 1972. *Home and office:* c/o Little Cajun Books, 4182 Blecker Drive, Baton Rouge, La. 70809.

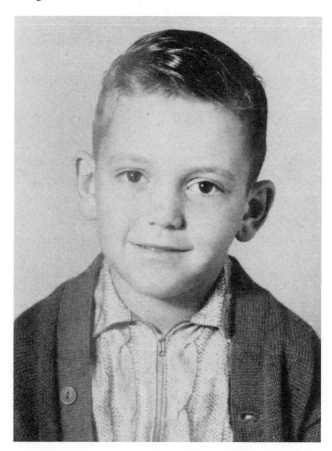

This is the only publicity photo used by Timothy Edler. Although he refuses to be photographed, he will don his Crawfish-Man costume for interviews.

CAREER: Little Cajun Books, Baton Rouge, La., publisher and author, 1977—; Louisiana State University, La., mail order instructor for the continuing education department, 1983—; *Awards, honors:* Official Ambassador of Goodwill for the State of Louisiana.

WRITINGS:

JUVENILE; ALL SELF-ILLUSTRATED, EXCEPT AS NOTED

Maurice the Snake and Gaston the Near-Sighted Turtle: Tim Edler's Tales from the Atchafalaya, Little Cajun Books, 1977.

T-Boy and the Trial for Life: Tim Edler's Tales from the Atchafalaya Series, Little Cajun Books, 1978.

The Adventures of Crawfish-Man, Little Cajun Books, 1979.

T-Boy in Mossland, Little Cajun Books, 1979.

T-Boy the Little Cajun (illustrated by Van Judice), Little Cajun Books, 1978.

Crawfish-Man Rescues Ron Guidry, Little Cajun Books, 1980.

Dark Gator, Little Cajun Books, 1980.

Santa's Cajun Christmas Adventure, Little Cajun Books, 1981.

Crawfish-Man's Fifty Ways to Keep Your Kids from Using Drugs, Little Cajun Books, 1982.

Cooncan: Boy of the Swamp, Little Cajun Books, 1983.

Rhombus, the Cajun Unicorn, Little Cajun Books, 1984.

Crawfish-Man's Night Befo' Christmas, Little Cajun Books, 1984.

Crawfish-Man Rescues the Ol' Beachcomber, Little Cajun Books, 1985.

ADAPTATIONS:

CASSETTES

"Maurice and Gaston," Little Cajun Books, 1978.

"T-Boy, the Little Cajun," Little Cajun Books, 1979.

"T-Boy and the Trial for Life: Tim Edler's Tales from the Atchafalaya Series," Little Cajun Books, 1979.

"T-Boy in Mossland," Little Cajun Books, 1979.

"The Adventures of Crawfish-Man," Little Cajun Books, 1979.

"Crawfish-Man Rescues Ron Guidry," Little Cajun Books, 1980.

"Dark Gator," Little Cajun Books, 1980.

"Santa's Cajun Christmas Adventure," Little Cajun Books, 1981.

"Crawfish-Man's Fifty Ways to Keep Your Kids from Using Drugs," Little Cajun Books, 1982.

"Cooncan: Boy of the Swamp," Little Cajun Books, 1983.

"Rhombus, the Cajun Unicorn," Little Cajun Books, 1984.

"Crawfish-Man's Night Befo' Christmas," Little Cajun Books, 1984.

"Crawfish-Man Rescues the Ol' Beachcomber," Little Cajun Books, 1985.

WORK IN PROGRESS: Three novels; five children's books "on the drawing board; I have been researching the lifestyles of the swamp people of the Atchafalaya Swamp for the last ten years. I will publish a Tom Sawyer-type story set in the 1920s in that area."

SIDELIGHTS: In 1977 Edler wrote and published his first book, *Maurice the Snake and Gaston the Near Sighted Turtle,* which was originally a bedtime story told to his children. "I started writing in 1974 in secret. They say there's diamonds in your backyard. There's no diamonds in my backyard. Heck, all they had in my backyard when I was growing up was moss and crawfish and turtles and snakes.

"And then I said, 'Well, now I know what they mean when they say there's diamonds in your backyard.' That's what you talk about, that's what you write about.

"They say you can paste your bedroom walls with rejection slips. I said, 'I'm not going to get a single one because I'm going to publish the books myself.' I started publishing when I published my first book myself. The people you see writing books are mostly with white hair and over sixty-five, so when I was twenty-eight, twenty-nine I said I was going to do it. So I quit my engineering job and started writing. I have over 100,000 books in print. I'm proud of that. I do one or two books a year.

"Anybody can write a book, anybody can publish a book, but nobody can sell a book. It's very, very hard. I do a little bit of everything in order for me to continue writing my stories.'"[1] To support himself, his wife, and five children, Edler makes handmade cypress cooking spoons and helps his wife in her jewelry business besides running his publishing company, Little Cajun Books.

Inspired by the swamps and everyday things in his native Louisiana, Edler created a super hero, Crawfish-Man. "In 1979, I was watching the 'Incredible Hulk' on television and I said to myself, 'Why don't we have a super hero in Louisiana?' I just sat down at a table and drew Crawfish Man.'"[1] He has described the hero as part man, part crustacean with special powers.

"I am scheduled to tour Europe in March, 1989. I am visiting schools to speak about anti-drug abuse, etc. I will carry letters from Louisiana kids to European kids, and vice versa. Did you know that anyone who touches Crawfish-Man's cape will NEVER USE DRUGS?''

FOOTNOTE SOURCES

[1]Gail Garcia, "Look! Out in the Swamp! It's Crawfish Man!," *Sunday Advertiser* (Lafayette, La.), May 11, 1986.

FOR MORE INFORMATION SEE:

Junior Scholastic, February 23, 1987 (p.1).

EDWARDS, Margaret (Alexander) 1902-1988

OBITUARY NOTICE: Born October 23, 1902, in Childress, Tex.; died following a stroke, April 19, 1988. Educator, librarian, and author. Though she taught high school English and Latin in Texas and Maryland, Edwards will be best remembered for her service as coordinator of young adult services for the Enoch Pratt Free Library in Baltimore, Maryland, from 1932 to 1962. An authority on library services for teenagers, she gave lectures on the subject for students of library science at many universities. "I am concerned," she said, "that the great potential in modern youth become a force for constructive change in America." Edwards wrote *The Fair Garden and the Swarm of Beasts: The Library and the Young Adult.*

FOR MORE INFORMATION SEE:

A Biographical Directory of Librarians in the United States and Canada, 5th edition, American Library Association, 1970.

OBITUARIES

School Library Journal, June/July, 1988.

ESTES, Eleanor   1906-1988

OBITUARY NOTICE—See sketch in *SATA* Volume 7: Born May 9, 1906, in West Haven, Conn.; died of complications after a stroke, July 15, 1988, in Hamden, Conn. Children's librarian and author. Since books were of utmost importance to Estes, it was natural for her to work in the children's department of the New Haven Public Library following high school graduation. After working there for seven years, she won a scholarship to the Pratt Institute Library School in Brooklyn. She subsequently worked at the New York Public Library from 1932 to 1941, the year her first book, *The Moffats,* was published. Her earliest books—*The Moffats, The Middle Moffat,* and *Rufus M.*—were fictionalized accounts of her childhood in West Haven, Connecticut at the turn of the century. Many of her books were self-illustrated, such as *Ginger Pye* and *The Moffat Museum.*

From the publication of her first book through her last one, *The Curious Adventures of Jimmy McGee,* in 1987, Estes gained a reputation as a popular writer of books for children (nineteen in all, as well as one adult novel). She won several literary prizes, including a 1952 Newbery Medal for *Ginger Pye.* About her children's books, Estes once remarked: "In my writing I like to feel that I am holding up a mirror, and I hope that what is reflected in it is a true image of childhood."

FOR MORE INFORMATION SEE:

Junior Book of Authors, H. W. Wilson, 1951.
Newbery Medal Books: 1922-1955, Horn Book, 1955.
Eleanor Cameron, *The Green and Burning Tree: On the Writing and Enjoyment of Children's Books,* Little, Brown, 1969.
John Rowe Townsend, *A Sense of Story: Essays on Contemporary Writers for Children,* Lippincott, 1971.
Lee Bennett Hopkins, *More Books by More People,* Citation, 1974.
Linda Metzger and Deborah A. Straub, editors, *Contemporary Authors: New Revision Series,* Volume 20, Gale, 1987.

OBITUARIES

New York Times, July 19, 1988.
Publishers Weekly, August 26, 1988.

FERRIS, Jean   1939-

PERSONAL: Born January 24, 1939, in Fort Leavenworth, Kan.; daughter of Jack W. (a major general in the armed services) and Jessie (a housewife; maiden name, Wickham) Schwartz; married Alfred G. Ferris (an attorney), September 8, 1962; children: Kerry Ordway, Gillian Anne. *Education:* Stanford University, B.A., 1961, M.A., 1962. *Home:* 2278 San Juan Rd., San Diego, Calif. 92103.

CAREER: Veterans Administration Hospital, San Francisco, Calif., clinical audiologist, 1962 63; San Diego Speech and Hearing Association, San Diego, Calif., clinical audiologist, 1963-64; clinical audiologist in a doctor's office in San Diego, 1975-76; free-lance writer, 1977—; secretary and office assistant in San Diego, 1979-84. *Member:* Society of Children's Book Writers, Southern California Council on Literature for Children and Young People, Authors Guild. *Awards, honors:* Grant from the Society of Children's Book Writers, 1984, for *Invincible Summer,* and 1987, for *Across the Grain;* Award for Outstanding Work of Fiction for Young Adults from the Southern California Council on Literature for Children and Young People, chosen one of American Library Association's

JEAN FERRIS

Best Books for Young Adults, one of *School Library Journal*'s Best Books of the Year, and one of *Booklist* Editor's Choices for Young Adults, all 1987, all for *Invincible Summer.*

WRITINGS:

YOUNG ADULT

Amen, Moses Gardenia, Farrar, Straus, 1983.
The Stainless Steel Rule, Farrar, Straus, 1986.
Invincible Summer, Farrar, Straus, 1987.

OTHER

Looking for Home, Farrar, Straus, 1988.
Across the Grain, Farrar, Straus, 1989.

WORK IN PROGRESS: A young adult novel about a family of American Basques.

SIDELIGHTS: "I'm very interested in the future of our young people. I try, in my work, to give them hope for the future and some guideposts for achieving a satisfying life, even when circumstances seem bleak and/or dismaying!

"I'm fascinated by the teenage years. There's so much going on then, so many emotional changes, decisions for the future, social problems. I remember my own teenage years vividly and they weren't all beer and skittles.

"*Amen, Moses Gardenia* was suggested by the attempted suicides of a couple of young people with whom my children were acquainted. I began to wonder how many other kids were feeling this way and why a young person would decide that there would never be anything worth living for in the long future. I became—and remain—deeply concerned about teenage depression, and wrote *Amen, Moses Gardenia* to give some hope and humor to kids who feel depressed and frightened enough to contemplate ending their lives. There is so much

"Well, come on, give. What happened?" ■ (From *Invincible Summer* by Jean Ferris. Illustrated by Michele Chessare.)

time ahead for situations to change; there is so much reason for hope. And *Amen, Moses Gardenia* has a happy ending.

"I believe that what every youngster needs the most is *one* person who is absolutely bonkers about him or her, who attaches no strings to the love he or she offers the child. You'd think every child would have two such people—parents. Unfortunately, not so. Incidentally, this one loving person does not have to be a parent. It can be anybody—even, as in *Amen, Moses Gardenia,* someone as unexpected as the maid.

"I feel certain that I will continue to write for young people because I care so much about them and find them so brave and complex. I have a couple of 'grown-up' books in mind too, for sometime in the misty future, but my first love will always be writing for kids. They're great."

HOBBIES AND OTHER INTERESTS: Travel, reading, sewing, volunteer work.

FISCHER-NAGEL, Andreas 1951-

PERSONAL: Born May 29, 1951, in Berlin, Germany; married wife, Heiderose (a free-lance writer and editor), December 3, 1975; children: Tamarica, Cosmea. *Education:* University of Berlin, Diploma in Biology, 1977. *Religion:* Evangelical. *Home:* Brunnenstrasse 7, 3509 Spangenberg-Metzebach, West Germany.

CAREER: Editor at Neumann-Neudamm Publishers, Melsungen, West Germany; writer. *Member:* World Wildlife Federation, Gesellschaft Deutscher Tierfotografen. *Awards, honors: Life of the Ladybug* was chosen one of Child Study Association of America's Children's Books of the Year, 1986, and *Season of the White Stork,* 1987; received the Auswahlliste des Deutschen Jugendliteraturpreis, twice, and the Critici in Erba Prize from the Children's Book Fair, Bologna, seven times.

WRITINGS:

JUVENILE; WITH WIFE, HEIDEROSE FISCHER-NAGEL; ALL SELF-ILLUSTRATED

Life of the Ladybug, Kinderbuchverlag, 1981, Carolrhoda, 1986.
Life of the Honeybee, Kinderbuchverlag, 1982, Carolrhoda, 1985.
Birth of a Kitten, Kinderbuchverlag, 1982, translation by Andrea Mernan published as *A Kitten Is Born,* Putnam, 1983.
Life of the Butterfly, Kinderbuchverlag, 1983, translation by Noel Simon, Carolrhoda, 1987.
Birth of Puppies, Kinderbuchverlag, 1983, translation by A. Mernan published as *A Puppy Is Born,* Putnam, 1985.
Season of the White Stork, Kinderbuchverlag, 1984, Carolrhoda, 1986.
Inside the Burrow: The Life of the Golden Hamster, Kinderbuchverlag, 1984, Carolrhoda, 1986.
The World of the Ant, Kinderbuchverlag, 1984.
Der Tannenbaum (title means, "The Christmas Tree"), Kinderbuchverlag, 1985.
Kinderstube der Tiere—Katzen (title means "A Book about Kittens"), Loewes Verlag, 1987.
The Fly, Kinderbuchverlag, 1988.
The Donkeybook, Kinderbuchverlag, 1988.
Kinderstube der Tiere—Hunde (title means "A Book about Dogs"), Lowes Verlag, 1988.
A Look through the Mouse Hole, Carolrhoda, 1988.
Inside the Burrow: The Life of the Golden Hamster, Lerner, in press.

"ANIMAL PICTUREBOOKS" SERIES; WITH H. FISCHER-NAGEL

Tiere am Wasser (title means, "Animals on the Water"), Otto Maier, 1987.
Tiere auf dem Bauernhof (title means, "Farm Animals"), Otto Maier, 1987.
Tiere in der Wiese (title means, "Animals in the Meadows"), Otto Maier, 1987.
Tiere im Wald (title means, "Animals in the Forest"), Otto Maier, 1987.
Zootiere (title means, "Zoo Animals"), Otto Maier, 1987.
Haustiere (title means, "House Pets"), Otto Maier, 1987.

WORK IN PROGRESS: With wife, Heiderose Fischer-Nagel, *Das Glas* (title means, "Glass"), *Froesche* (title means, "Frogs"), and *Das Korn am Beispiel des Weizens.*

SIDELIGHTS: "My wife and I want to show children the natural wonders with our work, because we believe that a person is unable to understand the problems of nature if he or she hasn't learned about nature during childhood."

FISCHER-NAGEL, Heiderose 1956-

PERSONAL: Born May 27, 1956, in Berlin, Germany; married Andreas Fischer-Nagel (an editor and writer), December 3, 1975; children: Tamarica, Cosmea. *Education:* University of Berlin, Diploma in Biology, 1982. *Religion:* Evangelical. *Home:* Brunnenstrasse, 7, 3509 Spangenberg-Metzebach, West Germany.

Heiderose and Andreas Fischer-Nagel

CAREER: Free-lance editor and writer. *Member:* World Wildlife Fund, Gesellschaft Deutscher Tierfotografen. *Awards, honors: Life of the Ladybug* was chosen one of Child Study Association of America's Children's Books of the Year, 1986, and *Season of the White Stork,* 1987; received Auswahlliste des Deutschen Jugendliteraturpreis, twice, and the Critici in Erba Prize from the Children's Book Fair, Bologna, seven times.

WRITINGS:

JUVENILE; WITH HUSBAND, ANDREAS FISCHER-NAGEL; ALL SELF-ILLUSTRATED

Life of the Ladybug, Kinderbuchverlag, 1981, Carolrhoda, 1986.
Life of the Honeybee, Kinderbuchverlag, 1982, Carolrhoda, 1985.
Birth of a Kitten, Kinderbuchverlag, 1982, translation by Andrea Mernan published as *A Kitten Is Born,* Putnam, 1983.
Life of the Butterfly, Kinderbuchverlag, 1983, translation by Noel Simon, Carolrhoda, 1987.
Birth of Puppies, Kinderbuchverlag, 1983, translation by A. Mernan published as *A Puppy Is Born,* Putnam, 1985.
Season of the White Stork, Kinderbuchverlag, 1984, Carolrhoda, 1986.
Inside the Burrow: The Life of the Golden Hamster, Kinderbuchverlag, 1984, Carolrhoda, 1986.
The World of the Ant, Kinderbuchverlag, 1984.
Der Tannenbaum (title means, "The Christmas Tree"), Kinderbuchverlag, 1985.
Kinderstube der Tiere—Katzen (title means "A Book about Kittens"), Loewes Verlag, 1987.
The Fly, Kinderbuchverlag, 1988.
The Donkeybook, Kinderbuchverlag, 1988.
Kinderstube der Tiere—Hunde (title means, "A Book about Dogs"), Loewes Verlag, 1988.
A Look through the Mouse Hole, Carolrhoda, 1988.

Inside the Burrow: The Life of the Golden Hamster, Lerner, in press.

"ANIMAL PICTUREBOOKS" SERIES; WITH A. FISCHER-NAGEL

Tiere am Wasser (title means, "Animals on the Water"), Otto Maier, 1987.
Tiere auf dem Bauernhof (title means, "Farm Animals"), Otto Maier, 1987.
Tiere in der Wiese (title means, "Animals in the Meadow"), Otto Maier, 1987.
Tiere im Wald (title means, "Animals in the Forest"), Otto Maier, 1987.
Zootiere (title means, "Zoo Animals"), Otto Maier, 1987.
Haustiere (title means, "House Pets"), Otto Maier, 1987.

WORK IN PROGRESS: With husband, Andreas Fischer-Nagel, *Das Glas* (title means, "Glass"), *Froesche* (title means, "Frogs"), and *Das Korn am Beispiel des Weizens.*

SIDELIGHTS: "I was born and reared in Berlin. As a child I read with great enthusiasm, spending many an hour in libraries. My parents awakened in me an early interest in nature—my father being a passionate amateur photographer of animals."

After graduating from the public school system, Fischer-Nagel pursued the study of German at the University of Berlin. Influenced by her husband, she switched her major to biology. "Before graduation I supported Andreas' idea to do a picturebook for children. I wrote the text to his photos. Unfortunately the book did not find a publisher."

In 1981 their first book, *Life of the Ladybug,* was published by Kinderbuchverlag. The book was well received and opened the doors to a fruitful career for the couple. "It's very important for us to write and illustrate our books, to impart our

(From *A Kitten Is Born* by Heiderose and Andreas Fischer-Nagel. Illustrated by the authors.)

conservationistic and ecological thoughts and ideas to children, so that they will learn to love and understand their environment and be warned against living in discord with their surroundings. Only then is it possible for us and for the generations to come to keep our living space intact. How often do we destroy a part of nature through our ignorance, how often do we shut out the sad truths?

"The words of a Sioux chieftain left a deep impression on me: 'When you pollute the last river, when you have felled the last tree, killed the last fish—tell me: Will you be able to eat all your money in the bank?' It is worthwhile to give some thoughts to his words.

"My husband and I are happy that our books have found such a vast audience. Some have been translated into twelve languages. And we feel lucky indeed to have been able to pass on some of our environmental consciousness to children, positive awareness about the world around us."

FITZGERALD, John D(ennis)   1907-1988

OBITUARY NOTICE—See sketch in *SATA* Volume 20: Born in 1907, in Utah; died after a long illness, May 21, 1988, in Titusville, Fla. Journalist and author. During his long literary career, Fitzgerald wrote adult novels, short stories and essays, and worked as a publicity agent for MGM and as a foreign feature editor for United Press in Europe, Africa, Asia and Australia.

Before he turned to writing children's books, Fitzgerald wrote three memoirs, two books for professional writers, and one historical fiction book for young people. Stories that he told his friends about his brother Tom and his "Great Brain" became the basis for his first children's book, *The Great Brain*, which was published in 1967. It was followed by more books about brother Tom and their childhood in the Utah Territory at the turn of the century, including *The Great Brain at the Academy, The Great Brain Reforms, The Return of the Great Brain,* and *The Great Brain Does It Again*. About his series, Fitzgerald once remarked: "The memories of childhood are either elusive or vivid. My memories of Tom are very graphic because he swindled me so many times when I was a boy."

FOR MORE INFORMATION SEE:

Frances C. Locher, editor, *Contemporary Authors,* Volumes, 93-96, Gale, 1980.
Sally Holmes Holtze, editor, *Fifth Book of Junior Authors and Illustrators,* H. W. Wilson, 1983.

OBITUARIES

Publishers Weekly, August 26, 1988.

FLEMING, Ronald Lee   1941-

PERSONAL: Born May 13, 1941, in Los Angeles, Calif.; son of Ree Overton and Elizabeth Ann (Ebner) Fleming; married Renata von Tscharner (a planner and architect), November 9, 1978; children: Severine von Tscharner, Siena Antonia von Tscharner. *Education:* Pomona College, B.A. (cum laude), 1963; Harvard University, M.C.P., 1967. *Home and office:* Townscape Institute, 2 Hubbard Park, Cambridge, Mass. 02138.

CAREER: Marshall, Kaplan, Gans & Kahn, Boston, Mass., urban planner, 1969-71; Townscape Institute, Inc., Cambridge, Mass., designer and planner, 1971-79, president,

RONALD LEE FLEMING

1979—. Lecturer at Harvard University, Yale University, and Columbia University; visiting critic at University of Virginia; U.S. State Department lecturer in Europe. Legislative chairman of Massachusetts Roadside Council; founder and chairman of Cambridge Arts Council, 1975-79; chairman, One Per Cent for Public Art committee, 1979-83; board of overseers, Castle Hill Foundation, Ipswich, Mass., 1980-87, and Strawberry Banke, Portsmouth, N.H., 1980-84; board of directors, Victorian Society, Philadelphia, Pa., 1983—; appointee, Massachussetts Historical Commission, 1986—; member of advisory board, Trustees on Reservations, Beverly, Mass., 1986—. *Military service:* U.S. Army, Intelligence, 1966-68; served in Vietnam; became captain.

MEMBER: American Planning Association, Royal Society of Arts (fellow), American Institute of City Planners, Society of Architectural Historians, Massachusetts Historical Society, Society for the Preservation of New England Antiquities (member of board of trustees, 1974-80), Preservation Action (vice-chairman, 1979—), Massachusetts Horticultural Society (member of board of trustees, 1979-84), Somerset Club, Union Boat Club, Knickerbocker Club (New York City), Century Association (New York City), Harvard Club, Club of Odd Volumes, Tavern Club (Boston). *Awards, honors:* Environmental Heritage Fellow of Heritage Foundation, 1963; Grant from the U.S. State Department, 1975; First Prize in Architecture and Planning from Columbia University's Urban Film Competition, 1975, for "A Measure of Change"; Fellow at Salzburg Seminar on American Studies, 1978; Merit Award from the American Society of Landscape Architects, and from the U.S. Department of Transportation, both 1981, both for

Chelsea Center City Revitalization Project; various awards for *New Providence,* 1987-88.

WRITINGS:

JUVENILE

(With wife, Renata von Tscharner) *New Providence: A Changing Cityscape* (illustrated by Denis Orloff), Harcourt, 1987.

OTHER

(Editor) *Censored Laughter: Czech Political Cartoons from "Prague Spring,"* privately printed, 1976.
(Contributor) Luisa Kreisburg, editor, *Local Government and the Arts,* American Council for the Arts, 1979.
(With R. von Tscharner) *Place Makers: Public Art That Tells You Where You Are,* Hastings House, 1981, 2nd enlarged edition, Harcourt, 1987.
(With Lauri A. Halderman) *On Common Ground: Caring for Shared Land from Town Common to Urban Park,* Harvard Common, 1982.
Facade Stories: Changing Faces of Main Street Storefronts and How to Care for Them, Hastings House, 1982.

Also contributor of numerous articles to professional journals, including *Longwood Program Seminars.*

WORK IN PROGRESS: Oh Say Can You See, a book on visual reform in America.

SIDELIGHTS: "Ultimately, my work is concerned with the potential emotive authority of place. I am interested in how people form attachments to place and how design and management strategies can secure these attachments. My books explore how objects, spaces, and buildings can create feelings of proprietorship among those who use them, and how that sense of proprietorship becomes the basis for an ethic of care.

"I became interested in the built environment as a small child when I was encouraged by my parents to visit a ghost town in the West while building my own town on our property in Los Angeles. The fellowship I received when I graduated from Pomona gave me an opportunity to do a comparative town study which later influenced me to go into town planning with a particular emphasis on preservation of townscapes. Helping to start an arts council brought me in touch with artists and we now commission artists to work in collaboration on 'placemaking' urban design projects."

HOBBIES AND OTHER INTERESTS: Collecting urban design books, helping to support a lecture series at Pomona College on built environment, "enjoying conversation at several dining clubs I helped to found."

FORD, Barbara

PERSONAL: Born in St. Louis, Mo.; married an assistant director of personnel. *Education:* St. Louis University, B.A.; New York University, M.A. *Home:* Pleasant Valley Rd., Mendham, N.J. 07945.

CAREER: Free-lance writer, 1970—. Has worked as a writer for the American Museum of Natural History, New York, N.Y., and as senior editor and contributing editor for *Science Digest.* Consultant for the science supplement of *Saturday Review. Member:* Animal Behavior Society, Bear Biology Association, American Association of Zoological Parks and Aquariums. *Awards, honors: Can Invertebrates Learn?* was named one of Child Study Association of America's Chil-

BARBARA FORD

dren's Books of the Year, 1972, and *How Birds Learn to Sing,* 1975; New Jersey Authors Award from the New Jersey Institute of Technology, 1980, for *Animals That Use Tools; The Elevator* was named an Outstanding Science Book for Children by the National Science Teachers Association and the Children's Book Council, 1982.

WRITINGS:

JUVENILE

Can Invertebrates Learn? (illustrated by Haris Petie), Messner, 1972.
How Birds Learn to Sing (illustrated with photographs by Bob Combs), Messner, 1975.
Katydids: The Singing Insects (illustrated with photographs by William Jaber), Messner, 1976.
Animals That Use Tools (Junior Literary Guild selection; illustrated by Janet P. D'Amato), Messner, 1978.
(With Ronald R. Keiper) *The Island Ponies: An Environmental Study of Their Life on Assateague* (illustrated with photographs by R. R. Keiper), Morrow, 1979.
Why Does a Turtle Live Longer Than a Dog? A Report on Animal Longevity, Morrow, 1980.
Black Bear: The Spirit of the Wilderness, Houghton, 1981.
Country and Growing with Nature, Carlton, 1981.
Alligators, Raccoons, and Other Survivors: The Wildlife of the Future, Morrow, 1981.
(With David C. Switzer) *Underwater Dig: The Excavation of a Revolutionary War Privateer* (Junior Literary Guild selection), Morrow, 1982.
The Elevator, Walker, 1982.
Keeping Things Cool: The Story of Refrigeration and Air Conditioning, Walker, 1986.

Inventions That Changed Our Lives: The Automobile, Walker, 1987.
Wildlife Rescue, (illustrated with photographs by Steve Ross), A. Whitman, 1987.

ADULT

Future Food: Alternate Protein for the Year 2000 (adult), Morrow, 1978.

Contributor of over sixty science features to magazines.

SIDELIGHTS: Ford's family had an unusual interest in animals. ''My father and mother gave the family dogs as much attention as people, possibly even a little more. Our next-door neighbors used to say that if they could be reincarnated, they'd like to come back as one of our dogs! Not surprisingly, I read animal books by the score, particularly the Albert Payson Terhune dog books. At that time, few children's science books were available.

''No one in our family had gone to college before I did, so I didn't realize that scientific careers involving animals were a possibility. I graduated from St. Louis University with a B.A. in political science and later acquired an M.A. in English from New York University. Only when I took a position as a writer at the American Museum of Natural History in the mid-60s did I realize that people actually studied animals as part of their work. It was natural for me to turn to animal behavior when I began writing children's books in 1970. All my children's books center around animal behavior and show scientists working with animals in the field and in the laboratory. I have also written about animal behavior for *Science Digest.*

''*Animals That Use Tools* grew out of my membership in the Animal Behavior Society [ABS]. At two different ABS conferences, I heard Dr. Benjamin Beck of the Brookfield Zoo in Chicago describe his experiments with tool-using baboons. During the second conference, in 1975, I asked a scientist who was lunching at my table if other animals used tools. He reeled off the names of a number of tool-using beasts, which I quickly jotted down. Over the next year, I researched the subject in my spare time and concluded there was enough material for a book.''

FROEHLICH, Margaret Walden   1930-

PERSONAL: Born June 17, 1930, in New Kensington, Pa.; daughter of Lloyd Leighton (a hardware wholesaler) and Hazel (a housewife; maiden name, Mays) Walden; married John A. Froehlich (a mechanical engineer), April 12, 1955; children: Catherine Froehlich Ednie, Andrea Froehlich Carlson, Gregory, Carl, Kristin, Rosemary, David, Margaret. *Education:* College of Notre Dame of Maryland, B.A., 1951; Johns Hopkins University, M.Ed., 1955. *Religion:* Protestant. *Home:* 283 Redding Rd., West Redding, Conn. 06896.

CAREER: Second-grade teacher at elementary schools in Baltimore, Md., 1951-55; mother and homemaker, 1955—; author, 1975—. Presenter of preschool story hours at Mark Twain Library, Redding, Conn., 1969-76.

WRITINGS:

JUVENILE

Hide Crawford Quick (ALA Notable Book), Houghton, 1983.
Reasons to Stay, Houghton, 1987.

MARGARET WALDEN FROEHLICH

WORK IN PROGRESS: A novel for juniors about overprotection and independence.

SIDELIGHTS: ''I think I write for children in order to make sense of my own childhood. Impressions from my own early years lie within me whole waiting to be milled.

''One incident happened before I was three. Our kitchen was in the basement and had a cement floor. We had a little wicker chair hung from the rafters to use as a swing. Unfortunately, its seat had been sat out. One evening while my parents did dishes, I set my doll in the swing. Of course she fell through and her head smashed on the floor. I can remember being put out with Pollyanna because she didn't hold on better. I can remember being curious to see what the insides of her head looked like. I can remember my father sweeping her into the dustpan. Because he didn't holler at me, I seemed to know that he felt sad over Pollyanna's demise as I did. I didn't mourn for long. I had fourteen other dolls waiting for my attention.

''My mother read to us and recited poetry to us. Robert Louis Stevenson was her favorite. When I heard his poem 'Bed by Day,' it was the first time I was aware that people can express their feelings for others to share. I figured Robert Louis Stevenson hated his mother for making him go to bed at eight in the summer just as I hated my mother for making me go to bed at eight. All through childhood I seem to have kept careful account of how I felt in different situations.

''I remember being perplexed by the way people acted. In second grade, my best friend's name was Lois. She had hair ribbons and socks to match all her dresses and her socks always clung nicely to her ankles. Every morning in school she and I raced to see who would finish writing the spelling words first. If Lois saw that I was getting ahead, she often reached across and drew a line down across my words. Then she kindly

Babe grew cold with fear for Mama. Mama wasn't getting better.■ (From *Reasons to Stay* by Margaret Walden Froehlich.)

lent me her eraser to erase the line. By the time I finished erasing, she was finished with her work. I wondered not only about Lois' behavior but about the fact that even though she caused me such suffering, I still wanted her for my best friend.

"The only writing I remember doing as a child was a series of four line poems. I begged the use of my mother's typewriter to copy them and decided that I would do it without mistakes. I remember well the crick in the neck that accompanies perfection.

"This is not to say that I didn't invent stories as a child. One of my sisters and I had pretend families—families with enormous quantities of children. For years, we were hardly ourselves as we assumed the identities of all those children and lived their lives.

"I guess I still need pretend children although I've had eight of my own and have cared for fourteen foster children. Always, in the background, are vivid memories of my own childhood. I know the territory! I guess that's why I like writing for children.

"When I first decided to be a writer, Gracie and Lizzie from *Hide Crawford Quick* were characters in an early story. It was about three children who spent a winter's morning making such an impressive gingerbread boy that they couldn't bear to eat it when it was done. However, they couldn't resist showing it off to a crabby neighbor who had come to visit. Didn't she

break off one of the gingerbread boy's legs and eat it! I sent the story out and got back a rejection slip. They said they didn't think the readers of their magazine would be interested in that story. Well, I was interested in Gracie. She became the main character of a novel which I sent out five times and it was rejected five times. One editor offered the advice that I should not *tell* a story—I *should show it happening.*

"I decided to rewrite the book. Meanwhile, years were passing. I sent the manuscript out four more times. This time, I got personal letters of rejection instead of printed forms. An editor at Houghton Mifflin told me in great detail just what was wrong with the book. I started all over again and a year later wrote and asked if she would read the new version. I mailed the manuscript on July 13th. On October 30th, I received a very small letter which began 'I am very sorry. . . .' 'Sorry'—I had heard that many, many times. However, the letter went on to say that she was sorry she had been so slow to answer. She said she was very impressed with the book and that Houghton Mifflin would be proud to publish it. October 30, 1981 ranked right up there among the happiest days of my life."

HOBBIES AND OTHER INTERESTS: "I enjoy refinishing decrepit old furniture. I love patchwork and quilting and in the summer—gardening. I've decided to limit my gardening to herbs and flowers, vegetables get out of hand and I don't like to cook!"

GANLY, Helen (Mary) 1940-

PERSONAL: Born March 7, 1940, in Cookham, England; daughter of Geoffrey Favatt (an artist and publisher) and Helen (a teacher; maiden name, Whatley) Robinson; married Charles Fabian Ware (divorced); married Michael Roy Ganly (in business), March 11, 1967; children: Daniel, Benjamin. *Education:* Attended Slade School of Fine Art, University College, 1958-62. *Home:* Oxford, England. *Agent:* Andre Deutsch Ltd., 105-106 Great Russell St., London WC1B 3LJ, England.

CAREER: Artist and art teacher, 1962—; author and illustrator, 1986—. Artist-in-residence, Djerassi Foundation, Woodside, Calif., 1987. *Exhibitions*—Group shows: London Young Contemporaries, London, England, 1959, 1960, 1961; Ruskin School Staff Shows, Oxford, England, 1965-74; Oxford Printmakers Co-operative, 1976-86; Mercury Gallery, London, 1976-86; British Artists, Oxford, 1981; Westgate Shopping Centre, Oxford, 1981; Christchurch Gallery, Oxford, 1981, 1986; Central Library, Oxford, 1982; Green College, Oxford, 1982; Oxford Gallery, Oxford, 1982; Museum of Modern Art, Oxford, 1983, 1986, 1987; Christ's Hospital Arts Centre, Sussex, England, 1983; Quay Arts Centre, Newport, Isle of Wight, 1984; "Pandora's Box" (touring exhibition), England, 1984-85; Frauen Museum, Bonn, West Germany, 1986, 1988; Kunstlerforum Museum, Bonn, West Germany, 1987; Septentrion Galerie, Lille, France, 1987; Minories, Colchester, England, 1987; Oxford Printmakers Co-operative, British Council, Peru, 1987.

One woman shows: Chapel Gallery, Bladon, Oxfordshire, England, 1973; Mercury Gallery, London, 1976; Balliol College, Oxford, 1978; Pentonville Gallery, London, 1982, 1984; St. Giles Church, Oxford, 1982; The Old Fire Station, Oxford, 1984; Cumberland Road Day Centre, Newham, England, 1985; Asian Women's Association, Ilford, England, 1985; West

HELEN GANLY

London Institute of Higher Education, 1986; Sanderson, London, 1986; Haymarket Theatre, Leicester, England, 1987.

MEMBER: National Association of Artists (member of management committee), Institute of Contemporary Arts, Oxford Printmakers, Oxford Artists Group, Friends of the Royal Academy of Arts, Friends of the Museum of Modern Art (Oxford). *Awards, honors:* Shortlisted for Smarties Prize for Children's Books, and shortlisted for the Other Award, both 1986, both for *Jyoti's Journey.*

WRITINGS:

Jyoti's Journey (self-illustrated juvenile), Dutton, 1986.

ILLUSTRATOR

Phillippa Pearce, *The Toothball* (juvenile), Deutsch, 1987.

WORK IN PROGRESS: Writing and illustrating another children's book to be published by Deutsch; a series of paintings and prints "inspired by Virginia Woolf's *A Room of One's Own.*"

SIDELIGHTS: "I was born into a family of artists. My parents had met at art school; my grandfather had been an illustrator, as were his two brothers. . . .I drew from an early age and was writing and illustrating my own books from the age of four years old. I was fortunate in being encouraged by my parents. I was always drawing, won prizes at school and in local shows, and when I was fourteen, won two national painting competitions. At seventeen, I won a scholarship to the Slade and left school early to take up the place. I think this positive rein-

forcement at an early age has helped me to cope with subsequent rejections and frustrations. I have vivid memories of the Slade, but I was shy, straight from school, and although I took in everything, I missed many opportunities through lack of confidence in myself. At art school, one develops a self-critical faculty. This can be a very painful and an inhibiting experience. Mystification can be used to confuse and undermine a young artist, but if the inner necessity to paint and draw or sculpt is powerful enough, it will continue through what for many students can be a daunting experience.

"I was always criticised for a lack of consistency of approach, but I have now come to terms with the fact that there are about four strands to my work which can all be worked on and expressed simultaneously. This may be a characteristic common to many artists. With regard to male or female art and imagery, I am doubtful as to whether one can make very clear distinctions. It seems to me that people tend to see what they want to see and conveniently ignore evidence which does not suit their particular argument. I know plenty of women artists whose work is non-figurative and large scale, whose work is strong and bold, as well as those whose work is small scale, delicate and illustrative. I also know men whose work is as varied as the women's. If anything, I feel that there is a greater freedom for women to slalom between different poles of expression, but I do not know whether this is due to the greater freedom to be found within their marginal position or whether it is due to specifically female characteristics.

"Apart from one period of several years when I explored the formal problems of non-figurative painting, I have worked in a figurative idiom, and I have always responded to my environment by making objects, drawings or paintings as a way of making sense of my life and the world around me. A 'theme' is always sparked off by a visual stimulus, but as the theme is developed, taken up and creatively explored, using the means and scale appropriate to its requirements, other patterns of thought may develop and can take me off on a separate line of enquiry.

"I did far less work when my children were young, but when they went to school, I did more, only this time unhampered by outside expectations. I was able to experiment more freely. I taught in an art school for ten years; I taught adult evening classes, in comprehensive schools, prep and public schools, in a mental hospital, a prison and I now teach in sixth form colleges. I am also a 'visiting artist' and lecturer to undergraduates in Oxford. In this latter role, I try to advise my students on how to survive as an artist. I believe that this has always been, and is now, very difficult, and that those who have worked out different strategies for survival can give strength and support to others.

"As I earn my living through teaching, I have complete freedom to do anything I like in my work, even if this sometimes means that certain projects are rejected by galleries as uncommercial. My freedom of expression and social mobility are essential to me as an artist.

"At the moment, I share a small studio with a number of artists, men and women, and I am a founding member of the Oxford Printmakers' Co-operative. Small scale work I do at home.

"I am interested in breaking down barriers between people in a positive way and show my work in shopping centres, libraries, housing estates, schools, hospitals, as well as in art galleries. I like to arrange exhibitions in which the spectators

This is Jyoti. She is eight years old. She was born in a village in India. ■ (From *Jyoti's Journey* by Helen Ganly. Illustrated by the author.)

can become active participants because I believe that all human beings have untapped creative potential.

"I believe artists are part of society and therefore, whether they are aware of the fact or not, cannot avoid having their work read 'politically' even if their aims are not political. I know that my work not only reflects my involvement in my own community, it also reflects my working situation in the studio, my developing awareness of the women's movement and my personal situation. But as I have already stated, I have been expressing myself through a visual medium from the age of four, and that inner need is the over-riding factor."[1]

Ganly has been featured on "The Summer of '76," produced by the British Broadcasting Corporation, "Out of Oxford," a documentary for Central Television, 1986, and "Helen Ganly: The Many Faces of a Woman Artist," for the Arts Council of Great Britain, 1986.

"*Jyoti's Journey* was originally an 'art work' and part of an exhibition in the Pentonville Gallery in London. I was doing very large collages using wallpaper remnants. My inspiration was the Asian community in East Oxford. I lived there, had Muslim and Hindu friends, and taught their children. I made a story without words, a picture narrative, in an old wallpaper book as part of this exhibition. It was seen by Marina Warner who encouraged me to show it to Pam Royds at Andre Deutsch. They reduced the number of pages, I had to add a simple text, and it was published in 1986. It is used widely in schools in

different ways—as a visual expression of the isolation felt by many immigrant families and as an introduction to the medium of collage."

GEISERT, Arthur 1941-

PERSONAL: Born September 20, 1941, in Dallas, Tex.; son of Leonard (an engineer) and Doris (a homemaker; maiden name, Boland) Geisert; married Bonnie Meier (a teacher), June 1, 1963; children: Noah. *Education:* Attended Chouinard Art Institute, and Otis Art Institute; Concordia College, Seward, Neb., B.S., 1963; University of California, Davis, M.A., 1965; graduate study at Art Institute of Chicago. *Religion:* Lutheran. *Home and office:* P.O. Box 3, Galena, Ill. 61036.

CAREER: Printmaker and artist. Concordia College, River Forest, Ill., art teacher, 1965-70; Concordia College, Seward, Neb., art teacher, 1970-71. *Exhibitions*—Group shows: Minnesota Art Museum, St. Paul, 1979; Illinois Art Council Gallery, Chicago, 1980; National Museum of American Art, Washington, D.C., 1982; Society of American Graphic Artists, New York, 1986; American Academy and Institute of Arts and Letters, New York, 1986. One-man shows: Print Club, Philadelphia, Pa., 1986; Foxley Leach Gallery, Washington, D.C., 1986; Boston Public Library, 1986. Work represented in university and museum collections. *Member:* National Artist's Equity Association, Los Angeles Printmaking Society, Boston Printmakers, Society of American Graphic

ARTHUR GEISERT

Artists, American Academy and Institute of Arts and Letters. *Awards, honors: Pigs from A to Z* was selected one of *New York Times* Ten Best Illustrated Children's Books, and one of *New York Times* Notable Books, both 1986; Illinois Arts Council Artist's Fellowship, 1986.

WRITINGS:

JUVENILE; SELF-ILLUSTRATED, EXCEPT AS NOTED

The Orange Scarf (illustrated by Thomas Di Grazia), Simon & Schuster, 1970.
Pa's Balloon and Other Pig Tales, Houghton, 1984.
Pigs from A to Z, Houghton, 1986.
The Ark, Houghton, 1988.

WORK IN PROGRESS: Illustrating *Aesop's Fables,* for Houghton.

SIDELIGHTS: "I try to combine a classical etching style—Piranesi, Canaletto, Callot—with narrative and sometimes humorous subject matter.

"Over the years I've built two houses and one suspension bridge. This construction experience is one source for my art."

FOR MORE INFORMATION SEE:

New York Times Book Review, July 29, 1984, November 9, 1986.
Time, January 5, 1987.

GOODSELL, Jane Neuberger   1921(?)-1988

OBITUARY NOTICE: Born about 1921, in Portland, Ore.; died of bone cancer in Detroit, Mich., in September, 1988.

Writer and author. As a free-lance writer, Goodsell was a weekly columnist for the *Astorian Budget* and had a weekly column, "From Soup to Nonsense," which was syndicated by Press Associates of Washington, D. C. Goodsell also contributed articles to several magazines, including *Ladies' Home Journal, Reader's Digest,* and the *NEA Journal.* She was the author of the juvenile, *Toby's Toe,* and the children's biography, *The Biography of Daniel Inouye* which won the Carter G. Woodson Book Award in 1978.

FOR MORE INFORMATION SEE:

OBITUARIES

Detroit News, September 11, 1988.

GRACZA, Margaret Young   1928-

PERSONAL: Surname is pronounced *Grawt*-suh; born April 16, 1928, in St. Paul, Minn.; daughter of Harold Curtice (a painter and decorator) and Amanda (a housewife; maiden name, Garvik) Young; married Rezsoe Gracza (an engineering consultant), October 27, 1959; children: Susan, Edward. *Education:* Macalester College, B.A., 1950; Danish Graduate School for Foreign Students, Copenhagen, Fulbright scholar, 1952-53; Mankato State University, M.S. 1980. *Politics:* Independent. *Religion:* Episcopalian. *Home:* 15151 Victor La., Minnetonka, Minn. 55345.

CAREER: International Institute (community service organization), St. Paul, Minn., activities director, 1950-52; St. Paul Public Schools, Minn., high school teacher of English and art, 1954-56; Minneapolis Institute of Arts, Minneapolis, Minn., staff member in education department, 1956-62, now docent and supervisor of children's activities. Art consultant, North-

MARGARET YOUNG GRACZA

ern States Power Co., Minneapolis, 1973; instructor, Hopkins Community Education, 1980—. *Exhibitions:* Minneapolis Annual Uptown Art Fair, 1972-81; (two-woman show) Eden Prairie City Hall Gallery, Eden Prairie, Minn., 1981; (one-woman show) Chauncey Wright Griggs Mansion, St. Paul, Minn., 1984. *Member:* Twin Cities Watercolor Society.

WRITINGS:

The Ship and the Sea in Art, Lerner, 1964.
(Translator from the Danish) Grete Janus Hertz, *Hi, Daddy, Here I Am,* Lerner, 1964.
The Bird in Art, Lerner, 1966.
(With husband, Rezsoe Gracza) *The Hungarians in America,* Lerner, 1969.
Art: Looking Forward to a Career, Dillon, 1971.

Writer of twelve radio scripts for children's program on art for the University of Minnesota educational station, KUOM, 1959-61.

WORK IN PROGRESS: Book for young people on the country and culture of Hungary.

SIDELIGHTS: "I grew up in a large family—my parents, four brothers, two uncles and, off and on, grandparents, lived with us. We lived in a big house in the city, but it was once a farmhouse. When we moved into it, a huge red barn was still in the backyard. So, we had a chance to play in it before it was torn down to make room for a coal shed and a garage.

"Our house was situated on a dirt road that was an official city street but it never got paved. The front of the house faced a large woods about the size of two city blocks. So with the dirt road and the woods, the front was like the country.

"The back of the house faced an alley, and that alley was just a block from a busy, main street. So, the backyard was a part

of the city. About six blocks away was the Mississippi River. A railroad track ran along the shores of the river and there was also a small airport. In the backyard we heard the boat whistles, train whistles, the sound of small airplanes and the sounds of cattle squealing. The cattle were in the trucks that roared down the main street taking them to the slaughter house in the nearby town.

"The area facing the front of the house was called 'The Woods.' It was our territory and we knew each part of the terrain very well. There was 'the top of the hill,' 'the bumps,' 'the ravine,' 'the washout' and 'the dump.' Just about every year we made shacks. Sometimes they were underground shacks, usually they were on the ground like a house and sometimes they were in a tree. It was difficult to keep a shack very long because there were usually some roughnecks from another neighborhood who would come and wreck it.

"It was legal to build fires then, so we often had our own picnics. We roasted wieners and marshmallows and put the potatoes under the coals in the fire. The skins of the potatoes got coal black, but the inside of the potato was always tasty. Since anyone could build a fire in 'the woods' anytime, the woods often caught on fire. Just about every fall we would watch the fire department rig, parked on the dirt road and the firemen running up into the woods with hoses.

"My father was an artist. He worked as a decorator of churches. He created original designs and religious symbols and then painted them on the church walls. He inspired all of us to value art and to realize the importance of being a good craftsman. There were often lively discussions on art as well as many other subjects.

"As soon as we were old enough, we all worked on part-time jobs, cutting lawns, delivering newspapers and working in the drugstore. We did this to earn money, of course, but my parents always stressed that each job had something to teach us.

"My parents always encouraged the delight of learning. I find that this is one of the most joyous parts of writing. It is a

(Cover illustration by Kirsten Jensinius from *Hi, Daddy, Here I Am* by Grete Janus Hertz. Translated by Margaret Young Gracza.)

wonderful adventure to take on a new subject and then go on a search in a library to find out all you can about the subject. And then you have to think a lot about the subject before you sit down to compose on the typewriter.

"It is fun to write books for young people because you have to make things clear and have the satisfaction that you are sharing your knowledge. It is like teaching school. You just have a little more time to think things through.

"In the upstairs of our house, we had a room called the 'art room.' It was unheated and had bookcases and shelves made from apple crates. There were also a homemade easel and a homemade table. That is where we did a variety of art projects from model airplanes to posters and oil paintings.

"The home that I live in now with my husband is a little like the one I grew up in. Instead of an upstairs art room, we have a basement 'workshop' that takes up half the basement. There we make pottery, frame pictures and do carpentry work. We spend many happy hours there working on art or craft projects."

GRAEBER, Charlotte Towner

PERSONAL: Born in Peoria, Ill.; married Vance Graeber, 1963. *Education:* Attended University of Illinois. *Home:* Elgin, Ill.

CAREER: Author of children's books. *Awards, honors:* Friends of American Writers Juvenile Book Merit Award, older category, 1980, for *Grey Cloud;* Irma Simonton Black Award from the Bank Street College of Education, 1982, and West Virginia Children's Book Award from the Wise Library, West Virginia University, 1986, both for *Mustard; The Thing in Kat's Attic* was selected one of Child Study Association of America's Children's Books of the Year, 1984.

WRITINGS:

JUVENILE

Grey Cloud (Junior Literary Guild selection; illustrated by Lloyd Bloom), Four Winds Press, 1979.
Mustard (illustrated by Donna Diamond), Macmillan, 1982.
The Thing in Kat's Attic (illustrated by Emily Arnold McCully), Dutton, 1984.
Fudge (illustrated by Cheryl Harness), Lothrop, 1987.
The Fluff Puff Farm, Worlds of Wonder, 1988.

"I LOVE TO READ" SERIES; ILLUSTRATED BY JACK STOCKMAN

Up, Down, and Around the Raintree, Chariot Books, 1984.
In, Out, and About the Catfish Pond, Chariot Books, 1984.

"MR. T AND ME" SERIES; ALL ILLUSTRATED BY JOE BODDY

The Hand-Me-Down Cap, T. Nelson, 1985.
The Somebody Kid, T. Nelson, 1985.
The Silver Squawk Box, T. Nelson, 1985.
The Best Bike Ever, T. Nelson, 1985.
Phoney Baloney, the Counterfeit Kid, T. Nelson, 1985.
The Sidewalk Mockers, T. Nelson, 1985.
The Hard Luck Mutt, T. Nelson, 1985.
My Mr. T Doll, T. Nelson, 1985.
The Not-So-Great Place, T. Nelson, 1985.
Tackle Block Stop, T. Nelson, 1985.
I'm So-So, So What?, T. Nelson, 1985.
The Muscle Tussle, T. Nelson, 1985.

"SPEAK FOR ME" SERIES; ALL ILLUSTRATED BY NEIL PINCHBECK

Jonah, Speak for God, T. Nelson, 1986.
Moses, Speak for God!, T. Nelson, 1986.

CHARLOTTE TOWNER GRAEBER

Paul, Speak for God, T. Nelson, 1986.
Peter, Speak for God, T. Nelson, 1986.

Contributor of articles and stories to periodicals.

ADAPTATIONS:

"The Fluff Puff Farm" (cassette), Worlds of Wonder, 1988.

SIDELIGHTS: "As soon as I learned to print I began filling notebooks with sad and tearful poetry. By the time I reached fifth grade I was adding notebooks of short stories to the ones filled with poetry in my large closet. But it wasn't until high school that my writing came out of the closet when I realized I was *required* to write poems and essays for the English classes I was *required* to take. Soon I was not only writing my own assignments but was correcting and completing English assignments for a classmate who panicked at the sight of a compound sentence. In exchange I was patiently and painfully steered through high school algebra and geometry with passing grades.

"Shortly after high school my father relocated our family in the Chicago area, where I worked at a dime store, a bank, and an oil company before starting college. Then I began commuting on the Northwestern railroad into the city, riding the elevated train around the Chicago loop, then transferring onto a streetcar that eventually deposited me at the University of Illinois Chicago campus at Navy Pier on Lake Michigan. During the hours of travel to and from the campus I collected bits of dialogue, impressions, and background for my English composition assignments by observing my fellow commuters. To this day I find myself eavesdropping and making up stories about the strangers I observe.

"In 1963 I married Vance Graeber and we settled his two children and dog and my two children and cat in an old house on the Fox River in Elgin, Illinois, where we still live. Here wild geese, ducks, possums, muskrats, raccoons, and other wildlife share our river bank. Through the years we further populated our home with a tame crow, a pet skunk, a flying squirrel, white mice, several canaries, a parrot, numerous cats, kittens, tropical fish, and a second dog.

"Still I always managed to find an unoccupied corner to write in—though often I worked with a cat on my lap, a bird on my shoulder, or a dog lying on my feet. During those years I sold my stories to various juvenile and denominational magazines. Eventually my husband converted an old shed on the edge of the river into a small workshop where I now write.

"A few years ago my husband introduced me to a man who breeds and races homing pigeons. At the time we had five cats, one dog, a parrot, a skunk, and a tankful of fish. My easy-going husband put his foot down. 'Enough is enough.' I had to agree. But my interest in homing pigeons continued and I began to write the story that grew into my first book, _Grey Cloud_."

GROTH, John (August)   1908-1988

OBITUARY NOTICE—See sketch in _SATA_ Volume 21: Surname is pronounced "Growth"; born February 26 (one source says February 2), 1908, in Chicago, Ill.; died June 27, 1988, in New York, N. Y. Artist, illustrator, educator, journalist, and author. Groth, a contributor of illustrations to many books and magazines, was best known for his expressionistic style of drawing, particularly of battle and sports scenes. Hired by _Esquire_ magazine in 1933 as its first art director, Groth drew assignments in Mexico, Russia, England, and Germany that early demonstrated his strength as a graphic journalist. In 1936 he moved to New York City, where he freelanced as a sports cartoonist and editorial illustrator for various periodicals. During World War II, as an artist-correspondent for the _Chicago Sun_, Groth was present at several closing battles. These he documented in a 1945 book, _Studio: Europe;_ his subsequent coverage of the Korean and French Indo-Chinese wars culminated in a companion volume, _Studio: Asia._

After World War II, Groth was a frequent contributor of drawings to _Collier's, Esquire, Vogue, Saturday Evening Post, New Yorker, Fortune, Sports Illustrated,_ and many other periodicals. He also illustrated several classics, including Charles Dickens' _A Christmas Carol_, Leo Tolstoy's _War and Peace_, John Steinbeck's _Grapes of Wrath_, Erich Maria Remarque's _All Quiet on the Western Front_, and Ernest Hemingway's _Men without Women_, for which he wrote the introduction. "Usually when I illustrate a book," said Groth, "I read it two or three times, making notes while reading, then put the book away and proceed on my own, hoping to create a work of art that will complement the author's text." Groth also taught at the Art Students League of New York, the National Academy of Design, and elsewhere. His pictures are in several collections, including the Museum of Modern Art, the Library of Congress, and the Metropolitan Museum of Art.

FOR MORE INFORMATION SEE:

Contemporary Authors, Volume 101, Gale, 1981.
Who's Who in American Art, 17th edition, Bowker, 1986.
Contemporary Graphic Artists, Volume 2, Gale, 1987.

OBITUARIES

New York Times, June 30, 1988.

HAMILTON, Virginia (Esther)   1936-

PERSONAL: Born March 12, 1936, in Yellow Springs, Ohio; daughter of Kenneth James (a musician) and Etta Belle (Perry) Hamilton; married Arnold Adoff (an anthologist and author), March 19, 1960; children: Leigh Hamilton (daughter), Jaime Levi (son). _Education:_ Antioch College, B.A., 1955, attended Ohio State University, 1957-58, and New School for Social Research, 1959. _Address:_ Box 293, Yellow Springs, Ohio 45387. _Agent:_ Arnold Adoff, Arnold Adoff Agency, 1 Lincoln Plaza, 37U, 20 West 64th St., New York, N.Y. 10023.

CAREER: "Every source of occupation imaginable, from singer to bookkeeper"; author of books for young people. Whittall Lecturer, Library of Congress, Washington, D.C., 1975; visiting professor, Queens College, 1986-87.

AWARDS, HONORS: Nancy Block Memorial Award from the Downtown (N.Y.) Community School Awards Committee, 1967, for _Zeely; The House of Dies Drear_ was chosen one of Child Study Association of America's Children's Books of the Year, 1968, _The Time-Ago Tales of Jahdu_, 1969, _Time-Ago Lost_, 1973, _Paul Robeson_, and _M.C. Higgins, the Great_, both 1974, _Arilla Sun Down_, 1976, and _Junius over Far_, and _The People Could Fly_, 1985; Edgar Allan Poe Award from the Mystery Writers of America for best juvenile mystery, and Ohioana Book Award from the Ohioana Library Association, both 1969, both for _The House of Dies Drear._

The Planet of Junior Brown was chosen one of _School Library Journal_'s Best Books, 1971, and selected a Newbery Honor Book by the American Library Association, National Book

VIRGINIA HAMILTON

Award finalist, and received the Lewis Carroll Shelf Award from the University of Wisconsin, all 1972; *Book World*'s Children's Spring Book Festival Honor Book, 1973, for *Time-Ago Lost; Boston Globe-Horn Book* Award for Text, and chosen one of *New York Times* Outstanding Books of the Year and one of American Library Association's Best Young Adult Books, all 1974, National Book Award, and Newbery Medal, both 1975, Lewis Carroll Shelf Award, and International Board on Books for Young People (IBBY) Honor List for Text, both 1976, all for *M. C. Higgins, the Great; Arilla Sun Down* was chosen one of *School Library Journal*'s Best Books of the Year, 1976, and *The People Could Fly,* 1985.

The Gathering was chosen one of New York Public Library's Books for the Teen Age, 1982; *Sweet Whispers, Brother Rush* was chosen one of American Library Association's Best Young Adult Books, one of *New York Times* Outstanding Books of the Year, and one of *School Library Journal*'s Best Children's Books, all 1982, received the Coretta Scott King Award from the American Library Association for outstanding inspirational and educational contributions to literature for children and young adults, *Boston Globe-Horn Book* Award for Fiction, Certificate of Honor from the International Board on Books for Young People for outstanding example of literature with international importance, American Book Award finalist, and Newbery Honor Book, all 1983; Parents' Choice Award for Literature from the Parents' Choice Foundation, one of American Library Association's Best Young Adult Books, one of *School Library Journal*'s Best Books for Spring, and one of New York Public Library's Children's Books, all 1983, and Coretta Scott King Award Honorable Mention, 1984, all for *The Magical Adventures of Pretty Pearl;* Ohioana Book Award, 1984, for her body of work; *A Little Love* was selected one of American Library Association's Best Books for Young Adults, 1984, and Coretta Scott King Award Honorable Mention, 1985; *Willie Bea and the Time the Martians Landed* was chosen one of New York Public Library's Children's Books, 1984.

The People Could Fly was chosen one of *New York Times* Best Illustrated Children's Books, a *Booklist* Editors' Choice, and a Notable Childrens Trade Book in the Field of Social Studies from the National Council of Social Studies and the Children's Book Council, all 1985, and the Coretta Scott King Award, and Other Award (Great Britain), both 1986; Coretta Scott King Award Honorable Mention, 1986, for *Junius over Far.*

WRITINGS:

JUVENILE NOVELS

Zeely (ALA Notable Book; illustrated by Symeon Shimin), Macmillan, 1967.
The House of Dies Drear (ALA Notable Book; illustrated by Eros Keith), Macmillan, 1968.
The Time-Ago Tales of Jahdu (ALA Notable Book; illustrated by Nonny Hogrogian), Macmillan, 1969.
The Planet of Junior Brown (ALA Notable Book), Macmillan, 1971.
Time-Ago Lost: More Tales of Jahdu (illustrated by Ray Prather), Macmillan, 1973.
M. C. Higgins, the Great (ALA Notable Book; *Horn Book* honor list; teacher's guide), Macmillan, 1974, large print edition, G. K. Hall, 1976.
Arilla Sun Down (ALA Notable Book; *Horn Book* honor list), Greenwillow, 1976.
Jahdu (illustrated by Jerry Pinkney), Greenwillow, 1980, large print edition, 1980.
Sweet Whispers, Brother Rush, Philomel, 1982.
The Magical Adventures of Pretty Pearl (ALA Notable Book), Harper, 1983.

(Cover illustration by Jerry Pinkney for the paperback edition of Hamilton's award-winning novel.)

Willie Bea and the Time the Martians Landed (ALA Notable Book), Greenwillow, 1983.
A Little Love, Philomel, 1984.
Junius over Far, Harper, 1985.
The People Could Fly: American Black Folktales (ALA Notable Book; *Horn Book* honor list; illustrated by Leo Dillon and Diane Dillon), Knopf, 1985.
The Mystery of Drear House: Book Two of Dies Drear, Greenwillow, 1987.
A White Romance, Philomel, 1987.
The Mystery of Drear House: The Conclusion of the Dies Drear Chronicle, Macmillan, in press.

JUSTICE TRILOGY

Justice and Her Brothers, Greenwillow, 1978.
Dustland, Greenwillow, 1980.
The Gathering, Greenwillow, 1981.

OTHER

W. E. B. Du Bois: A Biography (ALA Notable Book), Crowell, 1972.
Paul Robeson: The Life and Times of a Free Black Man (ALA Notable Book), Harper, 1975.
(Editor) *The Writings of W. E. B. Du Bois,* Crowell, 1976.

(Contributor) *Once upon a Time. . .Celebrating the Magic of Children's Books in Honor of the Twentieth Anniversary of Reading Is Fundamental*, Putnam, 1986.

In the Beginning: Creation Stories from around the World, Harcourt, 1988.

Anthony Burns: The Defeat and Triumph of a Fugitive Slave, Knopf, 1988.

Also author of introduction of the *Newbery Award Reader*, edited by Charles G. Waugh and Martin H. Greenberg, Harcourt, 1974.

ADAPTATIONS:

''Virginia Hamilton Reads *Zeely*'' (cassette), Caedmon, 1974.

''Sweet Whispers, Brother Rush'' (listening cassette; filmstrip with cassette), Miller-Brody, 1974.

''M. C. Higgins, the Great'' (listening record or cassette; filmstrip with cassette), Listening Post, 1975.

''The Planet of Junior Brown'' (record or cassette; filmstrip with record or cassette), Miller-Brody, 1976.

''Time-Ago Lost'' (cassette and book).

''The House of Dies Drear'' (movie, starring Howard Rollins), ''Wonderworks Series,'' PBS-TV, November, 1986.

''The People Could Fly'' (cassette), Knopf, 1988.

The House of Dies Drear, M. C. Higgins, the Great, Paul Robeson, The Time-Ago Tales of Jahdu, W. E. B. Du Bois, and *Zeely* have been adapted into talking books, and *The House of Dies Drear* has been adapted into Braille.

WORK IN PROGRESS: ''A collection of short stories tentatively titled *Choices, Changes, Gambles and Games;* a book about the life of a runaway slave; a book on creation myth.''

SIDELIGHTS: Virginia Hamilton was the first black writer to win the Newbery Medal in recognition of *M. C. Higgins, the Great,* a novel published in 1974. Considered challenging, literary and thematically complex, Hamilton's oeuvre is often credited by critics with having raised the standards of American literature for younger readers.

''What personal self I have is in my books. Everything that might become neurotic or personally problematic I put into a narrative. My stories are little pieces of me.''[1]

''Most of my writing is flavored from my childhood experience; although I write about the rural present, there is much of the Depression thirties in everything I create. So when I write about the road, as I'm doing in a new book, I see what somebody might have seen when she traveled the road a long time ago. I see the empty spaces and billboards; I don't see the motels. I choose what I see, and what I see is another time. It's the same thing with my hometown. I write about the areas in and around Yellow Springs, Ohio, or southern Ohio, but since we've been there for generations, I see that locale through my eyes, my mother's eyes, and my grandmother's eyes. I can do that anytime I want to because I know the way they saw it, the way my mother still sees it, and she's 90: she has a very long vision. I can walk through the door of her house, and sometimes she sees me as an aunt. Well, that's all right—I'm my aunt, too. For me, it's all a continuum. . . .I'm afraid I'm unable to deal with one time frame when I'm writing: I seem not to be able to create a character in one dimension of time. . . .I think that living on the land that supported my ancestors has a lot to do with it.''[2]

''I am a teller of tales, in part, because of the informal way I learned from Mother and her relatives of passing the time, which they also utilize for transmitting information, for enter-

tainment, and for putting their own flesh and blood in the proper perspective. The Perrys are interesting talkers. They began as farmers who had been fugitives from injustice. Acquiring land and homes, place and time, was to them the final payment in the cause of freedom. After long days, a long history in the fields, they talked their way into new states of mind. They could appreciate a good story in the companionship of one another, not only as entertainment but as a way to mark their progress. Stories, talking, grew and changed into a kind of folk history of timely incidents. And these developed in lines of force that had beginnings, middles, and endings—a certain style. True memory might lapse, and creativity come into play. It was the same creativity and versatility that had helped the first African survive on the American continent. An uncle of mine told the most astonishing lies. An aunt whispered in perfect rememory the incident of Blind Martha and how she found her way down the dusty road to the spot where the log cabin had stood in which she was born. The day Uncle Saunders was killed, all of the ivy fell from the Pasony house. Pasonys were neighbors, quiet and shrewd. But they could not save the ivy.

''There's the story I remember always knowing about my Grandpaw Levi Perry and how his hand burned shut from a fire in the gunpowder mill where he worked. And from the time that his life and mine coincided, his hand was a fist with burn scars hidden in the tightly shut palm. I would lace my fingers over his closed fist when I was a child, and he would lift me up and up, swing me around and around—to my enormous delight. Ever after, the raised Black fist became for me both myth and history, and they were mine. Grandpaw Perry was John Henry and High John de Conquer. He was power—the fugitive, the self-made, the closed fist in which I knew was kept magic. . . .

''What is transformed from myth, history, and family narrative in my own fictions is not a play—pretty to be held in the hands of children. My fictions for young people derive from the progress of Black adults and their children across the American hopescape. Occasionally, they are light-hearted; often they are speculative, symbolic and dark, and brooding. The people are always uneasy because the ideological difference they feel from the majority is directly derived from heritage. In the background of much of my writing is the dream of freedom tantalizingly out of reach.''[3]

''One of my uncles, on my mother's side, made an annual pilgrimage down to Ripley, Ohio to the John Rankin House. John Rankin and his nine sons were Presbyterian abolishionists, former southerners who hated slavery. Their house stood high on Liberty Hill with a light and a bell for slaves coming across to freedom. My Grandpaw Perry was brought north by his mother, who then promptly disappeared. She was believed to be a conductor in the Underground Railroad. They came up through Virginia to Ripley to Jamestown, Ohio, about ten miles from Yellow Springs. I believe she was caught on one of her many trips. She was never heard from again. . . .

''My grandpaw sat his children down once a year and told them the story. 'This was what slavery was like, and why I ran away. . .I am telling you so that it will never happen to you.' He made an enormous impression on my mother. I have asked her, 'What did he say?' And she never has told.

''I have done some digging into the history of the Underground Railroad and runaway slaves. The things I've discovered. . .the books I can write!. . .''[1]

''I've noticed lately that I have been speaking more about my mother and her family than early on when I spoke mostly about

(Cover illustration by Symeon Shimin from *Zeely* by Virginia Hamilton.)

my father. I think that I'm beginning to come around. The males in my family were very dominant. I had two older brothers and my father, of course. The women were not as strong; it was a very traditional household. My father was the dominant one and also the very creative and sensitive one. He was the sun: we revolved around him.''[2]

"He was a musician. He played in mandolin clubs all over the country in the early nineteen hundreds. The clubs were racially integrated and allowed females as well. I have wonderful old photographs of them, and still have my father's mandolin, a Gibson 1902, Patent Pending, all ivory and white. He was a fine classical mandolinist.

"He was also a very moody man. Mother was his third wife. His dream was to be the most famous mandolinist of his time. But he was barred from all the great concert halls because he could not belong to the musicians' union as a Black man. He never forgave the unions for that. He worked outside the system, creating his own musical groups, performing on radio and in dance halls in mining towns where you checked your guns at the door.

"Yes, without a doubt, I idolized him, not merely because he was a flamboyant figure, but because he was deeply sensitive, literate and politically committed. A strong childhood memory is of the men who passed through our town during the Depression—men completely broke, many for years without jobs, men who were hungry. 'Do you have work?' they would ask.

My father would always find something for them to do. He would leave food by the side of the road for those passing by. 'If you give something to people who are hungry,' he'd say, 'they'll never steal anything from you.' We grew everything ourselves and had much more than we could eat.

"My father was also a great reader. He loved Wendell Wilkie, whose *One World* was one of his favorite books. He knew W. E. B. Du Bois, and subscribed to *Crisis* magazine, which Du Bois edited under the auspices of the NAACP. Du Bois and Franklin Delano Roosevelt were my father's heroes. He subscribed to *The New Yorker,* and talked about what he read. Books were an important part of our lives—Poe, de Maupassant, many of the classics. I didn't realize then how unusual it was for a man like my father to have such a library. It was an important factor in my education.

"I attended a small country school where we weren't taught much more than some English and history—no black history. As a matter of fact, I was the only black girl in my class until seventh grade or so. I did very well, but our curriculum was so limited it would be years before I felt reasonably well educated.

"Oh, how I wanted to leave the little town of Yellow Spring. Every night I lay in bed listening to the long, sad whistle of the train passing through from New York to Chicago. I wanted with all my soul to get to Manhattan, but it seemed I was trapped forever.

The House of Dies Drear / Virginia Hamilton

ILLUSTRATIONS BY EROS KEITH

MACMILLAN PUBLISHING CO., INC
New York

Thomas stared out at the steady rain and the mountains, which were no longer familiar. ■
(From *The House of Dies Drear* by Virginia Hamilton. Illustrated by Eros Keith.)

"My cousin Marleen and I were inseparable—we made stilts together, we roller skated, we explored, we picked berries. The day she got married, I remember saying to her, 'Let's go for a walk.' And she said, 'I can't leave my husband.' Those words marked an irreversible change in my life. I was just seventeen, and had the feeling my life was over. There was so much I wanted to do, but couldn't see my way clear.

"Well, that evening, after Marleen's wedding, the telephone rang and a high school teacher gave me the news that she had arranged for a five-year scholarship for college. A bolt from the blue. A dream I had thought beyond my grasp.

"I started off in my home town at Antioch College. Going away to school was out of my reach even with my tuition paid for. Antioch was one of the few schools then that had a major in writing. That was lucky for me, but still I was restless.

"One of my teachers told me that I really ought to leave school, go to New York and try to become published. I spent summers in New York, working as a bookkeeper. I could earn much more money there than in the Midwest. I often went back and forth between Ohio and New York, a semester on, a semester off. Finally, I took my teacher's advice and left before taking my degree.

"I don't have a clear recollection of the day I officially left home to go to New York. My plan was to find a cheap apartment, a part-time job, write, and have a good time. And it all came together. I took a place in the East Village, in what is today called Alphabet City. Mornings I was a cost accountant for an engineering firm; afternoons I wrote; and evenings I went out or read. I read everything I could get my hands on, tore through all the Modern Library classics. Mexican writers were very popular at the time and I steeped myself in that work, as well.

"New York was such a different scene in the fifties. The East Village was a mix of Polish and Ukrainian immigrants, young writers and artists. It was easy to meet people. The painters Raphael and Moses Soyer held a weekly salon, attended by everyone who was anyone. Today, I get the feeling that writers, artists and musicians operate pretty much in separate spheres. It wasn't like that then. We were all together. It was a completely integrated scene.

"I worked hard at my writing, but wasn't singularly fixed on it. The fact that it wasn't being published did not eat away at me. *The New Yorker* wrote me very encouraging letters and tried to help me. But I would never quite fit their mold. I was meeting all kinds of people and having a wonderful time. Seriousness came slowly.

"Still, I thought I should try to find out a little more about how publishing worked. When a friend told me she was going to be taking a writing course at The New School, I pricked up my ears. It sounded interesting, but only twelve students would be admitted on the basis of samples. I was intimidated. Well, my friend and I applied, and I got in and she didn't, which made me feel terrible. This class was taught by Hiram Hayden, a founder of Atheneum. Hiram loved my writing, and in a sense became my mentor. He was a terribly handsome, raw-boned man. All the women in class had a crush on him. For a farm girl from Ohio, class was quite a scene. At the time I was writing an adult novel, *Mayo,* which Hiram wanted very much to publish. Unfortunately, his partners didn't agree. If they had, I might never have become a writer of children's books.

"A few years later a college friend who was working at Macmillan asked, 'Whatever happened to that children's story you

Standing in the room, she didn't know she had begun to talk to herself. ■ (From *Zeely* by Virginia Hamilton. Illustrated by Symeon Shimin.)

wrote at Antioch?' 'What children's story?' I asked. I honestly didn't remember. But she was right, I had written such a piece. I began working on it again and at her prodding, I sent it to Susan Hirschman, head of their children's book department. I didn't even know there was such a thing as children's book departments!

"That children's story became *Zeely,* my first book. I wrote what became the final manuscript when my daughter was very young. We were together the whole time I worked on that book. I'd show her the typed pages and tell her what it was. I'd explain how I was sending it off, and when the galleys came back, we would look at them together. And then I'd send back the galleys and the proofs would come. Then, one day the book arrived with my name on the cover. Suddenly it all came together for her—the look on her face was wonderful.

"*Zeely* looks to Africa. For years, I had kept a scrapbook on Africa, and a map that I was constantly revising as nations won their independence from European powers. A lot of the material became part of *Zeely.*

"The plot centers on Elizabeth, who fancies that Zeely, a beautiful six-foot Black woman who does tenant farming and raises pigs on Elizabeth's uncle's farm, is in reality an African princess. Elizabeth, the young protagonist who idolizes Zeely, is much like I was as a girl. Many of my characters are loners, unsure of who they are, and given to wild imaginings.

''Because it was my first book, I have a special fondness for it. That said, it is hard for me to read it today; there are many things I would do differently.''[1]

''There's nothing really you can do about being referred to as a 'minority' or 'black' writer. For a long time, I tried to fight it, saying I'm a writer, *period*. But in a country like ours, there really is a dominant culture. I prefer the term 'parallel culture.' If you look at things globally, blacks and Latinos do not constitute a small minority.

''The sixties was a great time for children's books, and books in general. There was a lot of federal money around, and libraries and schools were able to acquire good-sized collections of so-called minority books. But it had its downside, too. There was a lot of infighting among people supposedly fighting for the same cause—namely, equality for *all*. Raising the consciousness about black heritage, black culture, black people was, and remains to be, of vital importance. But political work is very tricky for a writer. Writers need time alone. And the idea of a collective stance can be dangerous. There was a lot of violence during the sixties, not only in the streets, but in the rhetoric as well. Writers were called upon by the leaders of the movement to be violent in their poetry or prose. I had a lot of trouble with that. One of the best poems of the period has a line that goes, 'must I shoot the/white man dead/to free the nigger/in his head?' A very important point of view. Politically, I did what I could, but mostly, I just continued to write my books.''[1]

''I attempt in each book to take hold of one single theme of the black experience and present it as clearly as I can. I don't mean to make the writing of fiction sound cold or calculating—it isn't at all. . . .The black experience in America is deep like the rivers of this country. At times through our history it became submerged only to emerge again and again. Each time it emerges, it seems strong, more explicit and insistent.

''There are themes in my writing that are strains through the whole of black history. The strain of the wanderer, like the theme of Jahdu; the strain of the fleeing slave or the persecuted moving and searching for a better place becomes the theme of the Night Traveller in *Zeely*. And the black man hiding his true self, ever acting so that those who betray him will never touch him. . . .Perhaps some day when I've written my last book, there will stand the whole of the black experience in white America as I see it.''[4]

''I have consistently written nonfiction, as well as fiction. The nonfiction not only provides a rest from novels and stories, but satisfies a need to do ongoing research and to tell the factual, historical stories of our people. It makes perfect sense, in view of the stature he had in the home I grew up in, that I would one day write a biography of W. E. B. Du Bois.''[1]

Hamilton's 1972 biography of Du Bois received generally high praise, although a few critics had reservations about the author's overt didacticism.

She has also written a biography of Paul Robeson. ''I had hoped, by writing the personal history of a real individual through a disciplined presentation of facts, to create the illusion of total reality; to give readers the feeling that they walked along with the subject in his life; and through the creative use of source material, to allow the subject to speak as closely as possible in his own voice.

''In this respect, of the two biographies, the Robeson biography is the more successful. The research and study of the Robeson material took a number of years. When that phase of

He had thick, white hair and a full white beard. . . .He was somehow larger than dream or nightmare. ■ (From *The House of Dies Drear* by Virginia Hamilton. Illustrated by Eros Keith.)

the work was completed, I discovered it was possible during the day to evoke the Robeson spirit in my mind and to live with it as though the man were a guest in my house. I began to know Paul Robeson quite well, and slowly two aspects of him emerged to trouble me and to pose definite problems in the actual writing.

''The first problem, and the one easiest to deal with, was the problem of Robeson emerging not as a man but as a symbol. . .In my Robeson research, it was almost impossible to find a single newspaper account that did not depict the man as somehow supernatural and larger than life. . . .

''Hardly ever was Robeson described as a man. Rather, he was 'this giant,' 'that great, noble prince,' or 'the original stuff of the earth. . . .' Eventually, I learned to use these overwrought passages to an advantage. But it became necessary for me to write in a very tight, simple style; to write close up to the individual in the hope that a concise and straightforward revelation of his life would finally produce a composite of the man.

''The second problem was more difficult and became clear to me only after I had written a first draft of the book. Then Robeson still seemed elusive. . . .For the basic difficulty of writing about blacks in America was intensely a problem here: the origins of black American history is fundamentally different from that of traditional American history. . . .

"In order to understand Paul Robeson or Dr. Du Bois, it is necessary that we understand that what the majority viewed as radical in their time was quite a normal point of view for these men whose lives were profoundly restricted by a whole system of established mores. . .Furthermore, it became necessary to go beyond the usual thorough and traditional histories having to do with political America, Europe, and the rest of the world, such as those written by Commager and Leuchtenburg, and to search for and find those revisionist historians, like Gabriel Kolko, whose historical truths emerge as radically different from what we have taken for granted as the truth. . . .

"Paul Robeson's drift toward radicalism and the appeal radicalism had for him become understandable from the viewpoint of a colonized people. Robeson saw himself as a citizen of the world and identified himself, as did Du Bois, with the world's workers and colonized peoples, whom he deemed criminally exploited under capitalism. . . .

"Curiously, my studies in radical history and research into black life and history have tended to radicalize me not so much in terms of world political views as in fictional terms. I would be a rather useless individual in any revolutionary situation. I hate violence and tend to view it as a human aberration—certainly not a very radical point of view. . .In any case, for myself, I deliberately attempt a kind of literary radicalism in the hope of removing traditional prose restrictions and creating new ways to approach literary forms from a perspective other than that of the majority. It is a way of continuing to legitimize nonwhite literature, bringing it into full view to provoke curiosity and discussion."[5]

Hamilton, who teaches as well as writes, has strong ideas concerning genre. "Traditionally, the young adult, or YA category of books has been maligned. I believe this is due more to the way the so-called movers and shakers of publishing houses think about YA, than to the qualities of the books themselves. Ask most editors, and they will talk about novels for young adults as 'problem books.' Supposedly, adolescents should be able to read them for the answers to the questions that typically plague them at that time of their life. Of course books can, and do help us to live; and some may even change our lives, but it is not a good thing to put sociological/didactic considerations before literary ones. Besides, kids are very knowing. I tend to treat sexuality as a given, as something almost commonplace, in the lives of my characters. This leaves me—and my readers—free to concentrate on other things. I think about my story, characters, images, symbolism—the dynamics that hold those elements together in a pleasing sort of tension.

"There are certain technical advantages for writing for YA. You're allowed to linger over descriptions—words, rather than actions, may be in the forefront. I love setting up scenes, starting with a wide view and then gradually moving in for the close-up. You can develop characters in a more sophisticated way. I consider most of the novels I've written for adolescents to be classical romances. Certainly love figures prominently in romances, but there are other, equally important, themes. The protagonist is made to undertake a journey—physical, psychic or both. As a result of that journey, she grows and changes, a complicated, usually painful, process.

"My last book, *A White Romance,* is about two central couples—one white girl and boy; one black girl and white boy. The setting for the black girl's epiphany is a heavy-metal rock concert. I learned fascinating things in the course of this book, including that I find myself more frequently on the same wavelength with people a generation or so younger; and 'out of sync' with readers and editors my own age. At least for this book.

"My son, a musician, was an invaluable help to me. He spent long hours talking with me into a tape recorder, giving me the lingo, the sounds, the scents, all the hidden things you have to be adept to know. He made sure I always placed the band members on the correct side of the stage—no drummers where the bass players should be—and called the instruments and the techniques used for playing them by their proper names. I must confess that this book grew partly out of my own anxiety about the heavy metal scene. Our son went often to these concerts, coming home with urine on his shoes and telling the most amazing stories. It frightened me. It went against the grain, however, to ask him to stop attending the concerts. So we struck a deal: he could continue to go, if he told me all about it. I was as much intrigued as I was scared by them.

"And so, because Jamie is such a marvellous storyteller and has such an extraordinary eye, place and milieu have a central role in *A White Romance.* Apparently these concerts are absolutely *packed.* Kids wait all night, sleeping outdoors, in order to get to the box office in time to buy a ticket. Far greater than the danger of drugs, apparently, is the danger of being trampled inside. People get so wound up in the hard-hitting music, that there's no way to say, 'Excuse me, I'd like to go to the rest room;' you would be crushed. Jaime says the only possible (not probable) way to get out of your row during the concert is if you yell that you are about to vomit. He told me something else that flabbergasted me. Heavy metal music attracts a lot of Vietnam veterans, many of whom are missing limbs. He says the weirdest thing is that after a concert there are all these crutches, canes and walkers just left lying. It makes you wonder: did people have mystical experiences in which they regained their ability to walk unaided? It sounds far-fetched, but. . . .

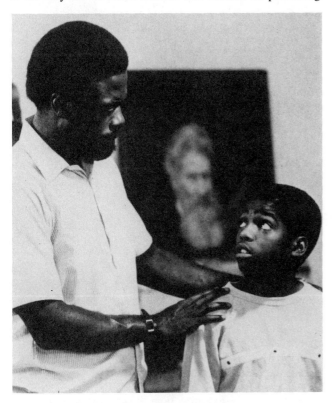

(From the television movie "The House of Dies Drear," starring Howard Rollins [left]. Presented on PBS "Wonderworks Series," November, 1986.)

(From "Raven the Creator" in *In the Beginning: Creation Stories from around the World* by Virginia Hamilton. Illustrated by Barry Moser.)

"All in all, this seemed to me a perfect place for a crucial epiphany. A number of readers of my generation have told me they don't know what to make of the book. A reviewer from a prominent magazine even called me, saying she felt totally over her head. (Needless to say, this didn't prevent her from writing a review.) But young people love the book. And that matters most to me.

"I wanted to 'test limits' in *A White Romance*. I was thoroughly tired of YA books filled with tantalizingly suggestive sex scenes. As though adolescents don't know what the score is. I wrote some very graphic scenes. I did have to make some cuts. For example, in one scene, I had the girl wrap her legs around her boyfriend's behind. That detail, as they say, ended up on the cutting room floor. But my big rock concert scene stayed in pretty much as I wrote it."[1]

Hamilton feels that another of her YA works—the *Justice Cycle*, including *Justice and Her Brothers, Dustland* and *The Gathering*—has suffered somewhat because of generic confusion. Although the books have all received glowing reviews, they have often been referred to as 'science fiction.' "I don't think of those books as science fiction, at all. They fall into the category of fantasy, and have elements of the cautionary tale. Science fiction is based on scientific fact; fantasy need not be. Someone did say that these books start with reality, turn into fantasy and end in science fiction. This may be true. I certainly did a lot of research for the third book. The original idea for the book was The Great Snake Race, which as a child I misunderstood in the same way that Justice does. Twins and clairvoyance are themes that have long fascinated me. So, too, has the theme of the alien, and the possibility of global disaster.

I feel less involved with my own heritage and more preoccupied with survivors of all kinds: Will the few who survive the cataclysm do so because they are genetically different? Is it possible that telepathy, prophecy, and genius are genetic mutations? Could the striking talents of a few be the means of survival for many? These are the questions I explore in *The Justice Cycle*."[1]

A book that means a great deal to Hamilton is *The People Could Fly*, a collection of American black folk tales with illustrations by Leo and Diane Dillon. "You see, the slaves—those former Africans— brought, chained, to this continent, had no power, no weapons to aid them in overcoming their oppressors. So it was that they used the folklore they created here to comment on their lives of servitude and to give themselves comfort and strength through endless hard times. Some of these tales are absolutely unique in the folk-tale genre. But how were they told—and where—is the question I asked myself again and again.

"There could not have been an easy way for them to develop over time. There was no safe place where, and no condition under which, the slaves could sit down and simply tell stories, except in the safety of the forests. Most of the southern country was forest. . . .Here they gathered under cover of darkness to pass gossip and to discuss what was beyond the forest. . . .Their meetings were so secret they dared not use their

It was the most exciting thing Buddy had ever seen. Big, fat and black Junior Brown playing classical music. ■ (Cover illustration by Jerry Pinkney from *The Planet of Junior Brown* by Virginia Hamilton.)

It was a long rowin time in the cold. ■ (From *The People Could Fly: American Black Folktales* by Virginia Hamilton. Illustrated by Leo and Diane Dillon.)

own names for fear the names would somehow reach the ears of the overseer. They dared not touch one another, lest the mere touching give away an identity.

"I've not found the research in black heritage and culture a cause for despair, however sorrowful some of the areas might seem. One feels like an explorer many times, tracking along the 'hopesteps' of beings dead and gone. Following trails of dogged courage and will beyond imagining across dangerous entrapments.

"Black folk tales, I believe, allow us to share in the known, the remembered, and the imagined together as Americans sharing the same history. . . .From teller to reader is the unbroken circle of communication. We all contribute to a construction of mere words. We are all together. That is what language does for us. That is what *The People Could Fly* may do for us. To say from one of us handed down to the other, you are not alone."[6]

FOOTNOTE SOURCES

[1]Based on an interview by Marguerite Feitlowitz for *Something about the Author*.
[2]Marilyn Apseloff, "A Conversation with Virginia Hamilton," *Children's Literature in Education*, winter, 1983.
[3]Virginia Hamilton, "Ah, Sweet Rememory!" *Horn Book*, December, 1981.
[4]V. Hamilton, "Portrait of the Author as a Working Writer," *Authors and Illustrators of Children's Books*, edited by Miriam Hoffman and Eva Samuels, 1972.
[5]V. Hamilton, *Illusion and Reality*, Library of Congress, 1976.
[6]V. Hamilton, "Coretta Scott King Award Acceptance," *Horn Book*, November/December, 1986.

FOR MORE INFORMATION SEE:

Top of the News, June, 1969, April, 1975.
Horn Book, February, 1970, February, 1972, December, 1972 (p. 563), June, 1973, December, 1974 (p. 671), August, 1975 (p. 337), December, 1978, October, 1982, June, 1983, February, 1984 (p. 24).
Elementary English, April, 1971.
Library Journal, September 15, 1971.
Christian Science Monitor, November 11, 1971, May 12, 1980, August 3, 1984.
Martha E. Ward and Dorothy A. Marquardt, *Authors of Books for Young People*, 2nd edition, Scarecrow, 1971.
Donnarae MacCann and Gloria Woodard, editors, *The Black American in Books for Children: Readings in Racism*, Scarecrow, 1972.
Washington Post Book World, November 10, 1974, November 11, 1979, September 14, 1980, November 7, 1982, November 10, 1985.
Lee Bennett Hopkins, *More Books by More People*, Citation Press, 1974.
Listener, November 6, 1975.
Francelia Butler, editor, *Children's Literature: Annual of the Modern Language Association Seminar on Children's Literature and the Children's Literature Association*, Volume IV, Temple University Press, 1975.
Lee Kingman, editor, *Newbery and Caldecott Medal Books: 1966-1975*, Horn Book, 1975.
Theressa Gunnels Rush and others, *Black American Writers Past and Present: A Biographical and Bibliographical Dictionary*, two volumes, Scarecrow, 1975.
Judith Wagner, "More Vivid than Daylight," *Cincinnati Enquirer* (Ohio), Januuary 5, 1975.
"Meet the Newbery Author: Virginia Hamilton," (filmstrip with record or cassette), Miller-Brody, 1976.
Barbara Nykoruk, editor, *Authors in the News*, Volume 1, Gale, 1976.
Doris de Montreville and Elizabeth D. Crawford, editors, *Fourth Book of Junior Authors and Illustrators*, H. W. Wilson, 1978.
Jacqueline S. Weiss, "Profiles in Literature" (videocassette), Temple University, 1978.
D. L. Kirkpatrick, editor, *Twentieth-Century Children's Writers*, St. Martin's, 1978, 2nd edition, 1983.
John Rowe Townsend, *A Sounding of Storytellers*, Lippincott, 1979.
Marilyn Apseloff, *Virginia Hamilton/Ohio Explorer in the World of Imagination*, State Library of Ohio, 1979.
Betsy Hearne, "Virginia Hamilton—An Eminent Writer for Children in the U.S.A.," *Bookbird*, number 2, 1980 (p. 22).
School Library Journal, February, 1980 (p. 21), May, 1980, April, 1983.
Lina Mainiero, editor, *American Women Writers*, Ungar, 1980.
Virginia Haviland, editor, *The Openhearted Audience: Ten Authors Talk about Writing for Children*, Library of Congress, 1980.
Mary Lystad, *From Dr. Mather to Dr. Seuss: 200 Years of American Books for Children*, Schenkman Books, 1980 (p. 179).
Betsy Hearne and Marilyn Kaye, editors, *Celebrating Children's Books: Essays on Children's Literature in Honor of Zena Sutherland*, Lothrop, 1981.
"Fanciful Words," *New York Times Book Review*, April 26, 1981.
Children's Literature Association Quarterly, fall, 1982 (p. 45), spring, 1983 (p. 17), winter, 1983 (p. 25).
Jim Roginski, compiler, *Newbery and Caldecott Medalists and Honor Book Winners*, Libraries Unlimited, 1982.
Publishers Weekly, July 6, 1983, February 26, 1988 (p. 115).
Donna Norton, editor, *Through the Eyes of a Child: Introduction to Children's Literature*, Merrill, 1983 (p. 500).
Seventeen, April, 1984.
Writer, August, 1984.
J. H. Dressel, "The Legacy of Ralph Ellison in Virginia Hamilton's 'Justice Trilogy,'" *English Journal*, November, 1984.
David Rees, *Painted Desert, Green Shade: Essays on Contemporary Writers of Fiction for Children and Young Adults*, Horn Book, 1984 (p. 168).
Dictionary of Literary Biography, Gale, Volume XXXIII, 1984, Volume LII, 1986.
Chicago Tribune Book World, November 10, 1985.
Anita Moss, "Mythical Narrative: Virginia Hamilton's *The Magical Adventures of Pretty Pearl*," *The Lion and the Unicorn*, Volume 9, 1985.
Children's Literature Review, Volume VIII, Gale, 1985, Volume XI, 1986.

HANSEN, Ron 1947-

PERSONAL: Born December 8, 1947, in Omaha, Neb.; son of Frank L. (an electrical engineer) and Marvyl (a stenographer; maiden name, Moore) Hansen; married Julie Vinsonhaler (an art historian), May 25, 1985. *Education:* Creighton University, B.A., 1970; University of Iowa, M.F.A., 1974; further graduate study at Stanford University, 1977-78. *Agent:* Liz Darhansoff, 1220 Park Ave., New York, N.Y. 10128.

CAREER: Stanford University, Stanford, Calif., Jones Lecturer in Creative Writing, 1978-81; author, 1975—; University of Michigan, Ann Arbor, affiliated with Michigan Society of Fellows, 1981-84; affiliated with the Writers Workshop, Uni-

The mayor's grand royal shadow had developed an annoying squeak in its knee. ■ (From *The Shadowmaker* by Ron Hansen. Illustrated by Margot Tomes.)

versity of Iowa, Iowa City, 1985, Cornell University, Ithaca, N.Y., 1985-86, University of Arizona, Tucson, 1986-88, and State University of New York (Binghamton) 1988—. *Awards, honors:* Two fellowships from the National Endowment for the Arts; PEN/Faulkner Award in Fiction finalist, 1984, for *The Assassination of Jesse James by the Coward Robert Ford;* *The Shadowmaker* was selected one of *New York Times* Notable Books, 1987.

WRITINGS:

Desperadoes, Knopf, 1979.
The Assassination of Jesse James by the Coward Robert Ford, Knopf, 1983.
The Shadowmaker (juvenile; Junior Literary Guild selection; illustrated by Margot Tomes), Harper, 1986.
(Editor) *You Don't Know What Love Is,* Ontario Review Press, 1987.
Nebraska, Atlantic Monthly, 1989.

SIDELIGHTS: "Some writers feel compelled to use contemporary settings in their novels because they need to explain their own lives to themselves or speak about public issues that are important to them. I've been too private for that sort of exploration. Historical fiction has given me the opportunity to say all I know about the Old West and about philosophical questions I thought were important, and it kept me away from a contemporary world that I found comparatively boring or implausible. And I liked the idea of using a popular genre,

such as the Western, as a way of expanding the appeal of my work to people who wouldn't otherwise pick it up."

Hansen's first novel, *Desperadoes,* is about the notorious Dalton gang, a group of outlaws that flourished in the West during the late 1800s. The Dalton Brothers started as peace officers in the Indian Territories but became disillusioned with the low wages and took up rustling. Later, they turned to robbing banks and trains. Hansen's version of the story is told in retrospect by the last of the gang's survivors, Emmett Dalton.

FOR MORE INFORMATION SEE:

Ron Hansen, *Desperadoes,* Knopf, 1979.
Chicago Tribune, April 8, 1979.
Newsweek, April 9, 1979, November 14, 1983.
New York, April 23, 1979.
Washington Post, May 4, 1979.
Esquire, May 8, 1979.
New York Times Book Review, June 3, 1979, February 5, 1984.
New York Times, June 13, 1979.
Los Angeles Times Book Review, November 20, 1983.
Christian Science Monitor, December 28, 1983.
Chicago Times Book World, March 18, 1984.

HARGREAVES, Roger   1935(?)-1988

OBITUARY NOTICE: Born about 1935; died September 12, 1988 of a heart attack in London, England. Author and illustrator. Hargreaves worked as a creative director of a London advertising agency before turning his doodlings into the popular "Mister Men" and "Little Miss" series of storybooks for children. He also wrote and illustrated a set of stories about animals in "Timbuctoo," including *Neigh, Oink, Snap, Puff,* and *Roar,* which were published in 1979. Among his "Mister Men" titles are: *Mr. Nonsense, Mr. Nervous, Mr. Lazy,* and *Mr. Tickle* and his "Little Miss" titles, including: *Little Miss Twins, Little Miss Late,* and *Little Miss Helpful.*

FOR MORE INFORMATION SEE:

OBITUARIES

Detroit News, September 16, 1988.

HARRISON, Edward Hardy   1926-
(Ted Harrison)

PERSONAL: Born August 28, 1926, in Wingate, Durham, England; son of Charles Edward (a coal miner and insurance agent) and Martha (a seamstress and housewife; maiden name, Thirlaway) Harrison; married Robina McNicol (an educator and design company director), November 12, 1960; children: Charles Edward. *Education:* Hartlepool College of Art, National Diploma in Design, 1950; King's College, University of Durham, Art Teacher's Diploma, 1951; University of Alberta, B.Ed., 1977. *Politics:* "Conservative leanings; liberal tendencies." *Religion:* "A lapsed Anglican." *Home and office:* 30 12th Ave. East, Whitehorse, Yukon Territory, Canada Y1A 4J6. *Agent:* George Maddison, 19 Glouster Grove, Toronto, Ontario M6C 1Z8, Canada.

CAREER: Slim School, Malaysia, housemaster, 1959-62; artist and writer, 1968—; Wingate Arts Ltd. (design firm), Whi-

EDWARD HARDY HARRISON

tehorse, Yukon Territory, president, 1972—. Lecturer. Fire chief in Carcross, Yukon Territory, 1968-71. *Exhibitions:* Children's Book Fair, Bologna, Italy, 1978. Work is represented in public and private collections, including Pemberton Securities Ltd., *Reader's Digest* (Canada), Yukon Territorial Government, Canadian Airlines International, ESSO Resources, Teleglobe, Amax Corporation, University of Alberta, Firestone, Interprovincial Pipeline, and Petrocan. *Military service:* British Army, Intelligence Corps, 1945-48; became sergeant. *Member:* Writer's Union of Canada, National Society of Art Education (United Kingdom).

AWARDS, HONORS: Children of the Yukon was named one of Child Study Association of America's Best Children's Books of the Year, 1977, and a Choice Book by the Children's Book Centre (Toronto), and one of Eight Canadian Books for Choice List by the International Youth Library for the 29th Annual International Exhibition, both 1978; Amelia Frances Howard-Gibbon Award runner-up from the Canadian Association of Children's Librarians, and Choice Book from the Children's Book Centre (Toronto), both 1982, and International Board of Books for Young People Honor List for Illustration, 1984, all for *A Northern Alphabet; The Cremation of Sam McGee* was selected one of *New York Times* Best Illustrated Books, 1987; Order of Canada, 1987.

WRITINGS:

UNDER NAME TED HARRISON

Children of the Yukon (juvenile; self-illustrated), Tundra, 1977.
The Last Horizon (adult), Merritt (Canada), 1980.
A Northern Alphabet (juvenile; self-illustrated), Tundra, 1982.
The Blue Raven (juvenile), Macmillan of Canada, 1989.

ILLUSTRATOR

Robert W. Service, *The Cremation of Sam McGee* (juvenile), Kids Can Press, 1986, Greenwillow, 1987.
R. W. Service, *The Shooting of Dan McGrew* (juvenile), Kids Can Press, 1987.

WORK IN PROGRESS: Illustrations for an educational videotape on the North for the National Film Board of Canada; an animated movie based on *The Blue Raven* to be produced by Intelevision Ltd., Toronto, Canada.

SIDELIGHTS: "Having been a teacher for twenty-nine years, I am interested in what motivates children to read and to learn. I consider the education and the educators of youth as vital concerns for humanity and its future. I abhor negativism in society and individuals, and regard the arts as a civilizing influence to be fostered. Good taste is paramount as is the cultivation of happiness and hopefulness.

"I was born in a coal mining town in England and have sought color, fresh air, and fantasy ever since. I have traveled and lived in India, Egypt, Kenya, Uganda, Malaysia, New Zealand, and Britain. I love to visit Germany and Austria and have visited Australia, Thailand, and Canada from east to west. I was the first European to paint the Buddha in a Chinese temple; I have danced a 'rongeng' in front of the King and Queen of Thailand and once had the occasion to design a national emblem of Thailand in paper sculpture for their majesties King Bumiphol and Queen Sirikit when they visited the Cameron Highland, Malaysia during the early 1960s. I was the first Canadian illustrator to have work shown at the Bologna Children's Book Fair. Designing the facade for the Yukon pavilion for 'Expo '86' in Vancouver, British Columbia was a recent enjoyable task.

"I originally began writing because the material being used to teach second-grade Cree children was highly unsuitable. They were being introduced to a white, middle-class world aeons removed from their experience. At first I manipulated stories to 'Indianize' them, but I was later forced to write about the culture and environment that surrounded and enveloped the reserve.

"I have been interested in art from my early days in an English elementary school. This interest ultimately enabled me to enter art school. However, my training was so rigorous and academic that I lost interest in painting until I left New Zealand in 1965. It was not until I moved to Carcross with my wife, Nicky and son, Charles, that I really became seriously interested in painting.

"My whole style changed to one more simple and colorful. Now I enjoy illustrating in the same bold vigorous style I have developed, and constantly seek new themes to explore.

"I feel that good illustration should leave something to the reader's imagination and increase their enjoyment of the text. It is through our imaginations that life can become more interesting.

"Children's literature, in my opinion, is extremely important as it encompasses a time when the mind is receptive to new experiences and can be encouraged to enjoy the world of books. Every little effort to reduce hatred, bigotry, racism, and selfishness in the world helps to widen the gap between civilized behavior and sheer barbarism. Good books can help."

HOBBIES AND OTHER INTERESTS: Reading (especially spy stories), fishing, spending time at our Carcross cabin, walking, traveling, lecturing on literature and art.

Talk of your cold! through the parka's fold it stabbed like a driven nail. ■ (From *The Cremation of Sam McGee* by Robert W. Service. Illustrated by Ted Harrison.)

FOR MORE INFORMATION SEE:

Northern Review, summer, 1988 (p. 90).

COLLECTIONS

De Grummond Collection at the University of Southern Mississippi.

HASSALL, Joan   1906-1988

OBITUARY NOTICE—See sketch in *SATA* Volume 43: Born March 3, 1906, in London, England; died March 6, 1988, in England. Wood engraver and illustrator. Hassall's illustrations earned her a reputation as one of the most accomplished of wood engravers in England. She was best known for her illustrations for the novels of Jane Austin, published by the Folio Society. Her father, John Hassall, was a prominent Edwardian poster artist and her brother, Christopher Hassall, was a well-known poet who helped to launch her professional career. "My first commission," said Hassall, "was. . .for my brother's book, *Devil's Dyke* after which I did not lack work." Since that first commission, Hassall illustrated more than forty books with engravings, woodcuts, and scraper-board, including Stevenson's *Child's Garden of Verses,* Whitlock's *All Day Long,* and Opies' *Oxford Book of Nursery Rhymes.*

Her work brought her numerous awards. In 1972, she became the first woman elected Master of Art Workers Guild. She was awarded a Bronze Medal for wood engraving in 1973 from the Paris Salon and an OBE (Order of the British Empire) in 1987.

FOR MORE INFORMATION SEE:

Bertha M. Miller, editor, *Illustrators of Children's Books: 1946-1956,* Horn Book, 1958.
M. S. Crouch, "Masters of Images," *The Junior Bookshelf,* August, 1988.

HEINLEIN, Robert A(nson)   1907-1988 (Anson MacDonald, Lyle Monroe, John Riverside, Caleb Saunders, Simon York)

OBITUARY NOTICE—See sketch in *SATA* 9: Surname rhymes with "fine line"; born July 7 (one source says October 21), 1907, in Butler, Mo.; died of heart failure, May 8 (one source says May 7), 1988, in Carmel, Calif.; cremated and ashes scattered at sea with military honors. Engineer and author. Considered one of the world's most creative and influential writers of science fiction, Heinlein authored more than forty-five books, some of which were made into motion pictures. His novels have been published in at least thirty languages and have sold more than forty million copies.

Ranked with Isaac Asimov and Arthur C. Clarke as a master of the science-fiction genre, Heinlein has been lauded for his ability to create entire societies in economical but convincing detail. He began to publish novels for young people in the 1940s. "When an editor assigned me the task of writing a juvenile novel," said Heinlein, "I entered the field with determination not to 'write down' to children." His fictional writings have often anticipated scientific and technical advances. Heinlein's stories introduced readers to such future commonplaces as waterbeds, atomic power plants, time travel and sex changes.

Prior to turning to writing full time, Heinlein worked as an architect, real estate agent, aeronautical engineer, and electronics company official, and he owned a silver mine. He also served as an aviation engineer with the U. S. Navy during World War II, a period in which he wrote several engineering textbooks. He once said that he had been "influenced by. . .everything I have ever seen, touched, eaten, endured, heard and read." Among Heinlein's most popular titles are *Strange Land, Double Star, The Green Hills of Earth, Citizen of the Galaxy, Day after Tomorrow,* and *Door into Summer.* Heinlein was also the author of two screenplays and contributor of many short stories and articles, some under pseudonyms, to *Saturday Evening Post, Analog, Galaxy, Astounding Science Fiction,* and other publications. Among his many awards and honors were four Best Science-Fiction Novel Awards from the World Science Fiction Convention in 1956, 1959, 1961, and 1966; an unprecedented four Hugo Awards, the "Oscars" of science-fiction writing; and the first Grand Master Nebula Award, given to him in 1975 by the Science Fiction Writers of America for his lifelong contribution to the genre. Heinlein was also a guest commentator with CBS-TV reporter Walter Cronkite during the Apollo space mission that put the first man on the moon.

FOR MORE INFORMATION SEE:

Who's Who in the World, 8th edition, Marquis, 1986.
Current Biography, H. W. Wilson, 1988.

OBITUARIES

Washington Post, May 10, l988.
Detroit News, May 10, 1988.
Los Angeles Times, May 10, l988.
New York Times, May 10, 1988.
Chicago Tribune, May 11, 1988.
Times (London), May 11, 1988.
Time (magazine), May 23, 1988.

HENSCHEL, (Elizabeth) Georgie

PERSONAL: Born in London, England; daughter of George (a musician) and Amy (a singer; maiden name, Louis) Henschel. *Education:* Studied in London, France, and Germany. *Home and office:* Ballintean, Kincraig, Kingussie, Invernessshire, Scotland.

CAREER: British Broadcasting Corp., London, England, overseas announcer, 1940-46; British Council, London, lecturer in Scandinavia, Finland, Switzerland, and the Netherlands, 1946-57; actress and writer, 1957—. Stud owner, riding instructor and dressage judge. *Member:* British Horse Society, British Equestrian Writers Association. *Awards, honors:* Cubith Award for services to pony club.

WRITINGS:

The Well-Dressed Woman, Phoenix House, 1955.
Careers with Horses, Stanley Paul, 1966.
Thomas, Werner Classen (Switzerland), 1977.
Illustrated Guide to Horses and Ponies, Ward, Lock, 1981.
Basic Riding Explained, Ward, Lock, 1981.
Kingfisher Guide to Horses and Ponies, Ward, Lock, 1981.
All about Your Pony (juvenile), Ward, Lock, 1982.
Horses and Ponies, Deans International, 1983.
Horses and Riding, F. Watts, 1986.

Author of series, "Murder after Dinner," broadcast by Swedish Radio. Contributor to British equestrian magazines, including *Riding, Horse and Hound, Pony Club,* and *Dressage.*

This young rider has been lucky enough to win a red rosette which is just visible on the pony's bridle. ■ (From *Horses and Riding* by Georgie Henschel.)

WORK IN PROGRESS: A book about her father, the first conductor of the Boston Symphony Orchestra, and herself.

SIDELIGHTS: "I began my career as a singer and gave several recitals in London, and then became the first woman announcer on the British Broadcasting Overseas Service. Since 1946 I have worked as a free-lance actress and writer.

"I always loved horses and riding; I first rode at age seven. On the death of my mother in 1956, I returned to live in Scotland and started a riding school and a stud of Highland ponies. I feel that today there is perhaps too much emphasis on competitive riding and not enough on the pleasure young people (and old) can get from riding and horses.

"I was encouraged to write about horses and ponies by Elweyn Hautly Edwards then of *Riding* magazine, and have done so now for some twenty years. I have always enjoyed writing.

"So many people own horses nowadays and know nothing about them! They try to ride without knowing how, and I feel compelled, for the sake of innumerable horses, to try to help them."

HOBBIES AND OTHER INTERESTS: Reading, travelling when possible.

HIRSCHI, Ron   1948-

PERSONAL: Name pronounced ''Hershey''; born May 18, 1948, in Bremerton, Wash.; son of Glenn W. (a lumbermill mechanic) and Doris (a homemaker; maiden name, Hoffman) Hirschi; married Brenda Dahl (a grocery clerk), July 19, 1969; children: Nichol. *Education:* University of Washington, B.S., 1974, graduate research in wildlife ecology, 1974-76. *Politics:* Independent. *Religion:* Independent. *Home:* 7003 NE Eisenhardt, Poulsbo, Wash. 98370. *Office:* Point No Point Treaty Council, 7850 NE Little Boston Rd., Kingston, Wash. 98346.

CAREER: Washington Game Department, Seattle, Wash., biologist, 1976-81; North Kitsap Schools, Poulsbo, Wash., counselor in Indian education program, 1984-85; author, 1985—; Point No Point Treaty Council, Kingston, Wash., biologist, 1988—. *Awards, honors: Headgear* and *One Day on Pika's Peak* were each chosen one of Child Study Association of America's Children's Books of the Year, 1986; Outstanding Science Trade Book for Children from the National Science Teachers Association, 1986, for *Headgear,* and 1987, for *City Geese, Who Lives in. . .the Forest,* and *What Is a Bird?*

WRITINGS:

JUVENILE

Headgear (illustrated with photographs by Galen Burrell), Dodd, 1986.

One Day on Pika's Peak (illustrated with photographs by G. Burrell), Dodd, 1986.

City Geese (illustrated with photographs by G. Burrell), Dodd, 1987.

What Is a Bird?, Walker, 1987.

Where Do Birds Live?, Walker, 1987.

The Mountain Bluebird, Dodd, 1988.

What Is a Horse, Walker, 1989.

Where Do Horses Live, Walker, 1989.

''WHERE ANIMALS LIVE'' SERIES

Who Lives in. . .the Forest? (illustrated with photographs by G. Burrell), Dodd, 1987.

Who Lives in. . .Alligator Swamp? (illustrated with photographs by G. Burrell), Dodd, 1987.

Who Lives in. . .the Mountains?, Putnam, 1988.

Who Lives on the Prairie?, Putnam, 1988.

Contributor to periodicals, including *Owl.*

WORK IN PROGRESS: A series of children's books for Dutton which will explore the seasons with a focus on wildlife and changing needs, colors, and conditions. ''As in many of my books, the relationship between animal and landscape is the emphasis''; another series of books for Bantam which are fun looks at several different landscapes. ''By asking 'Who am I?' the reader is invited into the landscapes to discover many animals that make up the community within each special place being explored. These will be illustrated graphically, my first non-photo illustrated books''; several other ideas, trying to create new ways to introduce young people to wildlife and wild places.

SIDELIGHTS: ''When I was growing up, I spent *all* my free time in the woods, at the beach, or out on the water in boats my father made for me. It was a wonderful childhood and a great way to learn about animals and their needs. So, I guess it was quite natural for me to major in wildlife ecology in college and when I graduated from the University of Washington, I worked as a wildlife biologist.

''It took a lot of work to get to college, work on my part and on the part of my wife, Brenda. We married young and since

RON HIRSCHI

Like weathered stones, these sheep are a part of the windswept ridges. ■ (From *Headgear* by Ron Hirschi. Photograph by Galen Burrell.)

we had little help from our family, I worked forty hours a week at night (at the post office) while attending college full time. Those were days during which we really appreciated any free time we had. Our daughter, Nichol, was born during the first years of my college career and the three of us often snuck away into the mountains to be together and to be in a place with wildflowers, clean air, and chipmunks. We also spent a lot of time in city parks near the University of Washington where I went to school. The inspiration for my book *City Geese* came from those days spent feeding geese and watching them in their city home.

"I also think that the inspiration to write children's books came during those years. Even though it was more than ten years before I even thought about writing as a profession, I did start creating stories for my daughter as she turned one, then two, then quickly five, then. . . .I really became enchanted by children's books as I read stories to Nichol, stories by Russell Hoban and Leo Lionni and Brooke Goffstein. Without realizing it, I became a student of children's literature as I bought books for Nichol and read and re-read them, carefully tracing the wonderful relationship between word and image.

"After college, I worked as a biologist, spending much time out in the field doing studies of relationships between plants and animals. I spent a lot of time writing reports too, especially reports that had an educational value. It seemed to me that there was a large gap between scientific knowledge and public knowledge. So, I tried to bridge gaps in as many ways as possible. I wrote some pamphlets, appeared occasionally on television, and wrote some natural history booklets for the local Audubon Society publication. Little by little, I was becoming a full-time writer.

"Still working as a biologist, I got involved in one project that changed my life. In the Pacific Northwest, where I was

working, people log forests as if no other forms of life need the trees. In the middle of a study in which we were trying to show otherwise, I got an idea. Here we were battling with words about the need to keep a few trees along streams (trees are important for fish and other wildlife, especially trees growing right at the bank of a river) and no one seemed to listen to scientific evidence. So, I thought, what if the trout really lived in the trees? What if a logger cut down a tree and the poor fish fell from the treetops? Then, I asked myself, would people see that trees were important for fish? So, I wrote a story called 'A Trout in Every Tree.'

"Even though that story has never been published, it inspired me to pursue a career as a writer. First, a few articles were published in local newspapers and fishing magazines. I am very proud of some of those articles since they attempt to show people the relationships between their actions and environmental consequences. And, the fishing articles also show fishers of trout that trees are important if they want to keep catching fish in the future.

"I submitted 'A Trout in Every Tree' and several other fiction picture book manuscripts to publishers. Actually, I submitted them to many, many publishers. Rejection slips piled up. I can't believe that didn't discourage me. Regardless, I was being published in children's magazines and I especially loved the work I did with *Owl*, the publication of the Canadian Young Naturalist Foundation.

"One idea I submitted to *Owl* was about horns and antlers. My editor, Sylvia Funston, thought it wasn't quite right for the magazine, but she liked the concept and wrote a few thoughts that triggered my imagination enough to rewrite the idea as a nonfiction book. Two or three months later, Rosanne Lauer at Dodd, Mead accepted the manuscript and *Headgear* became my first published book!

"Now, I write nonfiction almost exclusively. I still pursue some fiction and will have a picture book or two published in the near future. But, I remain a biologist and have a strong need to communicate through children's books all the ideas I have about our relationship with animals and the land.

"When I think about the inspiration for my books, the connection with my childhood experiences always come through. But, my recent experiences as a biologist are also important in shaping the book themes. For example, my series, 'Where Animals Live,' is based on a set of books I did for adults during the time I worked with the Washington Game Department.

"Still, I am intrigued by the way new ideas spring up every day. In the past few years I have spent a lot of time in the schools and I love the way kids respond to questions and talk about animals. Those days with students have shown me some ways to create books that allow the reader to participate more fully. That is one reason I write books with questions as titles and the main reason the text often asks questions, too.

"I have a lot of fun doing research for books since I get to spend a lot of time out in the mountains, at the beach, or in boats. Research for *The Mountain Bluebird* was especially enjoyable since my wife came along much of the time. We traveled to Montana and Wyoming several times to watch bluebirds at their nests, during migration, and in the late days of summer. During one of those trips to watch bluebirds, we camped in the Pryor Mountains of Montana. One morning, we followed some birds up a narrow canyon into the higher hills. On our walk back we heard horses. These weren't just

JUDY TAYLOR HOUGH

any horses though—they were wild horses, the first we had ever seen.

"I was overwhelmed on seeing the Pryor Mountain horses and have spent many days since then following them. I also began taking more photographs than I used to and enjoying that aspect of book creation. But, I usually rely on other photographers or illustrators to provide images for books and am working with a very talented photographer, Linda Younker, on two horse books published by Walker in 1989.

"As in my other books, the horse books attempt to bring us a little closer together—us, meaning the other creatures we share our world with as well as all the people, young and old.

"In June, 1988 I returned to work as a wildlife biologist after almost eight years away from the profession. I accepted an exciting job that allows me to work in the area in which I grew up. I have a little less time for writing now, but the job has inspired many new story ideas. I work for the Klallam Indian Tribe, attempting to protect their treaty rights to fish and wildlife, especially during logging activities. Once again, I am protecting trees along streams and the trout, salmon, eagles and other wildlife that need trees and healthy streams.

"The Klallam people lived in this area long before white people arrived and they have wonderful stories that tell of our relationship with animals and the land. As I listen to their stories, I realize the richness of their culture and I also realize how important it is to protect their way of life. One way they have of showing the relationships within their world is story. Another is artforms like the totem pole. Actually, the poles combine story and art in a way similar to a picture book. And, I hope to show this similarity in a picture book I am thinking about, one which combines images of people, animals, and creativity in a new way."

HOBBIES AND OTHER INTERESTS: "I enjoy spending extra time flyfishing; walking my dog, Swimmer; growing flowers; cooking; eating my daughter's pastries; and looking for special places to explore in Montana."

HOUGH, Judy Taylor 1932-
(Judy Taylor)

PERSONAL: Surname rhymes with "plow"; born August 12, 1932, in Murton near Swansea, South Wales; adopted daughter of Gladys Spicer Taylor (a teacher); married Richard Hough (a writer and naval historian), June 6, 1980. *Education:* Educated until the age of sixteen in the United Kingdom. *Politics:* Socialist. *Religion:* Church of England. *Home and office:* 31 Meadowbank, Primrose Hill, London NW3 1AY, England.

CAREER: Bodley Head, London, England, general assistant, 1951-55, specialist in children's books, 1955-80, director, 1967-84, deputy managing director, 1971-80; Chatto, Bodley Head & Jonathan Cape Ltd., London, England, director, 1973-80; Chatto, Bodley Head & Jonathan Cape Australia Pty Ltd., Sydney, Australia, and London, England, director, 1977-80; Frederick Warne, London, England, consultant on the licensing and commercial use of Beatrix Potter's creations, 1981—; writer, 1982—; Weston Woods Institute, Weston, Conn., associate director, 1984—. *Member:* Publishers Association (chairman of children's book group, 1969-72; member of council, 1972-78). *Awards, honors:* Member of the Order of the British Empire for services to children's literature, 1971.

WRITINGS:

ALL UNDER NAME JUDY TAYLOR

My First Year: A Beatrix Potter Baby Book, Warne, 1983.
Beatrix Potter: Artist, Storyteller, and Countrywoman, Warne (England), 1986, Warne (U.S.), 1987.

That Naughty Rabbit: Beatrix Potter and Peter Rabbit, Warne, 1987.
(With others) *Beatrix Potter, 1866-1943: The Artist and Her World*, Warne, 1988.
The Selected Letters of Beatrix Potter, Warne, 1989.

"SOPHIE AND JACK" SERIES; JUVENILE; ALL UNDER NAME JUDY TAYLOR; ALL ILLUSTRATED BY SUSAN GANTNER

Sophie and Jack, Bodley Head, 1982, Philomel, 1983.
Sophie and Jack Help Out, Bodley Head, 1983, Philomel, 1984.
Sophie and Jack in the Snow, Bodley Head, 1984.
Sophie and Jack in the Rain, Bodley Head, 1989.

"DUDLEY DORMOUSE" SERIES; JUVENILE; ALL UNDER NAME JUDY TAYLOR; ALL ILLUSTRATED BY PETER CROSS

Dudley Goes Flying, Putnam, 1986.
Dudley and the Monster, Putnam, 1986.
Dudley in a Jam, Walker, 1986, Putnam, 1987.
Dudley and the Strawberry Shake, Walker, 1986, Putnam, 1987.
Dudley Bakes a Cake, Putnam, 1988.

SIDELIGHTS: "I've worked in the children's book field all my life, first as an editor and publisher, now as a writer. My interest in Beatrix Potter began at my mother's knee, and continued through my collecting early children's books and my love of the Lake District where I was at boarding school. Now I'm inextricably involved!"

And Dudley had settled down for his long winter sleep before the jam had even begun to cool. ■ (From *Dudley in a Jam* by Judy Taylor. Illustrated by Peter Cross.)

HOBBIES AND OTHER INTERESTS: Collecting early children's books, gardening.

FOR MORE INFORMATION SEE:

Publishers Weekly, July 22, 1983 (p. 78), September 25, 1987 (p. 25).
Robert D. Hale, "Musings," *Horn Book*, January, 1988 (p. 100).

KAYE, Marilyn 1949- (Shannon Blair)

PERSONAL: Born July 19, 1949, in New Britain, Conn.; daughter of Harold Stanley (a retired microbiologist) and Annette (Rudman) Kaye. *Education:* Emory University, B.A., 1971, M.L.S., 1974; University of Chicago, Ph.D., 1983. *Politics:* Democrat. *Religion:* Jewish. *Residence:* Brooklyn, N.Y. *Agent:* Amy Berkower, Writers' House, Inc., 21 West 26th St., New York, N.Y. 10010. *Office:* Division of Library and Information Science, St. John's University, Grand Central and Utopia Parkways, Jamaica, N.Y. 11439.

CAREER: Library Quarterly, Chicago, Ill., editorial assistant, 1977-79; University of South Carolina, Columbia, instructor in library science, 1980-82; St. John's University, Jamaica, N.Y., began as instructor, associate professor in library and information science, 1982-86, professor of library and information science, 1986—. *Member:* American Library Association (chairman of Notable Children's Books committee, 1981-82), Beta Phi Mu. *Awards, honors: Will You Cross Me?* was selected one of Child Study Association of America's Children's Books of the Year, 1985; Children's Choice from the International Reading Association and the Children's Book Council, 1986, for *Wrong Kind of Boy*.

WRITINGS:

JUVENILE

Will You Cross Me? (illustrated by Ned Delaney), Harper, 1985.
Baby Fozzie Is Afraid of the Dark (illustrated by Tom Brannon), Weekly Readers Books, 1986.

"HELLO READER" MINI-SERIES

The Best Babysitter in the World (illustrated by Lauren Attinello), Scholastic, 1987.
Miss Piggy and the Big Gorilla (illustrated by L. Attinello), Scholastic, 1988.

"SISTERS" SERIES

Phoebe, Harcourt, 1987.
Daphne (Junior Literary Guild selection), Harcourt, 1987.
Lydia, Harcourt, 1987.
Cassie, Harcourt, 1987.

"ZOOBILEE ZOO" SERIES

Zoobilee Zoo: Big Mess (illustrated by Carol Hudson), Scholastic, 1987.

YOUNG ADULT NOVELS; "OUT OF THIS WORLD" SERIES

Max on Earth, Archway, 1986.
Max in Love, Archway, 1986.
Max on Fire, Archway, 1986.
Max Flips Out, Archway, 1986.
Max Goes Bad, Puffin, in press.
Max All Over, Puffin, in press.

MARILYN KAYE

UNDER PSEUDONYM SHANNON BLAIR

Call Me Beautiful, Bantam, 1984.
Star Struck!, Bantam, 1985.
Wrong Kind of Boy, Bantam, 1985.
Kiss and Tell, Bantam, 1985.

OTHER

(Editor with Betsy Hearne) *Celebrating Children's Books: Essays on Children's Literature in Honor of Zena Sutherland,* Lothrop, 1981.

Contributor of articles and reviews to library journals and newspapers, including *Booklist, New York Times Book Review,* and *Top of the News.* Editor of *Top of the News* (journal of the Association of Library Service to Children and Young Adult Services), 1982-84.

WORK IN PROGRESS: More stories in the "Sisters" series; a series about a group of girls at a sleepaway summer camp; a young adult novel dealing with a conflict of values in a family setting; a story for young readers about a tooth fairy; a "Hello Reader" book about Gonzo.

SIDELIGHTS: "I've been writing ever since I could make words out of letters and sentences out of words. As a child, I had fantasies of becoming a real professional writer when I grew up. But then, I also had fantasies of becoming a ballerina, a rock star, an airline stewardess, and the woman on television game shows who points at the prizes.

"My career options narrowed when it became apparent that I couldn't dance or sing, and that I was afraid of heights. I was also prone to extensive daydreaming, and I knew this would limit my potential as a television game show hostess.

"That left writing. Still, even though I liked writing, I couldn't really imagine anyone other than parents, teachers, and best friends wanting to read what I wrote. So I put my writing ambitions on the back burner, and channeled my love for books in other directions. After a while, I stopped thinking about writing.

"In college, I majored in English. Then I took a graduate degree in library science, and became a children's librarian. I enjoyed this, and I knew I belonged in the world of children, books, and libraries, but something was missing. I went back to school for a Ph.D., and then I became a teacher of children's literature. Now I was even closer to where I wanted to be—but still, something was missing.

"Still trying to figure out what that something was, I became more involved. I wrote articles about children and literature, I reviewed children's books, I went to children's literature conferences and meetings and discussion groups, and I served on committees that chose the best children's books of the year. And I was having a wonderful time. But every now and then, I'd think about that elusive something that I wasn't doing, something I was supposed to be doing.

"Then, one day, I remembered. I had been working on an article about the revival of teenage romances, and thinking about how much I'd enjoyed books like that when I was young. At the same time, a friend told me about an experience her teenage daughter was encountering. And all of a sudden, I knew I had a story to write.

"I wrote *Call Me Beautiful* under another name, Shannon Blair. I was still feeling insecure as a writer, and I thought I'd feel more comfortable hiding behind a pseudonym. But after writing three more books as Shannon Blair, I realized there were readers out there who liked what I was writing. And I felt brave enough to come out and take the credit—or the blame.

"I know there are many critics who think teenage romances are trivial and a waste of time. Obviously, I'm not one of them. I think we all need light, entertaining, escapist fiction. And just as I enjoyed reading these books when I was younger, I enjoyed writing them as an adult.

"After writing four romance books, I was ready to try something else. I created a series, 'Out of This World,' about an adolescent girl, Max, from another planet who comes to Earth and tries to fit in.

"Everytime I finish a book, or a series, I want to try something different. I've written some books for very young children, including books based on Muppet characters. And my most recent books are 'middle-grade' stories of contemporary family life. The 'Sisters' series deals with four very different siblings, their situations and their relationships.

"I suppose, in a way, there's something all my books have in common, and that's the fact that they were all written from my own experiences. No, I don't come from a family of four sisters, and I was never an alien or a Muppet. But every feeling I've written about, I've experienced. And I think that feelings—motives, reactions, responses, concerns—these are the core to any work of fiction.

"I write a lot. And when I'm not working on a book, I feel strange, the way I might feel if I wasn't eating or sleeping. That's why, when I'm not working on a book of my own, I'll write books for popular series. I've written books for the 'Couples' and 'Sweet Valley Twins' series and I've had fun doing them.

"Of course, I'm happiest when working on my own ideas, the stories and characters I've invented. And I'm always thinking about something different to try. Right now, I'm working on

(From *Will You Cross Me?* by Marilyn Kaye. Illustrated by Ned Delaney.)

an idea for an adult novel. But even if I decide to give it a shot, I don't think I'll ever stop writing children's books. I guess it's because the child in me is close to the surface, and she knows all the best stories.''

HOBBIES AND OTHER INTERESTS: Travel, listening to music (especially rock and rhythm and blues).

FOR MORE INFORMATION SEE:

Jim Roginski, editor, *Behind the Covers: Interviews with Authors and Illustrators of Children's and Young Adult Books,* Volume 2, Libraries Unlimited, 1989.

KEEPING, Charles (William James) 1924-1988

OBITUARY NOTICE—See sketch in *SATA* 9: Born September 22, 1924, in Lambeth, London, England; died May 16, 1988. Educator, artist, illustrator, and author. Widely regarded as the most brilliant and original British children's illustrator of his generation, Keeping also attracted considerable criticism for the often morbid quality of his pictures and for his routine rejection of conventional narrative. Leaving school at age fourteen, Keeping became a printer's apprentice, then served as a naval wireless operator in World War II. After the war he became a student at Regent Street Polytechnic, working in drawing, etching, engraving, and lithography. His lithographs

have been exhibited in several countries, and a number of museums and galleries own his work.

Keeping began work as an illustrator in 1956, commissioned by the Oxford University Press to illustrate stories by children's book author Rosemary Sutcliff. Among Keeping's other illustrations and drawings are two retellings of the Greek myths by Leon Garfield and Edward Blishen, *The God beneath the Sea* and *The Golden Shadow*; Alfred Noyes's poem *The Highwayman*, which won Keeping the 1982 Kate Greenaway Medal from the British Library Association (his second); and the Folio Society's *Complete Dickens*, which he began illustrating in 1981. His own picture books began to appear in the mid-1960s. Titles include: *Charley, Charlotte and the Golden Canary*, for which he received the 1968 Kate Greenaway Medal, *Joseph's Yard, Through the Window, The Spider's Web, The Railway Passage*, and *Willie's Fire Engine*—all closely based on the experiences of his own city childhood. ''I always had to stay in this little yard,'' said Keeping. In his yard, he ''watched spiders and flies and all sorts of things. . . .And all the while I was on my own, thinking.''

Besides illustrating books, Keeping was a visiting lecturer at several British art schools; created advertising art, wall murals, posters, comic strips, and book jackets; and worked on children's films for television. He was also runner-up for the 1974 Hans Christian Andersen International Children's Book Medal, awarded biennially for the most distinguished contribution to international children's literature.

FOR MORE INFORMATION SEE:

Who's Who, 139th edition, St. Martin's, 1987.
M. S. Crouch, "Makers of Images," *Junior Bookshelf*, August, 1988.

OBITUARIES

Times (London), May 20, 1988.
School Library Journal, August, 1988.

LANDON, Lucinda 1950-

PERSONAL: Born August 15, 1950, in Galesburg, Ill.; daughter of Roy Ned (a writer) and Barbara (Miner) Landon; married James Alan Egan (a photographer), August 27, 1977; children: Alexander, Eric. *Education:* John Cass School of Art, 1971; St. Lawrence University, B.A., 1972; attended Rhode Island School of Design, 1976-79. *Home:* 26 Tucker Hollow Rd., North Scituate, R.I. 02857. *Office:* Visualizations, 150 Chestnut St., Providence, R.I. 02903.

CAREER: Boston Center for the Arts, Boston, Mass., advertising assistant, 1974-75; special education teacher in Cambridge, Mass., 1975-76; Visualizations, Providence, R.I., artist, 1978—. *Awards, honors:* Special Edgar Allan Poe Award from the Mystery Writers of America, 1981, for illustrating *The Young Detective's Handbook*.

WRITINGS:

"MEG MACKINTOSH" SERIES; JUVENILE; SELF-ILLUSTRATED

Meg Mackintosh and the Case of the Missing Babe Ruth Baseball, Little, Brown, 1987.

LUCINDA LANDON

Meg Mackintosh and the Case of the Curious Whale Watch, Little, Brown, 1987.
Meg Mackintosh and the Mystery at the Medieval Castle, Little, Brown, 1989.

ILLUSTRATOR

William V. Butler, *The Young Detective's Handbook*, Atlantic Monthly Press, 1981.

WORK IN PROGRESS: Additional titles in the "Meg Mackintosh" mystery series, a series of illustrated, solve-it-yourself mysteries, with clues in the illustrations, for readers aged seven to nine, for Little, Brown.

SIDELIGHTS: "Writing the 'Meg Mackintosh' series gives me the opportunity to combine my love of drawing and mysteries. It's fun to design books with the clues hidden in both the text and the black and white illustrations. The reader is invited to match wits with Meg and try to solve the case by answering questions posed throughout the books. Meg's grandfather, her older brother Peter, and their dog Skip also help—and hinder—the process."

LEWIS, Mary (Christianna) 1907(?)-1988 (Mary Ann Ashe, Christianna Brand, Annabel Jones, Mary Roland, China Thompson)

OBITUARY NOTICE: Born December 17, 1907 (one source says 1909), in Malaya; died March 11, 1988. Author. Best known for her detective stories featuring Inspector Cockrill of the Kent County Police, Lewis wrote under various pseudonyms a number of adult mystery and suspense novels. She also wrote several children's books, notably a "Nurse Matilda" series of comic tales about a nanny; *The Brides of Aberdar*, a ghost story; and *Heaven Knows Who*, a nonfictional account of a nineteenth-century murder in Scotland. Furthermore, Lewis contributed to the anthology *Best Police Stories* and to various periodicals, including *Chicago Tribune, Saturday Evening Post*, and *Ellery Queen's Mystery Magazine*. Two of her stories won awards from the Mystery Writers of America. Prior to writing full time, Lewis worked at a number of odd jobs, among them governess, receptionist, dancer, model, sales clerk, and secretary. "We are what we remember," she once said. "We become a sort of sponge that soaks up our experience and emerges in what we have to say."

FOR MORE INFORMATION SEE:

Twentieth-Century Crime and Mystery Writers, 2nd edition, St. Martin's, 1985.

OBITUARIES

Times (London), March 14, 1988.

LLOYD WEBBER, Andrew 1948-

PERSONAL: Born March 22, 1948, in London, England; son of William Southcombe (a composer, director of the London College of Music, C.B.E. [Commander of the British Empire]) and Jean Hermione (a piano teacher; maiden name, Johnstone) Lloyd Webber; married Sarah Jane Tudor Hugill (a singer, clarinetist and pianist), July 24, 1971 (divorced, 1983); married Sarah Brightman (a singer and actress), March 22, 1984; children: (first marriage) Imogen, Nicholas. *Education:* At-

ANDREW LLOYD WEBBER

tended Oxford University, 1965, Guildhall School of Music and Drama, 1966-67, and Royal College of Music, 1967-68. *Religion:* Church of England. *Office:* 20 Greek St., London, W1V 5LF, England.

CAREER: Composer, author, and producer. The Really Useful Theatre Company (now The Really Useful Group), London, England, founder and non-executive director, 1978—. *Awards, honors:* Drama Desk Award, 1971, for "Jesus Christ Superstar"; Gold Record, London, 1977, for "Variations"; New York Drama Critics Circle Award for Best Musical, 1979, for "Evita"; Antoinette Perry "Tony" Award (two awards) for "Evita," 1980, (two awards) for "Cats," 1982, (seven awards, including Best Musical) for "The Phantom of the Opera," 1988; Grammy Award from the National Academy of Recording Arts and Sciences, 1981, for Best Cast Show Album of the Year, "Evita," and 1986, for Best Classical Contemporary Composition, "Requiem"; Lawrence Olivier Award, *Plays and Players* Award, and *London Standard* Award all for Best Musical, all 1986, all for "The Phantom of the Opera."

WRITINGS:

(With Tim Rice) *Evita: The Legend of Eva Peron, 1919-1952,* Drama Book Specialists, 1978.
(With T. Rice) *Joseph and the Amazing Technicolor Dreamcoat* (illustrated by Quentin Blake), Holt, 1982.
Cats: The Book of the Musical (photographs and drawings by John Napier), Faber & Faber, 1981, Harcourt, 1983.

PLAYS; COMPOSER OF STAGE SCORES

"Joseph and the Amazing Technicolor Dreamcoat" (lyrics by T. Rice), first produced at St. Paul's Junior School, London, 1968; first produced in America at the College of the Immaculate Conception, Douglaston, N.Y., 1970; also produced at the Albery, London, 1973, at the Brooklyn Academy of Music, December 23, 1976, at Entermedia Theatre (off-Broadway), and the Royale Theater (Broadway), November 18, 1981.
(With T. Rice) "Jesus Christ Superstar" (adapted from the Gospels), produced at Mark Hellinger Theatre, New York, October 12, 1971.

"Jeeves" (lyrics by Alan Ayckbourn), produced in London, 1975.
(With T. Rice) "Evita," produced at the Prince Edward Theatre (starring Elaine Paige and David Essex), London, June 21, 1978, at the Dorothy Chandler Pavilion, Los Angeles, spring, 1979, and Broadway Theatre (starring Patti LuPone and Mandy Patinkin), New York, September 25, 1979.
(And producer) "Cats" (adapted from T. S. Eliot's *Old Possum's Book of Practical Cats;* lyrics by Richard Stilgoe and Trevor Nunn), produced at the Palace Theatre (starring Elaine Paige), London, May 11, 1981, and Winter Garden Theater (starring Betty Buckley), New York, October 7, 1982.
"Song and Dance" (includes "Tell Me on a Sunday" [lyrics by Don Black] and "Variations") produced at Palace Theatre (starring Marti Webb and Wayne Sleep), London, 1982, produced on Broadway at Royale Theater (starring Bernadette Peters and Christopher d'Amboise), September, 1985.
"Starlight Express" (lyrics by R. Stilgoe), produced at Apollo Theatre, London, 1984, and Gershwin Theater, N.Y., 1986.
"The Phantom of the Opera" (based on book by Gaston Leroux; lyrics by Charles Hart and R. Stilgoe; starring wife, Sarah Brightman and Michael Crawford), produced at Her Majesty's Theatre, London, October 9, 1986, and Majestic Theater, N. Y., January 26, 1988.
"Aspects of Love" (lyrics by D. Black and C. Hart), first produced at Prince of Wales Theater, London, April, 1989.

Also composer of several unproduced plays, including "The Likes of Us" (lyrics by T. Rice), "Come Back Richard, Your Country Needs You" (with T. Rice), and "Cricket."

PLAYS; PRODUCER

"Daisy Pulls It Off," produced at Globe Theatre, London, 1983.
"The Hired Man," produced at Astoria Theatre, London, 1984.
"Lend Me a Tenor," produced at Globe Theatre, London, 1986.
"The Resistible Rise of Arturo Ui," produced at Queen's Theatre, London, 1987.

COMPOSITION

Variations (based on A Minor Caprice No. 24 by Paganini), Chappell, 1977.
"Requiem" (first produced at St. Thomas Church, New York City, January, 1985), Angel, 1985.

FILM SCORES

"Gumshoe," Columbia, 1972.
"The Odessa File," Columbia, 1974.

RECORDINGS

"Jesus Christ Superstar" (cast album featuring Yvonne Elliman's "I Don't Know How to Love Him") Decca, 1971, MCA Records, 1973.
"Joseph and the Amazing Technicolor Dreamcoat" (first record of completed work), MCA Records, 1974, (original Broadway cast) Crysalis, 1982.
"Evita" (London cast recording with Julie Covington), MCA Records, 1976, (Broadway cast album featuring Patti LuPone and Mandy Patinkin) MCA Records, 1979.
"Variations" (two recordings), MCA Records, 1978.
"Tell Me on a Sunday" (one-act musical featuring Marti Webb), Polydor, 1980.

"Cats" (London cast album), Geffen Records, 1981, Polydor, 1981, (Broadway cast album featuring Betty Buckley's "Memory"), Geffen Records, 1983.

"Starlight Express" (London cast album), Polydor, 1984, (music and songs from "Starlight Express"), MCA Records, 1987.

"Requiem" (Placido Domingo, Sarah Brightman and the Winchester Cathedral Choir; conducted by Lorin Maazel), EMI Angel, 1985.

"Song and Dance: The Song" (featuring Bernadette Peters), RCA Records, 1985.

"The Phantom of the Opera" (original London cast with Sarah Brightman and Michael Crawford), Polydor, 1987.

TELEVISION

"Tell Me on a Sunday," BBC-TV, 1980.
"Requiem," BBC-TV, 1985.

ADAPTATIONS:

"Joseph and the Amazing Technicolor Dreamcoat" (television), 1972.
"Jesus Christ Superstar," Universal Films, 1973.
"Requiem," American Ballet Theater, Chicago, Ill., February 7, 1986.

SIDELIGHTS: Lloyd Webber was born on **March 22, 1948,** the son of William Southcombe Lloyd Webber and Jean Her-

mione Johnstone. His younger brother, cellist Julian Lloyd Webber, was born in 1951. The family lived in South Kensington, London.

"My family was bohemian. My grandmother on my mother's side was divorced, when such things were quite unfashionable, from someone rather respectable in the Guards. My father's father was a plumber. There was no money on either side of the family, and, even though Granny had a bit of money to send Julian and I to private school, we would not have been able to stay if we hadn't won scholarships.

"My family was very much involved with music. My father was a professor of composition at the Royal College of Music, later becoming the director of the London College of Music. My mother taught privately, uncovering and encouraging children's musical ambitions. And, like all ambitious mums, she pointed me, and a little later Julian, into the direction of a musical instrument.

"I suppose it was natural for her to push us forward. She thought the violin was the instrument for me, but it didn't work out. Going through my old things recently, I was amazed to discover that I got a grade five in the violin when I was six. I can't imagine how, since I can't even remember how to hold one, let alone play it. I had much more fun with the French horn. I also learnt the piano. But I think I realised quite early on that my interest was the theatre, and it was not an area that my parents really knew.

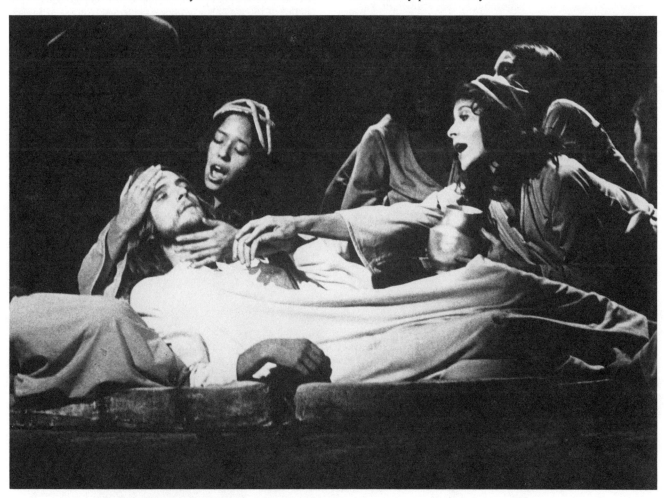

(From the stage production of "Jesus Christ Superstar," starring Jeff Fenholt and Yvonne Elliman. Lyrics and book by Tim Rice, music and orchestration by Andrew Lloyd Webber. Opened October 12, 1971 at the Mark Helliger Theatre.)

"I do know my father had a repressed side of him which liked popular music, though he dared not let it out. It's in his music in spades. He was a frustrated composer, really, but it would have been difficult for him to come out of the woodwork because the music he was writing was, by definition, terribly unfashionable. I think there was an element in him that would have liked the freedom to do what I do, but he was very wrapped up in running the Royal College of Music at the time.

"You have to think of his background. It was entirely working class: the scholarship at thirteen to music college; the feeling that he couldn't let that side down by doing anything out of the mainstream of academic music. Then the Second World War broke out and he had to go into the army; albeit not into the fighting army, but another part of it. There was a bit of resentment in him against people like Benjamin Britten who were allowed to opt out.

"After the war, he felt that composing was no longer possible for him. He was never prepared to take on board a composer like Britten. Probably wrongly, because he and Britten were greatly compared in 1937. With hindsight, I think his real gift was probably something far closer to popular music. He never disliked it. If he heard a tune of Richard Rodgers or a good pop record I might have brought home, he never said he didn't like it. But he never said anything about my music at all. It didn't occur to me that he would.

"I didn't know my father very well. I got to know him a little better when I was in my twenties, but I didn't know him really well until I had written 'Cats' when I was thirty-three.

"I remember listening to a piece he wrote called 'Aurora' on a 78 record. I was very influenced by its romanticism. My father was romantic at a time when romanticism was becoming more and more unfashionable. I wasn't aware of it in him personally, only through the music. Julian and I finally managed to get 'Aurora' included on my album of 'Variations' in 1987 with Julian playing and Lorin Maazel conducting. I think it emerges as a little gem.

"Such was the family background that we were allowed to get on with what we wanted to do in the most productive way. We weren't close to each other, Julian and I. We were united in one thing, which was that we both got a little bit jealous of the fact that John Lill was one of my mother's proteges and we slightly felt that we were no longer 'number one' at one point. But we never really worried about it. My great grandmother was the founder of what was called the Christian Communist Movement: first working in the East End of London, then running a transport cafe in Reading. My mum used to go down and work in Leyton, which is where she came across John, who then came to live with us. He was three or four years older than Julian and myself."

Lloyd Webber composed his first musical, "The Importance of Being Earnest," at age nine. Some of the songs were eventually published in *Music Teacher*. He also constructed his own model theatre, using a gramophone turntable to facilitate smooth scene changes. "My interest was in musical theatre. Luckily, my Aunt Vi, on my mother's side, was an actress, and introduced me to quite a lot of people on the fringe. I began to get a taste for how the theatre worked and how it might work for me. I can remember, very early on, going to see a touring opera company's production of 'La Boheme'—not, I would think, a very good one. I also saw most of the American musicals, because I kept asking to see them."

At twelve, he sent a fan letter to Richard Rodgers, and was invited to meet him at the Palace Theatre, London, where Rodger's "The Sound of Music" was playing.

1960. Won a scholarship to Westminster School, London, where he wrote two more musicals. These included one or two tunes developed in his later work. "My other interests were architecture and history. I really did think that perhaps I wouldn't go in for music at all, but something to do with architecture. I was always intrigued. I was interested in paradoxes within buildings, like why was there a cruciform church underneath Hexham Priory in the seventh century? It's there in excavations. When I was seven or eight, my dream was to go to places like that, so my parents very sweetly and dutifully took me around to look at buildings. I believe they thought that I would pursue architecture because my interest in music was not coming forward in a classical sense. Therefore, my mother was very keen to see that I did well at school in things to do with history and English, and didn't really push the music. I used to draw and write a lot about architecture. I'm a hopeless artist, so I couldn't draw anything very much, but I certainly used to write about it, entirely for myself."

1965. Despite doing badly on his "A" level exams, Lloyd Webber won an Open Award in history to Magdalen College, Oxford, mainly on the strength of a paper about Victorian architecture. He left Oxford after one term and came to London, where he met Tim Rice, a law student trying to peddle a book about pop stars through a publisher friend. He was later to say Tim was well worth leaving Oxford for. They collaborated, for the first time, on a musical based on the life of Dr. Thomas Barnardo, the founder of Victorian orphanages. "The Likes of Us" was not produced, but it proved they could work together. Lloyd Webber attended the Royal College of Music, but again chose not to complete his course.

1968. Asked by a schoolmaster friend to write a musical for St. Paul's Junior School in London, Rice and Lloyd Webber adapted the biblical story of Joseph and his brothers. They employed country and western, jazz, calypso, and rock music, while the Pharoah's "Song of the King" was written in homage to Elvis Presley. "Joseph and the Amazing Technicolour

Tim Rice with Lloyd Webber.

Dreamcoat'' was performed at the school and, two months later, at the Central Hall, Westminster where, unknown to the composers, Derek Jewell, the popular music critic of the *Sunday Times* (London) was in the audience. His enthusiastic review created sufficient interest for a recording to be made, and ''Joseph'' was expanded into a full-scale production in London. As a result, the collaborators were signed up by Sefton Myers—a businessman interested in directing show business talent with his partner, David Land—and given an annual salary of 3,000 pounds. ''Joseph'' was first performed in America in 1970 at the College of the Immaculate Conception in Douglaston, Long Island. It was revived in November, 1981, in New York's East Village, and subsequently transferred to Broadway's Royale Theater. Since its early success, ''Joseph'' has been performed almost constantly in schools and theaters worldwide.

''Joseph tells a story in one go. It was all music, and it was all a story. Also it had probably the funniest set of lyrics anyone could ever want to work with. It had Tim at his very best. In my opinion, his lyrics completely eclipse the music. There's a marvellous sense of bravura fun. Nobody other than Rice would ever have 'the dream you saw in your pajamas' rhyme with 'farmers'—only Tim. I think that's the very best side of him.''

They next wrote ''Come Back Richard, Your Country Needs You,'' based on the life of Richard the Lionheart. When no producer came forward to stage the work, they hid themselves in a Hertfordshire hotel for a week and wrote the bulk of their first major commercial success, ''Jesus Christ Superstar,'' the tale of the last seven days in the life of Christ, and as such, a contemporary passion play. Unable, once again, to find a producer, Lloyd Webber and Rice cut a demonstration disc for Decca. Released as a two-disc album, record sales, particularly in America, were enormous, creating a market for the stage production. Robert Stigwood signed them to a ten-year contract.

By the time ''Jesus Christ Superstar'' opened on Broadway on October 12, 1971, the record had sold over three million copies, rising eventually to an excess of ten. The show proved controversial, however, due to Tom O'Horgan's direction which featured Herod as a drag queen and suggested a carnal relationship between Christ and Mary Magdalene. Picket signs, carried by Christian and Jewish groups, fronted the theatre. Some critics even believed that it glamourized Judas. The composer and lyricist were unhappy with the production, even though it received seven Tony Awards and won Lloyd Webber a Drama Desk Award. The show closed on June 30, 1973 after 720 performances.

Meanwhile, the London version which had opened on August 9, 1972, was a huge success, running for 3,357 performances over an eight-year span. A film of ''Jesus Christ Superstar,'' shot in Israel and directed by Norman Jewison, was released by Universal in 1973. By the end of the 1970s, earnings from ''Superstar'' had exceeded $150 million.

1971. Married Sarah Jane Tudor Hughill.

1973. Lloyd Webber bought Sydmonton House, fifty-eight miles south west of London. A nearby village church became the home for the Sydmonton annual festival, where most of his subsequent musicals received their first performance. It also provides an opportunity for other musicians and writers to publicly air their work. ''My festival goes on every year, attended by roughly the first hundred people applying for tickets. It sort of emerged from many things, not just my things.''

''It provides a wonderful weekend for me, because it allows me to try out something new. It's also a great way to meet a lot of people whom I perhaps don't see as often as I would like to—a lot of them local. It's now, of course, slightly on the international map; making us a bit worried. Obviously, if I do a try-out of my next musical there, the whole world and its aunt are going to want to come and see and judge. And that's not what the festival is about. It's about the local people coming and seeing and judging.

''It's intended to be a sounding board for young artists, composers, writers—not necessarily young. A lot of young writers aren't given the opportunity to hear their own work. Sydmonton provides a short cut for people if they want to take it. If something of mine doesn't work at that weekend, I take it out. One knows from an audience, however small. Young people ought to do this more; get a group of people around they know—they may be quite ordinary, they may, in the end, be their Aunt Sally—but to sit them down and say, 'This is the show. We're going to play it on the piano for half an hour, do you like it?' It's also a weekend—usually the first in July—that a lot of friends of mine have etched in blood on their calendar.

''I'm very interested in any person of major talent who asks me to do a piece. I'm intrigued to see how you use people's abilities. One thing which depresses me is how often young performers, with everything to offer, go off in a direction that's not really right for them. It's often to do with management or the *appearance* of instant commercial success. I'm intrigued by performers more than anything else, because I'm not a performer myself.''

1975. Asked British playwright Alan Ayckbourne to provide the lyrics for ''Jeeves,'' based on P. G. Wodehouse's famous butler. The London show ran for only forty-seven performances and has not been revived, although Lloyd Webber hints that he may one day look at the piece again.

1977. Daughter, Imogen, born.

Composed ''Variations,'' based on the A Minor Caprice No. 24 by Paganini. ''It was written for my brother, Julian, on the cello. He asked me to do it, but I had wanted to write something for him anyway. As a piece, 'Variations' is very theatrical. I was writing for a very flamboyant performer—and Julian performed it superbly. (He is a very flamboyant performer whether he likes it or not.) There are few cellists who can hold a candle to Julian when he does 'Variations.' He's very knowing in that apart from being an absolutely brilliant musician—far better than me—he knows how to play an audience. I admire that quality in him, because he's very precise about how he does it. In fact, I'm writing a 'Phantom of the Opera' cello fantasia for him.''

1978. Lloyd Webber and Rice collaborated on ''Evita,'' a semi-fictional presentation of Eva Peron, wife of the Argentinian dictator, Juan Peron. Once again, the show was launched first as a record, and Julie Covington's version of ''Don't Cry for Me Argentina'' became a smash hit both in Britain and America. The London show opened at the Prince Edward Theatre on June 21, 1978. It starred Elaine Page as Eva and David Essex as Che Guevara.

Like the London show, the American production of ''Evita'' was directed by Hal Prince. It arrived at the Dorothy Chandler Pavilion in Los Angeles in 1979, and advance sales had exceeded two million by the time it opened at New York's Broadway Theater on September 25th. Despite some critics' concern that the show glamorized facism, "Evita" won the New York Drama Critics Award for Best Musical of the Year.

To gain control of his financial affairs, Lloyd Webber formed The Really Useful Theatre Company (subsequently part of The Really Useful Group), borrowing the name from the Really Useful Engine, a character in Wilbert Awdry's series of children's books. The company acts as a music publisher, a record label and a production company, running subsidiaries for books and films. Among the shows produced were the period comedy "Daisy Pulls It Off" which ran for three years in London, "Lend Me a Tenor," and a revival of Brecht's "Arturo Ui."

1979. Wrote "Tell Me On a Sunday" (the first-act precursor to "Song and Dance") with lyrics supplied by Don Black. First performed at the Sydmonton Festival, it was recorded (arranged and produced by Lloyd Webber) in 1980, sung by Marti Webb. In the same year, the BBC produced a TV-film version of the song-cycle. "It was a one-woman show. It intrigued me to see if I could write about a very ordinary person, and particularly a woman, having written 'Evita.' I thought, 'Well, I've written "Jesus Christ Superstar" and I've written "Evita," both with Tim Rice, all larger than life personalities.

Now I want to write about someone who's ordinary-sized, and in New York which is, frankly, a rather grizzly city.'

"I made up the story. It's never simple. To some degree, it's biographical in the sense that I knew the 'type of girl' I was writing about—I'd met her more than once. There are so many girls of that kind, who slightly drift through the world. In this case it was dictated by a character since I had a very particular idea in mind.

"With a one-woman show you're on your mettle. It's construction. What you can't do with a musical is say, 'I've written ten great tunes and that's it.' Half the art of making a musical work is what you're prepared to throw away. It's a funny thing people don't understand, certainly most of the critics working in musical theatre don't understand it. There could be a great melody that you don't allow to be developed and yet the audience feels comfortable with it. There are other people who work in a completely different way from me, many composers who would not rely on a melodic construction combined with a certain lateral construction."

1980. Son, Nicholas, was born.

(From the Broadway musical "Cats," a winner of seven Tony awards including one for Betty Buckley [above] for Best Supporting Musical Actress. Photograph by Martha Swope & Associates.)

(From the New York production of ''Evita,'' starring Mandy Patinkin and Patti LuPone, 1979. Photograph by Martha Swope & Associates.)

1981. Musical "Cats" produced at the Palace Theatre on May 11th. It was based on T. S. Eliot's *Old Possum's Book of Practical Cats* with additional unpublished poems and letters made available by the poet's widow, Valerie. Choreographed by Gillian Lynne, it was set in a giant rubbish dump, where all the characters were human-sized cats. Additional lyrics were supplied by Richard Stilgoe, but the show's most famous song, "Memory" was composed by Trevor Nunn, inspired by T. S. Eliot's poem "Rhapsody on a Windy Night." Nunn, an associate director of the Royal Shakespeare Company who had never before been involved in a large-scale commercial musical, directed the show, which was designed by John Napier, a theatre designer originally trained as a sculptor.

"Cats" has been Lloyd Webber's most successful musical to date. It opened in New York in October, 1982, at the Winter Garden Theater, and was still playing in 1988 when it had three touring companies in America, and productions in Europe, Japan, and Australia running simultaneously in addition to the original London production. By this time total box office receipts for the show exceed $425 million.

"We all thought we had a disaster on our hands with 'Cats,' we really did. We didn't have the money, we didn't have the investment. It was 1981. Things were very different then. Cameron Mackintosh was a new producer, and he hadn't produced anything of substance, other than things he'd done for the Arts Council. It was a very dangerous situation. We were half our investment short, and I had to take a second mortgage on my house. At that point I'd left Robert Stigwood, and all the money that had come from 'Superstar' and 'Evita' had been earned in Britain under a government where the top rate of tax was as high as ninety-eight per cent, so there wasn't a lot of money around to have a disaster with. The technical rehearsal hadn't gone well—it's always the way with musicals, and we were despondent. We thought we'd lost everything.

"We'd also lost our leading lady, Judi Dench, through injury during rehearsals. We really felt that we couldn't open and go forward. I remember it was Good Friday, we'd been rehearsing all day and met in Joe Allen's restaurant to decide what to do. There was Cameron, Trevor and myself. I will always owe everything to Trevor for saying, 'You've got to go on, you're just tired. Put up the money, Andrew. Get the second mortgage. I can't do it myself, but you must do it and we must open.' And we did.

"We had extended the previews, because of Judi Dench going out and Elaine Paige coming in. Preview one, on a Wednesday, went much better than we'd dared have a right to. The first act went very well; the second act went appallingly. Preview two went the other way round. By Friday evening I'd had enough. Instead of going to see the show, I went to a local restaurant. Everyone said, 'You've got the biggest hit of your career, Andrew,' and I thought they were joking. I went to see the end of the performance and the audience stood and cheered and cheered and cheered.

"Then we nearly lost it all. The first night had been put back, and there were a couple of hundred people who had bought tickets to make trouble because of the postponement—there always are people who will do that. So, when the 'Jellicle Ball' had been done, there was this great shout of 'Rubbish,' and we thought, 'Oh my God, we're going down the pan.' Then we had a bombscare. It was announced at the very end of the show, so we never knew what the first night applause would have been like because everyone just filed out of the theatre. Cameron and I thought we had the world crashing round our ears. Then we got the reviews—four phenomenal mainstream reviews.

"I chose Trevor Nunn to direct for a number of reasons. 'Cats' was not originally intended by me for the theatre because all I had were the poems to work with. I wanted to extend frontiers, to see whether I could write to existing verse, where there was no possibility of my being able to alter them or phone up a lyricist and say, 'Look, Buster, those words don't fit.'

"I remembered reading the cat poems in bed during childhood. Later, I'd play them on the piano for reaction from interviewers or friends. Finally, I put them together and did them at Sydmonton in the same way I did 'Starlight Express' a year later. When another poem emerged—as well as letters Eliot wrote about them—I realized the structure was there for a major musical.

"[The genesis of 'Cats'] has to be set in historical context. *Dance* was happening in Britain. I remember taking Hal Prince to see [contemporary dance group] Hot Gossip when we were in preview with 'Evita,' and he said, 'That's what Bob Fosse should be doing.' I took him to meet Arlene Phillips [the dance group's founder], whom I didn't know at all. Things were beginning to bubble. At the same time, Wayne Sleep, who came out of the ballet because of his size, was also making dance popular.

"Then I read T. S. Eliot's letter imagining an event in which cats danced a Jellicle Ball, with one cat eventually selected to go to the heavyside lair [cat heaven]. I discovered the story he'd written about Grizebella too (that was too sad for children and not in the book). All sorts of disparate things began to come together. When Eliot did the book, he originally thought it was going to be about dogs as well, which is why the poems about the Pollicle dogs is there, I presume, but the sequel was never written.

"Thinking there was something extraordinary here, I talked it over with Cameron Mackintosh whom I'd not met before. He was a young unknown producer, and, like me, 'mental' about musicals. We thought it would be a terrific idea to approach Trevor Nunn. It's ironical—now that he seems to have more musicals running than I do—that it took us three months to woo him. He had a definite command of popular showmanship, as I'd seen in his direction of 'Comedy of Errors' and 'Once in a Lifetime.' I felt very strongly that he would not betray Eliot.

"What he did was go through the main body of Eliot's work with me, where we found many other cat references—legion in Eliot's work. That is what made it all happen."

1982. "Song and Dance," a combination of "Variations" (second act) and "Tell Me On a Sunday" (first act) opened at the Palace Theatre, London, with Marti Webb in the starring role. The show came to New York's Royale Theater in September, 1985, with Bernadette Peters in the lead.

1983. Marriage to Sarah Tudor ended in divorce.

The Really Useful Theatre Company acquired the Palace Theatre, scene of the twelve-year-old's meeting with childhood idol, Richard Rodgers. The 1.3 million pounds purchase was financed from the profits of Lloyd Webber's own musicals. "Jesus Christ Superstar" had played at the Palace for eight years, and "Song and Dance" was housed there. "Pinocchio," a children's musical written by Lloyd Webber's father was given a performance. Later The Really Useful Theatre Company co-produced the Palace Theatre's revival of Richard Rodgers' 1936 musical, "On Your Toes."

(From the Broadway musical ''Starlight Express,'' which opened at the Gershwin Theatre, 1986. Photograph by Martha Swope & Associates.)

1984. Married Sarah Brightman, former member of the Hot Gossip dance group. Her soprano voice was to be an inspiration for his future compositions. At this time, Lloyd Webber became the first composer to have three shows running concurrently in London's West End and on Broadway.

That same year, "Starlight Express" was staged by Trevor Nunn and John Napier, with lyrics by Richard Stilgoe. It told the story of a race to find the fastest engine on the old American railroad. Choreographed by Arlene Phillips, the cast was asked to perform on roller skates. London's Apollo Theatre and the Gershwin Theater on Broadway were transformed into giant race tracks.

"'Starlight' was intended to be an animated film—the story of Cinderella as a cartoon: the steam train was Cinderella; the diesel and electric trains the ugly sisters; the Midnight Train, the fairy godmother who said, 'You may borrow my equipment, but you must be back by midnight because the Midnight Train has to go on time.' There was an engine trial; the little steam train dropped a piston in its haste to go back; and the prince traveled across America to find the train to which the piston fitted. It was supposed to be a children's fairy story, but it was blown up wildly.

"There can be a time when you don't want to stay with something, and if other people come up with another conception, you let them have a go. Who am I to complain? It certainly isn't what I thought. It's become very brutalist. It's become about racing, and it isn't fun in the same sense. On the other hand it's extremely exciting, and I think they were trying to introduce theatre to a modern generation of kids.

"There are many ways you can hold an audience. In the case of 'Starlight Express' I don't think it's me really holding them. It's the production itself. If it had been developed more in the way I'd conceived it, it might have held them in a completely different way. It had a performance at my festival with no scenery and no costumes, and it was considered great fun. I wrote it because I wanted to write something for my kids."

1985. "Requiem" received its premiere in New York in January at St. Thomas' Church, Fifth Avenue. Lorin Maazel conducted the English Chamber Orchestra and the Choir of Westminster Cathedral, and the solo roles were sung by Sarah Brightman, Placido Domingo and twelve-year-old chorister Paul Miles-Kingston. The BBC transmitted the entire New York performance on 'Omnibus,' screened in England, and the same cast later repeated the concert in Westminster Abbey.

As the most personal of Lloyd Webber's work to date, "Requiem" was dedicated to his father, and drew together his passions for music and church architecture. The piece received a Grammy Award for Best Classical Contemporary Composition. An extract from "Requiem," "Pie Jesu," sung by Sarah Brightman, became a top-selling record in England and America.

Two events set "Requiem" in motion. The first was the death of his father in 1982 and the second was a story about Cambodia in an obscure corner of the *New York Times,* concerning a boy who was faced with the choice of killing his mutilated sister or being killed himself. Cambodia has no musical influence on the score, but it did give Lloyd Webber the idea of scoring the "Requiem" for a boy, a girl, and a man: treble, high soprano, and tenor.

"Working on 'Requiem' was different partly because I was working on my own. I'd done that before with 'Variations,' but then I'd had my brother, Julian, as a guinea pig. I suppose

Sarah's voice put the lid on what I was coming to anyway, taking me towards 'Requiem' and 'Phantom.' She has a soprano voice.

"To put it simply, a man has two voices: his ordinary voice and a falsetto voice. So does a woman. She can sing in either soprano or what is called 'chest.' There's a break in a woman's voice, a point where it actually breaks. A soprano's training is to take that break out and go as smoothly as possible from the lowest note that a woman can sing to the highest. A singer like Elaine Paige or Liza Minelli sings in 'chest' or 'belt voice,' pushing only up to the point where the voice breaks, pushing that break as high as they possibly can. Ethel Merman is probably the best known example of someone who sang in chest, along with 99.9 percent of pop singers (and a thrilling noise it is too), but there are only about fifteen useable notes. With a soprano's voice you have an extra octave.

"If you look at the tunes of Richard Rodgers, the greatest melodist of all time, it's extraordinary how limited the range is—usually within ten notes—because he was working within the range of the performers available to him. His gift was so extraordinary that he was able to find a melody within such a small number of notes. Most of my melodies in 'Evita' are more angular. 'Rainbow High' covers quite a lot of notes, and an interviewer once asked me, 'Why do you punish your singers with all those intervals?' But I wasn't really thinking that way, I was concentrating on how I wanted to hear them come in.

"I wrote 'Requiem' with Sarah's soprano voice in mind. I was originally commissioned in 1978 by the BBC to write it as a requiem for Northern Ireland, and then a lot of things in it became personal. I thought it would be a terrific idea if one could use modern texts interspersed with Latin, but I could find no way of doing it, and the idea was dropped. In many ways I think it was right that it was.

"It's very hard to articulate what my personal feelings are in that piece. I can put into words what I think my musical achievements and my musical failures are, but I can't really put into words what I finally believe was my reason for composing it. It's very personal, like a lot of music I've written that has not found a performance. There's a whole body of church music that I've either not allowed performed or have had performed privately. I am religious, yet I'm not. 'Requiem' is linked to my love of architecture and to the whole British music tradition, which is why I use the boy's choir.

"There is something that I don't think I've fulfilled in 'Requiem' yet. There were certain things right and certain things wrong. There is one moment which doesn't work—obviously intended to be Russia and America juxtaposed. When it becomes deliberately Russian it could be labelled pastiche, and that's a pity because it wasn't meant to be. The idea was about eternal tragedy, and I wanted to have the Americans saying, 'When the wicked are confounded' and the Russians answering with 'huic ergo' and all that. That was an idea that came from my theatre background, which in a sense demanded some kind of staging."

1986. Bought the 1,200-acre Sydmonton Estate on the Berkshire-Wiltshire border for three million pounds. The land covers most of the villages of Ecchinswell and Sydmonton, and stretches to the edge of Watership Down, appearing in the novels of Richard Adams. His other homes are in Belgravia, London, on a ten-acre property near Nice in France, and in New York's Trump Tower.

Prince Edward commissioned Lloyd Webber and Rice to write a piece as a present for the Queen on her birthday. They pro-

Lloyd Webber was featured on the cover of *Time* magazine, January 18, 1988.

duced "Cricket," a thirty-minute musical based on their shared passion for the sport. "It was written for the Queen, asked for by the Palace, and I feel quite strongly that it was a piece that was asked for privately. Whilst to do it at Sydmonton was fun and Prince Edward, who'd been very much involved with it as producer, came to do it again there, I don't think it's something we should do publicly."

Coming across a fifty-cent copy of Gaston Leroux's 1910 novel, *Le Fantome de l'Opera* in a New York second-hand bookshop, Lloyd Webber realized that the tale of a masked man living in the depths of the Paris Opera House masterminding the career of a young ingenue singer was perfect material for a musical. "Phantom of the Opera" opened in London on October 9, 1986 at Her Majesty's Theatre, directed by Hal Prince, choreographed by Gillian Lynne, designed by Maria Bjornson and with lyrics supplied by Richard Stilgoe and Charles Hart. It was an immediate success with the public despite the reservations of some critics. "Phantom" won the Laurence Olivier, *Plays and Players,* and *London Standard* Awards for Best Musical. It was the first musical ever to have four separate songs in the British Top Ten singles charts, and the cast LP was the first mainstream musical cast album to reach the top of the charts.

Sarah Brightman's soprano voice had once again been an inspiration, and it was she who starred in the role of Christine in the London production and in New York, where the show opened on January 26, 1988 at the Majestic Theater. Two actresses, Claire Moore and Rebecca Caine, took over her part in London. The role of the Phantom was played in both productions by the British actor, Michael Crawford. When the show opened in Manhattan, Lloyd Webber capped his own record and became the only composer ever to have twice had three shows running simultaneously on Broadway and in London. Before the "Phantom" opened on Broadway advance ticket sales had exceeded $16 million.

Many critics were taken back that Lloyd Webber had written a romantic musical, more conventional in form than his recent work for the theatre. "You can't categorize music, and anyone who tries is playing with fire. I don't think any audience of mine really knows what they're expecting to see. A lot of people came to 'Phantom' in London in the first two or three previews there, thinking the combination of Andrew Lloyd Webber, 'Phantom of the Opera' and comedy actor Michael Crawford was going to mean an evening of Crawford swinging around on ropes, like an up-market version of 'The Prisoner of Zenda.' Or they thought it would be very campy and very funny. Instead they got my most mainstream romantic score.

"Funnily enough, the audience was right-footed by it pretty quickly; they took to it at once. The critics, however, were a little bit unprepared and not quite certain what it was. One or two of the reviews made inane comments about how I didn't go into the murky depths of 'Sweeney Todd.' Well, I wasn't writing 'Sweeney Todd,' I was writing a mainstream romantic musical based on what I found in the book.

"'Phantom' has a very definite style within the story telling, both musically and visually. The music either ends a little earlier than it ought to and the production takes it over on the next beat, or the other way round. So we wrong-foot the audience on practically every occasion—or like to think we do. But again, it comes back to one thing; what 'Cats,' 'Evita,' 'Jesus Christ Superstar,' 'Tell Me On a Sunday,' 'Variations,' and 'Phantom' have in common is construction. Construction is the one common ingredient binding all those shows together. It's the rhythm of musical theatre. I think you can take any

subject for musical theatre provided you do it in a way that people can actually respond to.

"I have strong views about what my shows should look like. I was baptized by fire with 'Jeeves,' an appalling disaster. Apart from it not being right as a show, which is another matter, it was not helped that it looked absolutely frightful. It's complex, however. You can't dictate to a designer how something should look to the point where you're stopping him from creating."

1987. Composed the Conservative Party election theme music to help Mrs. Thatcher to her third successive victory in the British General Election.

1988. Prince Edward signed on as a production assistant to The Really Useful Theatre Company.

Lloyd Webber is presently at work on his musical "Aspects of Love," adapted from David Garnett's 1955 novel of the same name. Don Black is collaborating with Charles Hart on the lyrics. "I take a very long time coming to the conclusion that I'm going to write something. Very often I write it, abandon it, do it again in two years time, then find there was a reason for not doing it at first. 'Cats' was like that. I started it back in 1978-79, got as far as performing four of the cat poems at my festival, abandoned it, then came back to it again. 'Aspects of Love' was the same.

"I have an interesting problem in 'Aspects of Love' in that I know that the part of the older man is never going to be sung by anyone who could be remotely considered operatic and, funnily enough, I'm finding that organically his songs are not demanding that kind of range. You hope that an audience would never know that such problems existed. If the entire audience throws bricks at 'Aspects of Love' when we do it at my festival in the summer, Charles and I will be the first people ankling away with the score to a safe distance, and it will not be subjected to a wider public.

"It's very much a constant process of thinking how you can actually make the story work in musical construction. There is a definite sense of the musician beginning to dictate how the story develops. I mean a Verdi or a Puccini or any of the major opera composers of the more popular kind, even Britten, would actually dictate to the librettist what should be going on at any given point. I find I'm doing that more and more now. I did that very much with 'Superstar.' I knew exactly what we should be doing and how to edit and take us through the whole thing. It's crucial. I read 'Aspects of Love' for the first time and had no idea how to do it. I may be wrong with what I'm doing now, but a style has evolved to tell the story. It may be that whoever directs it won't go along with the style. I've no idea whether it's got any kind of major commercial appeal. You don't know until it happens." "Aspects of Love," will have its premiere at the Prince of Whales Theatre in London in the spring of 1989.

"I very rarely go to my shows when they open, very rarely go to first nights. I just turn up cosmetically at the door, have someone fill my seat, and then go away. There are so many forces that come into play, and not all of them nice. So many people want to see one go down. I've gone a lot further than a lot of people thought. There are one or two people I know who've had the luck of a legendary first night where everybody says unanimously that it's all fantastic. That's never happened to me."[1]

FOOTNOTE SOURCES

[1]Based on an interview by Catherine Courtney for *Something about the Author.*

FOR MORE INFORMATION SEE:

BOOKS

Christopher Headington, *The Performing World of the Musician*, Silver Burdett, 1981.

Who's Who in the Theatre: A Biographical Record of the Contemporary Stage, 17th edition, Gale, 1981.

Contemporary Literary Criticism, Volume 21, Gale, 1982.

Current Biography Yearbook 1982, H. W. Wilson, 1983.

International Who's Who, 48th edition, Europa, 1984.

Gerald McKnight, *Andrew Lloyd Webber*, St. Martin's, 1985.

Mark White, *'You Must Remember This—': Popular Songwriters 1900-1980,* Scribner, 1985.

PERIODICALS

Melody Maker, October 10, 1970, March 3, 1973, June 16, 1973.

Time, November 9, 1970, September, 30, 1985, January 18, 1988, February 8, 1988.

Newsweek, November 16, 1970, October 25, 1971, October 8, 1979, October 11, 1982, September 30, 1985.

Rolling Stone, December 2, 1970, June 24, 1971, August 2, 1973, April 7, 1977.

New York Times, October 12, 1971, October 24, 1971, October 31, 1971, September 5, 1972, December 31, 1976, September 26, 1979, February 10, 1982, October 8, 1982, July 19, 1987, February 2, 1988.

Daily News (New York), October 13, 1971, September 21, 1979, September 26, 1979, January 10, 1988.

James R. Huffman, "'Jesus Christ Superstar'—Popular Art and Unpopular Criticism," *Journal of Popular Culture,* fall, 1972.

James M. Wall, "'Jesus Christ Superstar': A Surprising Film Success," *Christian Century,* June 27, 1973.

William S. Pechter, "Politics on Film: 'Jesus Christ Superstar,'" *Commentary,* September, 1973.

John Simon, "Films: 'Jesus Christ Superstar,'" *Esquire,* October, 1973.

Eric Salzman, "Another Little Eva Altogether," *Stereo Review,* April, 1977.

M. Gottfried, "Two Shots in the Arm for the London Stage," *Saturday Review,* October 14, 1978.

New Yorker, October 8, 1979, March 11, 1985.

G. Loney, "Don't Cry for Andrew Lloyd Webber," *Opera News,* April 4, 1981.

L. Bennetts, "Lloyd Webber's Third Broadway Show," *New York Times Biographical Serivce,* September, 1982.

Horizon, September, 1982, October, 1985.

School Library Journal, September 27, 1983.

"From the Bible to Back Alleys, Broadway's Hottest Composer Strikes all the Right Notes," *People Weekly,* December 27, 1982.

M. Hoyle, "Chatting to a Choo Choo," *Plays and Players,* March, 1984.

Alan Rich, "Sing-Out at the OK Chorales," *Newsweek,* March 18, 1985.

Roger Wolmuth, "Pop Singer Sarah Brightman and Composer Andrew Lloyd Webber Make a Classic Match," *People Weekly,* March 3, 1986.

Betsy Bauer, "Keeping Big Spenders on a Leash," *U.S. News & World Report,* February 23, 1987.

Dennis Polkow, "Andrew Lloyd Webber: From Superstar to Requiem," *Christian Century,* March 18-25, 1987.

Pamela Young, "The Multimillion-Dollar Music Man," *Maclean's,* June 8, 1987.

John Rockwell, "Andrew Lloyd Webber Superstar," *New York Times Magazine,* December 20, 1987.

(From the Broadway production of "The Phantom of the Opera," starring Michael Crawford and Sarah Brightman. Crawford won 1988's Tony for Best Actor in a musical.)

Patricia Morrisroe, "Here Comes the Phantom: A Haunting Smash Stalks Broadway," *New York,* January 18, 1988.
Variety, October 12, 1988 (p. 183).

LUCAS, George (Walton)   1944-

PERSONAL: Born May 14, 1944, in Modesto, Calif.; son of George (a retail merchant) and Dorothy Lucas; married Marcia Griffin (a film editor), February 22, 1969 (divorced, 1984); children: Amanda. *Education:* Modesto Junior College, A.A., 1964; University of Southern California, B.A., 1966. *Residence:* San Anselmo, Calif. *Office:* c/o Jane Bay, P.O. Box 186, San Anselmo, Calif. 94960.

CAREER: Worked as film editor for U.S. Information Agency; assistant to Francis Ford Coppola for "Finian's Rainbow" (editor and cameraman), 1967, and for "The Rain People" (assistant art editor and assistant cameraman), 1969; director of motion pictures and writer, 1971—; founder of Lucasfilm Ltd., San Anselmo, Calif. *Member:* Writers Guild of America, Academy of Motion Picture Arts and Sciences, Screen Directors Guild.

AWARDS, HONORS: Received Third National Student Film Festival Award, 1967-68, for "THX 1138"; Best Screenplay Award from the New York Film Critics, and from the National Society of Film Critics, and nominations from the Academy of Motion Picture Arts and Sciences for Best Screenplay, Best Director, and Best Film, all 1973, all for "American Graffiti"; Best Film Award from the Los Angeles Film Critics, nominations from the Academy of Motion Picture Arts and Sciences for Best Director and Best Film, all 1977, all for "Star Wars"; numerous other film awards.

WRITINGS:

American Graffiti, Grove, 1974.
Star Wars, Ballantine, 1976.

George Lucas, February, 1969.

SCREENPLAYS

(With Walter Murch; and director) "THX 1138," Warner Bros., 1971.
(With Gloria Katz and Willard Huyck; and director) "American Graffiti," Universal, 1973.
(And director) "Star Wars" (starring Mark Hamill, Harrison Ford, Alec Guinness and Carrie Fisher), Twentieth Century-Fox, 1978.
(And executive producer) "The Empire Strikes Back" (sequel to "Star Wars"), Twentieth Century-Fox, 1980.
(And executive producer) "Raiders of the Lost Ark," Lucasfilm, 1981.
(And producer) "Return of the Jedi" (third episode of "Star Wars" trilogy), Twentieth Century-Fox, 1983.
"Ewok and Star Wars Droids Adventure Hour" (weekly television show), ABC-TV, 1985.

PRODUCER

"More American Graffiti," Lucasfilm, 1979.
"The Ewok Adventure" (television film), ABC-TV, 1984.

EXECUTIVE PRODUCER

"Indiana Jones and the Temple of Doom" (sequel to "Raiders of the Lost Ark"), Paramount, 1984.
"Labyrinth" (starring David Bowie), Tri-Star, 1986.
"Howard the Duck," Universal, 1986.
(Author of original story; collaborator of screenplay with Ron Howard and Bob Dolman) "Willow," Lucasfilm, 1988.
"Tucker" (starring Jeff Bridges), Zoetrope Studios, 1988.
(With Steven Spielberg) "The Land Before Time," Universal, 1988.

Also author of three alternate "Star Wars" scripts; developer of unproduced script, "Apocalypse Now."

WORK IN PROGRESS: A third movie about Indiana Jones.

SIDELIGHTS: **May 14, 1944.** Born George Walton Lucas Jr. in Modesto, California. "I was very much aware that growing up wasn't pleasant, it was just. . .frightening. . . .I was unhappy a lot of the time. Not really unhappy—I enjoyed my childhood. But I guess all kids, from their point of view, feel depressed and intimidated. . . .My strongest impression was that I was always on the lookout for the evil monster that lurked around the corner."[1]

"My favorite things were Republic serials and things like Flash Gordon. . . .There was a television program called 'Adventure Theater' at 6:00 every night. We didn't have a TV set, so I used to go over to a friend's house and we watched it religiously. It was a twenty-minute serial chapter, and the left over minutes of the half hour was filled with 'Crusader Rabbit.' I loved it. . . ."[2] Lucas rarely went to feature-length movies, "and when I did it was to meet girls. . . ."[3] He loved comic books, however. "I read Tommy Tomorrow and, of course, lots of (other) comics. . . .Mostly DC comics—Batman and Superman. But I was also real keen on Donald Duck and Scrooge McDuck. . . ."[2] "What I enjoy most about Uncle Scrooge is that he is so American in his attitude. . . .That kind of greed attracts all young kids, because you want to have all this stuff!. . .

"I loved Disneyland. I wandered around, I'd go on the rides and bumper cars, the steamboats, the shooting galleries, the jungle rides. I was in heaven."[1] School was less than heaven. "I was never very good in school, so I was never very enthusiastic about it. . . .I always wanted to learn something other than what I was being taught. I was *bored*."[1]

(From the movie "American Graffiti," starring Ron Howard [right]. Copyright © 1973 by Universal Pictures.)

1960. Moved to a thirteen-acre ranch in Modesto. The reclusive teenager found refuge in rock 'n' roll music. "For teenagers, the person closest to them is a fantasy character. That's the disc jockey. It's like younger kids who have make-believe friends. A lot of teenagers have a make-believe friend in a disc jockey, but he's much more real because he talks to them, he jokes around. Especially a really excellent disc jockey like Wolfman Jack. He's part of the family. You listen to him every day, you're very close to him, you share your most intimate moments with him.

"When we were cruising, we could get Wolfman Jack from Tijuana. He was a really mystical character, I'll tell you. He was wild, he had these crazy phone calls, and he drifted out of nowhere. He was an outlaw, which of course made him extremely attractive to kids."[4]

"That was my period when I hung out with a real bad element [1950's greasers, with leather jackets and greased back hair— the real life version of the Pharoahs in 'American Graffiti'.]...The only way to keep from getting the s— pounded out of you was to hang out with some really tough guys who happened to be your friends....They'd send me in and wait until somebody would try to pick a fight with me. Then they would come in and pound 'em. I was the bait. I was always afraid that I was gonna get pounded myself."[1]

A car and "cruising" changed his life. "I was always going around picking up girls and hoping for the best....Nobody

knew who I was. I'd say, 'Hi, I'm George,' but after that night I'd never see the girls again. It wasn't like school, where you'd have to sit with them."[1]

"I wanted to be a race car driver at sixteen. I was a mechanic in a foreign car service, and my ambition was to be a race driver—sports cars, Formula One. That was it. My whole life. I lived, ate, breathed cars! That was everything to me."[5]

"I had my own life once I had my car. Along with the sense of power and freedom came the competitiveness to see who was the fastest, who was the craziest, and who was the bravest."[1] Anticipating this, George Lucas Sr. bought his son a Fiat Bianchina with a "sewing machine motor in it. It was a dumb little car. What could I do with that?..."[1]

June 12, 1962. "I was in an accident the day before I was going to graduate from high school. I spent some time in the hospital, and I realized that it probably wouldn't be smart for me to be a race driver....Before that first accident you are very oblivious to the danger and don't realize how close to the edge you are. But once you've gone over the edge and you realize what is on the other side, it changes your perspective...."[5]

Lucas nearly died in the crash. His life was saved when his seat belt broke, throwing him free from the car. "You can't have that kind of experience and not feel that there must be a reason why you're here. I realized that I should be spending my time trying to figure out what that reason is and trying to fulfill it. The fact is, there is no way I could have survived that accident if I'd been wrapped around that tree. Actually, that seat belt never should have broken, under any circumstances. . . .I began to trust my instincts. . . ."[1]

Entered Modesto Junior College. "When I went to Junior College I got very interested in the social sciences—psychology, sociology, anthropology. . . ."[5] "It was very hard, and I didn't have the background I needed—I couldn't even spell.

"If it hadn't been for the self-discipline that made me chain myself to my desk and do it, my work would have never gotten done. I felt there were a lot of kids that never figured that out. . .they just sort of whiled away their lives and woke up one day to find out they were thirty-five years old and hadn't amounted to much."[1]

June 9, 1964. Graduated junior college. "I had always been interested in art, and I'd been very good at it. My father didn't see much of a career in being an artist, so he discouraged me from that whole thing. . . ."[5] "It was one of the few times I can remember really yelling at [him], screaming at him, telling him no matter what he said, I wasn't going into the business. . . .'and as a matter of fact, I'm going to be a millionaire before I'm thirty.'. . .It was one of those things that at the time I was shocked I had said. It sort of came out of left field. . . ."[1]

"A very close friend of mine who I grew up with since I was four years old, was going to USC [University of Southern California] and asked me to take the test with him. I was going to go to San Francisco State and become an anthropology major or something like that. And he said, 'They've got a film school down there, and it's great 'cause you can do photography.' So I said, 'Well, all right, but it's a long shot 'cause my grades are not good enough to get into a school like that.' So I went and took the test and I passed. I got accepted!

"About that same time, I had been working on a race car for [cameraman] Haskel Wexler [later Lucas' cinematographer on 'American Graffiti'], and I met him, and he influenced me in the direction of cinematography. . . ."[5]

September, 1964. Entered the University of Southern California as a junior. "I suddenly discovered how exciting films were. I was fascinated by all of the technical aspects of it. I never got over the magic of it all."[3]

"When I finally decided that I was going to be a filmmaker. . .I lost a lot of face because for hot rodders the idea of going into film was really a goofy idea. And that was in the early sixties. Nobody went into film at that time. At USC the girls from the dorms all gave a wide berth to the film students because they were supposed to be weird."[4] "All my friends laughed at me and warned, 'You're crazy, you're going to become a ticket-taker at Disneyland.'. . .

"The unique thing about being at film school then as opposed to now was that it didn't lead anywhere. You concentrated more on what you were doing and on the people you were with, rather than thinking, 'Gee, if I make this kind of film, somebody will see it and I can get a job.' That was such a remote possibility that you didn't structure your life around it. The focus was on the films people made.

"The [instructors] never taught us much, other than the basics. They opened the door, but we had to go inside and find out for ourselves. We students were learning things infinitely faster than the classes were teaching us. You had to in order to keep up with what was going on."[1]

"I went to USC as a photographer—I wanted to be a cameraman—but obviously at film school you have to do everything: cinematography, editing, and script writing. Well, I did terrible in the script writing classes, because I hated script writing. I hated stories, I hated plot, and I wanted to make visual films that had nothing to do with telling a story. I was a difficult student. I got into a lot of trouble all the time because of that attitude. I felt I could make a movie out of *anything;* I mean, give me the phone book, and I'll make a movie out of it.

"I learned editing. . .that sort of became my whole life. . .I loved what you could do with editing. . . ."[5]

"Whenever I broke the rules, I made a good film, so there wasn't much that the faculty could do about it. They were caught between the fact that it was the best film in the class and that I had broken all the rules. . . ."[1]

"My friends and I were the best student film makers around. If you went to any international film festival we were always there winning the first, second, or third prize. And it was that attention—especially one film festival where I wiped out every category—won first place in all categories—that led to some people saying, 'Hey, this kid's sharp.'"[6]

"There was a small group of us that were making films, while the rest of the class sat around and said, 'Gee, we can't make movies—the teacher won't let us do this, or I can't do that, or you never get a break around here.' While they were complaining about why they never got to make movies I made *eight* movies. . . ."[5]

Other members of the "small group" from USC who figured out how to do it were: writer/directors Matthew Robbins ("Dragonslayer"), John Milius ("Conan the Barbarian"), Willard Huyck ("French Postcards"), and Bob Zemeckis ("Who Framed Roger Rabbit"), writers David S. Ward ("The Sting"), and Dan O'Bannon ("Alien"), producers Howard Kazanjian ("Return of the Jedi"), editor Walter Murch ("Apocalypse Now"), and directors Randal Kleiser ("Grease") and John Carpenter ("Halloween").

"We were like foreigners living in a strange country and all speaking the same language, all of us banding together to beat on the doors of Hollywood. We would share resources—if you needed something a friend would tell you where to get it from. And we all looked at each other's work, mostly at student film festivals. That's how Steve Spielberg got to be a member of the group. . . .He was at Long Beach State, but we met through film festivals."[7]

August 6, 1966. Graduated from the University of Southern California and tried to enlist in the Air Force. Teenage speeding violations restricted him from becoming an officer in the photographic unit. "I wasn't really that enthusiastic about going [to Vietnam] in the first place. I was just doing it out of desperation."[1]

Lucas later escaped the draft because of his diabetes. "After film school I went out looking for a job and I couldn't find one anywhere and I worked as a grip—you know, a guy that carries things around—on a couple of independent productions. I worked as a freelance cameraman for various people. . . .Then I got a job cutting, as an assistant editor, on a USIA [United States Information Agency] project for President Johnson on his trip to Asia. Then I got moved up to being editor. . . ."[5]

Mark Hamill, Carrie Fisher and Harrison Ford aboard the *Imperial Death Star*.

The USIA objected to his style of editing of the Johnson footage on political grounds. "They said I made the South Koreans look a little too fascist. . . ."[1]

"I decided that I wanted to be a director. I really didn't like people telling me how to do this and how to do that—you know, carrying out someone else's ideas that I didn't really think were so great. . . ."[5] "[Film] is a director's medium, there's no getting around that. The writer provides a very important element, but the final product is ultimately left in the hands of the director."[1]

Met future wife, Marcia Griffin (later the editor of "Taxi Driver" and "New York, New York"), who worked with him as a fellow editor. "Marcia had a lot of disdain for the rest of us because we were all film students. She was the only real pro there.

"It wasn't that I saw her in the editing room and said, 'I'm going to get that girl.' It was more like 'This is another girl and we'll have fun and what the heck.' I certainly never expected I would marry Marcia. . . .I think my relationship with women is not very complex. Up until Marcia, it was a very animalistic attraction."[1]

"I was also teaching at USC—a class in photography—and then I decided to go back there to graduate school. I was there for one more semester and did many more movies, but still non-story-type films. . . ."[5]

Decided to make "THX-1138:4EB (Electronic Labyrinth)," a science-fiction drama concerning man's escape from the limitation of his own inhibitions. "The idea had been boiling around in my mind for a long time. It was based on a concept that we live in the future and that you could make a futuristic film using existing stuff."[1]

The film won the National Student Film Award and caught the attention of Hollywood and Lucas' peers. Steven Spielberg recalled, "He reminded me a little of Walt Disney's version of a mad scientist. He was so unassuming when I first met him that I couldn't immediately associate him with the power of 'THX,' which really moved and influenced me. I never had seen a film created by a peer that was not of this Earth—'THX' created a world that did not exist before George designed it. It was hard to believe that here was somebody who knew this side of the camera as well as I thought I did."[1]

Lucas had other distinctions. "I won a couple of scholarships at the end of that semester—one to watch Carl Foreman make 'McKenna's Gold' out in the desert and make a little behind the scenes movie, and the other was a Warner's scholarship where you observe movie-making for six months. . . .Well, it takes about a week of watching for you to get bored. After that you've seen all that you could possibly see about making a movie. . . ."[5]

July, 1967. Started apprenticeship at Warner Bros. and worked with Francis Ford Coppola on "Finian's Rainbow." "The day I arrived at Warner's was the day Jack Warner was leaving

R2-D2 and C-3PO.

because they had sold the studios to a big corporation. The whole place was shutting down, so I couldn't be assigned to the story department. . . ."[7] "[The] animation [department] was empty; there wasn't anybody there except one guy who was sort of the head of the department and he would just sit in his office and twiddle his thumbs all day. . . ."[5]

"I had already been through all of this on another scholarship, the Carl Foreman grant, so what I wanted to do was get into the animation department, steal some footage or whatever and start making a film. About three weeks into the picture I told Francis I was bored, but he said, 'Look, kid, stick with me and I'll give you things to do.' He did and it turned out that we complimented each other very well. I was essentially an editor and cameraman, while Francis is a writer and director—more into actors and acting."[7]

1968. Assisted Coppola on movie, "The Rain People," and made a short documentary about the on-location experience called, "Filmmaker." "[We] were like two halves of a whole. I was always putting on the brakes and he was always stepping on the gas. It was good for me, because it loosened me up and got me to take more chances. I realized that you can jump off the cliff and survive ninety-nine percent of the time. And the one percent of the time Francis didn't make it, he made it look like he did. We actually had a lot of fun on that trip. It was rugged, but for all us young clowns, it was a great time."[1]

"[Coppola] offered to have me make a feature version of a film I made as a student, 'THX 1138.' So being young and bearded, and Francis being young and bearded, I thought, 'Well, he understands my concerns.' But then he said, 'If you're going to direct, you have to learn to write, and not only

do you have to learn to write, but you have to get good at it.' . . ."[8]

"So they chained me to my desk and I wrote the screenplay. Agonizing experience! It always is. I finished it, read it and said, 'This is awful.' I said, 'Francis, I'm not a writer. This is a terrible script.' He read it and said, 'You're right. This is a terrible script.' So he and I sat down together and re-wrote it, and it still was a pretty bad script. I said, 'Look, we've got to get a writer.' So we hired a writer to work on the project. . . .He wrote a script, and it was all right—it just wasn't anything at all what I wanted the movie to be. . . .I realized that if the script was going to be written the way I wanted it, I was going to have to write it myself. So a friend of mine from school, Walter Murch, sat down with me, and we wrote the screenplay—and it was still pretty esoteric and weird, but it was good enough to make into a movie—the one that finally got made—'THX 1138.' Francis talked Warner Bros. into going with it, and that's how I really got into writing."[5]

February 22, 1969. Married Marcia Griffin.

November 14, 1969. Formed American Zoetrope, a production company with Coppola. "We more or less work together as collaborators. What we do is look at each other's scripts, look at the casting, then at the dailies, at the rough cut and the fine cut, and make suggestions. We can bounce ideas off each other because we're totally different. I'm more graphics-film-making-editing-oriented; and he's more writing and acting-oriented. So we complement each other. . . ."[4]

Wicket.

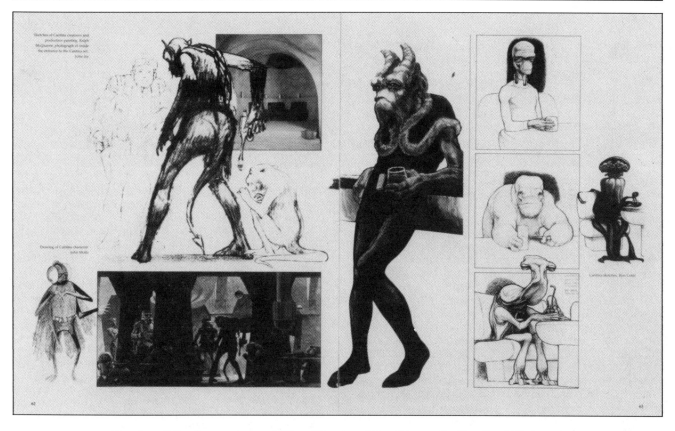

Sketches of Cantina creatures. ■ (From *The Art of Star Wars,* edited by Carol Titelman.)

"And then came Black Thursday."[8] On November 21, 1969, Warner Bros. cancelled it's deal with Zoetrope and took "THX 1138" away from Lucas to re-cut themselves. "Francis had borrowed all this money from Warner Bros. to set this thing up, and when the studio saw a rough cut of 'THX' and the scripts of the movies we wanted to make, they said, 'This is all junk. You have to pay back all the money you owe us.' Which is why Francis did 'Godfather.' He was so much in debt he didn't have any choice."[8]

March 11, 1971. Warner Bros. released "THX 1138" to a lukewarm reception. "The cuts didn't make the movie any better; they had absolutely no effect on the movie at all. It was a very personal kind of film, and I didn't think they had the right to come in and just arbitrarily chop it up at their own whim. I'm not really good with authority figures anyway, so I was completely outraged."[1]

"My second project was 'Apocalypse Now' which John Milius and I had been working on in school. . . .But we couldn't get it off the ground, and I wanted to do this rock and roll cruising movie. . . ."[5]

"I realized after 'THX' that people don't care about how the country's being ruined. . . .I would make a more optimistic film that makes people feel positive about their fellow human beings. It's too easy to make films about Watergate. And it's hard to be optimistic when everything tells you to be pessimistic and cynical. I'm a very bad cynic. . . .Maybe kids will walk out of the film and for a second they'll feel, 'We could really make something out of this country, or we could really make something out of our lives.' It's all that hokey stuff about being a good neighbor, and the American spirit and all that crap. There *is* something in it."[4]

"'THX' had taken three years to make and I hadn't made any money. Marcia was still supporting us, and I thought, 'Well

I'll do the rock and roll movie—that's commercial. Besides, I was getting a lot of razz from Francis and a bunch of friends who said that everyone thought I was cold and weird and why didn't I do something warm and human. I thought, 'You want warm and human, I'll give you warm and human.' So I went to Gloria and Bill Huyck and they developed the idea for 'American Graffiti,' and I took the twelve page treatment around. And it was turned down by every studio in town. The situation was pretty grim. Then I got invited to the Cannes Film Festival, because 'THX' had been chosen by some radical director's group. But Warner Bros. wouldn't pay my way. So, with our last $2000, [Marcia and I] bought a Eurail pass, got backpacks and went to Cannes."[8]

He was never informed of a press conference the French had scheduled for him. "I was barely able to get into my own picture, let alone go to a press conference. But for a number of years, the French thought I was a real snob."[1]

Upon his return from France, his deal with United Artists to make "American Graffiti" fell apart. "Bill and Gloria had a chance to direct their own movie, so I hired another friend to write the script. The first draft wasn't at all what I wanted. It was a desperate situation. I asked Marcia to support us some more. I was borrowing money from friends and relatives. I wrote the script in three weeks, turned it into UA, and they said 'Not interested.'. . .Then Universal said they might be interested if I could get a movie star. I said no. Universal said that even a name producer might do, and they gave me a list of names, and Francis [Coppola] was on the list. . . ."[8]

Coppola agreed to produce it. "We trust each other. . . .It's not like a producer telling you that you *have* to do something. Francis will say, 'Cut that scene out, it doesn't work at all.' And I may say, 'No, you're crazy. That's my favorite scene. I love it.' And he'll say, 'Okay, what do I care? You're an idiot anyway.' Actually, he calls me a stinky kid. He says, 'You're a stinky kid, do what you want.' And I may say the same thing to him. It works very well because you really need somebody to test ideas on. And you get a piece of expert advice that you value."[4]

Bill and Gloria Huyck helped Lucas write "American Graffiti." "They were cardboard cutouts in my script, non-people. Bill and Gloria made it one hundred percent better with a combination of wit, charm, snappy one-liners, and punched-up characters."[1]

"The film is about change. It's about the change in rock and roll, it's about the change in a young person's life at 18 when he leaves home and goes off to college; and it's about the cultural change that took place when the fifties turned into the sixties—when we went from a country of apathy and non-involvement to a country of radical involvement. The film is saying that you have to go forward. You have to be Curt, you have to go into the sixties. The fifties can't live.

"All good rock and roll is classic teenage stuff, and all the scenes were such classic teenage scenes that they just sort of meshed, no matter how you threw them together. Sometimes even the words were identical. The most incredible example—and it was completely accidental—is the scene where Steve and Laurie are dancing to 'Smoke Gets in Your Eyes' at the sock hop, and at the exact moment where the song is saying, 'Tears I cannot hide,' she backs off, and he sees that she is crying."[4]

1972. Directing "American Graffiti" proved to be a nightmare. "We'd start at 9:00 at night and end at 5:00 in the morning. In a regular movie, if you don't get what you're supposed to shoot one day, you can just throw up a few arc lights and shoot for another hour. On 'Graffiti,' when the sun came up, that was the end of the ballgame. We couldn't get one more shot. It was very hard on the crew. Nobody gets any sleep, so everybody's cranky. And it was very cold—like 40 degrees. We had to shoot it in 28 days, and sometimes we'd do as many as 30 setups in one night. . . ."[4] "I found myself saying, 'I don't really like directing that much. This is no fun!' What I really like is editing; that's what I can really sit and do and lose track of time and enjoy myself. . . ."[5]

"When I first screened 'American Graffiti,' one of the executives from Universal came up to me and said, 'This movie is not fit to show to an audience.' That is what he actually said. Well, Francis blew his cork. In my eyes, it was Francis' most glorious moment. He started screaming and yelling at this guy: 'How can you do this to this poor kid? He did this film for nothing, no money! He killed himself, and the first thing you tell him is that it's not fit to show to an audience. Couldn't you say, "Thank you, you did sort of a good job. Glad you brought it in on budget and on time."'" Francis kept yelling and yelling and he said, 'Well, I like this movie. I'll buy it. I'll give you a check for it right now.' Universal took the film, but we fought and fought. They wanted to take five minutes out of it. Five minutes in a movie is not going to make a difference. It was nothing more than an exercise in authority. . . ."[8]

"I expected 'American Graffiti' to be a semisuccessful film and make maybe $10 million—which would be classified in Hollywood as a success—and then I went through the roof when it became this big, huge blockbuster. And they said, well, gee, how are you going to top that? And I said, yeah, it was a one-shot and I was really lucky. I never really expected that to happen again. . . ."[9]

"I was thinking about quitting directing, but I had this huge draft of a screenplay and I had sort of fallen in love with it. Plus, I was a street filmmaker. I had never done a big, studio picture, so I thought, 'This'll be the last movie I direct.' I finally finished the script. I wanted to make a fairy tale epic, but this was like *War and Peace*. So I took that script and cut it in half, put the first half aside and decided to write the screenplay from the second. I was on page 170, and I thought, 'Holy smokes, I need 100 pages, not 500.' So I took that story and cut it into three parts. I took the first part and said, 'This will be my script. But no matter what happens, I am going to get these three movies made.'. . . ."[8]

"I wasted four years of my life cruising like the kids in 'American Graffiti' and now I'm on an intergalactic dream of heroism. In 'Star Wars,' I'm telling the story of me. It's fun—that's the word for this movie. Young people today don't have a fantasy life anymore; not the way we did. All they've got is Kojak and Dirty Harry. All these kids are running around wanting to be killer cops because the films they see are movies of disasters and insecurity and realistic violence. . . .I want 'Star Wars' to give people a faraway, exotic environment for their imagination to run free. I have a strong feeling about interesting people in space exploration. I want them to get beyond their basic stupidities of the moment and think about colonizing Venus and Mars. And the only way it's going to happen is to have some kid fantasize about getting his ray gun, jumping in his spaceship and flying off into outer space. . . .I wanted to make an action movie in outer space. I knew I wanted to have a big battle in outer space, a sort of dogfight thing. I knew I wanted to make a movie about an old man and a kid. And I knew I wanted the old man to be a real old man and have sort of a teacher-student relationship with the kid. I wanted the old man to also be like a warrior. I wanted a princess, too, but I didn't want her to be a passive damsel in distress. . . ."

"When I made the deal to write and direct 'Star Wars' at Fox, I obviously made it for nothing. All I had was a deal memo, no contract. Then 'Graffiti' came out, was a hit and suddenly I was powerful. Fox thought I was going to come back and demand all these millions of dollars and all these gross points. I said, 'I'll do it for the deal memo, but we haven't talked about things like merchandising rights, sequel rights.' I said I wasn't going to give up any of those. Fox said fine. They were getting me for less than $100,000."[8]

1976. Filmed "Star Wars" on location in Tunisia and on a soundstage in England. Formed his own special effects company, ILM—Industrial Light and Magic. "I was afraid that science-fiction buffs and everybody would say things like, 'You know there's no sound in outer space.' I just wanted to forget science. That would take care of itself. Stanley Kubrick made the ultimate science-fiction movie and it's going to be very hard for somebody to come along and make a better movie, as far as I'm concerned. I didn't want to make a '2001,' I wanted to make a space fantasy that was more in the genre of Edgar Rice Burroughs; that whole other end of space fantasy that was there before science took it over in the fifties. Once the atomic bomb came, everybody got into monsters and science. . . .I think speculative fiction is very valid but they forgot the fairy tales and the dragons and Tolkien and all the *real* heroes.

"Right when the film started, we hired two people—one was an artist, Ralph McQuarrie, and the other was the soundman, Ben Burtt. . . .Ben spent two years developing sound effects—he did all the ray guns, spaceships exploding, and toward the end he worked for. . .three or four months to come in with Artoo. I said I wanted to have beeps and boops and. . . .Well,

READ

and The Force is with you.

The American Library Association featured Yoda on its 1983 poster.

The Return of the Great Adventure.

Promotional ad for a Lucas/Spielberg collaboration.

(From the movie "Indiana Jones and the Temple of Doom," starring Harrison Ford and Kate Capshaw. Copyright © 1984 by Lucasfilm Ltd.)

it's easy to say that, it's another to take those beeps, boops and sounds and actually make a personality. He spent a long time coming up with sounds. And I would listen to it and I would say, no, no, we need something with a little more sensitivity, he needs to be sadder here, he needs to be happier there. We need to know he's angry here. . . .Ben had to write out the dialogue I never wrote. I just wrote, Threepio says, 'Did you hear that,' and the little robot goes 'beep-a-da-boop,' and Ben had to sit there and say, 'Hmm, well, of course I heard that, you idiot.' So then he'd take that and have to translate it. He did the same thing with the Wookie, a combination of a walrus and bear, and about five or six other animal sound effects that are all put together in a very sophisticated manner electronically to create one voice.''[9]

'''Star Wars' nearly broke me. I'm not a good general, and I had terrible conflicts between the role of general and the role of filmmaker. 'Star Wars' was so big that I couldn't control everything the way I did on 'THX' and 'American Graffiti.' Francis is good at delegating authority, but I'm not. I'm a craftsman; I'm a filmmaker, not a general.''[7]

'''American Graffiti' was unpleasant because of the fact that there was no money, no time and I was compromising myself to death. But I could rationalize it because of the fact that, well, it is just a $700,000 picture. . .and what do you expect, you can't expect everything to be right for making a cheesey, low-budget movie. But this was a big, expensive movie and the money was getting wasted and things weren't coming out right. I was running the corporation. I wasn't making movies like I'm used to doing. 'American Graffiti' had like 40 people on the payroll, that counts everybody but the cast. I think 'THX' had about the same. On 'Star Wars' we had over 950 people working for us and I would tell a department head and he would tell another department head, he'd tell some guy,

and by the time it got down the line it was not there. I spent a lot of my time yelling and screaming at people, and I have never had to do that before. I got rid of some people here and there but it is a very frustrating and unhappy experience doing that. . . .''[9]

''Directing is a reaction to everything—I have to make at least a thousand decisions a day. A thousand people coming up to you every day—and this is not an exaggeration—saying, 'Red or blue?' And you have to say, at that moment, with about fifteen seconds to make up your mind, 'OK, blue.' And if they have reasons that it should be different, they say so, and you have another fifteen seconds to analyze that. I guess that ultimately your level of success is how many of those are the right decisions and how many are the wrong decisions. If you can make the right decisions, you end up with a good movie. And if you make the wrong decisions, you end up with a terrible movie.

''For what it was, 'Star Wars' was made very inexpensively— a real low-budget movie—and it was very, very difficult getting things to work. The truth is that the robots didn't work at all. Three-PO works very painfully—and during the whole shooting of the picture I couldn't get R2 to go more than three feet without running into something. So you'll notice that in the film that he moves very little. The second unit came back here to ILM and rebuilt the robot, and we took him out to Death Valley and actually got some shots of him going more than three feet. So in the beginning there are actually a few shots of him going somewhere. You get the impression that he moves throughout the whole movie, but he doesn't. Everything was a prototype on the first movie, like, 'Gee, we're going to have to build this—we have no money, but we have to try and make this work.' But nothing really worked. . . .''[2]

"In special effects the key elements are time and money. Most of the special effects in 'Star Wars' were first-time special effects—we shot them, we composited them and they're in the movie. We had to go back and reshoot some, but in order to get special effects right, you really should shoot them two or three times before you go figure out how it should work, which is why it costs so much money. But most of our stuff was a one-shot deal. We did a lot of work but there is nothing that I would like to do more than go back and redo all the special effects."[9]

July 21, 1978. "Star Wars" released. "I'm sort of baffled by the movie, I have to admit. I mean, I expected it to be a moderately successful film—like a Disney movie. . . .I worked on the film right up until the day it opened. In fact, I was mixing the sound on the foreign versions of the film the day it opened here. I had been working so hard that, truthfully, I forgot the film was being released that day. My wife was mixing 'New York, New York' at night at the same place we were mixing during the day, so at 6:00 she came in for the night shift just as I was leaving on the day shift. So we ran over to grab dinner at the Hamburger Hamlet, which, by co-incidence, is right across the street from the Chinese Theater—and there was a huge line around the block. I said, 'What's that?' I had forgotten completely, and I really couldn't believe it. But I had planned a vacation as soon as I finished, and I'm glad I did because I really didn't want to be around for all the craziness that happened after that."[2]

Despite public adulation, the criticism of "Star Wars" ranged from Robert G. Collins': "[Taken for what it is, 'Star Wars'] functions as magic. With incredible audacity, it combines the stereotypes of modern pop literature and cinema with the Arthurian Romance," to Stanley Kauffman's: "About the dialogue there's nothing to be said. In fact, the dialogue *itself* can hardly be said: it sticks in the actors' mouths like peanut butter. . . ."

"Now, nobody likes critics. Stanley Kubrik told me he used to be concerned with what critics say. But he stopped getting upset when he realized that he spent three years developing an idea—working on it day and night—then somebody walks in and sees the film for two hours and spends a half-hour writing a review of it. So, the critic spends a total of 2 1/2 hours on something that you spent three years on. Kubrik said that after he realized that, critics held no interest for him. Critics are entitled to their opinions, and a lot of times what they say is true. It's just that they don't realize the effort and pain and struggling that went into something. . . ."[2]

The financial returns from "Star Wars" and it's subsequent merchandising sales allowed Lucas the freedom to produce the rest of his films through Lucasfilm, his own film production company, to build up his research and special effects division, Industrial Light and Magic, and to build Skywalker Ranch—an environment in which he and his elite friends can work to expand the art of filmmaking. "The ranch is a way of formalizing what we already have. I mean, before 'Star Wars' I was going to restore the building we're in—which was sort of run down. Then when the film was such a success I realized we could do this the way the original dream was, which was the dream for American Zoetrope, Francis Ford Coppola's film company, which is also based up here in Northern California. Meanwhile, Francis decided he'd rather be in the city. His original idea was to build a film studio—but my idea was to build a group of offices where my friends, and other Marin County filmmakers, could have a close proximity with each other."[6]

1979. Produced "More American Graffiti," directed by Bill W. L. Norton. "Actually, the inspiration we had for 'Apoc-alypse [Now],' things that are no longer in Francis' film, are going into 'More American Graffiti.' We're using the low-budget method we intended for Apocalypse and shooting it in 16mm, and the subject matter is all Vietnam.'"[7] The film failed, partially due to the fact the public already knew the fates of the "Graffiti" characters from the closing titles of "American Graffiti."

1980. Produced "The Empire Strikes Back," the second episode of the first "Star Wars" trilogy. After filtering out hundreds of directors, he decided on Irvin Kershner to direct. "When I visited the set in Norway and saw all the problems and the misery that Kershner was going through, wow, can you imagine being at the Arctic Circle at forty-five below zero? It's hard enough to just walk through it, let alone direct the actors, move the equipment. It was easy to let go of directing.'"[8]

"Finding a director is also very difficult, just like finding a writer. You need someone who technically knows what they're doing with extremely complicated movies—much more so than with any normal movie. I say that to people, and they don't really believe me. Even Irv Kershner didn't believe me. I said, 'You're in for a surprise on this one! I know you've been directing films for fifteen years, but you've never come across anything like this—believe me!' And he said, 'Oh, yeah, don't worry George.'. . .These films are not like regular movies. When you have that many special effects going on, and things have to be planned out so far in advance, and there are so many little pieces that have to fit together perfectly, and the chances of doing that are very remote—it drives you crazy."[6]

"I provided the story and technological advice, like does a robot do this or that? They shipped me the dailies and I looked at them. There were some problems. They were a little over budget, over schedule. That concerned me, because I only had so much money and I was afraid that if they used it all up, we wouldn't be able to finish the movie. But I knew they were doing the best job they could, and I thought the stuff looked terrific. It's truly Kershner's movie. Well, it's still my story. I just didn't have to do all the work. I feel Chewbacca is still my Wookie and R2-D2 is still my little robot."[8] "The Empire Strikes Back" was released and struck the same chord of success.

Lucas began collaboration with Steven Spielberg on "Raiders of the Lost Ark." "We have a great time together. He keeps saying it's my movie and I'll get blamed for it, and I keep saying it's his movie and he'll get blamed for it."[10]

The hero of "Raiders," Indiana Jones "has to be the kind of person we can look up to. We're doing a role model for little kids, so we have to be careful. We need someone who's honest and true and trusting."[1]

1981. "Raiders of the Lost Ark" found immediate success and monumental profit in international movie theaters. "I probably had more fun on that picture than on any other. I didn't have to do anything but hang out. I had all the confidence in the world in Steve and I was not at risk financially. I was hoping it would come in on budget, but if it didn't. . .well, for once, I wasn't at risk."[1]

Adopted a baby girl. Lucas began work on "Return of the Jedi," choosing Richard Marquand to direct the final episode of the first "Star Wars" trilogy—six more movies exist if Lucas decides to make them. The film had been titled "Revenge of the Jedi" right up until its release to stop the audience from guessing its plot. At the end of "Return of the Jedi," there is "no cliff hanger. The original idea kind of got segmented, and the fact that the story is a fairy tale kind of got

(From the movie ''Willow.'' Copyright © 1988 by Lucasfilm Ltd.)

lost, especially in the beginning, because the science fiction took over. I kept saying, 'Don't call it science fiction!' I think ['Return of the Jedi'], for better or worse, is going to put the whole thing in perspective. I don't know whether people are going to like it that much, but the truth of it is, that's the way the film's originally designed. . . .It's not nearly as complicated. [Luke Skywalker is the twin brother of Princess Leia. In the end, Luke touches the glimmer of good in their father, Darth Vader]. As I say, it started out as a simple fairy tale, and that's all it really is. . . .When it comes out, people will say, 'Oh, my God. How obvious! Why couldn't they think of something more interesting than that?' But I'm stuck with the way it was originally planned, and I can't suddenly go off on some tangent.''[2]

''Each film has accomplishments that I like. It's not that I didn't like the movies, but if I look at them now, each one falls a bit short of what I had hoped it to be—because I guess I either set my sights a little bit lower, or we actually do get a little bit better. You look at the Jabba the Hut scene and say, 'Oh, that's what he wanted the cantina [in 'Star Wars'] to be.' Or you look at the end battle, and you say, 'Oh, that's what the end battle was supposed to be in the first one.' But we couldn't have _done_ this movie then. I mean, it just was not humanly possible or even financially possible. So, a lot of these things I have finally worked out. I finally got the end battle the way I wanted it, I got the ground battle that I wanted, I got the monsters the way I wanted them.''[10]

1983. The success of ''Return of the Jedi'' insured more money for Skywalker Ranch. Lucas worked on the sequel to ''Raiders'' called ''Indiana Jones and the Temple of Doom,'' with Steven Spielberg and felt the increasing pressures of success. ''Running the company to me is like mowing the lawn. It has to be done. I semi-enjoy it, once in a while.''[1]

''My wife likes to have vacations. She doesn't like not to be able to go anywhere. She'd like to be able to say, 'Look, let's take off two or three weeks and just cool out.' So I _promised her_ that after 'Star Wars' every year we'd take two vacations—two or three weeks each year. That lasted for one year. Now, I try to get in one vacation a year, for a week or so. It always comes down to saying, 'Next week. Just let me get past this thing. . . .' By the time you get past this thing, there's always something else. . . .''[2]

''You spend ten years of your life on a picture and you say: 'Where is my life? Where is the normal—enjoying your weekends and your life with your friends?' You see everything just dropping away, and you sit and say, 'I don't see anybody anymore. I just don't have time for it.' And when you have a daughter, it changes things. You can't put a kid on hold and say, 'Wait, I've got one more picture to do; you just stay tight.' You know, she's only going to be two once, and she's great, and I'm not going to miss it.''[10]

Lucas still has thoughts about the next two ''Star Wars'' trilogies. ''After that, I can tell another story about what happens to Luke after this trilogy ends. All the prequel stories exist: where Darth Vader came from, the whole story about Darth Vader and Ben Kenobi, and it all takes place before Luke was born. The other one—what happens to Luke afterward—is much more ethereal. I have a tiny notebook full of notes on that. If I'm really ambitious, I can proceed to figure out what would have happened to Luke.''[10]

1984. Divorced Marcia. ''Indiana Jones and the Temple of Doom'' repeated the success of ''Raiders of the Lost Ark.''

1986. Produced ''Labyrinth,'' which was directed by Jim Henson [creator of the Muppets], and continued to work on his

Luke Skywalker and Darth Vader in a lightsaber duel. ■ (From the movie ''Return of the Jedi.'' Copyright © 1983 by Lucasfilm Ltd.)

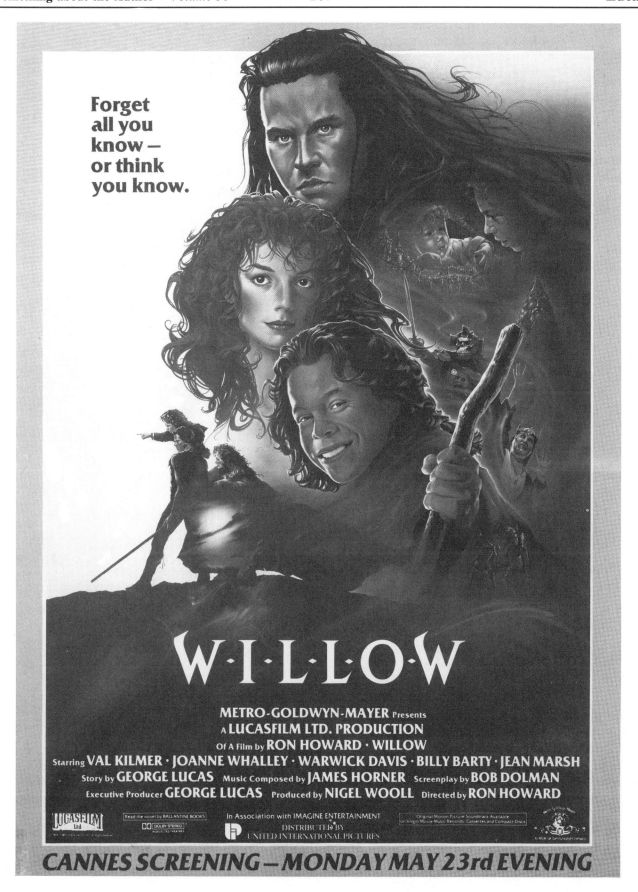

Promotional poster advertising 1988 Cannes screening of "Willow."

Preliminary sketch by Michael Whelan for the book *My Jedi Journal*. (From *Michael Whelan's Works of Wonder.*)

dream of Skywalker Ranch: "I'm going to sit down at a point when I feel very good about myself and do a lot of hard thinking. I may move on to something else or find out after a while that the only thing I really love to do is make movies. And I've always been interested in doing my strange little experimental films."[10]

1988. Lucas created the story for "Willow." The title character, Willow Ufgood—a three-foot member of the Nelwyn race—saves and protects a baby girl who will eventually undo evil queen Bavmorda. Lucas teamed up with director Ron Howard to produce this big-budget fairy tale. Although the critics were cool, the box office burned—making "Willow" another summer smash.

"Ever since I was in film school in the '60s, I've been on a train. Back then I was pushing a 147-car train up a very steep slope—push, push, push: I pushed it all the way up, and when 'Star Wars' came along in 1977, I reached the top. I jumped on board, and then it started going down the other side of the hill. I've had the brakes on ever since. My life since 'Star Wars' has been spent pulling back on all these levers, trying to stop this train from going down this very steep slope, with the wheels screaming and screeching all the way. It's been work, work, work."[11]

FOOTNOTE SOURCES

[1]Dale Pollack, *Skywalking: The Life and Films of George Lucas,* Harmony Books, 1983.

[2]Kerry O'Quinn, "The George Lucas Saga—Chapter One: A New View," *Starlog,* July, 1981.

[3]George Lucas, "Young Directors, New Films," *American Film Institute Report,* winter, 1977.

[4]Stephen Farber, "George Lucas: The Stinky Kid Hits the Big Time," *Film Quarterly,* spring, 1974.

[5]K. O'Quinn, "The George Lucas Saga—Chapter Two: The Cold Fish Strikes Back," *Starlog,* August, 1981.

[6]K. O'Quinn, "The George Lucas Saga—Chapter Three: The Revenge of the Box Office," *Starlog,* September, 1981.

[7]Audie Bock, "George Lucas: An Interview," *Take One,* May 15, 1979.

[8]Jean Vallely, "The Empire Strikes Back," *Rolling Stone,* June 12, 1980.

[9]Paul Scanlon, "The Force behind George Lucas," *Rolling Stone,* August 25, 1977.

[10]P. Scanlon, "George Lucas Wants to Play Guitar," *Rolling Stone,* July 21/August 4, 1983.

[11]Gerald Clarke, "'I've Got to Get My Life Back Again,'" *Time,* May 23, 1983.

FOR MORE INFORMATION SEE:

Stanley Kauffmann, "Films: THX 1138," *New Republic,* April 10, 1971.

New Republic, September 15, 1973.

Michael Dempsey, "Reviews: 'American Graffiti,'" *Film Quarterly,* fall, 1973.

Pauline Kael, "Un-People," *New Yorker,* October 29, 1973.

The 1988 holiday film campaign was lauched in _Daily Vanity._

Alice Sodowsky and others, "The Epic World of 'American Graffiti,'" _Journal of Popular Film,_ Volume IV, number 1, 1975.

New Yorker, May 30, 1977.

Time, May 30, 1977.

S. Kauffmann, "Films: 'Star Wars,'" _New Republic,_ June 18, 1977.

Robert Hatch, "Films: 'Star Wars,'" _Nation,_ June 25, 1977.

Richard A. Blake, "Two Histories of Film," _America,_ June 25, 1977.

Robert G. Collins, "'Star Wars': The Pastiche of Myth and the Yearning for a Past Future," _Journal of Popular Culture,_ summer, 1977.

Arthur Lubow, "A Space 'Iliad'—The 'Star Wars' War: I," _Film Comment,_ July-August, 1977.

Terry Curtis Fox, "Star Drek—The 'Star Wars" War: II," _Film Comment,_ July-August, 1977.

P. Kael, "Contrasts," _New Yorker,_ September 26, 1977.

Michael Pye and Lynda Myles, _The Movie Brats: How the Film Generation Took over Hollywood,_ Holt, 1979.

"Lucas, Wife Split," _Variety,_ June 22, 1983.

"Video," _People,_ March 26, 1984.

"Romance Comes between Mag and George Lucas," _New York Post,_ May 15, 1984.

William Scobie, "Spielberg, Lucas and 'Escapism,'" _Observer_ (London), June 10, 1984.

"Return of the Jedi Ewoks," _Daily News_ (N.Y.), October 23, 1984.

Daily News (N.Y.), May 7, 1985.

"Holt Will Publish Tie-Ins to 'Labyrinth,'" _Publishers Weekly,_ October 25, 1985.

"Forward-Thinking Lucas Leaves Door Open Anent More 'Wars' Features," _Variety,_ June 3, 1987.

Vernon Scott, "The Force Is Still with George Lucas," _Newsday,_ June 15, 1987.

LUSTIG, Arnost   1926-

PERSONAL: Born December 21, 1926, in Prague, Czechoslovakia; came to the United States in 1970; son of Emil and Therese (Lowy) Lustig; married Vera Weislitz, July 24, 1949; children: Josef, Eva. _Education:_ College of Political and Social Science, Prague, Czechoslovakia, M.A., 1951, Ing. Degree in Political and Social Sciences, 1954. _Home:_ 4000 Tunlaw Rd. N.W., Washington, D.C. 20007. _Agent:_ Elaine Markson Literary Agency, Inc., 44 Greenwich Ave., New York, N.Y. 10011. _Office:_ Department of Literature, American University, Washington, D.C. 20016.

CAREER: Radio Prague, Prague, Czechoslovakia and _Jewish Gazette,_ Prague, Arab-Israeli war correspondent, 1948-49; Czechoslovak Radio Corp., reporter in Europe, Asia, and North America, 1950-68; Barrandov Film Studios, Prague, screenwriter, 1960-68; writer in Israel, 1968-69; Jadran Film Studio, Zagreb, Yugoslavia, screenwriter, 1969-70; University of Iowa, Iowa City, member of International Writing Program, 1970-71, visiting lecturer in English, 1971-72; Drake University, Des Moines, Iowa, visiting professor of English, 1972-73; American University, Washington, D.C., visiting professor of literature, 1973-75, assistant professor of literature, 1976-77, associate professor of literature, 1977—. Head of the Czechoslovak film delegation to the San Sebastian Film Festival, 1968; member of the jury, Karlovy Vary International Film Festival, 1968; member of the jury, Newstadt International Prize for Literature. Visitor at Kibutz Hachotrim, Israel, 1968-69. Lecturer in film and literature at universities in Czechoslovakia, Israel, Japan, Canada, and the United States. *Member:* Authors Guild, Authors League of America, P.E.N., Film Club (Prague), Union of Czechoslovak Writers.

AWARDS, HONORS: First Prize from the Oberhausen Film Festival, 1961, and Best Short Story from the University of Melbourne (Australia), and First Prize from Amsterdam's Film School Festival, both 1962, all for "A Bite to Eat"; Best Book of the Year from Mlada Fronta Publishing House (Czechoslovakia), 1962, for *Diamonds of the Night*; First Prize from the Locarno Film Festival, 1963, for "Transport from Paradise"; First Prize from the Mannheim Film Festival, and from the Pesaro Film Festival, both 1964, both for "Diamonds of the Night"; First Prize of Czechoslovak Radio Corp., 1966, for radio play, "Prague Crossroads," and 1967, for radio play, "A Man the Size of a Postage Stamp"; Award from Dr. Vit Nejedly Competition from the defense ministry in Prague, for several literary works concerned with anti-fascist themes; First Prize at Monte Carlo Film Festival, 1966, and eight other international prizes, all for television film of "A Prayer for Katerina Horovitzova"; Clement Gottwald State Prize, 1966, and National Book Award finalist, and B'nai B'rith Award, both 1974, all for *A Prayer for Katerina Horovitzova*; Second Prize of San Sebastian Film Festival, 1968, for the film, "Dita Saxova"; Prize from Prague Spring Music Festival, 1968, for symphonic poem "Night and Hope."

National Jewish Book Award, 1980, for *Dita Saxova* and 1986, for *The Unloved*; Emmy Award for News and Documentary Outstanding Individual Achievement, 1985, for PBS film "The Precious Legacy"; honorary doctor of Hebrew Letters from Spertus College of Judaica, 1987.

WRITINGS:

IN ENGLISH

Nac a nodeje (short stories), Nase Vojsko, 1958, translation by George Theiner published as *Night and Hope,* Dutton, 1962 (also see below).

Demanty noci (short stories) Mlada Fronta, 1958, translation by Irish Urwin published as *Diamonds of the Night,* Artia, 1962 (also see below).

Dita Saxova (novel), Ceskoslovensky Spisovatel, 1962, translation by G. Theiner published as *Dita Saxova,* Hutchinson, 1966, translation by Jeanne Nemcova, Harper, 1979.

Nikoho neponizis, Nase Vojsko, 1963, published as *Indecent Dreams,* Northwestern University Press, 1988.

Modlitba pro Katerinu Horovitzovou (novel), Ceskoslovensky Spisovatel, 1964, translation by J. Nemcova published as *A Prayer for Katerina Horovitzova,* Harper, 1973.

The Unloved: From the Diary of Perla S., Arbor House, 1985.

COLLECTED WORKS; "CHILDREN OF THE HOLOCAUST" SERIES

Darkness Casts No Shadow, translation by J. Nemcova, Inscape, 1977, 2nd revised edition, Northwestern University Press, 1986.

Night and Hope, Inscape, 1977, new edition, Northwestern University Press, 1985.

Diamonds of the Night, translation by J. Nemcova, Inscape, 1977, 2nd revised edition, Northwestern University Press, 1986.

ARNOST LUSTIG

OTHER

Ulice ztracenych (title means "The Street of Lost Brothers"), Mlada Fronta, 1949.

Muj znamy Vili Feld (novel; title means "My Acquaintance Willi Feld"), Mlada Fronta, 1949.

Bile brizy na podzim (title means "The White Birches in September"), Ceskoslovensky Spisovatel, 1966.

Horka vune mandli (title means "The Bitter Smell of Almonds"), Mlada Fronta, 1968.

Milacek (title means "Darling"), Ceskoslovensky Spisovatel, 1969.

Also author of text for Otmar Macha's symphonic poem, "Night and Hope." Libretto for "Beadle of Prague" cantata, music by H. Berlinski. Also author of unproduced screenplays, "The Golem" with Zbynek Brynych, "The Excursion" with Jan Kadar, "The Street of Lost Brothers" with Jan Nemec, "The White Birches in the Fall" with Jaromil Jires, and a screenplay about the International Writers Program at the University of Iowa. Author of a short filmscript, "A Bite to Eat," directed by J. Nemec, 1960. Correspondent for literary magazines in Czechoslovakia, 1950-58; editor, *Mlady svet* (youth magazine; title means "The Young World"), 1958-60.

ADAPTATIONS:

SCREENPLAYS

"Transport from Paradise" (based on *Night and Hope*), Studio Barrandov (Prague), 1963.

"Diamonds of the Night," Studio Barrandov, 1964.

"Dita Saxova," Studio Barrandov, 1968.

TELEVISION SCRIPTS

"The Blue Day," T.V. Prague, 1960.
"A Prayer for Katerina Horovitzova," T.V. Prague, 1965.
(With Ernest Pendrell) "Terezin," ABC-TV, 1965.
"Stolen Childhood," for TV-Rome, 1966.
(Co-screenwriter) "The Precious Legacy," PBS-TV, 1984.
(With Robert Gardner) "The Triumph of Memory," PBS-TV, 1988.

RADIO SCRIPTS

"Prague Crossroads," Radio Prague, 1966.
"A Man the Size of a Postage Stamp," Radio Prague, 1967.

WORK IN PROGRESS: Screenplay adaptation of "The Unloved"; new screenplay, "A Prayer for Katerina Horovitzova"; a book of short stories, *Don Juan in Iowa City.*

SIDELIGHTS: Arnost Lustig was born on December 21, 1926 in Prague, Czechoslovakia. In 1942, he was sent with his parents to Theresienstadt, then to Auschwitz-Birkenau (where his father died in the gas chambers), then to Buchenwald. "Nine out of ten survivors of Auschwitz-Birkenau gain safe distance from it during the day, but at night when the will is suspended they inevitably return to it. . . .Auschwitz-Birkenau. . .[is] with them. In them.[1]

Years after his internment, Lustig returned to the former concentration camp. ". . .A new horror took possession of me. Auschwitz-Birkenau as a museum, as a giant reservation com-

"**He started shooting,**" said the first boy. ■ (Jacket design by Rufus Wells III from *Darkness Casts No Shadow* by Arnost Lustig.)

memorating human brutality, does not evoke in one's imagination even a shadow of the fear, anxiety, and hopelessness which a single moment of this death factory induced while still in full operation. Auschwitz-Birkenau, this empty, silenced camp, the largest man ever built for man, has the effect of a calm burial ground. The dead do not talk. The land is almost beautiful, whether grassy or covered with snow. Memory that serves the living betrays the dead. It is not in the power of the living to give voice to the dead. Time works against the innocent. Time toys with what happened yesterday. Time clears the mind to gain space for what will happen tomorrow. The image of the dead a person has who loiters in a cemetery is no image of the dead but only their faded picture.

"I rage at my impotence to express in words the weakness of memory. . . .Balzac is supposed to have said that evil which is too great can never be punished. How to bring this to terms with the four million dead who saw their last sun, stars, and moon here, with the mothers who saw the last of their children? How at least to breathe afterlife into them? Each one had been someone—my mother, my father, my brother, my sister. . . .

"Once I was a prisoner here. Why do I feel the same way as those who were never here, never saw Auschwitz-Birkenau? How can I call back to life the feeling of the dead?

"Was I really at the ramp when the orchestra, made up of the finest musicians of occupied Europe, played the French hit *J'attendrai* for those who were going to the gas, for those servicing the crematoria, for the workers at the Buna Werke or in the Auto Union or in the delousing station? Once a trio sang the German version of a hit for those who had attempted to escape. *'Komm zurueck, denn ich warte auf dich, denn du bist fuer mich all mein Glueck':* Come back to me, I am waiting for you—for you who are my happiness.

"In the orchestra I had a friend, Ota S., who used to play at the Esplanade Hotel in Prague and in the Est Bar. While he was playing, he watched his wife and three little boys go to the crematorium. On the day that his family was murdered, he was playing 'A Jew Had a Little Wife' and a song about a young man's unrequited love and a song about a wedding under the sky and how merry the wedding guests were and about how the bride and bridegroom's parents danced.

"Was I really standing here in the wind when two friends of mine, the older T. and the younger T., in a soccer game against eleven SS men, were told to play as best they could but not to win, and to remember that any injury they might inflict on the Germans, or even on themselves, would send them into the chimney? Surviving, they received a loaf of German commissary bread and a half-pound of blood pork pate. I watched the older T.'s clothes and shoes until they were through playing. It was almost like home—two teams, dressing rooms, lines, a field, goals, and a round ball. However, as Tadeusz Borowski later wrote, between the starting and final whistle of the referee, a stone's throw from the soccer field, three thousand people went to the gas.

"Was I really in the Gypsy camp, which SS men 'cleaned out' the night and day before we arrived from Terezin, 'the city Adolf Hitler gave the Jews;—and where only a few Gypsy children escaped death by digging themselves into the ground like worms and where the Gypsy boys stoned us as if we had caused their parents' deaths?

"Did I really talk with the twins Pavel and Peter on whom Dr. Mengele performed experiments and whom he castrated? Back in Terezin, at the Home for Youth, the twins gave me three ounces of sugar in exchange for a collection of poems by the Catholic poet Otakar Brezina. When I asked where their parents were, they replied that they had flown through the chimney in Crematorium No. 2 as if telling me they had taken the Orient Express to Istanbul.

"I remember little Rene G. from Prague who felt privileged because his sister was allowed to serve in the SS bordello and could bring him milk, bread, and sugar. He knew he would live only as long as his sister was there. But the gas and the chimney and the ashes would greet the two of them as soon as she was used up.

"I remember how in September 1944 I got through the gate onto the ramp in Auschwitz-Birkenau. We felt what animals feel during a solar eclipse or a forest fire or an approaching earthquake; within several minutes, all children under fifteen, women and men above forty, the sick, and the ones with glasses or grey hair were in bathrooms where Zyklon B came out of the sprinklers instead of water. In half an hour, a greasy fire was flashing from Chimneys No. 2 and No. 3, followed by smoke which gave off the pungent smell of human bones like from a glue or soap factory. Mothers waiting their turn had to watch their toddlers being thrown like chickens into the furnace. On the bathroom wall was written: *Baths of Eternal Forgetting.*

"I understand how difficult it is to write about this in primers and textbooks for children who were born years after the time when the swastika flag fluttered above Auschwitz-Birkenau

(From *Diamonds of the Night* by Arnost Lustig.)

headquarters. Sometimes I wish that all men and women wherever they live on earth, would have to visit Aushwitz-Birkenau for a day, an hour, or even a single second during the time when Hitler, Himmler, Eichmann, or Baldur von Schirach swelled with pride at what they had commissioned German architects, planners, and builders to do. . . . .Auschwitz-Birkenau must be at the beginning of all questions that torment us, and instead of providing answers it can only lead to further questions.

"I remember an afternoon in September 1944 when I stood in the Gypsy camp by the high-voltage wires, surrounded by bare Polish plains and forests. A thin transparent fog enveloped the ground and the people. It penetrated the soul. We could see Crematoria No. 2 and No. 3 where our relatives were burning. From the other side, smoke came from large pits where the dead from Hungary, for whom there were not enough furnaces, were burning in their own fat. A purple fire was flashing from the chimneys, soon glowing a deeper purple before turning into evil-reeking black smoke. Everything stank. The smoke became a cloud, and slowly a black rain—ashes—dropped down from it. Like everyone else I wished the wind would lift or the earth reverse its direction. The ashes had a bitter taste. Also the gas in the shower rooms had the bitter smell of almonds. These ashes were not from coal or burnt wood, rags or paper.

"They fell on us—mute, deaf, relentless ashes, in which human breath, shrieks, and tears could be felt. I stood at a concrete fence post with white porcelain insulators, taking it all in like an hallucination. A tune from Johann Strauss's 'Die Fledermaus' was going through my head. But this was no dream. It was real.

"A couple of days earlier I had heard it at a cabaret with my father, in the attic of the fire station in Terezin. Now my father was soap. Ashes. Smoke tasting of bones. The fog, as white as swan's wings, turned black, and song, sky, and ashes fused into one. The curve of the melody and the plait of the lyrics suddenly acquired a new meaning: *Gluecklich ist, wer vergisst, was doch nicht zu aendern ist.* Happy the one who forgets what cannot be changed. I was singing. My friends dragged me into the hut before prisoner count so I would live at least until the next day.

"It was exactly what the men of the SS wanted for those who still lived in Auschwitz-Birkenau: to feel as insane and lonely, as lost and helpless, as in a nightmare, to regard the absurd as normal and the normal as absurd. But the loneliness among the dead is still better than the loneliness of the living. Sometimes I would go to the concrete fence post and wires just as one might visit a cemetery, save only that our dead did not have graves. I would only catch the ashes in the palm of my hand or watch the chimney smoke day and night.

"Once, standing by the wires again, I saw a little herd of completely naked women. It was October and a cold wind blew on them as they each carried shoes and a bundle of effects under their arms. Their heads were shaven bare. The last twenty wore transparent shirts. All were barefoot.

"Since my father had become soap, ashes, and the echo of Strauss's 'Die Fledermaus,' I could not get rid of the thoughts that it would perhaps be better if my mother joined him. That way I would not have to watch her walk barefoot on the muddy October ground, through the wet patches of snow. I watched the chilled women, one after another, to see if my mother was among them. I felt relief when I went over the naked ones with my eyes to find that she was not there, and then over the ones in shirts to see that she was not walking among them

Katerina Horovitzova could feel the debility which emanated from the huddle of human beings there beside her. ■ (From *A Prayer for Katerina Horovitzova* by Arnost Lustig. Illustrated by Juan Svarez.)

either. Only when the last two came into view did I see that the next to the last was my mother.

"I was glad she failed to notice me. She did not even watch where she was going. I was sad that she had not been sent to the bath of eternal forgetting. Before they stole her clothes, shoes, and underwear and shaved her head, she had been beautiful. I was unable to call to her. The wires began to attract me again. A touch would have been enough. I did not want to imagine what was in store for my mother apart from torture, gas, fire. I watched until she disappeared into the fog. I woke up the next day with the consoling thought that she must have frozen before she reached the end of the road between the wires. Snow and rain kept falling. In my mind, I buried my mother too with the song in which one is happy when he forgets what cannot be changed. I did not want her to be with me once I became so terribly lonely again.

"In the middle of a clear day I can close my eyes and see shadows. They are not specters but the hunched figures of men and women, children and old people. It is the ramp in Auschwitz-Birkenau, the baths where *Disinfection* is written in German. They are going to the gas. This is the Germany I carry within me. This is the Germany I carry within me even though I wish I could be more like my mother, who spoke its language before Auschwitz-Birkenau became the measure of everything German for her."[1]

No, the relief he had expected to feel did not come. ■ (Jacket design by Rufus Wells III from *Night and Hope* by Arnost Lustig).

Years later "...I came home with the intention to write a story about American Jews who got in the hands of the German army during the American troops disembarkment on Sicily in the year 1943....I began writing at 7 P.M. that day, continued through the night and whole next day. In the evening of that day I was done. The following ten days I could not sleep. I had the impression I had been constantly meeting the devil."[2]

The result was *A Prayer for Katerina Horovitzova.* "My personal payment for the six million dead of whom each represents to me one innocently killed human being, father, brother, sister, friend. Every one of them had been someone. I reject Balzac's wisdom, saying that if evil is massive enough it cannot be punished, for a great evil exceeds the framework of criminal law. Such evil must be punished and my attempts to punish and try is this story."[2]

And with those haunting memories, Lustig grew up and spent the next two decades as a journalist and screenwriter in postwar Communist Czechoslovakia, encouraged by the glimmers of freedom demonstrated by the liberal era of Dubcek. "I was in love with my country, to tell the truth. It's a beautiful country, a very romantic country. Prague is a mystical and romantic city. Just to walk through the streets makes you feel something special. And I felt it. If somebody had told me in the first half of 1968 that I would leave, I would have laughed at him. The idea of leaving my country was not in the least milli-millimeter of my mind.

"People in Czechoslovakia love to read, and if you are a writer, they like you. This is the only country where a poet can make a living, because people stand in line for books of poetry. This was a good country for writers. For instance, I didn't write on very popular themes. I wrote on suffering in camps, about the war, but they published over a half million copies in ten years. And this is a small nation of ten million people. Hemingway is published in Prague—150,000 copies; Fitzgerald—200,000 copies. Everybody knows who Faulkner is, sometimes more than they do [in the U.S.]. Steinbeck, whom I met once in Prague, is a favorite of Czech readers, because they know his best books.

"So to live in such a country, you don't have to be a hero; it is enough to be a writer. You feel that your life has meaning; you are working as well as you can, and people are reading your work. You don't need more. You can make a living. For a writer, it is not good to be very poor, but neither is it good for him to be very rich. Somewhere midway. This was my situation in Prague when we left. I felt like a prince."

With the Soviet invasion in 1968, however, "almost no books were published except by mistake." For instance, 22,000 copies of a collection of three of Lustig's novels were published in 1970, and were banned almost immediately, even though one of the novels had been reprinted seven times since 1964. "Suddenly the regime thought that my descriptions of Nazi concentration camps might be an allegory for life under the present regime in Czechoslovakia. For what can you publish in these countries, if you try to be as honest as possible, yet want to avoid a situation comparable to jumping on the tail of a snake so that he can still whirl around to bite you with his teeth? The only way is to write about the past. . . .

"Once everything was lost, when the country was invaded, I was declared by the last congress of the Communist party an 'enemy of the state,' an 'imperialist agent,' a 'Zionist.' They said all my books and films were paid for by some world conspiracy, and my books were confiscated."

When conditions became intolerable, Lustig and his family moved to the United States. "Being an exile you have to start all over again, from the bottom of life—you have no money, no country, just your hands. And for such a person this country is very good. You have to prove yourself to survive. It was your Jack London who said that in literature, only the best survive. So far I have survived a lot, and hope I can go on surviving."[3]

"Under those circumstances it is better to be in a strange country, to start again, and to prove to yourself that you are a real writer. To be a writer under the best circumstances is not so difficult. To remain a writer under worse circumstances is, I think, a good test for a writer.

"Every writer has a duty to be as good as he can as a writer, to tell stories he likes in the best way he can. What he likes—this is his personal approach to life. I like stories about brave people, about how they survived under the worst cirumstances. I like people who are fighting for their fate, and who are better in the end, richer, in a sense, than they were in the beginning. I think that each writer has a certain duty—to imagine himself in theory as perhaps the last human being under certain circumstances and that perhaps his testimony will be the last one. He is obliged to deliver that testimony."

Lustig's books and stories have been translated into more than twenty languages, including German, Spanish, Japanese, Polish, Hebrew, Hindi, Esperanto, French, Estonian, Norwegian, Italian, and Yiddish.

FOOTNOTE SOURCES

[1]Arnost Lustig, "Auschwitz-Birkenau," translated by Josef Lustig, *Yale Review*, spring 1983.
[2]A. Lustig, *A Prayer for Katerina Horovitzova*, Harper, 1973.
[3]"PW Interviews: Arnost Lustig," *Publishers Weekly*, February 21, 1977.

FOR MORE INFORMATION SEE:

Kirkus Reviews, August 1, 1973.
Best Sellers, October 15, 1973.
New York Times Book Review, October 21, 1973.
Booklist, November 1, 1973.
Proteus, spring, 1974.
Choice, fall, 1974.
Southwest Review, winter, 1974.
Washingtonian, May, 1977.
World Literature Today, autumn, 1979 (p. 636), summer, 1981.
Byron L. Sherwin and Susan G. Ament, *Encountering the Holocaust: An Interdisciplinary Survey*, Impact Press, 1979.
Insight, June 16, 1986.
The Jewish Week, June 3, 1988.

McCONNELL, James Douglas Rutherford 1915-1988 (Douglas Rutherford; Paul Temple, a joint pseudonym)

OBITUARY NOTICE—See sketch in *SATA* 40: Born October 14, 1915, in Kilkenny, Ireland; died April 29, 1988. Educator, editor, and author. McConnell was a longtime Eton College teacher and writer of instructional books, war stories, and many crime novels. Under the name Douglas Rutherford he published most of his crime fiction, including *Gunshot Grand Prix*, *Killer on the Track*, and *Rally to the Death*. He also collaborated with Francis Durbridge on crime novels such as *The Pig-Tail Murder*, *A Game of Murder*, and, under the joint pseudonym Paul Temple, *The Tyler Mystery*.

FOR MORE INFORMATION SEE:

OBITUARIES

Times (London), May 5, 1988.

METTER, Bert(ram Milton) 1927-

PERSONAL: Born August 14, 1927, in New York, N.Y.; son of Harry W. (a salesman) and Rosella (a homemaker; maiden name, Fischbein) Metter; married Roslyn H. Reiser (a homemaker), January 11, 1952; children: Joel, Lawrence, Daniel. *Education:* Brooklyn College, B.A., 1949; Columbia University, M.A., 1952; Harvard Business School, A.M.P., 1980. *Religion:* Jewish. *Home:* 41 Nutmeg Dr., Greenwich, Conn. 06831. *Office:* J. Walter Thompson Co., 466 Lexington Ave., New York, N.Y. 10017.

CAREER: Daily Mirror (newspaper), New York, N.Y., writer, 1953-56; *Newsweek* (magazine), New York, N.Y., writer, 1956-59; J. Walter Thompson Co. (advertising agency), New York, N.Y., writer, 1959—, vice-president, 1965-73, senior vice-president, 1973-78, creative director, 1974-85, executive vice-president, 1978-85, vice-chairman, 1985-88; chairman, 1988—. *Awards, honors:* Has received numerous advertising awards.

BERT METTER

WRITINGS:

Bar Mitzvah, Bat Mitzvah: How Jewish Boys and Girls Come of Age (illustrated by Marvin Friedman), Clarion, 1984.

SIDELIGHTS: "I've always wanted to be a writer. But instead of traveling the path of book authorship, I became an advertising writer. The pace is fast, the work is fun, the pay is good. So I've earned my living writing television commercials and print ads at one of the country's top ad agencies. While you get huge audiences for your work, ad writing is anonymous—and your goal is to sell products, but you have to be creative to be effective.

"I've always wanted to try my hand at books or movies—but hadn't had the time or motivation. My children helped me. I have three sons and they all went through a Bar Mitzvah ceremony. Each time it happened, I felt I should know more about the meaning of the ceremony—and went looking for a short, clear explanatory book. I couldn't find one and decided to fill the need myself.

"Now that I've tasted the experience, I don't think my first book will be my last."

FOR MORE INFORMATION SEE:

New York Times, October 11, 1984.
Adweek, September 2, 1985.

MOSER, Barry   1940-

PERSONAL: Born October 15, 1940, in Chattanooga, Tenn.; son of Arthur Boyd and Wilhelmina Elizabeth (Haggard) Moser; married Kay Richmond (an artist; divorced, April, 1978); children: Cara, Romy, Maddy. *Education:* Attended Auburn University, 1958-60; University of Chattanooga, B.S., 1962;

graduate study at University of Massachusetts, 1969-70; studied with George Cress, Leonard Baskin, Jack Coughlin and Harold McGrath. *Home and studio:* Bear Run, North Hatfield, Mass. 01066. *Agent:* Jeff Dwyer, 30 Pleasant St., P.O. Box 1149, Northampton, Mass. 01061. *Office:* Pennyroyal Press, Inc., P.O. Box 1149, Northampton, Mass. 01061.

CAREER: Artist, engraver, book designer, printmaker, illustrator, teacher, lecturer. Pennyroyal Press, Northampton, Mass., founder and major domo, 1968—. Visiting artist, University of Tennessee, 1972, 1975, Rhode Island College, 1976, University of Nebraska at Omaha, 1976, University of Nebraska at Lincoln, 1976, California College of Arts and Crafts, Oakland, 1977, 1982, 1983, University of Washington, Seattle, 1981, Carnegie Mellon University, Pittsburgh, Pa., 1986, and Ringling School of Art and Design, Sarasota, Fla., 1986; lecturer. Has taught at Williston-Northampton School, Easthampton, Mass. Juror, Fifty Books of the Year, American Institute of Graphic Arts, 1981.

EXHIBITIONS—Group shows: Dixie Annual, Montgomery, Ala., 1964, 1965; Winston-Salem Annual, Winston-Salem, N.C., 1965; Twenty-second American Drawing Biennial, Norfolk, Va., 1966; Westfield State College Annual, Westfield, Mass., 1970; Leverett Craftsman Association, Leverett, Mass., 1971, 1973; Second Cape Cod Annual, Barnstable, Mass., 1971; Boston Printmakers, Brandeis University, Waltham, Mass., 1972; Berkshire Museum Show, Pittsfield, Mass., 1972, 1973; "Six Printmakers," Spectrum Gallery, Brewster, Mass., 1972; Optik Gallery, Amherst, Mass., 1973; Oklahoma National Print and Drawing Show, Oklahoma City, 1974; Los Angeles National Print Show, Otis Art Institute, Los Angeles, Calif., 1974; New Hampshire International Print Exhibition, New Hampshire Graphics Society, 1974; Fifteenth Annual Bradley Print Show, Bradley University, Peoria, Ill., 1974.

Library of Congress National Print Exhibition, Washington, D.C., 1975; "Printmaking West," Utah State University, Logan, Utah, 1975; Krakow Invitational, Krakow, Poland, 1975; "Woodblock Prints," ADI Galleries, San Francisco, Calif., 1975; Smith College Library, Northampton, Mass., 1976; Silvermine, New Canaan, Conn., 1976; "Modern Greek Typography," Wellesley College Library, Wellesley, Mass., 1976; University of Wisconsin, Milwaukee, Wis., 1976; "History of the Printed Books," San Francisco Public Library, Calif., 1976; "Recent Acquisitions," Houghton Library, Harvard College, Cambridge, Mass., 1976; Footprint International Small Format Exhibition, Seattle, Washington, 1977; Fourth International Exhibit of Botanical Art, Pittsburgh, Pa., 1977-78; "Regional Small Presses," Keene State College, Keene, N.H., 1978; "Calligraphy, Past and Present," George Walter Vincent Smith Museum, Springfield, Mass., 1979; "Printers' Choice," Grolier Club, New York City, 1979; "Private Presses, The Book as Art," Liberty Gallery, Louisville, Ken., 1979; "American Printmakers as Illustrators," Pratt Institute, New York City, 1979.

"Seventy from the Seventies," New York Public Library, New York City, 1980; "Fifty Books of the Year," American Institute of Graphic Arts, New York City, 1981-86; "Visage d'Alice," Centre National d'art et de culture Georges Pompidou, Paris, France, 1983; Smithsonian Institution, Washington, D.C., 1985.

One-man shows: Hunter Gallery, Chattanooga, Tenn., 1964; Graphic Arts Society, Springfield, Mass., 1969; Unitarian Society, Amherst, Mass., 1969; University of Tennessee, Chat-

BARRY MOSER

tanooga, 1970, 1975, 1980; Optik Gallery, Northampton, Mass., 1971, 1973; American International College, 1972; Main Street Gallery, Nantucket, Mass., 1973, 1974, 1985, 1986; Springfield Public Library, Springfield, 1973; Berkshire Museum, Pittsfield, Mass., 1973; Rhode Island College, Providence R.I., 1975; Smith College, Northampton, Mass., 1976; Boston Athenaeum, Boston, Mass., 1976; University of Nebraska, Omaha, Neb., 1976; Wenniger Graphics, Boston, Mass., 1977, 1983; Holyoke Museum, Holyoke, Mass., 1977, 1983, 1984; New Hampshire Technical Institute, Concord, N.H., 1977; Trinity College, Hartford, Conn., 1977.

Galleriaforma, Genoa, Italy, 1980; University of Wisconsin, River Falls, Wis., 1980; Museum of Fine Arts, Springfield, 1982; Mary Ryan Gallery, New York City, 1982, 1983, 1985, 1987; LaSalle University Union, Philadelphia, Pa., 1983; University Press Books Gallery, Berkeley, Calif., 1984, 1985; University Research Library, University of California at Los Angeles, 1984; International Galleries, Northampton, Mass., 1985, 1986; Mark Twain Memorial, Hartford, Conn., 1985; Schiller-Wapner Galleries, New York City, 1985; Glenn Books and Crown Center, Kansas City, Mo., 1985; Bluxome Art Gallery, San Francisco, Calif., 1985, 1986; Atlantic Gallery Ltd., Washington, D.C., 1986; World College West, Petaluma, Calif., 1986; Carnegie Mellon University Library, Pittsburgh, Pa., 1986.

Works are in more than one hundred private and public collections, including the Library of Congress, Beinecke Library at Yale University, Berkshire Museum, Boston Athenaeum, Brown University, University of California at Los Angeles, Dartmouth College, Cambridge University, Georgetown University, Grolier Club, British Museum, New Britain Museum of American Art, New York Public Library, Houghton Library at Harvard University, London College of Printing, Minneapolis Society of Fine Arts, National Library of Australia, New York Botanical Gardens, Princeton University, Stanford University, Syracuse University, University of British Columbia, University of North Carolina at Chapel Hill, and Vassar College Library.

MEMBER: American Printing History Association (charter member); National Academy of Design. *Awards, honors:* Purchase Prize, and Faculty Purchase Prize, both from the Westfield State Annual, both 1970; Second Prize from the Cape Cod Annual, 1971; Award of Merit from the New Hampshire International, 1974; Award of Merit from the American Institute of Graphic Arts, 1982-86; American Book Award for Pictorial Design, and included in the American Institute of Graphic Arts Book Show, both 1983, both for *Alice's Adventures in Wonderland;* Award of Merit from Bookbuilders West, 1983-86; Award of Merit from *Communications Arts,* 1984-86; *Frankenstein* was included in the American Institute of Graphic Arts Book Show, 1984; *Jump! The Adventures of Brer Rabbit* was named one of *School Library Journal*'s Best Books for Young Adults, 1986, and was selected one of Child Study Association of America's Children's Books of the Year, 1987; *Jump Again!* was selected one of *New York Times* Best Illustrated Books of the Year, and one of *Redbook*'s Best Picture Books of the Year, both 1987.

The Tar-Baby, she sat there, she did. ■ (From *Jump Again! More Adventures of Brer Rabbit* by Joel Chandler Harris. Illustrated by Barry Moser.)

Ma told me to wash and get ready to eat. ■ (From *I Remember Grandpa* by Truman Capote. Illustrated by Barry Moser.)

WRITINGS:

SELF-ILLUSTRATED

(With Parrot) *Cirsia and Other Thistles*, Pennyroyal Press, 1978.
Notes of the Craft of Woodengraving, Pennyroyal Press, 1980.
A Family Letter, Pennyroyal Press, 1980.
Pan, Pennyroyal Press, 1980.

ILLUSTRATOR

Ely, *Too Black, Too White*, University of Massachusetts Press, 1969.
The Red Rag, Castalia Press, 1970.
The Death of the Narcissus, Castalia Press, 1970.
Bacchanalia, Pennyroyal Press, 1970.
Cautantowitt's House, Brown University Press, 1970.
E. M. Beekman, *Homage to Mondrian*, Pennyroyal Press, 1972.
The Oyster and the Eagle, University of Massachusetts Press, 1973.
Twelve American Writers, Pennyroyal Press, 1974.
Thirteen Botanical Woodengravings, Pennyroyal Press, 1974.
Mugwumps, Morals and Politics, University of Massachusetts Press, 1975.
Modern British Fiction, University of Texas Press, 1975.
E. M. Beekman, *Carnal Lent*, Pennyroyal Press, 1975.
Robert Frost, a Living Voice, University of Massachusetts Press, 1975.
Goudy Greek, Pennyroyal Press, 1976.
J. Waldsorf, *Men of Printing*, Pennyroyal Press, 1976.

Steinberg and McGuigan, *Rhode Island: An Historical Guide*, Rhode Island Bicentennial Commission, 1976.
The Poetry of Octavio Paz, University of Texas Press, 1976.
Paul Smyth, *Thistles and Thorns*, University of Nebraska, 1976.
Paul Ramsey, *Eve Singing*, Pennyroyal Press, 1977.
Marcia Falk, *Song of Songs*, Harcourt, 1977.
Bellot, *William Knox*, University of Texas Press, 1977.
J. Chametzky, *From the Ghetto*, University of Massachusetts Press, 1977.
Osip Mandelstam, University of Texas Press, 1977.
Manvell, *Chaplin*, Little, Brown, 1977.
Smith, *Elizabeth Tudor, Portrait of a Queen*, Little, Brown, 1977.
Bishop, *St. Francis of Assisi*, Little, Brown, 1977.
E. M. Beekman, *The Killing Jar*, Houghton, 1977.
Arthur MacAlpine, *Man in a Metal Cage*, Pennyroyal Press, 1977.
Sprich and Nolan, *The Whispered Meanings*, University of Massachusetts Press, 1977.
Allen Mandelbaum, *Chelmaxims*, Godine, 1977.
Paul Mariani, *Timing Devices*, Pennyroyal Press, 1977.
Jane Yolen, *The Lady and the Merman*, Pennyroyal Press, 1977.
Lawrence Ferlinghetti, *Director of Alienation*, Main Street Press, 1977.
William Stafford, *Late Passing Prairie Farm*, Main Street Press, 1977.
Louis Simpson, *The Invasion of Italy*, Main Street Press, 1977.
Nancy Bubel, *The Adventurous Gardner*, Godine, 1977.
Stephen Brook, *Bibliography of the Gehenna Press*, J. P. Dwyer, 1977.
Mark Twain, *1601*, Taurus Books, 1978.
David Smith, *Goshawk and Antelope*, University of Illinois Press, 1978.
The Esthetic of Jean Cocteau, University Press of New England, 1978.
Walter Chamberlain, *Woodengraving*, Thames & Hudson, 1979.
M. W. Ryan, editor, *Irish Historical Broadsides*, J. P. Dwyer, 1979.
Vernon Ahmadjian, *The Flowering Plants of Massachusetts*, University of Massachusetts Press, 1979.
Herman Melville, *Moby-Dick; or, the Whale*, Arion Press, 1979.
John Brown's Body, Doubleday, 1979.
In Praise of Sailors, Abrams, 1979.
A. Mandelbaum, *A Lied of Letterpress*, Pennyroyal Press, 1980.
Dante, *Volume One: The Inferno, the Divine Comedy of Dante Alighieri, a Verse Translation with Introduction and Annotations by Allen Mandelbaum*, University of California Press, 1980.
Virgil, *Aeneid*, translated by A. Mandelbaum, University of California Press, 1980.
P. Smyth, *The Cardinal Sins: A Bestiary*, Pennyroyal Press, 1980.
Galway Kinnell, *The Last Hiding Places of Snow*, Red Ozier Press, 1980.
Homer, *Odyssey*, translated by T. E. Shaw, Limited Editions, 1980.
D. Smith, *Blue Spruce*, Tamarack Editions, 1981.
G. Kinnell and Diane Wakoski, *Two Poems*, Red Ozier Press, 1981.
Gene Bell-Villada, *Borges and His Fiction*, University of North Carolina Press, 1981.
Dante, *Purgatorio*, translated by A. Mandelbaum, University of California Press, 1982.
Lewis Carroll, *Alice's Adventures in Wonderland*, University of California Press, 1982.
L. Carroll, *Through the Looking Glass, and What Alice Found There*, University of California Press, 1982.

It was some time before the Cowardly Lion awakened. ■ (From *The Wonderful Wizard of Oz* by L. Frank Baum. Illustrated by Barry Moser.)

Robert Bly, *The Traveller Who Repeats His Cry,* Red Ozier Press, 1982.

Mary Shelley, *Frankenstein, or the Modern Prometheus,* University of California Press, 1983.

D. Smith, *Gray Soldiers,* Stuart, 1983.

R. Bly, *The Whole Misty Night,* Red Ozier Press, 1983.

(Contributor) *Visages d'Alice ou les illustrateurs d'Alice,* Gallimard, 1983.

Lewis Carroll, *The Hunting of the Snark,* Pennyroyal Press, 1983.

William Carlos Williams and Romantic Idealism, University Press of New England, 1984.

Dante, *Paradiso,* translated by A. Mandelbaum, University of California Press, 1984.

Paul Mariani, *A Usable Past,* University of Massachusetts Press, 1984.

E. M. Beekman, *Totem and Other Poems,* Pennyroyal Press, 1984.

Robert Francis, *The Trouble with God,* Pennyroyal Press, 1984.

Mark Taylor, *Erring,* University of Chicago Press, 1984.

Robert Penn Warren, *Fifty Years of American Poetry,* Abrams, 1984.

Mark Twain, *The Adventures of Huckleberry Finn,* University of California Press, 1985.

Anne Frank, *Anne Frank: Diary of a Young Girl,* Pennyroyal Press and Jewish Heritage, 1985.

Richard de Fournival, *Master Richard's Bestiary of Love and Response,* translated by Jeanette Beer, University of California Press, 1985.

L. Frank Baum, *The Wonderful Wizard of Oz,* University of California Press, 1985.

Giants and Ogres, Time-Life Books, 1985.

Sylvia Plath, *Above the Oxbow,* Catawba Press, 1985.

Richard Michelson, *Tap Dancing for the Relatives,* University Press of Florida, 1985.

M. Falk, *It Is July in Virginia,* Scripps College Press, 1985.

Joel Chandler Harris, *Jump! The Adventures of Brer Rabbit,* adapted by Van Dyke Parks and Malcolm Jones, Harcourt, 1986.

Stephen Crane, *The Red Badge of Courage,* Harcourt, 1986.

Washington Irving, *Two Tales: Rip Van Winkle [and] The Legend of Sleepy Hollow,* Harcourt, 1986.

Barbara Stoler Miller, translator, *The Bhagavad-Gita,* Columbia University Press, 1986.

The Fall of Camelot, Time-Life Books, 1986.

Nathaniel Hawthorne, *The Scarlet Letter,* Harcourt, 1986.

Editors of American Heritage Dictionary, *Word Mysteries and Histories: From Quiche to Humble Pie,* Houghton, 1986.

The Strange Case of Dr. Jekyll and Mr. Hyde, Pennyroyal Press, 1986.

Robert D. Richardson, Jr., *Henry David Thoreau: A Life of the Mind,* University of California Press, 1986.

Eudora Welty, *The Robber Bridegroom,* Pennyroyal Press, 1987.

J. C. Harris, *Jump Again! More Adventures of Brer Rabbit* (ALA Notable Book), adapted by Van Dyke Parks, Harcourt, 1987.

Truman Capote, *I Remember Grandpa,* Peachtree, 1987.

Virginia Hamilton, *In the Beginning: Creation Stories from around the World,* Harcourt, 1988.

Also illustrator of *Une Ecraseuse,* 1978, *An Alphabet,* and *Liber Occasionum.* Contributor to periodicals, including *Audubon, Massachusetts Review, New York Review of Books, New York Times Book Review, Parabola, People's Express, Publishers Weekly, Yankee,* and *Polity,* the Journal of the Northeastern Political Science Association.

WORK IN PROGRESS: Biddy Early, by Nancy Willard, for Knopf; *The Guild Shakespeare,* for Doubleday; *Tom Sawyer* and *Tales of Edgar Allan Poe,* for Morrow Junior Books.

SIDELIGHTS: "I began my formal education, so to speak, in military school, where I stayed for six years from the seventh grade through the twelfth. To be an artist in a southern male-oriented family like mine was not the thing to do. We played ball, went hunting, and I could identify every car made between 1940 and 1958. I got busted at school from corporal down to private for drawing naked women on blank pages of my Spanish textbook. I can't remember now whether I got that punishment for not paying attention in class—although that

One eye had lost its pupil, and was glaring and spectral, but the other had the gleam of a genuine devil in it. ■ (From *Two Tales: Rip Van Winkle and The Legend of Sleepy Hollow* by Washington Irving. Illustrated by Barry Moser.)

ALICE WAS BEGINNING TO GET very tired of sitting by her sister on the bank, and of having nothing

(From *Alice's Adventures in Wonderland* by Lewis Carroll. Illustrated by Barry Moser.)

would have been a real severe penalty—or for defacing a textbook—it was, after all, my book—or for drawing dirty pictures. My sense tells me it was the latter.

"After military school I went to Auburn and studied mechanical engineering; that's about building cars, so it was acceptable. My family wouldn't hear of me going north to school; they're true Faulknerian southerners. I lasted at Auburn for two years, or until my folks' money ran out, and then returned home to study painting at the University of Chattanooga. This time I was footing the bills so the family had nothing to say about what I did.

"I suppose that I was a constant source of disapproval. I even married a 'Yankee' from Missouri, just across the line, who 'talked funny.' It never occurred to any of them that maybe we might talk a little funny.

"After I got married I took a job teaching at another military school. It must sound like I am of the military mind, having spent so much of my life around their institutions, but I'm not that way at all. I hate the military mentality, but I took the job to support us when I got married. I graduated from college, got married, started work as a teacher and we had our first daughter all in the same year, 1962.

"I worked at the school for five years and then, well, I didn't exactly get sacked but the closest thing to it. I was hired to teach typing and mechanical drawing—with a few classes in art during the last two years—but finally I was refused an annual raise that was automatic at the school. The headmaster explained that I had a 'lackadaisical attitude' toward teaching typing and he didn't much like my approach to coaching weightlifting either. I was also accused of putting away my football team's equipment while it was still wet. That did it: I applied for teaching jobs in Colorado and New England, as far away from Tennessee as I could get.''[1]

Subsequently Moser taught in Hampshire, Mass. and continued studying everything he could about printmaking, engraving and, especially drawing. One of his teachers was Leonard Baskin. ''I met him through mutual friends soon after I moved here. The first print I ever bought was one of his. He asked me what I would like to learn from him, and I said, 'From you, drawing.' I consider him to be one of the master draftsmen of the twentieth century. He said, 'All right, go draw a tree, and I want to see everything there is to see in that tree.' That was the beginning of lesson one. I made a drawing of a tree, brought it back to show him, and he asked, 'Why did you draw such a small tree on such a large piece of paper?' I remember replying, 'Damn, I knew you'd say that, because I would have said the same thing to one of my students.' End of lesson one.

''I went and made another drawing and he said, 'Do it again,' and again and again until I had made about six drawings and had six lessons. Leonard never said much more than 'Do it again,' until the last one. Then he said, 'That's a nice drawing. I would buy that drawing.' End of my studies with Leonard Baskin. He taught me a lot, though, about using fine paper, crowquill points, drawing and something about persistence.''[1]

In 1968 Moser founded the Pennyroyal Press. Working out of a Northhampton, Massachusetts printshop, he, master printer Harold McGrath, and Jeff Dwyer have issued over forty-nine imprints, many of them first editions of contemporary writers illustrated with Moser's original wood engravings and etchings.

Moser produced his first wood engraving in 1968 and today is considered one of the finest graphic artists in the United States. He has illustrated over eighty books, appeared in over sixty group shows and forty one-man shows, and has work in over one hundred public and private collections, including the British Museum, New York Public Library, the Library of Congress and major colleges and universities. He has illustrated such diverse works as *Moby-Dick*, *Alice's Adventures in Wonderland*, *Through the Looking Glass and What Alice Found There*, *Frankenstein*, *Huckleberry Finn*, and *The Wonderful Wizard of Oz*.

''I think I bring freshness to every project I do because just about every book I've decided to illustrate I just read for the first time. You have to understand I spent six years in military school. . .and never read a book if I could help it. I was not a good student. I had no intellectual curiosity whatsoever until I was 25. I went through four years of college and never read a book. That is the honest-to-God truth. All I did was play ball and make pictues of naked women. I just never read. The only book I illustrated that I read while I was in school was *Frankenstein*.

''Now when I come to a project, I come to it fresh, and what back in the 50s was an aggravation to my instructors, is to me today—as a maturing artist—something of great benefit. It's a great benefit, you see, because I come to it without any preconceived notions, no prejudices whatsoever.''[2] Once he accepts an assignment, he will read a book over and over again. ''After a while, I can quote these books at length by heart.''[2]

Now the ground was covered with a thin powdering of snow. ■ (From *Around the World in Eighty Days* by Jules Verne. Illustrated by Barry Moser.)

''A text I choose must seed my mind and have a market. I know it is not popular for an artist to talk about money, but as far as I'm concerned there is no reason to choose a text that has a limited market when you can choose a text that has a broad one.

''The illustrated book, which is different from the typographic book, does not belong to any one person, neither to the author any more than, on a different level, to the craftsman who had manufactured its paper, to the designers and punch-cutters who had drawn and cut the punches for its type, to the compositors who had composed the type, to the impositors who had imposed it, any more than it belongs to the pressman who has midwifed the book to a physical reality, nor to the binder, who ultimately cradles it between its boards to give it a substance that allows it to go out to be held in the hand to be read. The art of the book is an act of solidarity and collegiality. It is more closely akin to the theater or architecture than to painting or sculpture. Designer and illustrator are craft-fellows to typographers and printer, to papermakers and bookbinders, to editors and publishers. The *whole book* is spawned in a community of peers.

''The book is an organic whole, a single voice, a single form. When I see my images (from a book) tacked up on a wall they look out of place. They need to be tied together because that's what they have been designed for.

"I don't know where ideas come from. One moment you have none, the next moment you do. Deadline pressure seems to make them flow more readily. Happily, with the *Alice* books I had all kinds of ideas. The creation of illustrations is often a merging of the theoretical and the practical. This was the case of one *Alice* illustration idea I had for the falling-down-the-well dream scene. I discussed this with people in the theater department of Smith College, who were helping me design an authentic period costume, about making an apparatus inside the costume consisting of a pungee cord to which I could hook up one of my daughters. The theory was to attach her to a hanging ring in a gymnasium with me lying flat on my back, taking pictures underneath her, and have her bounce up and down on the cord trying to create a falling effect. But, in practice, it never would have worked, since the gestures of a human form falling in space are different from those of a secured weight on which gravity is acting.

"Although I wanted to explore it, I was diverted by information I came by that was to change the nature of my approach. From a concordance to *Alice* then being written by a scholar at the Univerity of Colorado, I was astonished to learn of the number of times the words "death" and "dying" and "lone" and "lonely" came up in the text. It came to me then that reality was the key, not the dream scenes. So I abandoned

We poked our heads out. . .and looked up, and down, and across. ■ (From *The Adventures of Huckleberry Finn* by Mark Twain. Illustrated by Barry Moser.)

the falling idea and of ever seeing Alice except when she's awake. The only time we see Alice within the dream is when she sees herself in the looking glass, which is an announcement of the book, *Alice through the Looking Glass*. I used the mirror image to play the two books against each other—images from one book being identical in position and outline with images in the other. If you lay the two *Alice* books side by side and flip the pages simultaneously from the back of one book and the front of the other, you find that some illustrations are exact mirror images—duplications. In *Alice in Wonderland*, ten pages from the back, there is a double spread of the jury that is at the bottom of the page, with two large hats going up into the margin. Close the pages and those two hats close on top of each other and are, in fact, mirror images. Ten pages from the front of *Alice through the Looking Glass* are two chess sets that do exactly the same thing. In fact, if you pile the books one on top of the other and drive a nail through them both, it would pass through exactly similar points, particularly eyes, in both books. The hatter and the hare in *Alice* and the hatter and the hare in *Looking Glass* are based on the same two images, and if one traced them both they would be identical and the tracings could be interchanged.

"Mary Wollstonecraft Shelley's *Frankenstein*. . .was a difficult book to do. It was the first one I did using color in the image. I 'see' in black and white and I create my images in black and white. But *Frankenstein* changed all that. The book contains ten color plates and its typography is rigidly black and white. There are no paragraph breaks. Instead, I used tiny crosses for paragraph marks, so there are little black spots all the way through, but the pages are always a rectangle and always mechanically the same, each page thirty-one lines long. Even at the end of a volume (the book is written in three volumes), I designed the layout of the last page so as to end in a triangular point of type that is thirty-one lines from the top line.

"Color is nonexistent in the book except as it relates to the monster. Ugliness in *Frankenstein* is the book's psychological basis, and I used color to bring it out in a structural sense. I decided the monster had to be very ugly, and in meeting the problem head on I decided to go to color to give him special intensity.

"In the middle of the work, the monster comes back and in a monologue tells Frankenstein what he has been doing over the past two or three years. During that monologue, I have shown the monster eight times in what I call conversational portraits—his head turns slightly, gestures change, the light changes. In them, the monster's color becomes more and more complex—the first image is one color under black, then two colors under black, then three colors. Then I play yellow over red over a second red, then the second red over the first red over the yellow, playing it in reverse order. And I continue building color for the subsequent portraits. The frontispiece—a tree being blown apart by lightning—is the motif of the book and is a pale blur overprinted with black. In the book's last image—the last thing the monster says is 'farewell'—his face is literally going out of the picture, thrown way up into a corner; his back is also printed with blue.

"Once an idea is in place, the search for the image begins. Images can emerge from a lot of research. Some I do in my library, which contains visual material rather than books purely for reading—history, objects, costumes, anatomy, curiosities and the like. This kind of material comes in handy when I'm called in to handle just one aspect of a job, like cutting the woodblocks for *Moby-Dick*. That wasn't my book and I didn't create the illustration concept, but was hired because my hands

Her final employment was to gather sea-weed, of various kinds, and make herself a scarf, or mantle, and a head-dress. ■ (From *The Scarlet Letter* by Nathaniel Hawthorne. Illustrated by Barry Moser.)

"Then you should say what you mean," the March Hare went on. ■ (From *Alice's Adventures in Wonderland* by Lewis Carroll. Illustrated by Barry Moser.)

could cut the blocks. The publisher felt that no one should interfere with, or interpret, Melville's novelistic art. The illustrator should do nothing more than build 'stage sets' for it, that is, simply illustrate for the reader authentically detailed elements of whaling at that time. So my woodengravings are of harpoons, tackle, long boats, whales and the like. At the time I thought the approach was a good one. But I have my own ideas about the illustrating of *Moby-Dick* and am longing for a chance to do the book again, but from a dramatic point of view, interfering, as it were, with Melville's work.

"In researching I go as far down into a project as I possibly can. In doing *Huckleberry Finn*, for instance, in order to depict a trip down the Mississippi River I sat on a boat in the middle of the river with a camera to capture the essence of the scene. (I use a camera as a tool to record in a permanent way what my eyes see.)

"I may not use a single piece of research I come up with, but it's there. It's part of the well I have to dip into. And no matter what I find, whether I use it or not, it all makes the final work richer.

"In creating the image of the monster in *Frankenstein*, I did not rely on conventional research. For instance, I didn't turn to a memory of Boris Karloff, who played the monster in the original film version. To avoid stereotyping and to give the image true ugliness, my eighteen-year-old daughter and I took a human skull, built up areas with plasticene, covered it with chicken skin and then sewed it with coarse black thread to create the suture lines. I must have taken over 300 pictures of it, and it was from those pictures that the image was created.

"I bought a 500mm lens for my camera, which I am using specifically to capture faces of outpatients at the State Mental Hospital in Northampton, Mass., for the day I do my own *Moby-Dick*. I want to use such faces as the crew of the *Pequod*. I can't capture them by sketching, because I'm not that fast or that good. But standing unobtrusively at a distance with a 500mm lens, I can do it.

"When I get into a project I live an intense life. When I did *Alice*, I'd get up at four o'clock in the morning and work for seventeen hours a day, seven days a week, for eight or nine months and damn near killed myself. As Bernard Shaw said, 'Wiskey makes it possible.'"[3]

FOOTNOTE SOURCES

[1]"Barry Moser, Designer, Illustrator and Publisher," *Communication Arts*, September/October, 1985.
[2]Nicholas A. Basbanes, "Barry Moser: A Noted Artist and Illustrator Plans to Enter the Twentieth Century," *Worcester Sunday Telegram*, November 16, 1986.
[3]"Illustrator at Work: Barry Moser," *Publishers Weekly*, July 6, 1984.

FOR MORE INFORMATION SEE:

Chattanooga Times, October 26, 1975.
Daily Hampshire Gazette, September 23, 1976.
Joseph Blumenthal, *The Printed Book in America*, Godine, 1977 (p. 129).
Springfield Republican, June 25, 1978.
Fine Print, July, 1978 (p. 65), July, 1982.
Yankee, October, 1978 (p. 138).
David M. Sander, *Wood Engraving*, Viking, 1978 (p. 34).
Printing News, February 10, 1979 (p. 13).
Publishers Weekly, March 19, 1979, August 1, 1986 (p. 31).
Horticulture, April, 1979 (p. 27).
Christian Science Monitor, February 2, 1982.
Newsweek, March 1, 1982.
Eunice Agar, "Wood Engravings by Barry Moser," *American Artist*, April, 1982 (p. 68).
Lynne Baranski, "Wood Engraver Barry Moser Carves a New and Darker *Alice in Wonderland*," *People Weekly*, April 12, 1982.
English Language Notes, December, 1982.
Village Voice, April 26, 1983.
Sunday Post (Bridgeport, Conn.), June 26, 1983.
Chicago Tribune Magazine, January 27, 1985.
New England Monthly, September, 1985.
Book World, September 8, 1985.
San Francisco Examiner, May 7, 1986.
Five Owls, November/December, 1986.

NEWMAN, Matthew (Harrison) 1955-

PERSONAL: Born July 22, 1955, in St. Petersburg, Fla.; son of Harry Gerald (a salesman) and Sesame (a singer and actress; maiden name, Smith) Newman; married Karyn Tonkinson, August 12, 1983 (divorced, August 19, 1986), married Shawn K. Murphy (a paralegal), November 21, 1987. *Education:* University of California—Berkeley, B.A., 1978. *Politics:* Democrat. *Religion:* Catholic. *Home and office:* 322 West Miner, Apt. 3-A, Arlington Heights, Ill. 60005.

CAREER: Society for Visual Education, Chicago, Ill., staff writer and producer of filmstrips, book cassettes, and micro-

MATTHEW NEWMAN

software, 1979-83; author of books for children and young adults, instructional designer of microcomputer software, and writer/producer of industrial training materials including videos, filmstrips, and user guides, 1983-87; Coronet/MTI Film & Video, Chicago, supervising producer, 1987—. Professional musician; lead guitar player for Chicago-based new wave group, Rant/Chant. *Member:* Independent Writers of Chicago Association. *Awards, honors: Learning* magazine Audio-Visual Award for Best Filmstrip, 1980, for ''The Human Reproductive Systems''; Filmstrip Award Honorable Mention from the National Educational Film Festival, 1983, for ''Listening Skills'' and ''The Holiday Adventures of Ted E. Bear;'' Best Filmstrip Award from the National Educational Film Festival, 1984, for ''The Olympic Games.''

WRITINGS:

JUVENILE

Watch/Guard Dogs, Crestwood House, 1985.
Dwight Gooden, Crestwood House, 1986.
Patrick Ewing, Crestwood House, 1986.
Larry Bird, Crestwood House, 1986.
Lynette Woodard, Crestwood House, 1986.
Mary Decker Slaney, Crestwood House, 1986.

ADAPTER; BOOK WITH CASSETTE

Goldilocks and the Three Bears, Society for Visual Education, 1980.
Little Red Riding Hood, Society for Visual Education, 1980.
The Selfish Giant, Society for Visual Education, 1980.
Thanksgiving for King, Society for Visual Education, 1980.
The Wide-Mouthed Frog, Society for Visual Education, 1980.
Leo the Lop, Society for Visual Education, 1982.
The Cucumber Princess, Society for Visual Education, 1982.

FILMSTRIPS FOR CHILDREN

''The Human Reproductive Systems,'' Society for Visual Education, 1979.

''Developing Self-Esteem,'' Society for Visual Education, 1980.
''Insurance: How to Buy and Why,'' Society for Visual Education, 1981.
''Listening Skills,'' Society for Visual Education, 1982.
''The Olympic Games,'' Society for Visual Education, 1983.
(Adapter) ''The Holiday Adventures of Ted E. Bear,'' Society for Visual Education, 1983.
''Basic Chemistry,'' Encyclopaedia Britannica, 1985.
''Contemporary Issues: Terrorism,'' Encyclopaedia Britannica, 1986.
''The Modern Presidency,'' Coronet/MTI, 1988.
''Moments in History,'' Coronet/MTI, 1989.

MICROCOMPUTER TEACHING GAMES

''Guiness World Records Problem Areas in Addition,'' Society for Visual Education, 1982.
''Fractions,'' Society for Visual Education, 1983.
''Guiness World Records Problem Areas in Multiplication,'' Society for Visual Education, 1984.
''Run for President,'' World Book, 1984.

EDUCATIONAL MUSIC SOUNDTRACKS

''Spinners and Slugs,'' Scott, Foresman, 1984.
''Sound,'' Encyclopaedia Britannica, 1985.
''Winter,'' Encyclopaedia Britannica, 1986.

WORK IN PROGESS: Fiction; plays; original music.

SIDELIGHTS: ''I was born in St. Petersburg, Florida in 1955, the second of six children. In the same year, my family moved to California, where I spent the next twenty odd years growing up in different cities up and down the California coast. We lived in Los Angeles, Azuza, Tin Can Beach, Palm Springs, West Hollywood and El Monte, all within the space of a few years. At about age ten, my parents split up and we went from having a home and a pool in Palm Springs to being alone with our mother on welfare, refugees from suburbia, boat people on the Venice canals. I ended up spending the better part of my grade school years in Venice, which was then a washed out bohemian beach town.

''In Venice, I shined shoes, sold newspapers and panhandled as a way to make money for corn dogs and ice cream. My brothers and sisters and I spent most of our days on the boardwalk at the beach, hopping trams, riding waves, and sneaking into Pacific Palisades Park. We found ways to entertain ourselves without any money, such as by inventing a 'Man from Uncle' Club, complete with 'Man from Uncle' tests such as jumping off lifeguard towers, climbing up piers, and riding elevators to the top of strange buildings. All the while I was trying to find my niche among the odd mixture of artists, gypsies, street people, burnt-out lifeguards, surfers, gangs, preachers, retirees, political activists, and L.A. Beautiful People who made up the Venice scene in the late 60s.

''Originally a Catholic homemaker from Brooklyn, it took my mother many years and six children before she discovered that she was really an artist, and an idealist, at heart. After divorcing my father, and after living in Venice for a few years, the bohemian side of her personality was unleashed. As she developed her own singing and acting talents, she also encouraged her children to develop artistically. She was the first to expose us to people who cared more about artistic integrity than anything else. To be sure, I never grasped the value of our bohemian upbringing at the time; I had an entirely different view of what life on the 'Boardwalk' was supposed to be. I know now, however, that life in Venice taught me what it took to be artistic and idealistic; her bearded, barefooted friends introduced me to a kind of personal integrity that was mys-

There are times when even a star like Lynette has to sit on the bench! ■ (From *Lynette Woodard* by Matthew Newman. Photograph courtesy of *Focus on Sports*.)

teriously intriguing, and gave me an awareness that there was power in being outside the mainstream of art and politics, a richness in being poor, and a strength in being different from everyone else. At the time, however, I simply felt that these 'hippies' were 'weird,' even as I became one myself.

"My first artistic endeavors were dramatic and musical. I remember writing plays for my brothers and sisters to act out for my parents, many of which took place at exciting locales such as McDonald's restaurants. One year, I got a guitar and my brother got a drum set for Christmas (my father sold musical instruments). My brother and I formed a band called 'Solo and the Termites.' I named the band after one of my television heroes, a secret agent called Napoleon Solo from the old "Man from Uncle" show.

"I had always loved reading, and as a boy I read lots of biographies. At age thirteen, I wrote a letter to President Lyndon Baines Johnson suggesting that he should create holidays for Benjamin Franklin, Thomas Edison, and Thomas Jefferson, all of whom were my heroes. I'll never forget coming home from school one day to find an envelope addressed from the White House; I think that was the first time that I understood the power of writing, and how putting words to paper could make people and places as magical and mysterious as the President, and the White House as real as a young boy could ever hope them to be.

"In the 1970s my mother moved me and my brothers and sisters to another decaying counter-culture scene; Haight-Ashbury in San Francisco. Still, I did not appreciate the tragic romantic character of the scene, and at age fifteen, I escaped across the bay to live with a kindly Berkeley professor (with my mother's blessing). The professor let me bang on his piano and encouraged me to enroll at an alternative high school in

Berkeley. In between endless games of basketball, I fell in love with the works of Dylan Thomas, J. D. Salinger, and Anton Chekov. In 1973, I enrolled at the University of California at Berkeley and eventually got a degree in Rhetoric. Aristotle, Plato, Cicero, and Quintillian taught me about the roots of writing and about how the art of persuasion is at the bottom of any piece of writing. At the same time, I formed another two-man band and was active in the drama department.

"After graduation in 1978, I had tired of what was by then a jaded Berkeley scene and sought a fresh start in Chicago, Illinois. I have found Chicago to be a place which has more heart and less glitz than California; a place where neighborhood and family roots run so deep that natives either feel hopelessly loyal or hopelessly strangled; a place where visitors from either coast are viewed as either freaks or deities, depending on whether the person likes or resents Chicago. What has kept me here is the work, which has yet to let up after eight years, and the city's heart, a little piece of which I have captured in a lady named Shawn Murphy.

"After a year of working as a bill collector and a mailroom clerk, I landed a staff writer/producer position at Society for Visual Education. I held this job for four years before going free-lance in 1983. In 1987, I became the coordinating producer for Walt Disney Educational Media, which is distributed by Coronet/MTI Film & Video. Later I became supervising producer.

"I enjoy educational writing, largely because it allows me to constantly learn about new subjects. I encourage all aspiring writers, actors, musicians, and other artists to believe in themselves and to avoid becoming too practical too soon. Believe in your abilities and you will find a way to earn a living. You must decide early on, however, whether you really want to be a writer, or whether you are simply intoxicated with the mystique of being a writer. Almost everyone, it seems, fancies him or herself worthy of a book; the romantic myths suggest that writing is something which is both as natural as breathing and as glamorous as fiction. In reality, a career in writing involves years of unrewarded and unrecognized effort. Even when you begin to gain success, the business of getting published, largely a systematic process of compromise, often diminishes the idea or inspiration that got you writing in the first place. By the time you have a finished product, you may recognize only a small portion of your original work. True, this piece gets larger the longer you are around, as do the financial rewards. Somehow, however, one's skin never quite gets tough enough, and the money seldom justifies the effort. Seeing your words in print, however, and knowing that someone somewhere may be touched in an important way by your ideas, does help to even everything out.''

NICKL, Barbara (Elisabeth) 1939- (Binette Schroeder)

PERSONAL: Born December 5, 1939, in Hamburg, Germany; daughter of Hans Heidermann (a businessman) and Barbara (a costume designer for stage; maiden name, Semper) Schroeder; married Peter Nickl (a children's author, jurist and organizer of craft exhibitions and fairs), August 30, 1971. *Education:* Allgemeine Gewerbeschule Basel (Switzerland), Certificate, 1966. *Home:* Southern Bavaria, West Germany.

CAREER: Free-lance illustrator and photographer, 1968—; free-lance writer, 1969-71. *Member:* Bund Deutscher Grafikdesigner, Bund Deutscher Buchkuenstler. *Awards, honors:* Prix loisirs jeunes (France), 1970, Golden Apple from the International Biennale of Children's Book Illustration (Bratislava,

Czechoslovakia), Silver Medal from the International Book Fair (Leipzig), and German Youth Literature Prize Best Books List, all 1971, all for *Lupinchen; Florian and Tractor Max* was named one of Child Study Association of America's Children's Books of the Year, 1972; *Krokodil Krokodil* was selected one of the Most Beautiful Books of the Year in Switzerland, and a Best Illustrated Children's Book of the preceding four years from *Graphis,* both 1975, and received the Owl Prize (Japan), 1977; *Muenchhausen* was named one of the Most Beautiful Books of Switzerland, 1977, one of *New York Times* Best Books, and on the German Youth Literature Prize Best Books List, both 1978, and received honorable mention from the International Book Art Exhibition (Leipzig), 1982; *The Wonderful Travels and Adventures of Baron Muenchhausen* was named one of *New York Times* Best Illustrated Books, 1980.

WRITINGS:

ALL UNDER NAME BINETTE SCHROEDER; ALL SELF-ILLUSTRATED

Lupinchen, Nord-Sued, 1969, Delacorte, 1970, published as *Flora's Magic House,* North South Books, 1986.
Archibald und sein kleines Rot (title means ''Archibald and His Little Red''), Ellermann Verlag, 1970.
Florian und Traktor Max, Nord-Sued, 1971, translated by Esther Stonkas, published as *Florian and Tractor Max,* Putnam, 1972.
Lelebum (title means ''Little Elephant''), Thienemanns Verlag, 1972.
Zebby Swims, Walker, 1981.
Zebby Gone with the Wind, Walker, 1981.
Zebby's Breakfast, Walker, 1981.
Zebby Shops, Walker, 1981.
Run Zebby Run, Walker, 1981.
Tuffa and the Picnic, Dial, 1983.
Tuffa and the Bone, Dial, 1983.

BARBARA NICKL

(From *Beauty and the Beast*, translated by Ann Carter. Illustrated by Binette Schroeder.)

Tuffa and Her Friends, Dial, 1983.
Tuffa and the Snow, Dial, 1983.
Tuffa and the Ducks, Dial, 1983.

ILLUSTRATOR; ALL UNDER NAME BINETTE SCHROEDER

Peter Nickl, *Ratatatam, die seltsame Geschichte einer kleinen Lok,* Nord-Sued, 1973, translated from the German by Michael Bullock, published as *Ra Ta Ta Tam: The Strange Story of a Little Engine,* Merrimack, 1984.
P. Nickl, *Krokodil Krokodil,* Nord-Sued, 1975, translated from the German by Ebbitt Cutler, published as *Crocodile, Crocodile,* Scribner, 1977.
P. Nickl, reteller, *Baron Muenchhausen,* Nord-Sued, 1977, translated by Elizabeth Buchanan Taylor, published as *The Wonderful Travels and Adventures of Baron Muenchhausen,* Chatto & Windus, 1979.
Michael Ende, *Die Schattennaehmaschine* (title means "The Shadow Sewing Machine"), Thienemanns, 1982.
P. Nickl, *Das traeumende Haus* (title means "The Dreaming House"), Edition Weitbrecht, 1982.
Madame Leprince de Beaumont, *Beauty and the Beast,* retold from the French by Ann Carter, Crown, 1986.
Wilhelm Grimm and Jakob Grimm, *Der Froschkoenig oder der eiserne Heinrich,* Nord-Sued, 1989, published as *The Frog King,* North South Books, 1989.
M. Ende, *Die Vollmondlegende* (title means "The Full Moon Legend"), Deutscher Taschenbuchverlag, 1989.

TELEVISION

"Muenchhausen" (five-episode television series), Norddeutscher Rundfunk, 1976.

ADAPTATIONS:

"Lupinchen" (puppet play), Compagnie de Manifole (France), 1971, (television segment), Bayerischer Rundfunk, 1979.

"Ratatatam, die seltsame Geschichte einer kleinen Lok" (television segment), Bayerischer Rundfunk, 1975.

SIDELIGHTS: "From childhood on I was fascinated with my grandfather's art books, especially Bosch and Brueghel. Later, the art of the surrealists Max Ernst, Chirico, and Magritte were important to me. The vast surrealistic landscapes remind me of the northern landscapes of my country and are one of the most important elements in my work. . . .The magical mystery about things. The integration of dreams into reality.

"I have travelled in England, France, Switzerland, Austria, Poland, Czechoslovakia, Moscow, Hungary, Italy, Spain, the Netherlands, the United States, Canada, Virgin Islands, Namibia, Thailand, Burma, Nepal and China. From the artistic point of view, the countries I enjoyed most were Italy, Namibia, Burma, Nepal and China. I speak English, French and a little Italian. My many trips to Italy since I was eighteen have become part of my book *Beauty and the Beast* which I set in the Italian Renaissance. A trip to Namibia and to the fantastic Namib Desert was like coming home into one of my 'free' paintings—as was my last trip to China. (In my free paintings I paint rather surrealistic.)

"When I was ten I started to draw children's picture books for my little cousins. I was chosen godmother of my youngest cousin when I was fourteen, and as a gift I gave him a picture book—a mixture of childish naivete and a bit of Walt Disney with a big family of apes and a very lovely fairy. Throughout all my years of studies I never left the idea to do children's picture books one day.

"The principles of artistic education in the Allgemeine Gewerbeschule Basel were based on those of the Bauhaus and the time I spent in that school were of great importance for

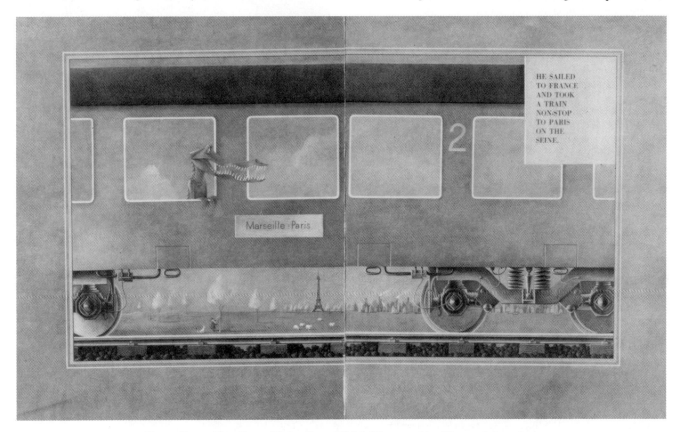

(From *Crocodile, Crocodile* by Peter Nickl. Illustrated by Binette Schroeder.)

me. Still it was not easy to get away from the severe school style and find my own.

"*Lupinchen*—my 'first' and still most successful book—came out of a kind of very melancholic mood one sleepy summer day in Berlin. It is my first book and it still is my favorite one—because it's the book where I found 'my style.' I see my illustrations like a kind of stage in which all the events of the story happen. I want the vast horizons to tempt children to walk into the book, and I want them to long to discover what's behind those fading hills and mountains. I want the objects and actors on these stages to look very clear as if it would be easy to grasp them. Shadow and the light is very important in my work. I love things to look transparent, as if glowing from inner light. I love a magical atmosphere and a certain kind of gloominess. I myself as a child never was attracted by bright and 'happy' paintings but by the dark and mysterious ones.

"When I worked on *Ratatatam*, everybody protested when I showed one special illustration out of this book: the one where the little engine drives through the night, a greenish night. . . . 'It's much too gloomy for children, they will hate it!' was said. One day a friend of mine visited with her three-year-old son, a very joyful vivacious little boy. I just happened to have spread out all the illustrations on the floor for a kind of last check. The little boy looked at all of them, quickly but very intensely at the same time—and he stopped in front of the gloomy one and said: 'That is the most beautiful one!'

"It always occurs to me as very strange when I hear what *grown-ups* think children like (or should like?) and when I see what *children* like. . . .

"I work with gouache colours, sometimes using a bit of aquarell for special effects. I use the gouaches in a transparent technique with very thin layers of colour."

FOR MORE INFORMATION SEE:

Graphis 155, Volume 27, Graphis Press, 1971-72.
Bruno Duborgel, "Images et Temps, quatre etudes sur l'espace du sens," *Etude 3: Fleur-de-Lupin ou l'escargot mythique,* Universite de Saint-Etienne (France), 1985.
Illustration (Japan), number 10, 1985.
Mechthild Lobisch, "Binette Schroeder—Buehnen der Phantasie oder die Kunst Traeume zu baendigen," *Beisszangerl* (West Germany), July, 1985.
Annemarie Verweyen, "Die phantastische Bilderwelt der Binette Schroder. Ihr Koennen am Beispiel ihres Werkes *Beauty and the Beast*," *Eselsohr, Informationsdienst fuer Kinder- und Jugendmedien* (West Germany), July 7, 1985.

OLDFIELD, Margaret J(ean) 1932-

PERSONAL: Born September 23, 1932, in Waukegan, Ill.; daughter of Roger Erwin (an electrical engineer) and Ragna (a housewife; maiden name, Heffta) Olson; married Freeborn Robert Oldfield (an accountant and publisher), January 4, 1965. *Education:* North Dakota State College, B.S., 1955. *Home:* 5200 Gorgas Ave., Minneapolis, Minn. 55424.

CAREER: North Dakota State College Library, part-time while a student, 1951-55; Hallmark Cards, Inc., Kansas City, Mo., greeting card artist, 1955-56; Gibson Card Co., Cincinnati, Ohio, free-lance greeting card artist, 1957-67; North East Neighborhood School, Minneapolis, Minn., teacher, 1958-60; author and illustrator of children's books, 1965—. *Member:*

MARGARET J. OLDFIELD

"I belong to many animal welfare and conservation organizations."

WRITINGS:

ALL SELF-ILLUSTRATED CHILDREN'S BOOKS

Tell and Draw Stories, Creative Storytime Press, 1961.
Tell and Draw Animal Cut-Outs, Creative Storytime Press, 1963.
Aloysious Alligator, Creative Storytime Press, 1964.
More Tell and Draw Stories, Creative Storytime Press, 1969.
Costumes and Customs of Many Lands, Creative Storytime Press, 1970.
The Adventures of Tabby Sue and Her Sister, Abigail, Creative Storytime Press, 1971.
It's Tough to be a Fish Nowadays, Creative Storytime Press, 1972.
Lots More Tell and Draw Stories, Creative Storytime Press, 1973.
Fat Cat and Ebenezer Geezer, the Teeny Tiny Mouse, Creative Storytime Press, 1974.
Tell and Draw Paper Bag Puppet Book, Creative Storytime Press, 1976.
Tulip Tabby Cat, Creative Storytime Press, 1978.
Finger Puppets and Finger Plays, Creative Storytime Press, 1979.
Tell and Draw Cut-Outs, Creative Storytime Press, 1988.

Contributor of children's stories and illustrations to *Child Life, Children's Activities,* and *Highlights for Children.*

WORK IN PROGRESS: A book entitled *Costumes and Customs of South America.*

SIDELIGHTS: "I began writing children's stories while teaching in my college lab-school, and continued writing my own materials while teaching nursery school and kindergarten classes. *Aloysious Alligator* was my first effort at storytelling. The children in my lab-school class loved it, and their acceptance encouraged me to submit the story and illustrations to a children's magazine. *Aloysious* received a nicely written rejection slip. A few years later I submitted an illustrated story to the magazine *Children's Activities,* and it was accepted and published. Subsequent illustrated stories were accepted by *Highlights for Children* and *Child Life. Aloysious Alligator* was published in l964 as a picture book.

"I enjoy writing gentle stories about animals and their relationships and experiences with children. When I was a child, our family had many pets and I was exposed to kindness, love, and gentleness toward animals. At times I try to gently coax my readers to my view of conservation and consideration for pets and wildlife.

"Since my husband and I were married, three cats have been a part of our family: Tabby Sue, Abigail, and Pickles. They were the inspiration for many of my stories and illustrations. Tabby Sue lived with us for seventeen years. Abigail is still with us, she is approaching her eighteenth birthday but still acts like a kitten at times. Tabby Sue and Abigail inspired the books, *The Adventures of Tabby Sue and Her Sister, Abigail* and *Fat Cat and Ebenezer Geezer, the Teeny Tiny Mouse.*

"*Tell and Draw Stories* began when I remembered a story and drawing from my childhood. The story was about a pig who became lost in a snowstorm. I drew a simple pig figure on the blackboard while telling the story, and my pre-school class loved it. That pig story inspired fifty more original *Tell and Draw Stories* written over a period of fifteen years.

"Teaching young children gave me a good idea as to the type of stories and drawings they relate to and enjoy. Children's natural curiosity about the habits and homes of friends (both animal and human) is marvelous, and curiosity can awaken in them a love of stories and a love of reading. Young children can be a wonderful and a critical audience."

ORAM, Hiawyn   1946-

PERSONAL: Born September 28, 1946, in Johannesburg, South Africa; daughter of John Woollerton (in business) and Eileen (Hargraves) Shilling; married Gavin T. Oram (a stockbroker), April 7, 1973; children: Maximilian, Felix. *Education:* University of Natal, B.A., 1966. *Home:* 41 Crestway, London SW15 5DB, England.

CAREER: Natal Performing Arts Council, Durban, South Africa, actress, 1966; Young Advertising, Johannesburg, South Africa, copywriter, 1967-68; De Beers/Charter Consolidated, London, England, public affairs assistant, 1968-69; J. Walter Thompson (advertising agency), Johannesburg, copywriter, 1970-72; Leo Burnett (advertising agency), London, copywriter, 1972-74; free-lance writer, 1974—. *Awards, honors:* Mother Goose Award, 1983, for *Angry Arthur.*

WRITINGS:

JUVENILE

Skittlewonder and the Wizard, Dial, 1980.
Angry Arthur (illustrated by Satoshi Kitamura), Harcourt, 1982.
Ned and the Joybaloo (illustrated by S. Kitamura), Anderson Press, 1983, David & Charles, 1988.
In the Attic (illustrated by S. Kitamura), Andersen Press, 1984, Holt, 1985.
Jenna and the Troublemaker (illustrated by Tony Ross), Holt, 1986.
What Stanley Knew (illustrated by Lesley Arkless), David & Charles, 1987.

Also author of stage play, "Enemies Within"; a television situation comedy, "A Working Woman"; and screenplays, "The Woman and the Idol," and "The Lucifer March."

WORK IN PROGRESS: A novel; children's books; a screenplay; a television drama series.

SIDELIGHTS: "An early sense of loss plus early indignation at the widespread injustice in the universe (both man-made and natural) drew me toward the empires of the imagination where I could rearrange and control the component parts. Writing is an extension of that process. The vital subject for me is the interface between fact and fiction, between the conscious and subconscious worlds, and the human animal's seeming dependence on fiction (ideologies, religions, dreams, and images) for his motivation and fulfillment.

"Works that have had formative effects include Walt Disney's 'Snow White,' as my first film, F. H. Burnett's *The Secret Garden,* the poetry of T. S. Eliot and William Blake, Henry James's *Portrait of a Lady,* Dostoevski's *Crime and Punishment,* Romain Gary's *Dance of Genghis Cohn,* Oriana Fallaci's *A Man,* R. W. Fassbinder's films, especially 'Saturn's Brew,' Robert Bresson's 'Pickpocket' and 'A Gentle Creature,' and Nellie Kaplan's *A Very Curious Woman* and *Nea.*"

OTFINOSKI, Steven   1949-

PERSONAL: Surname is pronounced *ott-fin-a-ske;* born January 11, 1949, in Queens, New York; son of Anthony (a retired insurance salesman) and Helen (a housewife; maiden name, Zaspel) Otfinoski; married Beverly Larson (a free-lance writer, editor, and harpist), April 18, 1981; children: Daniel, Martha. *Education:* Attended Boston University, 1967-69; Antioch College, B.A., 1972. *Home and office:* 34 Warwick Ave., Stratford, Conn. 06497. *Agent:* Susan Cohen, c/o Writer's House, 21 West 26th St., New York, N.Y. 10010.

CAREER: Hartford Times, Hartford, Conn., news reporter, 1972-73; Field Publications, Middletown, Conn., assistant editor for *Read* magazine, 1974-75; free-lance author, 1975—. *Member:* Fairchester Playwrights, Dramatists' Guild. *Awards, honors:* One-Act Play Award from Quaigh Theatre, 1983, and Westchester County Playwriting Competition runner-up, 1985, both for "The Bookworm"; Playwriting Award from the Community Children's Theatre of Kansas City, Mo., 1985, for musical play "The Princess and the Pea."

WRITINGS:

FOR YOUNG READERS

The Monster That Wouldn't Die and Other Strange but True Stories, Field Publications, 1976.

The Troublemaker was a hard man, but he was not made of iron.
"All right, my dear," he sighed. "Come to the field behind my house
at midnight tomorrow. And bring your Troubles with you."

(From *Jenna and the Troublemaker* by Hiawyn Oram. Illustrated by Tony Ross.)

STEVEN OTFINOSKI

(With Diane Carlson) *The Blood Suckers and Other True Animal Stories*, Field Publications, 1976.

The Rubber-Soled Kid and Other Funny Superstars, Field Publications, 1976.

Plays about Strange Happenings, Field Publications, 1976.

The World's Darkest Days: Stories of Great Tragedies of the Past, Field Publications, 1977.

The Red Ghost and Other True Animal Stories, Field Publications, 1977.

(Compiler) *Fun for All: Jokes and Cartoons to Make You Laugh*, Field Publications, 1977.

High Flier and Other Fast Action Stories, Field Publications, 1977.

The Third Arm and Other Strange Tales of the Supernatural, Field Publications, 1977.

Monsters to Know and Love: Stories of Chills and Fun, Field Publications, 1977.

Sky Ride and Other Exciting Stories, Field Publications, 1977.

The Verlaine Crossing (illustrated by Stanley Flemming), Pitman, 1977.

Tony, the Night Custodian, Janus Books, 1977.

Plays for Group Reading, Field Publications, 1977.

Space Trucker and Other Science Fiction Stories, Field Publications, 1978.

The Zombie Maker: Stories of Amazing Adventures, Field Publications, 1978.

Village of Vampires (illustrated by Chris Kenyon), Pitman, 1979.

Fun to Read Funny Stories, Playmore, 1979.

(With Annie Mueser) *Cobra in the Tub and Eight More Stories of Mystery and Suspense*, Field Publications, 1980.

(Editor and contributor) *Face at the Window and Other Stories of Suspense and Adventure*, Field Publications, 1980.

(Contributor) *My Giant Story Book*, Playmore, 1981.

(Contributor) *Christmas Fun World*, Playmore, 1981.

(Compiler and contributor) *Know Power: Everything to Know about Everything*, Playmore, 1981.

The Screaming Grave, Weekly Reader Books, 1982.

History Alive! (plays), Educational Insights, 1982.

Midnight at Monster Mansion (multiple adventure novel; illustrated by Michael Racz), Scholastic, 1984.

TV Superstars Scrapbook 1, Weekly Reader Books, 1984.

TV Superstars Scrapbook 4, Weekly Reader Books, 1985.

Superworld (adventure), Scholastic, 1985.

James Bond in Barracuda Run (multiple adventure novel), Ballantine, 1985.

TV Superstars '86, Weekly Reader Books, 1986.

Wild on Wheels, Weekly Reader Books, 1986.

Carnival of Terror (multiple adventure novel), Weekly Reader Books, 1986.

Cosby, Punky, Kate and Allie, Weekly Reader Books, 1986.

The Secret of Pirate Island, Weekly Reader Books, 1986.

Master of the Past (multiple adventure novel), Weekly Reader Books, 1987.

The Shrieking Skull, Weekly Reader Books, 1988.

(Contributor) *Hispanic American Biographies*, Globe Books, 1988.

Hispanics in American History, Volume 2, *1865 to the Present*, Globe Books, 1989.

PLAYS

"A Revolution Relived: In Word and Song," touring production at schools and churches in Conn., 1976.

"At Crazy Jayne's" (one-act comedy), first produced at Stagelights Theatrical Club, New York City, 1978.

"Love of Frankenstein" (comedy), first produced at Actor's Playhouse, New York City, 1978.

"Great Moments from the Good Book" (comedy sketches), first produced at Arts Cafe, Hartford, Conn., 1982.

"The Bookworm" (one-act comedy), first produced at Quaigh Theatre, New York City, 1983.

"The Ventriloquist" (musical comedy), first produced at Quaigh Theatre, New York City, 1983.

"Stooge Night" (drama), first produced at Quaigh Theatre, New York City, 1985.

"Wedding Bell Blues" (one-act comedy), first produced at American Theater of Actors, New York City, 1986.

"Cutting Edge" (one-act adaptation of a short story) first produced at American Theater of Actors, New York City, 1987.

"Conscience" (one-act adaptation of a short story), first produced at American Theater of Actors, New York City, 1987.

"We the People" (musical; music by Richard Amend and Mary Lang), first produced in Stratford, Conn., 1987.

CHILDREN'S MUSICALS

"The Birdfeeder" (music), first produced at Quaigh Theatre, New York City, 1982.

"The Ghosts of Gloomy Manor" (music by Karl Blumenkranz), first produced at Quaigh Theatre, New York City, 1982.

"The Christmas Santa Lost His Ho! Ho! Ho!" (music by Mary Lang), first produced at Quaigh Theatre, New York City, 1983.

"Snow White" (music by M. Lang), first produced at Calliope Storybook Theatre, Eatontown, N.J., 1984.

"Mrs. Claus to the Rescue!" (music by K. Blumenkranz), first produced at Quaigh Theatre, New York City, 1984.

"Sleeping Beauty" (music by Richard Amend), first produced at Club Bene Theatre, Sayerville, N.J., 1985.

"The Princess and the Pea" (music by R. Amend), first produced at Club Bene Dinner Theatre, Sayerville, N.J., 1985.

"Rumpelstiltskin Is My Name!" (music by M. Lang), first produced at Club Bene Dinner Theatre, Sayerville, N.J., 1985.

ADAPTATIONS:

"Cobra in the Tub and Eight More Stories of Mystery and Suspense" (cassette for the blind), Field Publications, 1980.

WORK IN PROGRESS: Hispanic Pride, a series of twelve biographies of well-known Hispanic Americans for elementary students, to be published by Rourke Enterprises; "Still Life with Dead Grizzly," a serious drama based on the life of American explorer Meriwether Lewis; a biography on Mikhail Gorbachev to be published by Cloverdale Press for their "Great Lives" series.

SIDELIGHTS: "I was raised in Farmingdale, Long Island, the eldest of three boys. When I was ten, our family moved to my father's hometown of Middletown, Connecticut. I was an introspective boy and spent much of my time reading books, watching television, and daydreaming. I fell in love with horror and suspense movies at an early age and have turned to them for inspiration for many of my books, stories, and plays for young readers.

(From *Midnight at Monster Mansion* by Steven Otfinoski. Illustrated by Michael Racz.)

"Although I wrote comics, stories, and poems throughout my childhood, it wasn't until studying a year abroad in London while in college that I truly discovered the joys of writing. I kept a journal and wrote down descriptions of places and people and my thoughts and feelings of the life around me.

"After graduation back in the states, I quickly got my first writing job, as a reporter for the now-defunct *Hartford Times.* Newspaper writing with its tight deadlines and emphasis on clear, precise writing was excellent training for me, as it is for most writers. However, I soon grew tired of writing about town meetings and car accidents, and quit after only a year.

"I traveled for the summer and returned home to my parents' house that fall determined to start a spectacular career as a free-lance writer. Spectacular it wasn't. My efforts at writing witty greeting cards and spine-tingling short stories for mystery magazines were doomed to failure. As the rejection slips piled up on my writing desk, I decided I'd better get a full-time job doing anything to earn money before I tried my dear parents' patience beyond endurance. Fortunately, Xerox Educational Publications, home of *My Weekly Reader* and many other school periodicals, was located in my hometown. Unfortunately, they had no immediate openings in their editorial department. So, I took a job working in the mail room and after getting to know some of the editors on a number of periodicals was offered the job of assistant editor on *Read* magazine, an English and reading periodical for secondary students. I enjoyed the mixture of editing and creative writing and might be there still, if I wasn't laid off in one of several notorious staff cutbacks after only a year on the job. My boss cried openly at the suddeness of my 'termination,' but I was actually quite happy. I knew working in an office wasn't for me and I was already looking forward to once again trying my hand at being an independent freelancer.

"This time, with my experience at Xerox Educational Publications and the contacts I'd made there, my efforts were more successful. And I've been at it ever since. I never set out to become a writer for young people. It just sort of happened by accident, and I've never regretted it. Their interests in adventure, the mysterious, and the supernatural, are my interests as well. And when I sit down to write I don't ask whether my readers will like what I'm writing. I try to please myself first. If I'm interested in what I'm writing, I take it for granted that they'll be interested too. And nine times out of ten I'm right.

"However, there is another side to my career. Since my first attempts at creative writing, I have always found it easier to write dialogue than descriptive narrative. I was fascinated by the stage and turned to playwriting at an early age. I have written about one hundred published classroom plays for young people as well as over thirty 'serious' plays for the legitimate stage. About half of these have been produced Off-Off Broadway and in regional theater. I've written a number of stage adaptations of familiar fairy tales that have been produced for family audiences. I say 'family' because I don't believe there should be such a thing as 'children's theatre.' I wrote these plays to appeal to both adults and young people. After all, children don't usually go to these productions alone, and my off-beat humor keeps the parents who are dragged along from getting bored.

"Where do I get my ideas? One major source is the vast treasure chest of literature, movies, and theatre that is our cultural heritage. I enjoy adapting famous works and sometimes spoofing them. In other cases I draw on my own childhood and experiences as a student. If there's a germ of truth and real experience in the story, it's always easier to write and make believable to others. Of course, there are times when I don't have to think up the idea at all. It's handed to me by the publisher. A good instance of this is one of my favorite books, *The Screaming Grave*. The publisher called, gave me the title, a one-sentence description about a boy walking through a graveyard at night and hearing a scream, and asked me to write the book in about four weeks. From this meager beginning, I came up with a plot and characters and wrote the thing. My 'inspiration' was that if I didn't meet the deadline I might not get paid!

"Being a professional writer means being able to write well, quickly, and sometimes, on demand. Sometimes its frustrating, but, all in all, I wouldn't want to be doing anything else."

PALECEK, Josef 1932-

PERSONAL: Born February 25, 1932, in Jihlava, Czechoslovakia; son of Josef (a customs officer) and Marta (Mistova) Palecek; married wife, Libuse (a writer and art director), December 19, 1958; children: Veronika. *Education:* Graduated from Charles IV University, Prague, Czechoslovakia, 1955. *Religion:* Roman Catholic. *Home:* Nad Zamecnici 15, 15000 Prague 5, Czechoslovakia. *Agent:* Dilia Vysehradska, 12824 Prague, Czechoslovakia.

CAREER: Painter, illustrator, graphic artist. Has worked in tapestry and with mobils, has collaborated on animated films and worked with scene design in television. Has exhibited in one-man and group shows in Czechoslovakia, Japan, France, Switzerland, Canada, Germany, and Austria.

AWARDS, HONORS: Outstanding Book Prize from Albatros Publishers (Czechoslovakia), 1968, for *Jake oci ma vitr*, and 1976, for *The Poppy-Seed Man; The Ugly Duckling* was selected one of Child Study Association of America's Children's Books of the Year, 1972, and *The Magic Grove*, 1986; Kinder-

JOSEF PALECEK

und Jugendbuchpreis der Stadt Wien (Austria), 1972, for *"Das ist eine wunderschoene Wiese,"* sagt Herr Timtim, 1976, for *Michael hat einen Seemann*, and 1979, for *Claudia mit einer Muetze voll Zeit;* Diplome Loisirs Jeunes, 1973, for *Das Haesliche Entlein;* Anniversary Prize of the Supraphon Publishing House (Czechoslovakia), 1974; Grand Prix de Treize, 1974, for *Mir gefaellt es nicht ueberall; Tell Us, Spring* was selected one of the Most Beautiful Books of the Year from the Ministry of Culture, the Slovakian Center for Book Culture, the National Writer's Archives, and the Slovakian Language and Culture Association (Czechoslovakia), 1977; Anniversary Prize from the Albatros Publishing House, 1977; Cena ministerstva kultury CSR, 1979, for *Klavirni skolicka;* Premio di letteratura per L'infanzia, 1981, for *Piccoli concerti della sera;* Cena Narodni galerie v Praze za animovany film Kouzelny sad, 1983; Cestne uznani v soutezi o Premio Critici in erba, 1986, for *Koulelo se, koulelo*.

ILLUSTRATOR:

Miroslav Florian, *Jake oci ma vitr* (title means "What Kind of Eyes Has the Wind"), SNDK (Prague), 1968.

J. V. Svoboda, *Dandelion*, Albatros (Prague), 1971.

Hans Christian Andersen, *Das Haesliche Entlein*, Nord-Sued, 1972, published in England as *The Ugly Duckling*, Abelard, 1972.

W. Harranth, *"Das ist eine wunderschoene Wiese,"* sagt Herr Timtim, Jungbrunnen (Austria), 1972, published in England as *The Wonderful Meadow*, Dobson, 1981.

Libuse Palecek, *Mir gefaellt es nicht ueberall* (title means, "I Don't Like It Everywhere"), Nord-Sued (Switzerland), 1973.

L. Palecek, *Who Is the Mightiest in the World*, Nord-Sued, 1973.

Kurt Baumann, *The Three Kings*, Nord-Sued, 1973.

V. Fiser and P. Eben, *Elce pelce kotrmelce* (title means "Eeny-Meeny"), Supraphon (Czechoslovakia), 1973.

W. Harranth, *The Last Thief*, Jungbrunnen, 1973.

Z. Adla, *Stars over the Lonely House*, Albatros, 1974.

J. V. Svoboda, *A Butterfly Net*, Albatros, 1974.

L. Huwe, *Child, My Child*, Dausien (Germany), 1974.

K. Born, *Ignatius and the Butterfly*, Nord-Sued, 1974.

W. Harranth, *Michael hat einen Seemann*, Jungbrunnen, 1974.

Hans Christian Andersen, *The Emperor's New Clothes*, Nord-Sued, 1974, Faber, 1979.

L. Palecek, *Der lustige Mann* (title means, "The Merry Gentlemen"), Jungbrunnen, 1974.

L. Palecek, *The Little Tiger*, Gakken (Japan), 1974, published in England as *The Timid Little Tiger*, Hutchinson, 1980.

L. Palecek, *Tylinek*, Albatros, 1975.

L. Palecek, *The Little Hippo Pummel*, Nord-Sued, 1975.

H. C. Andersen, *Thumbelina*, Nord-Sued, 1975.

Z. Adla, *The Magician's Garden*, Albatros, 1976.

M. Borova, Z. Janzurova and L. Sluka, *Klavirni skolicka* (title means, "The Little Piano School"), Panton (Czechoslovakia), 1976.

Frantisek Nepil, *Makovy muzicek* (title means "The Poppy-Seed Man"), Albatros, 1976.

M. Florian, *Tell Us, Spring*, Albatros, 1976.

L. Palecek, *Tralala*, Gakken, 1977.

J. Palecek, *Merry Pictures*, Albatros, 1978.

W. Harranth, *Claudia mit einer Muetze voll Zeit* (title means "Claudia with a Cap Full of Time"), Jungbrunnen, 1978.

H. C. Andersen, *Three Fairy Stories*, Nord-Sued, 1979.

L. Palecek, *The Mightiest Mouse in the World*, Lutterworth, 1980.

L. Palecek, *The Bird of Happiness*, Lutterworth, 1980.

L. Palecek, *Piccoli concerti della sera* (title means, "Little Evening Music"), Quadragono (Italy), 1980.

K. Capek, *A Doctoral Fairy Story*, Shuei-Sha (Japan), 1980.

(From *Das Lied vom Apfelbaum* by Jaroslav Seifert. Illustrated by Josef Palecek.)

V. Adlova, *Changing Loves,* Albatros, 1980.

H. C. Andersen, *The Little Mermaid,* Merrimack, 1981.

D. Lhotova, *Annie under the Coloured Hill,* Albatros, 1981.

L. Palecek, *The Surprise Kitten,* Scholastic Book Services, 1981.

H. Baumann, *My Friends,* Nord-Sued, 1982.

E. Lorenz, *Sylvia in a Tree,* Jungbrunnen, 1982.

L. Palecek, *The Magic Orchard,* Neugebauer Press (Austria), 1983, published in America as *The Magic Grove: A Persian Folktale,* Picture Book Studio, 1985.

J. Brukner, *The Key of the Kingdom,* Albatros, 1983.

Jaroslav Seifert, *Das Lied vom Apfelbaum* (title means "The Song of the Apple Tree"), Bohem Press, 1985.

J. Seifert, *Koulelo se, koulelo* (title means "Rolling, Rolling"), Bohem Press, 1985.

J. Suchl, *Eskimos Fairy Tales,* Albatros, 1985.

Sergei Prokofiev, *Peter and the Wolf,* translated by Patricia Crampton, Picture Book Studio, 1987.

Brothers Grimm, *Bremen Town Musicians,* translated by Anthea Bell, Picture Book Studio, 1988.

ANTHOLOGIES

We Are Little, Jungbrunnen, 1982.
We Are Growing Bigger, Jungbrunnen, 1982.

ANIMATED FILMS

"The Little Tiger," State Film Studio (Czechoslovakia), 1974.
"Tylinek," State Film Studio, 1978.
"Magic Grow," State Film Studio, 1982.

Also illustrator of numerous additional books.

WORK IN PROGRESS: With wife, Libuse, another picture book entitled *The Little Path.*

SIDELIGHTS: "I started working as an illustrator in Prague. . . .The situation in my country is rather special because many of the best poets write verse for children. These are by no means old rhymes, but true poetry. And this is a delightful offer and challenge to an artist's imagination and intellect."

Palecek illustrates almost exclusively for children. He started working for children's magazines, moved on to illustrate texts, and now lends his own concepts to illustrating children's verse and picture books. He believes that these picture books, where so much depends on the interplay between words and picture, should be written and illustrated by one person.

Several of his books are a collaborative effort with his wife, Libuse. "Our first joint picture book came into being when our daughter was about six. And as Veronika grew, the number of books grew too. . .and although [she is grown up], we have the text of a couple more books waiting in a drawer. When our daughter was at the autograph album age we wrote: 'Never try to be happy at someone else's expense. That is our wish for you and ourselves.' And that is really the message our books bring to others, whether they are children or adults."

The Paleceks perceive the main aim of these little books as the solution of ethical problems: relationships, tolerance, jealousy, parasitism, overcoming fear, and the search for happiness. Philosophical problems are for the couple the basis for enchanting stories which link dreams to certainties.

Palecek's approach to his art is to compose a book as a graphic whole. "I tackle each book differently, deciding the means according to the story. Sometimes oil pastels seem most suitable, at other times watercolors, or tempera or India ink. My illustrations are paintings rather than drawings." He plans the color schemes of the double pages which support the ideas of the theme, and only afterwards fills in the complimentary details of his pictorial compositions.

"I love working for children. Time with them is more fun. . .more fantastic. . . .The happy moments spent with them is not enough to wet one's palate. You have to free yourself from the shell of your own adulthood—and that seems to me almost beautiful.

"I love illustrating texts that have their own literary scenic fantasy. I take them as an inspiration for free graphic expression on the theme that I have accepted. . . .The creation of a picture book is full of exciting moments—to hit on the right idea, the right little story to put across, and then to draw and write the text. . .and then the first print-off of the book comes into existence. It's exciting: In the beginning there is only a pile of paper and at the end we hold a little book of which maybe twenty thousand copies have been printed."

FOR MORE INFORMATION SEE:

Jugend und Buch, International Institute fuer Jugend (Austria), numbers 3 and 4, 1985.

PATON, Alan (Stewart) 1903-1988

OBITUARY NOTICE—See sketch in *SATA* Volume 11: Born January 11, 1903, in Peitermaritzburg, South Africa; died of throat cancer, April 12, 1988, in Botha's Hill (near Durban), Natal, South Africa. Political and social activist, educator, academic administrator, and author. Paton was probably best known for his 1948 novel, *Cry, the Beloved Country,* in which he vividly portrayed the horrors of South Africa's racist apartheid system. Paton worked as a high school teacher in the 1920s and 1930s and as a reformatory principal from 1935 to 1948. He began writing *Cry, the Beloved Country* in 1947 while touring European and American prisons and reformatories. The novel concerns a black minister's loss of religious faith as he searches for his son, a suspected murderer, in the vast Johannesburg ghetto. Though some critics found *Cry, the Beloved Country* pretentious and occasionally awkward, the book proved enormously successful, and Paton was soon perceived as a figurehead for South Africa's anti-apartheid movement. The book was later adapted into a movie, "Cry, the Beloved Country," starring Sidney Poitier and into an opera, *Lost in the Stars.*

In the early 1950s, Paton founded the Liberal Party of South Africa and increased his opposition to his country's racist policies. His actions prompted retaliation from the South African Government in the 1960s, when it effectively banned the Liberal Party and revoked Paton's passport. Paton, however, continued to oppose apartheid, though in his later years he was sometimes perceived as a conservative for his protests against foreign sanctions and disinvestment. Among his other writings are the novel *Too Late the Phalarope,* the short story collection *Tales from a Troubled Land,* and the posthumously published *Journey Continued* (title listed in one source as *Journey's End*).

FOR MORE INFORMATION SEE:

Current Biography, H. W. Wilson, 1952, May, 1988.

OBITUARIES

Los Angeles Times, April 12, 1988.
Chicago Tribune, April 13, 1988.

New York Times, April 13, 1988.
Times (London) April 13, 1988.

PAUL, David (Tyler)   1934-1988

OBITUARY NOTICE: Born November 18, 1934, in New York, N.Y.; died of lung cancer, March 28, 1988, in Willow Grove, Pa. Publishing executive, producer, editor, and author. An account supervisor at Meridien Gravure Company from 1959 to 1960, Paul then worked successively as an art or design director for Macmillan Company, *Popular Boating* magazine, Parents Magazine Press, and Random House until 1969. He subsequently served as vice-president and managing editor, then president, of Abelard-Schuman and Criterion Books from 1969 to 1971; publisher of Drake Publications from 1973 to 1974; and co-founder and editor of *Fire Islander* magazine from 1975 to 1977. Between 1976 and 1981 he was managing editor successively of *Northeastern Industrial World* magazine and of Cambridge Book Company, for which he was also executive editor for video and audiovisual. Thereafter he was an independent television producer. Paul was also director of Photo-Media Limited and proprietor of Graphics Consultations by D. T. Paul. An author of children's books, he wrote *Harbor Tug* and *Tugboat Adventure.*

FOR MORE INFORMATION SEE:

Who's Who in America, Supplement to 44th edition, Marquis, 1987.

OBITUARIES

New York Times, March 31, 1988.

PERRINS, Lesley   1953-

PERSONAL: Born January 26, 1953, in Birmingham, England; daughter of Joseph Edward and Margaret (Tombs) Wright; married Andrew Perrins (in government service), April 8, 1978; children: Louise Margaret, Ian Roger. *Education:* St. Hugh's College, Oxford, B.A. (with first class honors), 1974. *Home:* 17 Windmill Ave., Ewell, Surrey KT17 1LL, England. *Agent:* Threshold Book Ltd., 661 Fulham Rd., London SW6 5P2, England.

CAREER: London Borough of Enfield, London, England, careers officer, 1975-78; Epsom Borough Council, Surrey, England, careers officer, 1978-79; Manpower Services Commission, London, writer and researcher, 1979-81; Paper and Paper Products Industry Training Board, London, writer and researcher, 1981-82; free-lance writer, 1982—. *Member:* Institute of Careers Officers.

WRITINGS:

How Paper Is Made (juvenile), Facts on File, 1985 (published in England as *How It Is Made: Paper* [illustrated by A. Lockwood], Faber, 1985).

SIDELIGHTS: "I was asked to write the book about paper following my study of the industry when working for the Training Board. In researching the project I became an expert on the fascinating differences between making toilet paper and high-grade writing paper. The book is directed at the nine-to-fifteen age range, but I hope it is an interesting read for adults, too.

"My career is in temporary suspension because of motherhood. I have many projects in mind for the future, though, including a novel, tutoring for Open University by correspondence, and possibly historical research on my favorite author, Dante, and the period in which he lived. Professionally I am interested in the betterment of young people through vocational advice and in women's issues."

PETERSON, Lorraine 1940-

PERSONAL: Born July 10, 1940, in Red Wing, Minn.; daughter of Bertil Milton (a farmer, insurance agent and realtor) and Gladys (a homemaker; maiden name, Skog) Peterson. *Education:* North Park College and Theological Seminary, B.A., 1962. *Religion:* "Believer in Jesus Christ." *Home:* Pilar Presa 4764, Colonia Benito Juarez Auditorio, Municipio Zapopan 45199, Jalisco, Mexico. *Agent:* Bethany House Publishers, 6820 Auto Club Rd., Minneapolis, Minn. 55438.

CAREER: Glenview Junior High School (now Springman Junior High School), Glenview, Ill., teacher of American history and English, 1962-65; American School, Quito, Ecuador, teacher of English and civics, 1965-66; Edison High School, Minneapolis, Minn., history teacher, 1966-79; author, 1978—; Northeast Junior High School, Minneapolis, teacher, 1979-81; American School of Guadalajara, Guadalajara, Mexico, teacher of history and English as a second language, 1981-86. *Member:* Mexican Teachers of English to Speakers of Other Languages. *Awards, honors:* Gold Medalin Book Award, 1984, for *Why Isn't God Giving Cash Prizes?;* Gold Medalin Book Award of Merit, 1986, for *Real Characters in the Making.*

WRITINGS:

FOR YOUNG ADULTS

If God Loves Me, Why Can't I Get My Locker Open?, Bethany House, 1980 (also published as a study guide, 1982, and as a teacher's guide, 1983).
Falling Off Cloud Nine and Other High Places (illustrated by LeRoy Dugan), Bethany House, 1981.
Why Isn't God Giving Cash Prizes? (illustrated by L. Dugan), Bethany House, 1982.

LORRAINE PETERSON

Real Characters in the Making, Bethany House, 1985.
Dying of Embarrassment and Living to Tell about It (illustrated by Nevil Ahlquist), Bethany House, 1988.
Anybody Can Be Cool, but Awesome Takes Practice, Bethany House, 1988.

If God Loves Me, Why Can't I Get My Locker Open? has been translated into Spanish and Chinese, and *Falling Off Cloud Nine and Other High Places* has been translated into Chinese.

WORK IN PROGRESS: "I'm presently writing a book for teens on overcoming temptation. I'm attempting to answer some of their most often asked questions on this topic."

SIDELIGHTS: "I grew up on a farm near Ellsworth, Wisconsin. From my parents I received the ethic that anything worth doing is worth doing well and the idea that getting a good education was extremely important. With few close neighbors, my sister and I had to invent our own fun—dressing our cats in doll clothes, getting Fido to perform in our circuses, and even co-authoring an unfinished work which we entitled 'The Rose Twins.' When I was six years old I made the most important decision of my life—I gave my life to Jesus Christ. My faith has given me stability and purpose throughout my life.

"When I was in high school I entered a writing contest. The American Legion Committee awarded second place to my essay but there were only two contestants—my girlfriend and myself. Since her father was editor of the *Red Wing Daily Republican Eagle,* our pictures duly appeared on the front page of the newspaper. I was thoroughly embarrassed by the entire ordeal. Mostly my English teachers complained about my atrocious spelling. *Six Minutes a Day to Perfect Spelling* failed me so I decided my themes would have to be good enough to receive As in spite of mispelled words. One teacher told me I'd never get through college unless I improved my spelling. At least I proved her wrong.

"My father was determined that his children would receive the university education which the Great Depression had denied him. In college, history was the subject I loved—and I found great freedom in writing essay tests in which misspelled words weren't counted against me. Because I've *always* wanted to be a teacher, I could patiently endure my education courses.

"And, for me, teaching was almost like the career I'd always dreamed of. I loved going to work, and except for a few snags, it was a lot of fun. I became deeply involved with my students and wanted them to be able to share the joy my faith in Christ had given me. The chemistry teacher, Mike Minnima, shared my vision. Receiving permission from the school administration, we put up posters advertising our meetings at the Y.M.C.A. We had Bible studies zeroing in on making personal faith in Christ work in the life of a teenager. Avoiding doctrinal issues, we worked with high schoolers from all denominations and backgrounds. We had parties such as the annual June in January picnic, kite flying contests, and the biggest ice cream sundae in the world. (A washtub holds a lot of ice cream!) In order to help some of the girls in a small group setting, I invited them to my apartment for a Bible study (after first sending out letters for parent permission). I wanted these girls to read their Bibles daily, a practice that has been a source of guidance, encouragement, and peace in my own life. I looked for a devotional book for teens. What I wanted didn't exist.

"I considered writing some devotional material myself. God is my friend and I ask him for specific guidance when I make decisions. My prayer was this: 'Lord, if this is your will I want someone to say, "Lorraine, *you* should write a book!"'

We sponsored a student life retreat. With the devotional guide I had written and their Bibles, we sent high schoolers into the woods to spend a half hour alone with God. To my surprise, everyone participated enthusiastically. Some came back late. Then fellow counselor Colleen Watson remarked, 'Lorraine, *you* should write a book'—so I did and I've been writing ever since.

"Mainly my books are a product of my own personal prayer and Bible study. I write about spiritual truths that have helped me in my own life. Once I select a topic, I read what others have written on the subject. Combining all the information, I rework it and translate it into 'teenese.'

"*If God Loves Me, Why Can't I Get My Locker Open?* and *Falling Off Cloud Nine and Other High Places* deal with specific teen problems—dating, getting along with parents, self-image, etc. *Why Isn't God Giving Cash Prizes?* deals with Christian doctrine. What is God like? Who is Jesus Christ? *Real Characters in the Making* shows the history teacher in me. I feel teens have a need for positive role models and that, indeed, we can learn from history. In this book I use Old Testament characters to teach teens pitfalls to avoid and examples to follow. *Dying of Embarrassment and Living to Tell about It* presents an answer to the old question, 'Who Am I?' in strictly biblical terms.

"I love teenagers. They are fascinating, and I never cease to learn from the students I teach. My goal as a writer is to try to help them through this difficult period of life by pointing out that Christian faith can be relevant to the teenager's world. As I worked closely with teens, I looked for the right book to give them to read. When I couldn't find it, I wrote it! Since I had never written anything before, I consider my books to be examples of God's miracles, and I thank him.

"I started writing during my summer vacation in 1978. By the end of the summer I had a stack of hand-written snatches on scratch paper of various sizes and colors. The next summer I discovered that just putting down ideas was fun but that organizing and finalizing my writing was *work*. When I sent my samples to Bethany House Publishers, they were accepted— the only catch was that I had to redo my work and put it into a different format for a book. Since I've always held a full-time teaching position, I use whatever blocks of time are available to me. Parts of my books have been written while riding on buses, in airports, and while waiting for friends.

"As a teenager I had a lot of questions and found that adults were surprised that I had interests in topics, such as biblical doctrine, eternity, the meaning of existence, and the attributes of God. When I became a teacher, I found that many teens had those same interests. As an adviser for the nondenominational club called Student Life, I worked with a lot of different kinds of kids—football heroes, unwed mothers, intellectuals, kids on drugs, and average students. I learned a lot about their world. When I write, I often think of those kids and answer questions they'd ask me.

"I think the most serious problems facing young people today include not being given absolute standards of right and wrong, insecurity, having nothing to believe in, not being listened to, and not being taken seriously. In my own life I've found that knowing Jesus Christ and receiving God's power are the answers to these problems. I've seen teenagers change completely because of having made a life commitment to Jesus Christ. I write because I believe there is an answer to life, and I want teenagers to know about it."

HOBBIES AND OTHER INTERESTS: Travel, ancient and "any other kind" of history, decorating cakes, sports, raising plants, jogging.

PHELAN, Terry Wolfe 1941-

PERSONAL: Born May 26, 1941, in New York, N.Y.; daughter of Jack (in trucking business) and Lillian (a dietician; maiden name, Goldberg) Wolfe; married Arnold Phelan (an attorney), August 4, 1963; children: Jackie, Rebecca. *Education:* New York University, B.S., 1963; Brooklyn College of the City University of New York, M.Ed., 1968. *Home:* 36 Hadler Dr., Somerset, N.J. 08873. *Agent:* Don Farber, 99 Park Ave., New York, N.Y. 10016.

CAREER: New York City Board of Education, New York, N.Y., elementary school teacher, 1963-66; writer, 1966—. *Member:* Society of Children's Book Writers, League of Women Voters. *Awards, honors:* New Jersey Institute of Technology Authors Award, 1981, for *The S. S. Valentine.*

WRITINGS:

JUVENILE, EXCEPT AS NOTED

The Week Mom Unplugged the T.V.s (illustrated by Joel Schick), Four Winds Press, 1979.
The S. S. Valentine (illustrated by Judy Glasser), Four Winds Press, 1979.
Best Friends, Hands Down (illustrated by Marilyn Hafner), Four Winds Press, 1980.
Making Half Whole, Signet, 1985.
A.M./P.M. Lovetime (young adult), Signet, 1986.

SIDELIGHTS: "I feel the only things I know well are about children. Maybe it's because I never really grew up. My success in getting a manuscript accepted was due to a course in writing for children given by Patricia Gauch at Rutgers. I learned to face myself, feel confident and what it really is to write for children.

"The ideas for my books come mostly from events that happened to me. I was the mother who unplugged the T.V.s. Other times I've written on a subject because I felt there was a need for it. *The S. S. Valentine* is about normal children getting to know a child in a wheelchair. It was my contention that so-called 'normal' children have great difficulty relating to children who are handicapped."

HOBBIES AND OTHER INTERESTS: Travel (including Europe and Israel), playing tennis and bridge.

PIKE, E(dgar) Royston 1896-1980

OBITUARY NOTICE—See sketch in *SATA* Volume 22: Born April 9, 1896, in Enfield, Middlesex, England, died June 6, 1980. Editor and author. Pike worked for Amalgamated Press as an associate editor from 1932 to 1944 and as editor of its *World Digest* throughout the 1950s. He wrote such works as *The Story of the Crusades: A Popular Account, Temple Bells; or, The Faiths of Many Lands, Slayers of Superstition, Round the Year with the World's Religions*, and *Encyclopedia of Religion and Religions.*

FOR MORE INFORMATION SEE:

Times Literary Supplement, March 2, 1967, August 31, 1967.
Library Journal, May 18, 1970, October 7, 1970.

The audience gasped. This was probably the neatest play they had ever seen. ■ (From *The S. S. Valentine* by Terry Wolfe Phelan. Illustrated by Judy Glasser.)

QUIXLEY, Jim 1931-

PERSONAL: Born December 13, 1931, in Melbourne, Australia; son of Charles Valentine (a real estate agent) and Olive (a homemaker; maiden name, Disney) Quixley. *Education:* Melbourne University, B.A., 1963; Royal Melbourne Institute of Technology, A.L.A.A. (Associate of the Library Association of Australia), 1967; University of Western Ontario, M.L.S., 1970. *Politics:* "Leftish." *Home:* 40 Homewood Ave., #2114, Toronto, Ontario, Canada M4Y 2K2. *Office:* Frost Library, Glendon College, 2275 Bayview Ave., Toronto, Ontario, Canada M4N 3M6.

CAREER: Camberwell Public Library, Melbourne, Australia, librarian, 1963-65; Latrobe University Library, Melbourne, librarian, 1965-69; Frost Library, Glendon College, Toronto, Ontario, Canada, head librarian, 1970-78, librarian, 1979—. Worked at various jobs traveling around the world, 1952-56, and general office work, 1957-58. *Member:* Canadian Library Association. *Awards, honors: Cross Canada Writers Quarterly* Annual Writing Competition Award, Playwrighting Section, and commendation from the Ontario Playwrights Showcase Competition, both 1980, both for "Queer Masquerade."

WRITINGS:

"The Bottle," Australian Broadcasting Commission, 1969.
Willie Won't Fly (juvenile; illustrated by Clarence Barnes), Borealis, 1978.

UNPUBLISHED PLAYS

"The Amazing Case of the Lovely Lady Orangeutan" (one-act), 1979.
"Queer Masquerade" (two-act), 1980.
"We're Just Beautiful; That's All" (juvenile; one-act), 1981.
"Last Night at the Baths" (two-act), 1986.
"Heaven at Haverfella" (two-act), 1987.

Contributor of poems to periodicals, including *Ciao, Deviance,* and *Mouth of the Dragon.*

WORK IN PROGRESS: Of the Lillies, a novel about the striving of an inner city family in Melbourne, Australia during the 1920s and 1930s.

SIDELIGHTS: "I grew up in Australia in a fairly happy household, with my older brother and sister, my father and an aunt who took care of us. My mother was an alcoholic and my parents were divorced when I was still quite young. Although my father provided quite well for us, looking back, I think we occasionally lacked some things that money can't buy. Perhaps, because of this, my stories are inclined to be a bit grimmer than most.

"The endings are happy and hopeful, but only after struggle—real struggle—not some minor inconvenience or problem that in no way threatens the permanent happiness that so many middle class people assume is their birthright.

JIM QUIXLEY

"Culturally, we were a working class family, but vaguely interested in a 'richer' life. However, as an adult, I was soon dissatisfied with this. Finally I found the world of books, theater, etc. I can still remember the revelation of discovering, when I was in my early twenties, the 'classics' of literature and music. A whole new world opened up as I devoured Dumas' *The Three Musketeers,* Dostoevski's *Crime and Punishment,* the poetry of T. S. Eliot and the worlds of opera and ballet. I was the first member of my family to go to high school (and finish, and go to university, albeit belatedly) so I was 'on my own' with such very high-brow interests.

"For as long as I can remember, I've dreamed of being a writer, but until recently, I thought it was something way beyond my reach. I did a little writing in Australia, almost all unpublished. Then, for experience in the broadest sense, I moved to Canada in 1969. After a while, I'd gained sufficient confidence to suddenly decide to try to make my dream a reality.

"I think it's the child in me that writes my children's work, and I notice that much of it seems inclined to be another version of the ugly duckling, a character I feel an affinity to.

"Because I am gay, I'm particularly interested in all aspects of gay life. Most of my work for adults is concerned with this.

"For the past several years, I almost ceased writing so that I could use all my spare time to fulfill another of my dreams, to learn a second language—in my case, French. I'm fairly bilingual now, so am back to writing, mostly adult material, especially plays."

HOBBIES AND OTHER INTERESTS: Theater, opera, ballet, swimming, hiking, cycling.

RADIN, Ruth Yaffe 1938-

PERSONAL: Born October 8, 1938, in Hartford, Conn.; daughter of Simon M. and Molly A. Yaffe; married Sheldon H. Radin (a professor), June, 1960; children: one son, two daughters. *Education:* Hartford College for Women, A.A., 1958; Connecticut College for Women (now Connecticut College), B.A., 1960; Southern Connecticut State College, M.S., 1963. *Religion:* Jewish.

CAREER: Elementary schoolteacher in Meriden, Conn., 1960-63, and Bethlehem, Pa., 1963-66; Congregation Keneseth Israel, Allentown, Pa., librarian, 1982—; author. Certified reading specialist, 1980. *Awards, honors: Tac's Island* was selected one of Child Study Association of America's Children's Books of the Year, 1986.

WRITINGS:

JUVENILE

A Winter Place (ALA Notable Book; "Reading Rainbow" selection; illustrated by Mattie Lou O'Kelley), Little, Brown, 1982.
Tac's Island (illustrated by Gail Owens), Macmillan, 1986.
Tac's Turn (illustrated by G. Owens), Macmillan, 1987.

WORK IN PROGRESS: High in the Mountains, to be published by Macmillan.

RUTH YAFFE RADIN

RICHARDS, Walter (Jr.)   1907-1988

OBITUARY NOTICE: Born March 11, 1907, in Springfield, Ill.; died May 23, 1988, in Burbank, Calif. Business executive, producer, and scriptwriter. Richards was a producer and administrator at several radio stations in the Midwest until World War II, when he became head of the U. S. Marine Corps Radio Unit. He then worked as an editor and writer for NBC-Radio's "Calvacade of America" for two years before becoming president of R-Star Productions in Burbank, California. Richards also served as president of Micro Products Corporation beginning in 1956 and as a consultant to Marshall Field Communications during the 1960s. He wrote scripts for radio shows such as "Lux Radio Theater" and for television programs. One of his most popular scripts was published as a children's book, *Santa's Own Story of the First Christmas: The Gift of the Little Shepard.*

FOR MORE INFORMATION SEE:

Who's Who in the West, 17th edition, Marquis, 1980.

OBITUARIES

New York Times, May 31, 1988.
Chicago Tribune, June 2, 1988.
Los Angeles Times, June 3, 1988.

ROCKWELL, Harlow   1910-1988

OBITUARY NOTICE—See sketch in *SATA* 33: Born in 1910; died after a long illness, April 7, 1988. Illustrator and author. Before turning to children's books, Rockwell worked as an art director, magazine illustrator, printmaker, package designer, and a new products designer. He wrote and illustrated many children's books, including *ABC Book, My Doctor, My Nursery School, My Dentist,* and *Our Garage Sale.* Rockwell shared a studio with his wife, Anne, in their Greenwich, Connecticut home, where they also collaborated on writing and illustrating many other books for children. Rockwell won the Art Directors Club Gold Medal three times, and his prints, watercolors, and woodcuts have been exhibited at the Library of Congress Print Show and the Audubon Artists Annual.

FOR MORE INFORMATION SEE:

Lee Kingman, and others, *Illustrators of Children's Books: 1967-1976,* Horn Book, 1978.

OBITUARIES

Publishers Weekly, May 20, 1988.
Horn Book, July, 1988.

ROHMER, Harriet   1938-

PERSONAL: Born May 19, 1938, in Washington, D.C.; daughter of Ben and Hilda (Rotenberg) Dorfman; children: two. *Office:* Children's Book Press, 1461 Ninth Ave., San Francisco, Calif. 94122.

CAREER: Author and editor, 1975—; Children's Book Press, San Francisco, Calif., founder and director. Pioneered third world cultural programs at UNESCO in Paris, France. *Awards, honors:* Coretta Scott King Award Honor Book, 1987, for *The Invisible Hunters.*

HARRIET ROHMER

WRITINGS:

Seven Circles That Danced the World, and Twenty-Four Other Magic Tales to Read Aloud, (illustrated by Josie Grant), Children's Book Press, 1974.

ADAPTER

(With Mary Anchondo) *The Magic Boys: Los ninos magicos,* (illustrated by Patricia Rodriguez), Children's Book Press, 1975.

(With Jesus Guerrero Rea) *The Treasure of Guatavita: El tesoro de Guatavita,* (illustrated by Carlos Loarca), Children's Book Press, 1976.

(With J. Guerrero Rea) *Cuna Song: Cancion de los Cunas* (illustrated by Irene Perez), Children's Book Press, 1976.

(With J. Guerrero Rea) *Atariba and Niguayona* (illustrated by Consuelo M. Castillo), Children's Book Press, 1976.

(With M. Anchondo) *The Little Horse of Seven Colors: El caballito de siete colores* (illustrated by Roger I. Reyes), Children's Book Press, 1976.

(With M. Anchondo) *How We Came to the Fifth World: Como vinimos al quinto mundo* (illustrated by Graciela C. de Lopez), Children's Book Press, 1976.

(With M. Anchondo) *The Mighty God Viracocha: El dios poderoso Viracocha* (illustrated by Mike Rios and Richard Montez), Children's Book Press, 1976.

(With J. Guerrero Rea) *Land of the Icy Death: Tierra de la muerte glacial* (illustrated by Xavier Viramontes), Children's Book Press, 1976.

The Legend of Food Mountain: La Montana del Alimento (illustrated by Graciela Carrillo), Children's Book Press, 1982.

(With Octavio Chow and Morris Vidaure) *The Invisible Hunters: Los cazadores invisibles* (illustrated by Joe Sam), Children's Book Press, 1987.

(With Dorminster Wilson) *Mother Scorpion Country: La tierra de la Madre Escorpion* (illustrated by Virginia Stearns), Children's Book Press, 1987.

EDITOR

(With M. Anchondo) *Skyworld Woman: La mujer del mundo-cielo* (illustrated by R. I. Reyes), Children's Book Press, 1975.

(With M. Anchondo) *The Headless Pirate: El pirata sin cabeza* (illustrated by Ray Rios), Children's Book Press, 1976.

Tran-Khan-Tuyet, *The Little Weaver of Thai-Yen Village* (picture book), Children's Book Press, 1977, revised edition, 1987.

Maria Garcia, *Connie and Diego* (illustrated by Malaquias Montoya), Children's Book Press, 1978, revised edition, 1987.

Richard Garcia, *My Aunt Otilia's Spirits,* Children's Book Press, 1978, revised edition, 1987.

Margo Humphrey, *The River That Gave Gifts,* Children's Book Press, 1978, revised edition, 1987.

ADAPTATIONS:

"Read-along with *Atariba and Niguayona*" (cassette), Children's Book Press, 1988.

"Read-along with *The Legend of Food Mountain*" (cassette), Children's Book Press, 1988.

WORK IN PROGRESS: Stories from Central America; a Pacific Rim series; and more stories and art work by Afro-American artists.

SIDELIGHTS: Rohmer founded Children's Book Press to help fill a gap in children's literature. "At the present moment what is considered children's literature comes from four or five Northern European countries. In large cities, more than fifty percent of children are not of Northwestern European origins. Nothing includes them."[1]

Her interest in folk tales from Latin America, Vietnam and the Afro-American tradition began when her son was in a Head Start program in a Spanish-speaking center in San Francisco. At that time there were no books available that represented the cultures of these children. "They could not see themselves or their culture in a book that could be read to them. The same was true of Asian, Black and Native American children. The white children were missing out on tremendously rich cultures.

"Often times Latin American or Afro-American culture is either a blank space, or presented in a negative way. There are no longer blatantly biased textbooks or children's books, but missing pieces are still there.

"In recent studies, they have documented how exposure to literature and drama affects emotional life, and how that affects decisions. We want these children to grow up to be adults who will be compassionate with all groups of people. This is a subtle thing, but will they grow up to see certain people as more 'people' than others? Will they have a world view? Will they have genuine compassion for people from other parts of the world? This is important for those who will grow up to be leaders."[1]

Several criteria are important to Rohmer when choosing a folk tale for a book. "It has to be exciting, and not a run-of-the-mill adventure. Something new has to be introduced, and it has to be resolved, as with any good story for children or adults.

"It has to represent some important concept for the culture, and it has to have strong, positive images of children and women. In some of the stories, a woman might be a minor character, but it's been legitimate to expand her part of the story. . . .I always did this based on interviews and research."[1]

Another criterion is that the story has to focus on families right up to the present time, one reason why the books are bilingual. "In some of these families the mother is monolingual in one language and the children are monolingual in English. It's sad and tragic, but it can also be something funny."[1]

Researching folklore tradition in libraries as well as in person included travel to Nicaragua. "It was rumored that the oral tradition was almost dead there. . .I had the help of the Catholic bishop on the coast, and the priests and teachers in the Catholic church. They wrote letters of introduction to the village leaders. I went and stayed there and spent time talking with the old people. They had fragments of stories."[1]

A manuscript which had been handed down in a family led to *Mother Scorpion Country.* "The story comes from the matriarchal tradition, which was pre-Christian. The manuscript came from the perspective of a Victorian man of the cloth. Mother Scorpion never appears in his version. By reading other stories and talking to the old people, I was able to put together a lot of pieces.

"If I was working in the oral tradition, I had to work in the public art tradition. In Latin America, the great mass of people don't have access to book stores or libraries. And they don't have access to museums or picture books. But they do have access to mural art. The history of these people is written large on walls in Mexico and Central America."[1] Rohmer's first books were illustrated by local Latino women muralists, and later by Joe Sam, a Harlem-born artist and Margo Humphrey, who wrote as well as illustrated *The River That Gave Gifts.*

Rohmer plans to do more stories from Central America, a Pacific Rim series, and more stories and art work by Afro-American artists. "The point is that these are fascinating stories. They are for the children of North America, to entertain and teach them, and to delight them always."

FOOTNOTE SOURCES

[1]Carol Fowler, "Folk Tales for Children," *Contra Costa Times,* November 10, 1987.

FOR MORE INFORMATION SEE:

Horn Book, June, 1979 (p. 331).

SANDERS, Scott R(ussell) 1945-

PERSONAL: Born October 26, 1945, in Memphis, Tenn.; son of Greeley Ray (in farming and industrial relations) and Eva (an artist and homemaker; maiden name, Solomon) Sanders; married Ruth Ann McClure (a lab technician), August 27, 1967; children: Eva Rachel, Jesse Solomon. *Education:* Brown University, B.A. (summa cum laude), 1967; Cambridge University, Ph.D., 1971. *Politics:* Liberal. *Religion:* Christian. *Home:* 1113 East Wylie St., Bloomington, Ind. 47401. *Agent:* Virginia Kidd, Box 278, 538 East Harford St., Milford, Pa. 18337. *Office:* Department of English, Indiana University, Bloomington, Ind. 47405.

SCOTT R. SANDERS

CAREER: Indiana University-Bloomington, assistant professor, 1971-74, associate professor, 1975-80, professor of English, 1980—. *Member:* Science-Fiction Writers of America, Friends of the Earth, Sierra Club, Society of Friends, Phi Beta Kappa. *Awards, honors:* Woodrow Wilson fellow, 1967-68; Danforth fellow, 1967-71; Marshall scholar, 1967-71; Bennett fellow in creative writing, 1974-75; National Endowment for the Arts fellow, 1983-84; *Bad Man Ballad* was selected one of *School Library Journal*'s Best Books for Young Adults, 1986; Award in Creative Nonfiction from the Associated Writing Programs, 1987, for *The Paradise of Bombs*.

WRITINGS

D. H. Lawrence: The World of the Major Novels, Viking, 1974.

Wilderness Plots: Tales about the Settlement of the American Land, Morrow, 1983, new edition, Ohio State University Press, 1988.

Fetching the Dead: Stories, University of Illinois Press, 1984.

Wonders Hidden: Audubon's Early Years, Capra, 1984.

Terrarium, Tor Books, 1985.

Stone Country, Indiana University Press, 1985.

Hear the Wind Blow: American Folksongs Retold (illustrated by Ponder Goembel), Bradbury, 1985.

Bad Man Ballad, Bradbury, 1986.

The Paradise of Bombs, University of Georgia Press, 1987.

The Engineer of Beasts, Orchard Books, 1988.

The Invisible Company, Tor Books, 1989.

Also contributor to anthologies. Author of column, "One Man's Fiction," *Chicago Sun-Times,* 1977-83. Fiction editor, *Cambridge Review,* 1969-71, and *Minnesota Review,* 1976-80.

Contributor to literary journals and popular magazines, including *North American Review, Georgia Review, Omni, Isaac Asimov's Science-Fiction Magazine, Ohio Review, Transatlantic Review, Sewanee Review, Michigan Quarterly Review, New York Times Book Review,* and *New Dimensions.*

WORK IN PROGRESS: Audubon, a novel; *The Pure Products of America,* a collection of essays; *The Gordon Milk Suite,* a collection of stories; *The Dreamlife of Science,* a series of narratives about the human side of science.

SIDELIGHTS: "I have long been divided, in my life and in my work, between science and the arts. Early on, in graduate study, this took the form of choosing literary studies rather than theoretical physics. When I began writing fiction in my late twenties, I wanted to ask, through literature, many of the fundamental questions that scientists ask. In particular, I wanted to understand our place in nature, trace the sources of our violence, and speculate about the future evolution of our species. My writing might seem diverse in form—realistic fiction, science fiction, folktales, stories for children, personal essays, historical novels—yet it is bound together by this web of questions. In all of my work, regardless of period or style, I am concerned with the ways in which human beings come to terms with the practical problems of living on a small planet, in nature and in communities. I am concerned with the life people

The Indians meandered through their deserted hunting grounds like spirits of the unburied dead. ■ (From "White Man's Game" in *Wilderness Plots: Tales about the Settlement of the American Land* by Scott R. Sanders. Illustrated by Dennis B. Meehan.)

make together, in marriages and families and towns, more than with the life of isolated individuals.

"I do not much value experimentation in form and style, if it is not engendered by new insights into human experience. I do value clarity of language and vision. Much of my writing deals with the lives of rural people, with children, with the elderly, with outcasts, with figures who are neither literary nor intellectual; and I would like the real-life counterparts of those people to be engaged and moved by my fiction.

"I have worked on several literary magazines, and feel their health is a good gauge of the health of literature at any given time. I have also worked against the Vietnam war, nuclear weapons, and the militarization of America, and in favor of environmental protection and wilderness preservation. Marriage and child-rearing are important influences on the shaping of my imagination."

HOBBIES AND OTHER INTERESTS: Building, hiking, bicycling, wild flowers, voyaging.

SCHWARTZ, Alvin 1927-

PERSONAL: Born April 25, 1927, in Brooklyn, N.Y.; son of Harry (a taxi driver) and Gussie (Younger) Schwartz; married Barbara Carmer (a learning disabilities specialist), August 7, 1954; children: John, Peter, Nancy, Elizabeth. *Education:* Attended City College (now City College of the City University of New York), 1944-45; Colby College, A.B., 1949; Northwestern University, M.S. in Journalism, 1951. *Politics:* Independent. *Home and office:* 505 Prospect Ave., Princeton, N.J. 08540. *Agent:* Marilyn Marlow, Curtis Brown Ltd., 575 Madison Ave., New York, N.Y. 10022.

CAREER: Newspaper reporter, 1951-55; writer for nonprofit and commercial organizations, 1955-59; Opinion Research Corp., Princeton, N.J., director of communications, 1959-64; Rutgers University, New Brunswick, N.J., adjunct professor of English, 1962-78; free-lance writer and author of books for adults and children, 1963—. Trustee, Joint Free Library of Princeton, 1972-74. Member of National Council, Boy Scouts of America, 1972-74. *Military service:* U.S. Navy, 1945-46. *Member:* Authors League of America, Authors Guild, American Folklore Society.

AWARDS, HONORS: New Jersey Institute of Technology Award, 1966, for *The Night Workers*, 1968, for *The Rainy Day Book*, 1969, for *University*, 1972, for *A Twister of Twists, A Tangler of Tongues,* 1977, for *Kickle Snifters and Other Fearsome Critters*, 1980, for *When I Grew Up Long Ago*, 1980 and 1981, for *Chin Music*, 1981, for *Ten Copycats in a Boat and Other Riddles,* and 1987, for *Tales of Trickery from the Land of Spoof.*

New York Times Outstanding Books, 1972, for *A Twister of Twists, A Tangler of Tongues,* and 1973, for *Tomfoolery;* National Council of Teachers of English Citation, 1972, for *A Twister of Twists, A Tangler of Tongues,* and 1975, for *Whoppers;* American Library Association and the National Endowment for the Humanities Bicentennial Book, 1972, for *The Unions,* and 1973, for *Central City/Spread City; Central City/ Spread City* was selected a Notable Children's Trade Book in the Field of Social Studies from the National Council for Social Studies and the Children's Book Council, 1973, *Cross Your Fingers, Spit in Your Hat,* 1974, *Whoppers,* 1975, *Chin Music,* 1979, and *Flapdoodle,* 1980; *Witcracks* was selected one of Child Study Association of America's Children's Books

ALVIN SCHWARTZ

of the Year, 1973, *Central City/Spread City* and *Cross Your Fingers, Spit in Your Hat,* 1974, *Whoppers,* 1975, and *Tales of Trickery from the Land of Spoof, There Is a Carrot in My Ear and Other Noodle Tales, In a Dark, Dark Room,* and *Ten Copycats in a Boat and Other Riddles,* all 1987; *Cross Your Fingers, Spit in Your Hat* was selected one of the International Reading Association and Children's Book Council's Children's Choices, 1975, *Whoppers,* 1976, *Kickle Snifters and Other Fearsome Critters,* 1977, and *Ten Copycats in a Boat,* 1981; *Kickle Snifters and Other Fearsome Critters* was named one of *School Library Journal*'s Best Books of the Year, 1976.

Witcracks was chosen one of New York Public Library's Books for the Teen Age, 1980, and *Cross Your Fingers, Spit in Your Hat,* 1980, 1981, and 1982; *In a Dark, Dark Room and Other Scary Stories* was selected as a Notable Children's Book by the Association for Library Service to Children (American Library Association), 1984; Buckeye Children's Book Award from the State Library of Ohio, and Colorado Children's Book Award, both 1986, and Arizona Young Readers Award from Arizona State University, 1987, all for *Scary Stories to Tell in the Dark;* Buckeye Children's Book Award, Washington Children's Choice Picture Book Award from the Washington Library Media Association, Virginia Children's Book Award, and Garden State Children's Book Award from the New Jersey Library Association, all 1986, all for *In a Dark, Dark Room and Other Scary Stories;* honored for body of work by Rutgers University School of Communications, Information and Library Studies, 1986.

WRITINGS:

A Parent's Guide to Children's Play and Recreation, Collier, 1963.

How to Fly a Kite, Catch a Fish, Grow a Flower and Other Activities for You and Your Child (illustrated by Mary Weissfeld), Macmillan, 1965.

America's Exciting Cities: A Guide for Parents and Children, Crowell, 1966.

The Night Workers (juvenile; illustrated with photographs by Ulli Steltzer), Dutton, 1966.

What Do You Think? An Introduction to Public Opinion: How It Forms, Functions, and Affects Our Lives (juvenile), Dutton, 1966.

The City and Its People: The Story of One City's Government (juvenile), Dutton, 1967.

Museum: The Story of America's Treasure Houses (juvenile; ALA Notable Book), Dutton, 1967.

The People's Choice: The Story of Candidates, Campaigns, and Elections (juvenile), Dutton, 1967.

To Be a Father: Stories, Letters, Essays, Poems, Comments, and Proverbs on the Delights and Despairs of Fatherhood, Crown, 1968.

Old Cities and New Towns: The Changing Face of the Nation (juvenile), Dutton, 1968.

The Rainy Day Book, Simon & Schuster, 1969.

University: The Students, Faculty, and Campus Life at One University (juvenile), Viking, 1969.

Going Camping: A Complete Guide for the Uncertain Beginner in Family Camping, Macmillan, 1969, 2nd revised edition published as *Going Camping: A Complete Guide for the Family Camper,* 1975.

(Compiler) *A Twister of Twists, A Tangler of Tongues: Tongue Twisters* (juvenile; illustrated by Glen Rounds), Lippincott, 1972.

(From *The Cat's Elbow and Other Secret Languages,* collected by Alvin Schwartz. Illustrated by Margot Zemach.)

Hobbies: An Introduction to Crafts, Collections, Nature Study and Other Life-Long Pursuits (illustrated by Barbara Carmer Schwartz), Simon & Schuster, 1972.

The Unions: What They Are, How They Came to Be, How They Affect Each of Us (juvenile), Viking, 1972.

(Compiler and reteller) *Witcracks: Jokes and Jests from American Folklore* (juvenile; illustrated by G. Rounds), Lippincott, 1973.

(Compiler and reteller) *Tomfoolery: Trickery and Foolery with Words, Collected from American Folklore* (juvenile; illustrated by G. Rounds), Lippincott, 1973.

Central City/Spread City: The Metropolitan Regions Where More and More of Us Spend Our Lives (juvenile), Macmillan, 1973.

(Compiler and reteller) *Cross Your Fingers, Spit in Your Hat: Superstitions and Other Beliefs* (illustrated by G. Rounds), Lippincott, 1974.

(Reteller) *Whoppers: Tall Tales and Other Lies Collected from American Folklore* (juvenile; illustrated by G. Rounds), Lippincott, 1975.

Stores (illustrated with photographs by Samuel Nocella, Jr.), Macmillan, 1976.

Kickle Snifters and Other Fearsome Critters Collected from American Folklore (juvenile; illustrated by G. Rounds), Lippincott, 1976.

(Editor and compiler) *When I Grew Up Long Ago: Family Living, Going to School, Games and Parties, Cures and Deaths, a Comet, a War, Falling in Love and Other Things I Remember; Older People Talk about the Days When They Were Young* (illustrated by Harold Berson), Lippincott, 1978.

Chin Music: Tall Talk and Other Talk (juvenile; illustrated by John O'Brien), Lippincott, 1979.

Flapdoodle: Pure Nonsense from American Folklore (juvenile; illustrated by J. O'Brien), Lippincott, 1980, large print edition, 1980.

(Compiler) *Ten Copycats in a Boat and Other Riddles* (juvenile; illustrated by Marc Simont), Harper, 1980.

(Reteller) *Scary Stories to Tell in the Dark: Collected from American Folklore* (juvenile; illustrated by Stephen Gammell), Lippincott, 1981.

(Compiler) *The Cat's Elbow and Other Secret Languages* (juvenile; ALA Notable Book; illustrated by Margot Zemach), Farrar, Straus, 1981.

(Reteller) *There Is a Carrot in My Ear and Other Noodle Tales* (juvenile; illustrated by Karen Ann Weinhaus), Harper, 1982, large print edition, 1982.

Busy Buzzing Bumblebees and Other Tongue Twisters (juvenile; illustrated by Kathie Abrams), Harper, 1982, large print edition, 1982.

(Compiler) *Unriddling: All Sorts of Riddles to Puzzle Your Guessery Collected from American Folklore* (juvenile; ALA Notable Book; illustrated by Susan Truesdell), Lippincott, 1983.

(Reteller) *In a Dark, Dark Room and Other Scary Stories* (juvenile; ALA Notable Book; illustrated by Dirk Zimmer), Harper, 1984, large print edition, 1984.

More Scary Stories to Tell in the Dark: Collected and Retold from Folklore (juvenile; illustrated by S. Gammell), Lippincott, 1984.

(Reteller) *Fat Man in a Fur Coat and Other Bear Stories* (juvenile; illustrated by David Christiana), Farrar, Straus, 1984.

(Reteller) *All of Our Noses Are Here and Other Noodle Tales* (juvenile; illustrated by K. A. Weinhaus), Harper, 1985.

(Reteller) *Tales of Trickery from the Land of Spoof* (juvenile; illustrated by D. Christiana), Farrar, Straus, 1985.

Telling Fortunes: Love Magic, Dream Signs and Other Ways to Learn the Future (illustrated by Tracey Cameron), Lippincott, 1987.

A boy was digging at the edge of the garden when he saw a big toe. ■ (From "The Big Toe"
in *Scary Stories to Tell in the Dark: Collected from American Folklore* by Alvin Schwartz.
Illustrated by Stephen Gammell.)

(Reteller) *Gold and Silver, Silver and Gold: Tales of Hidden
Treasure* (illustrated by D. Christiana), Farrar, Straus,
1988.
I Saw You in the Bathtub and Other Folk Rhymes (illustrated
by Syd Hoff), Harper, 1989.

Contributor to numerous periodicals, including *Redbook, Co-
ronet, Parade, Parents', Public Opinion Quarterly, Journal
of Marketing, New York Times,* and *New York Herald Tribune.*

ADAPTATIONS:

"Tongue Twisters" (cassette), Caedmon, 1974.
"Scary Stories to Tell in the Dark" (record or cassette), Caed-
mon, 1986.
"More Scary Stories to Tell in the Dark" (cassette; with teach-
er's guide), Listening Library, 1986.
"In a Dark, Dark Room" (cassette), Harper, 1986.

WORK IN PROGRESS: Various books for young people dealing with folklore and other subjects.

SIDELIGHTS: **April 25, 1927.** Born in Brooklyn, New York.
The son of a cab driver, Schwartz and his sister grew up in
"a series of modest apartments. . . .Actually my family was
far larger than this. There were dozens of aunts, uncles, and
cousins who lived within a mile or two of us. They were so
lively and intriguing that, when I was eleven or twelve, I
devoted my first piece of writing to them. It was a newspaper

filled with the news and gossip of this extended family. Since
my typewritten manuscript was the only copy, I rented it by
the day to anyone who wanted to read it."[1]

"When I was a boy, I wanted to be an archeologist or a
journalist. Both involved digging out and understanding the
unknown. But journalism also involved writing, and at some
point when I was in high school, it was in that direction that
I moved."[2]

"I first became interested in folklore when most of us do, in
childhood. But at that time I had no idea that the games,
sayings, songs, rhymes, taunts, and jokes I knew; the things
I wrote on walls; the superstitions I relied on; the tales I heard
and learned; the customs we practiced at home; or the ways
we had of doing things were all folklore.

"I also did not realize that much of this lore gave my life
structure and continuity, that these games, songs, jokes, tales,
and customs were often very old, that ordinary people like me
had created them, and that all this had survived simply and
remarkably because one person had told another. With each
retelling the result—be it a tale or a taunt—often changed
slightly to reflect the circumstances of the individual involved.
In fact, when one considers the countless variants of any joke,
saying, tale, ballad, or song, it is almost as if one were encountering the assembled impressions of a series of prints pulled
from a stone—all are the same, yet each is different.

"It also did not occur to me as a child that the folklore we create, pass on, and change says a good deal about us, about the times in which we live, and about the needs we have. Our jests provide pleasure, but they also provide emotional release. When they deal with racial and ethnic groups and with parents and siblings, they provide weaponry. The tall tales which so amuse us spring from the vastness of a frontier wilderness where life was brutal and the people diminished and fearful. They created incredible lies in which individuals were larger and taller than life and could not fail, no matter what. Our superstitions provide answers to things we do not understand and cannot explain. Even today, when we know so much, we turn for answers to astrology and to the occult; and like our ancestors, we continue to cross our fingers, wish on stars, and knock on wood."[3]

1941-1951. Pursued an interest in journalism in high school, college and graduate school. "I went through a series of editorships in high school and college, went on to graduate school, worked briefly for *Newsweek,* and I got a job on a newspaper in upstate New York."[2]

1963. Turned to free-lance writing. "With a family of my own, I felt a thirst for more income and took a series of quick jobs as speech writer and publicist. Then one day I got on my bicycle and went home from the last of those jobs and never went back. I was not going to do that again. Which brings us to the beginning.

(From "The Viper" in *Scary Stories to Tell in the Dark: Collected from American Folklore* by Alvin Schwartz. Illustrated by Stephen Gammell.)

"I brought out a book called *A Parent's Guide to Children's Play,* then others of that genre. In 1966 my first children's book was published. It was called *The Night Workers.* It was a study of people who work at night. It was followed by a half-dozen books that dealt with urban life, government, and public opinion. I had gone back to journalism."[2]

"When I began writing kids' books, they were concerned basically with the kinds of things that fascinated me as a journalist....I initially was concerned with social issues and American institutions and things of that sort. I did books ranging from how public opinion functioned and formed to a book on the labor movement and how it functioned. The market for them was really supported by the funding from the Elementary and Secondary Education Act in 1965. When that funding began to die in the early 1970s, I realized that this was not a practical avenue. I liked to do these books, but I was not going to support myself and have the freedom that I had gained, if I continued to write them, at least as many."[4]

1972. Began collecting folklore after his successful book *Tongue Twisters* appeared. "I've always been interested in wordplay. I decided I was going to pursue this. I did a book of tongue twisters and in the process of collecting this material (being a journalist, I naturally decided to find some expert resources), I determined who the President of the American Folklore Society was and I called him up. He happened to be in the folklore department at the University of Pennsylvania, actually, and I've used that department ever since as a resource. He has followed my work and been very helpful. Many folklorists across the country have also been cooperative. That's what happened. The first book was a national bestseller. My feeling was, my goodness, if this is the response, I certainly must pursue this! And that's what happened."[4]

"I cannot explain why writing, compiling, and 'finding out' have had such an attraction for me. My interest in folklore is easier to explain. I grew up with ethnic roots but not much knowledge of American traditions.

"So exploring my national folklore has been a great and satisfying adventure."[2]

Schwartz's rigorous research has resulted in numerous collections of folklore. His work has been recognized by *School Library Journal,* the American Library Association, the National Endowment for the Humanities, the National Council of Teachers of English, and the National Council for the Social Studies. "I am frequently asked where I obtain the folklore I include in my books for young people. Whenever it is feasible, I collect material from the folk—particularly from children, our strongest, most cohesive folk group, and from the elderly, who in many respects are as important. I do my collecting in schoolyards, in classrooms, in summer camps, on street corners, at church picnics, in city homes, in country stores, on farms, in shopping centers. Some days I find little or nothing, for this search is very much like prospecting. But other days I strike gold. I also rely on regular contacts with a half dozen schools, each in a different kind of community, which I visit at intervals or with whose pupils I correspond. And clearly I rely on archives and libraries.

"My collections include folklore ranging in age from a few weeks to thousands of years. The 'Peter Piper' twister recently observed its three hundredth anniversary in print, but it seems far older. The ethnic joke has its roots in ancient days. The hoary tale 'The Man with the Golden Arm'—which Mark Twain called a lovely scare story—was old when it arrived here two centuries ago from England. And over the years countless variations have developed as one person has told it to another.

During a. . .summer at a children's camp in New England, my. . .daughter learned a version of the Golden Arm tale I had not earlier encountered. When she got home, she told it to a friend. In her retelling she added her imprint, which is one of the traditional functions of any member of a folk group. And in doing so, she performed another traditional function: She transmitted the lore.''[3]

The process that Schwartz goes through in writing a typical book involves thorough research before the actual writing. ''I overlap my work—sometimes I'm working on three things at once, and I do that for practical reasons. One of the reasons is that I might 'block' or simply become very bored with what I am doing if I work with it too intensively. Then I will move to something else, and in the process, my mind clears when it comes to the first project.

''Basically, what I do with every book, is learn everything I can about the genre. This will involve a lot of reading and

scholarly books and journals and sometimes discussions and scholarly folklorists. I do a lot of my work at Firestone Library at Princeton University. I live about a half mile from there, and this is one of the reasons we live in Princeton. It's really a fine library. In the process of accumulating everything on a subject, I begin setting aside things that I particularly like. What's interesting is that eventually patterns emerge. What I'm looking for is not only what I like, but things that typify the genre. So there is a range of material and there always will be.

''In working with 'scary story' material, one finds five or six or seven typologies. I was not aware of this with *Scary Stories* until I began searching the material and putting it together. Sometimes I will go so far as to study the structure of an item to see how it works, because this is important in making selections and it's also interesting to people to understand this, I think.

(From *A Twister of Twists, A Tangler of Tongues* by Alvin Schwartz. Illustrated by Glen Rounds.)

"Then having done the research, I begin putting the book together. If there is writing involved, then that comes next. Generally, one of the short books, an 'I Can Read' book, takes me six months to do, about half the time in research and half the time in writing. The writing is very important to me. Everything I write is read aloud three or four times in the bathroom because the acoustics are so good. I'm listening to the way the sounds link up and work together, so I will lock myself in the bathroom and read the book aloud and put big red circles around those things that are not working in terms of sounds. Since a lot of this material is going to be *told,* the sounds are important. But, what I'm also after here, when I'm dealing with tales, are stripped down tales—right down to the essentials, because traditionally, storytellers will take such a tale and embellish it themselves. I want them to be able to do this. Now I've discovered that professional storytellers are using my stuff. And librarians use it in this way, I hope. They should be. After all, every time you sing a folksong, it changes. That's essentially what I do.

"The older books take a long time. They generally take a year or more. A book I did called *Fat Man in a Fur Coat and Other Bear Stories* was an experiment. I began, for the first time, using mixed media. I was using folktales and some poetry, including an Abraham Lincoln poem. I used some journalism—I developed the story on the air force research using bears. There is some historical material in the book and there's hyperbole and so on. The idea was to use all of these media to reflect the nature and texture of the varied relationships, fanciful and otherwise, that we have with bears.

"Sometimes it's all very easy. When I did *The Cat's Elbow and Other Secret Languages,* I was brash enough to sign a contract without really looking to see what there was. I as-

sumed, well, there just had to be stuff, and I could just find it. I became quite nervous after three months because I was finding very little. And then one day I was on C Floor of Firestone Library, staring at a very brief reference to secret languages in the *New York Folklore Journal* which referred me to a science magazine from 1890, which referred me to a defunct German folklore publication, which was published in the 1890s! The editor had an interest in secret languages, and he had made periodic requests of his readers for secret languages they knew. There was a trove of material there. I found all that in one morning! So I hired some graduate students who translated this stuff from the Old Norse and Swahili and Chinese and so forth. I think there are nine or ten of these secret languages which ended up in the book, including the title 'The Cat's Elbow.' I discovered on an airplane ride what it actually meant. It's from the German. I was riding out to Sacramento, and the man sitting next to me taught German literature at Wake Forest University. He said, 'What are you working on?' And I told him. He said, 'You know what that means? The ''cat's elbow'' means the funny bone.' The Germans refer to the funny bone as 'the cat's elbow.' So when I got off the plane I called my editor in New York. They were putting the book together, and we worked it into the text.''[4]

In each of Schwartz's books explanatory notes, sources and a bibliography are included. "We tend to think of folkore as old-fashioned. But whenever people interact and share problems, possibilities, solutions, and pain, they continue to create and use the stuff of folklore to deal with their needs. This process is at work on farms, in city neighborhoods, in hospitals, in jails, in factories and stores, in the armed forces, on playgrounds, in schools, and in many other places. Yet, for several reasons, we have come to depend less on folklore. As our technology has advanced we have come to rely increas-

On her way home from the market, the woman took a short cut through the cemetery. ∎
(From ''Cemetery Soup'' in *More Scary Stories to Tell in the Dark: Collected from Folklore,* retold by Alvin Schwartz. Illustrated by Stephen Gammell.)

Then a big voice said,   **"And *ME!*"**

(From "The Pirate" in *In a Dark, Dark Room and Other Scary Stories,* retold by Alvin Schwartz. Illustrated by Dirk Zimmer.)

ingly on other people for goods, services, and entertainment and less on ourselves and on those we know. The extended family and the traditions it preserved have disappeared. We move about the country to an extraordinary extent; each year one family out of four moves from one place to another. As a result of such changes, we have to a serious extent become alienated from our traditions and have lost a sense of place and a sense of self. If this perception is correct, we have altered the fabric of our society, and we are changing from something we were to something we have not yet become.

"In light of all this, what am I trying to say to a child who reads my books of folklore? Laugh when you can. As Josh Billings suggested, '[O]pen your mouth wide enough for the noise to get out without squealing, throw your head back as though you was going to be shaved, hold on to your false hair with both hands and then laugh till your soul gets thoroughly rested.'

"Understand that you are not very different from people who lived before you, despite the trappings of modern life. You experience the same joys, the same fears, the same anger, the same love, the same need for dignity, the same need for security.

"Understand that you are part of a living tradition to which you contribute and from which you draw. You are deeply rooted in the experience of the human race and are part of something remarkable and continuous—the folk. At a time when everyone and everything seem in transit, it is good to know this.''[3]

FOOTNOTE SOURCES

[1]Sally Holmes Holtze, editor, *Fifth Book of Junior Authors and Illustrators,* H. W. Wilson, 1986.

[2]Publicity, Farrar, Straus.
[3]Alvin Schwartz, "Children, Humor, and Folklore," *Horn Book,* August, 1977.
[4]"Profile: Alvin Schwartz," *Language Arts,* April, 1987.

FOR MORE INFORMATION SEE:

New York Times Book Review, May 6, 1973, January 17, 1982.
Horn Book, June, 1977 (p. 281), February, 1984.
Children's Literature Review, Volume III, Gale, 1978.
Martha E. Ward and Dorothy A. Marquardt, *Authors of Books for Young People,* supplement to the second edition, Scarecrow, 1979.

SCOTT, Ann Herbert 1926-

PERSONAL: Born November 19, 1926, in Germantown, Philadelphia, Pa.; daughter of Henry Laux (a newspaperman) and Gladys (a homemaker, singer and painter; maiden name, Howe) Herbert; married William Taussig Scott (a professor of physics), September 29, 1961; children: Peter Herbert, Katharine Howe; (stepchildren) Jennifer, Christopher (deceased), Stephanie, Melanie. *Education:* University of Pennsylvania, B.A., 1948, graduate student, 1948-49; Yale University, M.A., 1958. *Politics:* Democrat. *Religion:* Society of Friends. *Home and office:* 1425 Alturas Ave., Reno, Nev. 89503.

CAREER: Rider College, Trenton, N.J., teacher of English, 1949-50; New Haven State Teachers College (now Southern Connecticut State College), New Haven, part-time teacher of English, 1956-58; Wider City Parish, New Haven, coordinator of volunteer work, 1958-61; editor and writer, 1961—. Lec-

ANN HERBERT SCOTT

turer. American Friends Service Committee, Northern California Office, member of Reno area committee, 1966-84; cofounder and member, Children's Literature Interest Group, 1980—; founder and chairperson, Sierra Interfaith Action for Peace, 1986—; director, All the Colors of the Race, Nevada Humanities Committee Conference on Ethnic Children's Literature, 1983. *Member:* Society of Children's Book Writers, National Association for the Advancement of Colored People, Phi Beta Kappa, Mortar Board, Sphinx and Key. *Awards, honors: Sam* was chosen one of the American Institute of Graphic Arts Children's Books, 1967-68; *Not Just One* was selected one of Child Study Association of America's Children's Books of the Year, 1968, and *On Mother's Lap,* 1972; Nevada Arts Council Grant, 1987, to study old Nevada Buckaroos.

WRITINGS:

JUVENILE, EXCEPT AS NOTED

Big Cowboy Western (illustrated by Richard W. Lewis), Lothrop, 1965, new edition, Scott Foresman, 1966.
Let's Catch a Monster (illustrated by H. Tom Hall), Lothrop, 1967.
Sam (ALA Notable Book; illustrated by Symeon Shimin), McGraw, 1967, new edition, Open Court, 1977.
Not Just One (illustrated by Yaroslava), Lothrop, 1968.
Census, U.S.A.: Fact Finding for the American People, 1790-1970 (young adult), Seabury, 1968.
On Mother's Lap (illustrated by Glo Coalson), McGraw, 1972.
Some Day Rider, Clarion, 1989.

Contributor to periodicals, including *Reno Gazette-Journal,* and *Nevada Highways.*

ADAPTATIONS:

"Books about Real Things" (based on *Sam,* along with discussion of author's work; filmstrip with cassette), Pied Piper, 1982.

WORK IN PROGRESS: "I have a number of works in progress, including my first easy-to-read story and several manuscripts that have come out of my interviews with Nevada ranchers and cowboys."

SIDELIGHTS: "When I worked in New Haven in the 1950s, I was appalled by the lack of children's books picturing either urban neighborhoods or dark-skinned families. I initiated and directed LINK, a program designed 'to give inner-city children between the ages of eight and twelve the chance to become friends with a caring adult and, through an ongoing relationship, to widen their horizons and raise their aspirations.' I dreamed that someday I would write true-to-life stories that would be set in the housing project where I worked, stories in which my New Haven friends could find themselves. However, it was not until I had moved to Nevada that *Big Cowboy Western* evolved.

"This was the first children's story I had written since childhood. Like most of what I have written since, it began as a gift from a child. It was a result of the memories of years I had spent working in New Haven—an old produce peddler and his horse, a lonely, little boy in a cowboy hat sitting by himself on a bench, an irrepressible youngster who called himself Big Cowboy Western, and several families with many children where the mothers worked and there were no fathers at home.

"I have written all my life—mostly committee reports, minutes, grant requests, and doggerel for family birthdays. However, a few years ago I began looking for something worth doing that would be both income-producing and transportable since my husband's summer research takes us to different parts of the country. I decided that what I would most enjoy doing would be writing for young children and thought I would have a try at it.

"I believe the pull toward children's writing comes from something childlike within me. I've always enjoyed being around little children and wherever we've lived—farm, city, housing development—there have been a few small children who have been among my closest friends. The sense of delight and wonder little children bring to the here and now seems to awaken something deep in me. In contrast to writing for adults, which is often dreary and difficult for me, writing for children is often fun; it springs up unexpectedly in familiar places with some of the same spontaneous independence as forgotten daffodils in a leaf-covered bed.

"In general I work over material for some time, usually simplifying and resimplifying, often cutting out favorite phrases because they are not necessary to the thrust of the story. When there is something I am unsure about, six-year-old children's ideas about monsters, for example, I do a lot of talking with children. Otherwise I work from memory and imagination. I always *see* picture books as I write them; the sense of the graphics helps shape the development of the manuscript.

"*Sam,* a story of a boy too little to do anything, was a notable exception. It came as I was scrubbing out the bathtub after a visit from a particularly experimental young neighbor. I wrote it in a few minutes, made some minor changes the next day, and sent it off."[1]

Census, U.S.A. is a study of American census-taking. "This book started innocently enough when I took a job as a census taker on the Pyramid Lake Indian Reservation and stumbled into an almost completely neglected area of our national life.

"Peace and social justice are important matters to both my husband and me, and we are often up to our ears in mailing lists, mimeographed materials, and the other paper work of social action."[1]

"As a writer who specializes in picture books for young children, my work has peculiar aesthetic concerns. Although I am not an artist, I continually work with images in mind, leaving much of the telling to the skill of the illustrator. My work is often described as 'simple,' and so it is. However, it is the simplicity of discovering the organic shape of an idea, eliminating all that is unessential, depicting the large in the small. My manuscripts often go through twenty to thirty revisions.

"My reputation as a children's writer is based on books which evoke universal themes: the security of mother's love, the yearning to be big and important, the courage to deal with fear or jealousy. I am a realist, trying to faithfully depict life as I observe it, and I usually choose to explore important matters of the heart within the framework of everyday scenes from the lives of young children. Before beginning a story, I like to be as familiar as possible with what I am trying to portray.

"Recently I have been drawn to new themes and ideas linked to the life of remote Nevada, the buckaroos and ranchers, the

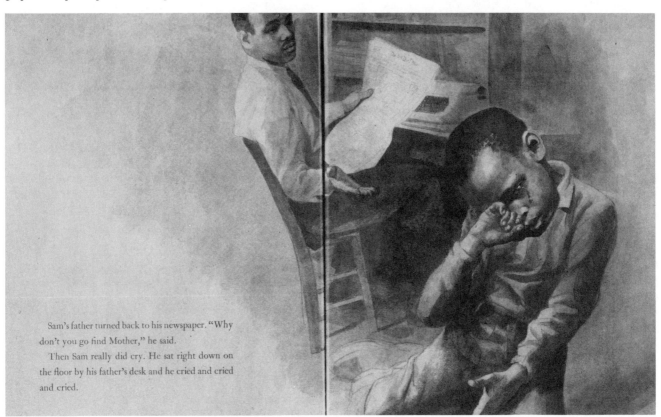

Sam's father turned back to his newspaper. "Why don't you go find Mother," he said.
Then Sam really did cry. He sat right down on the floor by his father's desk and he cried and cried and cried.

(From *Sam* by Ann Herbert Scott. Illustrated by Symeon Shimin.)

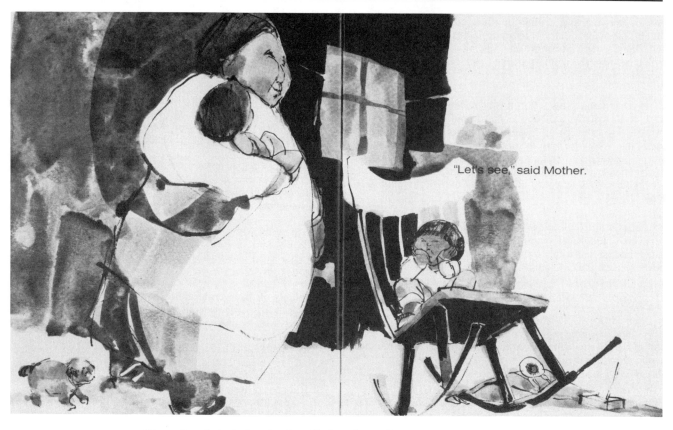

"Let's see," said Mother.

(From *On Mother's Lap* by Ann Herbert Scott. Illustrated by Glo Coalson.)

Paiute and Shoshone people. The book ideas evoked by these themes are not just for children but the sort of picture book one critic calls the 'Everybody Book.' An opportunity to interview a number of old buckaroos was provided by a Nevada State Council on the Arts grant in 1986-87, inspiring a number of partly finished stories and a book entitled *Some Day Rider*. Most recently a visit to the Duckwater Indian Reservation stirred the beginning of one Shoshone story and the foreshadowing of others.

"I also do editorial work for my husband who is writing a biography on Michael Polany."

In her spare time, Scott enjoys painting, both pictures and houses, talking with friends, poking around in the garden, cooking and eating, exploring, especially in the mountains, desert or beaches.

FOOTNOTE SOURCES

[1]Lee Bennett Hopkins, *Books Are by People*, Citation, 1969.

FOR MORE INFORMATION SEE:

Library Journal, February 15, 1968.
Christian Century, December 18, 1968.
Doris de Montreville and Elizabeth D. Crawford, editors, *Fourth Book of Junior Authors and Illustrators*, H. W. Wilson, 1978.
Dorothy A. Marquardt and Martha E. Ward, *Authors of Books for Young People*, 2nd edition supplement, Scarecrow Press, 1979.

COLLECTIONS

Kerlan Collection at the University of Minnesota.
University of Nevada Archives.

SIMAK, Clifford D(onald)   1904-1988

OBITUARY NOTICE: Born August 3, 1904, in Millville, Wis.; died April 25, 1988, in Minneapolis, Minn. Educator, journalist, and author. Simak, who was inducted into the Science Fiction Hall of Fame in 1973, was a prolific writer of science fiction novels and short stories. The recipient of three Hugo Awards, two Nebula Awards, and a Grand Master Award for his lifetime contribution to science fiction, Simak is best known for his books *City, Way Station,* and *The Visitors,* and for his collection *Skirmish: The Great Short Fiction of Clifford D. Simak.*

Besides writing, Simak also taught school and worked for several Michigan newspapers in his early career, then joined the *Minneapolis Star and Tribune* in 1939. He eventually became news editor and science editor of that publication, retiring in 1976. Simak's other works include the novels *The Creator, Special Deliverance,* and *Highway of Eternity,* the story collections *Strangers in the Universe* and *The Worlds of Clifford Simak,* and the nonfiction works *The Solar System: Our New Front Yard, Wonder and Glory: the Story of the Universe,* and *Prehistoric Man.*

FOR MORE INFORMATION SEE:

Contemporary Literary Criticism, Volume 1, Gale, 1973.
Dictionary of Literary Biography, Volume 8: "Twentieth Century American Science Fiction Writers," Gale, 1981.
The Writers Directory, 1988-1990, St. James Press, 1988.

OBITUARIES

New York Times, April 28, 1988.
Los Angeles Times, April 29, 1988.
Times (London), April 29, 1988.
Washington Post, April 30, 1988.

THALER, Michael C. 1936-
(Mike Thaler)

PERSONAL: Born in 1936, in Los Angeles, Calif.; son of Ben (a salesman, poet, and sculptor) and Jean (a homemaker; maiden name, Rosensweig) Thaler; married: Jackie Sweeny (a poet, teacher and author), September 29, 1985; children: Gabby, Matt. *Education:* Attended the University of California at Los Angeles. *Home and office:* Box 223, R.D.1, Stone Ridge, N.Y. 12484. *Agent:* Andrea Brown, 301 West 53rd St., Suite 13B, New York, N.Y. 10019.

CAREER: Author and illustrator, 1961—. Songwriter, sculptor, game designer, teacher, lecturer. Creator of "Letterman" for Public Broadcasting Service children's television series "The Electric Company." Teacher of workshops on riddle-making, creative book making, stories and creative dramatics. *Member:* PEN, American Society of Composers, Authors and Publishers. *Awards, honors: Moonkey* was selected a Children's Choice by the International Reading Association and the Children's Book Council, 1982.

WRITINGS:

JUVENILE; UNDER NAME MIKE THALER

The Magic Boy (self-illustrated), Harper, 1961.
The Clown's Smile (self-illustrated), Harper, 1962, new edition (illustrated by Tracey Cameron), 1986.
The King's Flower (self-illustrated), Orion Press, 1963.
Penny Pencil: The Story of a Pencil (self-illustrated), Harper, 1963.
Moonboy (self-illustrated), Harper, 1964.
The Prince and the Seven Moons (illustrated by Ursula Arndt), Macmillan, 1966.
(Editor with William Cole) *The Classic Cartoons: A Definitive Gallery of the Cartoon as Art and as Humor,* World Publishing, 1966.

MICHAEL C. THALER

The Rainbow (illustrated by Donald Leake), H. Quist, 1967.
The Smiling Book (illustrated by Arnie Levin), Lothrop, 1971.
My Little Friend (illustrated by A. Levin), Lothrop, 1971.
The Staff (illustrated by Joseph Schindelman), Random House, 1971.
How Far Will a Rubberband Stretch (illustrated by Jerry Joyner), Parents Magazine Press, 1974.
Magic Letter Riddles (self-illustrated), Scholastic, 1974.
What Can a Hippopatamus Be? (illustrated by Robert Grossman), Parents Magazine Press, 1975.
Wuzzles (self-illustrated), Scholastic, 1976.
Soup with Quackers! Funny Cartoon Riddles (Junior Literary Guild selection; self-illustrated), F. Watts, 1976.
Riddle Riot (self-illustrated), Scholastic, 1976.
(With W. Cole) *Knock Knocks: The Most Ever* (self-illustrated), F. Watts, 1976.
Funny Bones: Cartoon Monster Riddles (self-illustrated), F. Watts, 1976.
Silly Puzzles (self-illustrated), Xerox Publications, 1976.
Dazzles (self-illustrated), Grosset, 1977.
(With W. Cole) *Knocks Knocks You've Never Heard Before* (self-illustrated), F. Watts, 1977.
(With W. Cole) *The Square Bear and Other Riddle Rhymes* (self-illustrated), Scholastic, 1977.
Never Tickle a Turtle: Cartoons, Riddles and Funny Stories (self-illustrated), F. Watts, 1977.
There's a Hippopotamus under My Bed (illustrated by Ray Cruz), F. Watts, 1977.
What's Up Duck? Cartoons, Riddles, and Jokes (self-illustrated), F. Watts, 1978.
The Chocolate Marshmelephant Sundae (self-illustrated), F. Watts, 1978.
The Yellow Brick Toad: Funny Frog Cartoons, Riddles and Silly Stories (self-illustrated), Doubleday, 1978.
(With W. Cole) *Give Up? Cartoon Riddle Rhymes* (self-illustrated), F. Watts, 1978.
Madge's Magic Show (illustrated by Carol Nicklaus), F. Watts, 1978.
(With W. Cole) *Backwords* (self-illustrated), Random House, 1979.
Picture Riddles (self-illustrated), Random House, 1979.
Unicorns on the Cob (self-illustrated), Grosset, 1979.
Screamers (self-illustrated), Grosset, 1979.
Steer Wars (self-illustrated), Grosset, 1979.
The Nose Knows (self-illustrated), Grosset, 1979.
Grin and Bear It (self-illustrated), Grosset, 1979.
Toucans on Two Cans (self-illustrated), Grosset, 1979.
The Complete Cootie Book (self-illustrated), Avon, 1980.
My Puppy (illustrated by Madeleine Fishman), Harper, 1980.
Moonkey (illustrated by Giulio Maestro), Harper, 1981.
The Moose Is Loose (illustrated by Toni Gaffr), Scholastic, 1981.
A Hippopotamus Ate the Teacher (illustrated by Jared Lee), Avon, 1981.
Oinkers Away: Pig Riddles, Cartoons and Jokes (self-illustrated), Archway, 1981.
Scared Silly: A Monster Riddle and Joke Scare-a-Thon Featuring Bugs Mummy and Count Quackula (self illustrated), Avon, 1982.
Story Puzzles, Scholastic, 1982.
The Pac-Man Riddle and Joke Book (self-illustrated), Archway, 1982.
Paws: Cat Riddles, Cat Jokes and Catoons (self-illustrated), Archway, 1982.
(With William Cole) *Monster Knock Knocks* (self-illustrated), Archway, 1982.
Owly (illustrated by David Wiesner), Harper, 1982.
The Moon and the Balloon (illustrated by Madeleine Fishman), Hastings House, 1982.

(From *In the Middle of the Puddle* by Mike Thaler. Illustrated by Bruce Degen.)

Mike Thaler and friends.

Stuffed Feet (self-illustrated), Avon, 1983.

It's Me, Hippo! (illustrated by Maxie Chambliss), Harper, 1983, large print edition, 1983.

Riddle Rainbow (self-illustrated), Hastings House, 1984.

Montgomery Moose's Favorite Riddles (illustrated by Neal McPheeters), Scholastic, 1985.

Cream of Creature from the School Cafeteria (illustrated by J. Lee), Avon, 1985.

Funny Side Up! How to Create Your Own Riddles (self-illustrated), Scholastic, 1985.

Upside Down Day (illustrated by J. Lee), Avon, 1986.

King Kong's Underwear (self-illustrated), Avon, 1986.

Hippo Lemonade (illustrated by M. Chambliss), Harper, 1986.

Mr. Bananahead at Home (self-illustrated), Scholastic, 1987.

Hink Pink Monsters (illustrated by Fred Winkowski), Scholastic, 1987.

In the Middle of the Puddle (illustrated by Bruce Degen), Harper, 1988.

Pack 109 (illustrated by Normand Chartier), Dutton, 1988.

Come and Play Hippo, Harper, 1989.

The Teacher from the Black Lagoon, Scholastic, 1989.

Godzilla's Pantyhose, Avon, 1989.

ACTIVITY BOOKS; ALL WITH JANET PULLEN

The Riddle King's Giant Book of Jokes, Riddles and Activities, Modern, 1987.

The Riddle King's Jumbo Book of Jokes, Riddles and Activities, Modern, 1987.

The Riddle King's Super Book of Jokes, Riddles, and Activities, Modern, 1987.

The Riddle King's Book of Jokes, Riddles and Activities, Modern, 1988.

RECORDINGS

"The Riddle King Tells His Favorite Riddles, Jokes, Stories, and Songs with Steve Charney" (cassette), Caedmon, 1985.

"The Riddle King's Riddle Song Scholastic Songs with Steve Charney" (cassette), Scholastic, 1987.

"These Are the Questions" (cassette).

"My Blanket Is the Sky" (cassette).

"Sing Me a Rainbow" (cassette).

SOFTWARE

(With J. Pullen) "The Riddle King's Riddle Magic," Mindscape, 1987.

GAMES; ALL WITH J. PULLEN

"The Riddle King's Scrambled Legs," Playspaces, 1988.

"The Riddle King's Riddle Race," Playspaces, 1988.

"The Riddle King's Hink Think," Playspaces, 1989.

"The Riddle King's Riddlemania," Playspaces, 1989.

Also author of *Story Letters*, Grosset, and *Scared Silly*, Avon. Thaler's books have been published in England, Canada, France and Japan. Contributor of cartoons to *Harper's Bazaar, Horizon, Humpty Dumpty*, and *Saturday Evening Post*.

WORK IN PROGRESS: A television show; a softwear disc; a childen's novel; an "I Can Read" series for Harper; an easy reader series for Dutton; seven stories for Scribner's "Basic Reader Program"; articles for *Instructor* and *Learning* magazines.

SIDELIGHTS: An author of numerous children's books, Thaler has been drawing since his teens. "What I really hoped to earn a living at was doing cartoons for adults. Actually, they weren't even funny cartoons, they were the 'save-the-world' kind. Then one day Ursula Nordstrom, an editor at Harper & Row, saw a picture story I had done for *Harper's Bazaar,* of all magazines, and asked if I had ever thought of doing children's books.

"In 1961, I did my first book, *The Magic Boy,* about a little boy who could juggle rainbows, which he sometimes dropped, and elephants, which he never dropped—and here I am eighty books later.

"I. . .see language differently than many people. It is sort of like I am sitting in the balcony looking down on things."[1]

"I'm only just now learning to write, to feel words. Writing a story is like painting a picture. You put down one color, and then you put down a second color next to it, and it changes the first color. You put down words next to words and they change, too. So when you put two or three words together, there's an interaction. I write with my feelings."[2]

When writing Thaler looks to the child within ". . .I sort of feel like I am more of a receiver than an originator, that I am merely the radio the music plays through. It's like the stories are already there. I am simply putting them down on paper.

"There was a time in my life that everything had to be serious. Now I have learned that laughter is important, and I feel it is important for children to have a good body of humor, an intelligent body of humor. That is what I am working on."[1]

"I'm very bad at guessing other people's riddles, so it's easier to make them up. Most riddle books are just lists of riddles, but I like to play up the visual aspects. Every person has a great creative force inside him. I try to teach people to find their own potential. I'd rather have kids make up their own riddles and do their own drawings. My philosophy is that if you are in touch with your own creative potential, you can be in touch with anything. Education should be a flowering, a bringing out of each individual's creative potential."[3]

"When you do children's books, there can be no waste, no fat. It has to be all muscle and bone. There has to be character development, plot and depth, all in thirty-two pages. And it has to have beauty and energy. It has to give off energy. Words give an emotional feeling. They give you energy.

"I had always thought that children's books should have a message. But just the laughter of children is the message. Laughter is a message in itself."[2]

Thaler travels to schools across the country reading from his books and encouraging children to develop their own creativity. "I find riddles to be a valuable educational tool. They get

Not long thereafter, Eema and the princess were married. The king and the giant became good friends and played chess together every day.

(From *The Staff* by Mike Thaler. Illustrated by Joseph Schindelman.)

kids into all sorts of things—synonyms, rhythm, spelling syntax, syllables and, more importantly, into the dictionary, a marvelous source of riddles.

"I tell them with the simple riddle-writing system I have developed, it really is easier to write riddles than to guess the answers. It is a way of getting kids to learn to love language and to have fun with language." [1]

In his visits to schools Thaler encourages children to make up their own stories, draw their own cartoons and write their own books in order to help children appreciate laughter and their own creativity. "There is pure creativity when you are around kids. The energy of children is the most amazing, important source of energy in this whole country. It should be protected and helped to develop. Teachers to me are the most important people in the world because they are shaping the future. The possibilities of kids are the possibilities of the future.

"Every child has the potential to be a poet, a writer, an artist, but as people grow older, they put on overcoats until their intuitive spontaneity is covered up. When I do workshops for teachers I always have to spend time getting them to take those overcoats off." [1]

"I have a shirt that says, 'Kids are everyone's future.' They are! and teachers are the most valuable people in our society, because teachers are the ones who shape kids.

"If kids are going to learn about caring for learning, they'll learn it from teachers. Teachers are the most important people in our society, and they get so very little recognition. They are treated poorly by so many people.

"Basically, society is into power, and teachers don't represent power and success. But they are the real power in society because they have the power to shape the future. What a kid gives to society oftentimes depends on one teacher who took the time to shape that child. Teachers are the unsung heroes of society.

"Teachers have to be creative and loving in their teaching. Love and creativity are the two basic elements of life to me. If you put love and creativity into everything you do, you've got it made. This is the philosophy I live by, and the philosophy I teach." [2]

Thaler became known as "America's Riddle King." "I was out speaking at schools in Albuquerque, New Mexico. . .when a reporter came to interview me. The teacher introduced me by that name, and I figured it was a title no one else probably wanted so I accepted it." [1]

Thaler created the "Letterman" feature on "Electric Company" amd wrote over sixty segments for the show. "The Letterman segment really represents the two sides of me. Letterman is really this very sweet guy, the kind who always says things like, 'Drive carefully,' and Spellbinder is the trouble maker, but he never causes any trouble unless he knows Letterman is around to help him.

"Like, he wouldn't take the H away from the lady's heels and turn them into eels or add a W and turn them into wheels so she would roll down the hill unless he knew Letterman was around to put the word back together properly." [1]

"I believe that the most important two things that human beings have—and what *makes* them human—are love and creativity. This belief is the foundation of my books and my life. The

"All my friends have houses," he thought. "I would like a house too." ■ (From *It's Me, Hippo!* by Mike Thaler. Illustrated by Maxie Chambliss.)

awards and honors that are most important to me are children's laughter and creativity."

When he's not working on his many projects, Thaler enjoys collecting art, netsuke, model and toy race cars, t-shirts, and laughter.

FOOTNOTE SOURCES

[1] Deena Mirow, "Who Makes Children Feel Riddle-culous?," *Plain Dealer*, March 17, 1985. Amended by M. Thaler.
[2] Frederick P. Szydlik, "Q: What Do You Say to a Riddle King? A: Hello, Thaler!," *Knickerbocker News*, April 29, 1983. Amended by M. Thaler.
[3] *Junior Literary Guild Catalog*, September, 1976. Amended by M. Thaler.

FOR MORE INFORMATION SEE:

Cindy Kornetti, "A Kingdom of Riddles," *Trentonian*, June 14, 1985.
Jack and Jill, April/May, 1986.
Kathy Matter, "Power of Imagination," *Journal Courier* (Indiana), May 25, 1985.

THOMAS, Vernon (Arthur) 1934-

PERSONAL: Born January 29, 1934, in Calcutta, India; son of Basil Arthur (an executive) and Eileen (a teacher; maiden name, Almeida) Thomas. *Education:* Calcutta University, Bachelor of Commerce Degree, 1954; London Royal School

VERNON THOMAS

of Music, final grade in piano, 1954; further study at Regent Institute, London, 1971-72. *Religion:* Roman Catholic. *Home:* 129 Lenin Sarani, Calcutta 70013, West Bengal, India.

CAREER: Writer. Jessop & Company, Calcutta, India, accounts executive and departmental manager, 1954-76; fiction editor of *The Teenager,* 1985—; fiction editor of *Together,* 1988—. Has also taught piano. *Member:* Writer's Workshop Club, Calcutta (honorary member). *Awards, honors:* First prize in *Himmat Weekly* magazine (India) short story contest, 1971.

WRITINGS:

CHILDREN'S NOVELS, EXCEPT AS NOTED

The Little Girl of Dove Cot, Hemkunt Press (New Delhi, India), 1974, Better Yourself Books (India), 1986.
Tairy Fales (young adult), Hemkunt Press, 1975.
The Right to Love (young adult), Hemkunt Press, 1976.
The Wasted Years (adult), Better Yourself Books, 1977.
Tiny Tess and The Little Angels, Better Yourself Books, 1977.
The Mystery At Gul Mohur, Better Yourself Books, 1980.
Home Is Where the Heart Is (young adult), Better Yourself Books, 1980.
The Mystery at Lime Tree House (young adult), Better Yourself Books, in press.
The Three Friends, Better Yourself Books, in press.
The Mystery of the Secret Package, Better Yourself Books, in press.
The Mystery of the Missing Ornaments, Better Yourself Books, in press.
The Do-Gooders, Better Yourself Books, in press.

SHORT STORY COLLECTIONS

Roses for Remembrance (young adult), Better Yourself Books, 1973.
Hidden Beauty (young adult), Better Yourself Books, 1974.
Heart and Reason (young adult), Better Yourself Books, 1975.

Tides of Fortune (young adult), Better Yourself Books, 1975.
There Comes a Time (adult), Better Yourself Books, 1976.
Suddenly It's Christmas: A Collection of Yuletide Stories (adult; Writer's Workshop Greenbird Series), Writer's Workshop, 1977.
When Christmas Comes (young adult), Better Yourself Books, 1981.

RETELLER

Tales from the Panchatantra, Better Yourself Books, 1974.
Fifty Aesop Fables, Better Yourself Books, 1975.
Jataka Tales, Better Yourself Books, 1976.
Stories from the Arabian Nights (illustrated by R. K. Basu), Hemkunt Press, 1977, Auromere, 1979.
Folk Tales of India, Hemkunt Press, 1978, Auromere, 1979.
Fairy Tales from India, Hemkunt Press, 1978, Auromere, 1979.
Aesop's Fables (illustrated by Reboti Bhushan), Hemkunt Press, 1980, Auromere, 1981.
More Stories from the Arabian Nights (illustrated by R. K. Bose), Hemkunt Press, 1980, Auromere, 1981.
The Story of Jesus Christ, Hemkunt Press, 1980.
Legends of North India, Hemkunt Press, 1981.
More Legends from North India, Hemkunt Press, 1981.
More Stories from the Panchatantra, Hemkunt Press, 1981.
Robinson Crusoe, Better Yourself Books, 1981.
Kidnapped, Better Yourself Books, 1981.
Buried Alive, Better Yourself Books, 1981.
Tales of Birbal and Akbar, Hemkunt Press, 1982.
Tales from India, Hemkunt Press, 1982.
Bedtime Stories from India, Hemkunt Press, 1982.
Gulliver's Travels, Better Yourself Books, 1984.
Treasure Island, Better Yourself Books, 1984.
The Adventures of Hajji Baba of Ispahan, Better Yourself Books, 1984.
The Coral Island, Better Yourself Books, 1984.
Quo Vadis, Better Yourself Books, 1984.
Tales from Other Lands, Better Yourself Books, 1987.
Thirty Fables of La Fontaine, Better Yourself Books, 1987.
More Jataka Tales, Better Yourself Books, 1987.
More Tales from The Panchatantra, Better Yourself Books, 1988.
Fifty More Aesop Fables, Better Yourself Books, 1988.
Les Miserables, Better Yourself Books, 1988.
Ivanhoe, Better Yourself Books, in press.
The Fables of Phaedrus, Better Yourself Books, in press.
Famous Old Fairy Tales, Better Yourself Books, in press.
A Tale of Two Cities, Better Yourself Books, in press.
Tales from Eastern India, Hemkunt Press, in press.
The Story of Lord Mahavira, Hemkunt Press, in press.
Land and People of India, Hemkunt Press, in press.

Contributor to magazines in India, England, South Africa, Ireland and Bangladesh.

WORK IN PROGRESS: Short stories for magazines in India.

SIDELIGHTS: "An only child, I was born in Calcutta, India. I spent my early years of schooling at a Jesuit school, St. Xavier's, in the city. My final years of schooling were spent at St. Patrick's High School in Asansol, a country town in West Bengal, from where I passed the Senior Cambridge.

"During my school days I was always fond of writing and would take particular pride in my essays during English language classes. I wrote my first story in 1946 at the age of twelve. It was a children's story about two identical princesses. I showed it to my teacher and he asked me where I would like to send it for publication. 'To *The Illustrated Weekly of India,*' I replied. It was the leading magazine of the country at the time, and my teacher smiled, and told me that I must not be so ambitious. He advised me to send it to a smaller publication. But for me it was a case of the best or none at all. And so, I forgot about writing for the next twenty years, by which time I had long since graduated from college and was working as an accounts executive in a large engineering firm in Calcutta.

"Over the years, I was very fond of writing newsy and humorous letters to friends and relatives living in other parts of India and abroad. They would enjoy reading my letters and several advised me to take up writing as a hobby. A female cousin of mine was particularly encouraging. There was a column in one of our local newspapers in which humorous anecdotes were published. I often told my cousin that I could write such stuff, and she would encourage me to try.

"About this time I was hoping to marry a young lady, but she underwent a change of heart. One day she was seen out with another chap, who later became her husband. This intelligence left me rather devastated. I went to bed that night most miserable, and the next morning I sat down to write my first article. That was in 1967, and it was the start of my writing career. I have always felt grateful to that lady. I attribute my initiation into the literary field to her. Today she lives in Australia with her family, and we still exchange greetings at Christmas.

"I have not looked back since. One story followed another. Then in 1971-72 I took a postal course in the art of short story writing from the Regent Institute in London. Although by this time I had had a lot of success in Indian publications, in 1973 I had my first success abroad. A romantic short story of mine was published in a leading South African journal called *Personality*. Shortly after I sold the British Rights of this story to the D.C. Thomson magazine, *Story World*. Then at the end of 1973, my first book, *Roses for Remembrance*, a collection of short stories for teens, was published.

"In 1970 the editor of a youth magazine invited me to write for children. The thought was a bit alarming at first. Though I was very fond of children, I knew little about them. But I took up the challenge. I put on my thinking cap and soon my first children's novel, *The Little Girl of Dove Cot*, was produced. It is now in its second edition.

"Though most of my short stories are for adults and teens, my books are mainly for children and teens. My publishers have been very encouraging in this respect, and have given me many commissions for books of retold fiction. I find writing for children very stimulating. Over the years I have cultivated the habit of being a keen observer of them in action, both at play and in speech. That way I try to keep my characters in my original works as real as possible. I also try to keep my plots plausible. I try to make one sequence follow another as naturally as possible—no miracles or fantastic situations or outcomes.

"I don't believe in talking down to children. Though I try to tell my stories as simply as possible, I do not avoid big words if they convey more appropriately what I am trying to say. I find writing for children more difficult than writing for adults. I know several other writers who complain of this, too. So, in this respect, I don't feel alone or a rare sort of person!

"Ideas for stories can come to me from any source—at any time or place. Sometimes I have jumped out of bed at night to get an idea down on paper. Yet when I get an idea for a story or a book, I usually have to wait till the opening paragraphs start buzzing around in my head. Then I begin to write.

It takes me a few hours to get a story draft down on paper. It may take a week to get the draft of a children's book written. Thereafter, it can take anything from a few days to a few weeks to finalize a short story. It can take some months to finalize a book for children. My only adult novel took me a whole year to write.

"I am very particular about my writing. I never release a story till I am fully satisfied with it. Most times I find that when things are difficult, it is best to wait awhile before improving a manuscript. The choice of a single word can keep me thinking for a good half hour. Sometimes even a single paragraph can keep me busy for several hours. At times what sounds wonderful today can sound just awful the next day, which means I must tear the section to bits once more. For this reason I dislike working against a time schedule.

"In 1976 I gave up my accounts job to take on full-time writing. Over the twenty years of my writing career I guess I have faced the same difficulty most writers face—rejection. I remember at the start of my career, when I had my first rejection, my mother very kindly hid the envelope amongst her papers and handed it to me in secret, so that I would not be shamed before the rest of the family. But I have learned since there is no shame in rejection. What one journal may not take another one will; each manuscript sooner or later finds its place.

"I believe the ability to write comes as a God-given talent. I don't believe one can learn to write. The ability, like the seed which grows into a tree, must be there. Then only can it be cultivated. And determination is what every aspiring writer should have. Otherwise interest will flag in the face of rejection. To aspiring young writers I would say, if you feel the urge to write start right away. Write about anything you can think of, and ideas will gradually flow.

"I try to encourage young writers. As the fiction editor of a youth magazine, I always provide reasons in detail for rejecting a manuscript. At times I even go in for heavy editing, in order to make a manuscript suitable for use. That way young people feel rewarded to see their efforts in print.

"Regarding the illustrations for my books, I leave that to my publishers. I don't have a talent for drawing or painting. However, at times, with the permission of my publishers, I have encouraged several young artists to illustrate some of my books. On these occasions I have given my suggestions to them concerning what scenes to illustrate and how best to do so. The outcomes, of course, I have not been able to judge. The final word has always remained with my publishers.

"Being a writer has been hard work, frustrating at times, but nevertheless rewarding in the end. For this reason—even though I think at times that I should have branched out into some easier field—I conclude that were I to live my life over again, I would still choose the same line. I would opt for my pen."

HOBBIES AND OTHER INTERESTS: Gardening and collecting crockery and glassware. "I love entertaining and delight in planning meals for guests, and take pride in setting and decorating the dining table. I was once quite crazy about parties and loved dancing, but now I have grown too old and staid for such occupations!"

FOR MORE INFORMATION SEE:

Men of Achievement, International Biographical Centre of Cambridge (England), 1982.

THOMPSON, Hilary 1943-

PERSONAL: Born October 8, 1943, in Yorkshire, England; daughter of Thomas William (a design engineer) and Florence Ena (a homemaker; maiden name, Ironmonger) Allen; married Raymond H. Thompson (a university professor), September 12, 1966; children: Gareth, Katharine, Gawen David. *Education:* University of Alberdeen, M.A. (with honors), 1965; University of Alberta, M.A., 1967, Ph.D., 1972; attended Neighbourhood Playhouse Theatre School, New York, 1967. *Politics:* New Democratic Party. *Religion:* Anglican. *Office:* English Department, Acadia University, Wolfville, Nova Scotia, Canada BOP 1XO.

CAREER: University of Alberta, Canada, teaching assistant, 1965-67; Acadia University, Wolfville, Nova Scotia, Canada, lecturer, 1969-73, assistant professor, 1973—; writer. Secretary, Wolfville Children's Centre, 1972-74; member of executive board, Parent Teachers' Association, Kentville Schools, 1975-76. *Member:* Children's Literature Association, Children's Theatre Association of America, Association of Canadian University Teachers of English, Disabled Unite for Equality in Life (vice-president, 1984-85), Canadian Society of Children's Authors, Illustrators and Performers (Atlantic representative, 1984-85). *Awards, honors:* Honourable Mention for booklength children's prose, 1980, for "ION Adventure," second prize in adult short fiction, 1980, for "Landmarks," both from the Writers' Federation of Nova Scotia Writing Competition; honourable mention from the Ottawa Little Theatre Competition, 1980, for "The Flower That Fades."

WRITINGS:

Three Puppet Plays, Nova Scotia Dramatists' Co-op, 1976.
Anansi the Spider (puppet play), Nova Scotia Dramatists' Co-op, 1977.
Anancy and Lizard (puppet play), Nova Scotia Dramatists' Co-op, 1977.
The Quarrelling Quails (puppet play), Nova Scotia Dramatists' Co-op, 1977.
Warm Is a Circle (self-illustrated juvenile), Lancelot, 1979.
Madame Fou-Fou and the Apricot Mousse; or, Cinderella Comes of Age: A Play for Children or Puppets, Nova Scotia Dramatists' Co-op, 1979.

HILARY THOMPSON

Only So Far (adult), Fiddlehead Poetry Books, 1982.

UNPUBLISHED ADULT PLAYS

"Northern Lights," performed at Acadia University, 1979.
"The Flower That Fades," performed at Nova Scotia Dramatists' Co-op, Halifax, October, 1981.

Also author of "Jamie and the Lamb." Contributor to *Canadian Children's Literature* and *Survey of Science Fiction and Fantasy.* Poetry editor of *Atlantis,* 1978-86.

WORK IN PROGRESS: The Giant under the Mountain, a juvenile novel; *Turtle Diary and Dragonlands,* poetry; working in the field of children's theater in education; *Nova Scotian Children's Rhymes.*

SIDELIGHTS: "My concerns are with playwrighting for children which involves and absorbs this interest. To this end I spent a sabbatical year with Dorothy Heathcote, a specialist in Theatre-in-Education at the University of Newcastle-upon-Tyne.

"As a teacher and writer I allow the one activity to feed the other. My students, who are at Acadia University, give me many insights into their world, their concerns. These, in turn, become part of my own thinking as a writer. Always I am passionately convinced of the importance of imaginative activity and the revelation of truth through creativity, whether it be in works of literature I teach or in the poems and stories I choose to write."

FOR MORE INFORMATION SEE:

Alpha, spring, 1983 (interview).
Writers' News, summer, 1983 (interview).

TRIVELPIECE, Laurel 1926-
(Hannah K. Marks)

PERSONAL: Born January 18, 1926, in Curtis, Neb.; daughter of Leland S. (a farmer) and Eleanor (a nurse attendant; maiden name, Best) Trivelpiece; married Alfred D. Shapiro (an architect), November 14, 1953; children: Mitchell D., Matthew Alfred. *Education:* Modesto Junior College, A.A., 1946; University of California at Berkeley, B.A., 1948. *Home and Office:* 23 Rocklyn Court, Corte Madera, Calif. 94925. *Agent:* Curtis Brown Ltd., 10 Astor Place, New York, N.Y. 10003.

CAREER: Abbott Kimball, San Francisco, Calif., secretary and copywriter, 1949-50; Roy S. Durstine, San Francisco, copywriter, 1950-52; City of Paris, San Francisco, copywriter, 1952-53, 1953-57; Bergdorf Goodman, New York, N.Y., copywriter, 1953; free-lance writer, 1963—. Member of Marin Bilateral Nuclear Weapons Freeze and town committees of Corte Madera, Calif. *Member:* P.E.N., Sierra Club, Marin Poetry Society. *Awards, honors:* Second Prize for Short Fiction from the Pacific Northwest Writers Conference, 1977, for story, "Winning the Gold"; First Prize from Little Theatre of Alexandria National Competition, 1985, for "The New Job"; Second Prize from the Pioneer Valley Physicians for Social Responsibility Poetry Contest, 1985, for two poems on the nuclear dilemma; Marin Arts Council Creative Advancement Grant, 1985; Beatrice Hawley Poetry Award, 1987.

WRITINGS:

Legless in Flight (poems), Woolmer/Brotherson, 1978.
During Water Peaches (young adult novel), Lippincott, 1979.

This spring of 1943 the government was importing them to pick the peaches and apricots. . .because so many Americans were away at the war. ■ (From *During Water Peaches* by Laurel Trivelpiece. Illustrated by Kenneth Dewey.)

(Under pseudonym Hannah K. Marks) *Triad* (novel), Pocket Books, 1980.

In Love and in Trouble (young adult novel), Archway, 1981.

"The New Job" (one-act play), first produced in Ross, Calif., at Ross Alternative Theatre, November, 1984.

Trying Not to Love You (young adult novel), Archway, 1985.

Blue Holes (poetry collection), Alice James Books, 1987.

Just a Little Bit Lost (young adult novel), Scholastic, 1988.

Work represented in anthologies, including *The Best American Short Stories,* Houghton, 1971, 1974, 1983. Contributor of stories and poems to periodicals, including *Colorado Quarterly, Prairie Schooner, American Poetry Review, Ironwood, Carleton Miscellany,* and *Indiana Review.*

WORK IN PROGRESS: A poetic drama (screenplay) on the Wordsworths; plays.

SIDELIGHTS: "I was born in Curtis, Nebraska, one of five children, in what became a desperately poor farming family. When the farm, which belonged to my grandfather, all but blew away in the Thirties, my parents gave up farming and came, *a la* the Okies, to a better life in California. This was my mother's great effort: she was determined that her children were going to have the opportunity to get an education and, more basically, have enough to eat. Life was hard in the San Joaquin Valley, too, but all of us could work—picking fruit at first, then working in the canneries. My mother got work

as a practical nurse, my father as a milker, which provided us with a home of sorts. My sister worked for her room and board to attend junior college. My brother continued his lost, alcoholic ways, and I, the third, burned to grow up, get out of high school, and in some undetermined way, set the world on fire.

"We survived. I had always been interested in poetry, especially since the marvelous day when I was eight or nine and my doggerel appeared on the 'Aunt Hannah' page for children of the *Omaha World-Herald.* When I had managed, with the aid of a small scholarship and a collection of part-time jobs (there were no student loans in those far off days), to scrabble my way to the University of California, I timidly applied for a creative writing class. I was rejected and felt it was therefore official: I could not be a writer. Still, most impractically (it broke my mother's heart that I wasn't being trained to be a teacher), I continued to study English literature. After a trip to Europe, which I financed with secretarial work, I decided I probably could be a copywriter. But, I continued to write poetry, in fact, I took a workshop with Lawrence Hart, and that was the beginning.

"My passion for the Wordsworths was heightened by a providential opportunity (due to my husband's work) to spend the years 1978 and 1979 in England. I was able to visit the Lake District and climb the fells that the Wordsworths had climbed, to deepen my research there and at the British Museum.

"Hiking, in the Sierras particularly, and botany are two other passions which have a way of appearing in my novels, short stories, and poems. My current work in progress, *The Girl Is Lost,* is a young adult novel about a girl who gets lost in the Sierras. I was once lost there, for a few hours only, but it was enough."

UNSTEAD, Robert J(ohn)   1915-1988

OBITUARY NOTICE—See sketch in *SATA* Volume 12: Born November 21, 1915, in Deal, Kent, England; died May 5, 1988. Educator, publisher, editor, and author. Unstead was best known for his books on history, which he hoped would make the subject appealing for young readers. He was a schoolmaster in St. Albans, England, for four years and a headmaster in Letchworth, England, for ten. The historian retired from teaching in 1957 to become a free-lance author and to direct his own publishing company. His writings include *Looking at History: Britain from Cavemen to the Present Day, Pioneer Homelife in Australia, Living in Samuel Pepys' London, How They Lived in Cities Long Ago, A History of the World,* and the eight volume *History of the English-Speaking World.* Unstead also edited series of children's reference books for A. & C. Black and reviewed history books for the *Times Literary Supplement.*

FOR MORE INFORMATION SEE:

Who's Who, 140th edition, St. Martin's, 1988.

OBITUARIES

Times (London), May 9, 1988.

WALLACE, Ian   1950-

PERSONAL: Born March 31, 1950, in Niagara Falls, Ontario, Canada; son of Robert Amiens (a sales manager) and Kathleen (a homemaker; maiden name, Watts) Wallace. *Education:* Attended Ontario College of Art, 1969-74. *Home and office:* 370 Palmerston Blvd., Toronto, Ontario, Canada M6G 2N6.

CAREER: Kids Can Press, Toronto, Ontario, staff writer and illustrator, 1974-76; free-lance artist and author, 1974—; Art Gallery of Ontario, Toronto, Ontario, information officer, 1976—. *Exhibitions:* Art Gallery of Ontario, 1986. *Member:* Writers Union of Canada, Authors Guild of America. *Awards, honors:* Imperial Order of the Daughters of the Empire Book Award, 1984, Amelia Frances Howard-Gibbon Medal from the Canadian Library Association, 1985, and included on the International Board on Books for Young People Honor List, 1986, all for *Chin Chiang and the Dragon's Dance; Very Last First Time* was exhibited at the Bologna International Children's Book Fair, and chosen one of Child Study Association of America's Children's Books of the Year, both 1987.

WRITINGS

JUVENILE

Julie News (self-illustrated), Kids Can Press, 1974.
(With Angela Wood) *The Sandwich,* Kids Can Press, 1975, revised editon, 1985.
The Christmas Tree House (self-illustrated), Kids Can Press, 1976.
Chin Chiang and the Dragon's Dance (self-illustrated), Macmillan, 1984.
Sparrow's Song, Viking, 1986.

IAN WALLACE

Morgan the Magnificent (self-illustrated), Macmillan, 1988.

ILLUSTRATOR

Jan Andrews, *Very Last First Time* (Junior Literary Guild selection), Macmillan, 1985.
J. Andrews, *Eva's Ice Adventure,* Methuen, 1986.
Tim Wynne-Jones, *The Architect of the Moon,* Groundwood, 1988.

Contributor to periodicals, including *Canadian Books for Young People.*

SIDELIGHTS: "Like most children growing up in Niagara Falls, Ontario in the 1950s, Sunday afternoons were spent with my family driving leisurely through the countryside counting cows, cars and the many species of trees that my brothers and I could see through the back window of our father's car. This activity was far removed from the one carried out by a fair percentage of large city dwellers of the 80s, many of whom bring their children indoors on Sunday afternoons to expansive spaces we know as art galleries and museums. Free to roam those hallowed halls children count the numbers of Renoirs and Modigliani's or the stuffed horn-rimmed owls and the variety and colour of rare duck's eggs to be found in a single glass case.

"My first exposure to the world of art came not through pictures hung on gallery and museum walls, but through the picture books my brothers and I carted out of our local library. Contained within the covers of each book were worlds so foreign and exciting that we marvelled at the daring of the characters, thrilled to their singular and collective bravery, and were often chillingly jerked back by great waves of fear that flushed through our veins. For children growing up in small-city Ontario, these books and their images carried us out of our sheltered environment to places we never imagined and only discovered within those treasured pages. Just as important they made us keenly aware of the fact that a painter was not merely someone who, like our father, picked up a brush or roller and stroked or rolled it over the walls of our house whenever the rooms had grown tired around the edges. But rather, an artist was someone who made dreams real.

"From those years there are three resonant images I carry around in my hip pocket like a child saving a dried worm for that special day. From Kenneth Grahame's *Wind and the Willows* comes the first two images. It is of Toad gleefully flying his bright orange bi-plane just seconds after a death defying crash into a now crumbling chimney. That image still delights me with the deliciousness of having achieved a feat of which my parents would NEVER HAVE APPROVED. My recklessness and independent abandon for property and propriety are abruptly brought into check by the second image that can still bring me into line: a repentent Toad having escaped from jail, ball and chain shackled to his ankle standing at the edge of freedom. The quiet solemnity of that moment in illustration and my life, glows as strongly today with the moonlit light it emitted three decades ago.

"The third image is taken from a book that has fallen from grace of late, *Little Black Sambo* by Helen Bannerman. As a child I was not aware of the racist tones educators today say are present in this cherished little book. I had not been exposed to racism, or to black people at that point in my life and I loved Sambo, his Momma and Papa, and was especially admiring and envious of his bright lime green umbrella, fine red jacket, short blue pants, and odd pointed shoes. A suit of such colour and quality I never imagined would be mine. But ohhhhh, how I longed to have one just like Sambo's. Wouldn't I be grand when I walked around our neighborhood? Wouldn't everyone be envious of Me?

"The magic and power of that story, of course, is found in the act of the four tigers who having taken Little Black Sambo's clothes, grab hold of each others tails and quickly spin themselves into a frenzy, melting away 'and there was nothing left but a great big pool of melted butter (or ''ghi,'' as it is called in India) round the foot of a tree.' What delicious pancakes that butter made.

"Perhaps it was the power of those three images that captured my imagination as a child and forced me to draw the same magic with crayons and pencils over my bedroom walls, the sidewalk that ran from the front door of our house to the street, and even (sacrilege!) within the covers of books we had re-

As the dance went on, Chin Chiang's feet moved more surely.... ■ (From *Chin Chiang and the Dragon's Dance* by Ian Wallace. Illustrated by the author.)

ceived as gifts. Certainly they were a catalyst. However, looking at the scenarios from a broader perspective, they allowed me the chance to emulate what I had seen, attempting to capture with my own hand the magic, the drama, and the excitement of those images. Imitating those characters and worlds would later enable me to look at my own world and describe it through my own eyes as my talent emerged and developed. What better place to learn than at the feet of masters!

"My creative life hiccupped along dropping in and out with unpredictable regularity until the day at age thirteen when I gave up the notion of being a fireman and announced that I was going to be an artist. My parents' response was not surprising since they were consistently supportive of my brothers and me, no matter what wild dreams we espoused or what strange predicament we had managed to get ourselves into.

"'Of course you will,' they said.

"And that was that. The decision was made. And with it came the unconditional support of my parents, so crucial to anyone risking the possibility of living a creative life. This desire to become an artist did not diminish as my teenage years progressed, but helped to conquer those racing hormones, the battle against teenage angst and love, and the ability to pass countless hours alone in my room with only the sound of a pencil scratching over the surface of stacks of paper.

"My training has been mainly visual, but the single most important thing I've learned is that everything creative must have a purpose and a reason for its expression. My first three books were labors of love. Writing and illustrating do not come easily to me; the challenge is in the struggle. I have had the opportunity to read to 100,000 children across Canada, and I now understand how important books are to our lives. To watch children laugh or cry at a story with you is achieving a high level of communication."

Eva and her mother walked through the village. ■ (From *Very Last First Time* by Jan Andrews. Illustrated by Ian Wallace.)

Wallace wrote and illustrated *Chin Chiang and the Dragon's Dance* over a period of six years. "The first time I saw the dragon's dance I was overwhelmed by the dramatic images and exploding sounds. That New Year celebration felt as exciting that day as it must have been when first performed centuries ago. I decided then and there to tell a story encompassing this dance. Here was a tale steeped in tradition, passed down the generations. With every step, leap, twist, and curl of the dragon's tail those dancers breathed life into that mythic creature, bestowing favour on the Chinese community for the coming year. The animated faces of the crowd on that sunny February day told me not only was this an important celebration for the Chinese people, but also an expression of a universal human spirit.

"The task of creating this book was not completed in the short term, but over six years. Having endured that long gestation, I cannot stress enough the value of time—time to allow the right works to come forth, time to allow the drawings to formulate in the head before they appear on paper, and time to allow both to be as polished as a piece of rare jade.

"Visually, I wanted the illustrations to be the story's emotional barometer. This was achieved through the design, the changing perspectives, and the use of colour (watch the colour intensify toward the climax.)

"This is a story with which people of all ages and races can identify. Remember, whether we are six or sixty-six we all have fears that must be overcome. If we can rid ourselves of those basic fears, anything becomes possible."

Illustrated *Very Last First Time* by Jan Andrews. "I could not believe my good fortune to have been presented with a story that captured my imagination so immediately, and would test my artistry and skill as an illustrator. Possessed by the sweeping grandeur and by an inherent fear of the under-ice world, I realized the necessity of portraying the young Inuit girl, Eva Padlyat, with dignity and respect due a race of people who live in harmony with the land. It was in the spirit world, as integral a part of the Tundra landscape as the ice, the snow and the animals found there, that I discovered the emotional link of illustrator to story, and the story to its reader.

"As much as I am in need of solitude when I am lost in the activity of writing or illustrating, I am also a social creature by nature, enjoying the comraderie of friends and people in general. Writing and illustrating provide me with the former while storytelling provides me with the latter. At times my life does appear somewhat schizophrenic, but for the most part, I love the balance of the two activities; writing and illustrating or storytelling.

"What a luxury it is to wake up each morning and know that this new day will not be the same as the one before and never the same as those that come after."

HOBBIES AND OTHER INTERESTS: Walking, movies, travel, dining out.

FOR MORE INFORMATION SEE:

In Review, April, 1979.
Quill & Quire, February, 1985.
Emergency Librarian, February, 1985.
Canadian Children's Literature, number 48, 1987.

WATTS, Irene N(aemi) 1931-

PERSONAL: Born May 24, 1931, in Berlin, Germany; came

IRENE N. WATTS

to Canada in 1968; daughter of Sigmund (a salesman) and Margot (a welfare counselor; maiden name, Russ) Kirstein; married James Watts (a computer programmer), March 5, 1955; children: Julia, Tania (Mrs. Jean Gariepy), Adam, Vicki (Mrs. Bill Duncan). *Education:* University College, Cardiff, Wales, B.A. (with honors), 1953. *Religion:* Jewish. *Office:* 14834 N. Bluff Rd., #217, Whiterock, British Columbia, Canada V4B 3E3. *Agent:* Playwrights Union Canada, Toronto, Ontario, Canada.

CAREER: Citadel of Wheels and Wings, Citadel Theatre, Edmonton, Alberta, Canada, artistic director, 1969-1975; freelance director and theatre instructor, 1970—; Jabberwocky Theatre for Children, Vancouver, British Columbia, Canada, associate director, 1976; First Vancouver Heritage International Festival for Children, Vancouver, founding program director, 1977-78; Neptune Theatre, Halifax, Nova Scotia, Canada, director of educational programs and founding director of Neptune Theatre School and Young Neptune Touring Company, 1979-86; Arts Umbrella Performing Arts Centre, Vancouver, instructor and playwright, 1987-88; playwright for young people. *Member:* Canadian Actors Equity, Playwrights Union of Canada, Canadian Society of Authors, Illustrators, and Performers. *Awards, honors:* Achievement Award from the Province of Alberta, 1976, for drama; Playwright Award from the Pacific North West Writers, 1986, for "A Small Adventure."

WRITINGS:

A Chain of Words: A Play, Talon Books, 1978.

A Blizzard Leaves No Footprints and Three Other Participation Plays for Children, Playwrights Canada, 1978.

(Editor) *Tomorrow Will Be Better: The Writings of British Columbia Schoolchildren,* Playwrights Canada, 1980.

Martha's Magic, Playwrights Canada, 1981.

Tales from Tolstoy/Once upon a Time/The Taming of the Wild Things, Playwrights Canada, 1982.

(Compiler) *Beyond Belief: A Collage of the Supernatural,* Playwrights Canada, 1983.

Season of the Witch, Playwrights Canada, 1986.

(Adapter with Tom Kerr) *A Christmas Carol,* Playwrights Canada, 1986.

I Want to Be. . .and Other Creative Themes for Special Occasions, Pembroke, 1989.

Also author and director of scripts, including "Canada Speaks," 1975; "Martha's Magic," 1982; "The Rainstone," 1983; "A Small Adventure," 1986; and "Behind the Mask," 1988. Author of radio story, "Three Pairs of Underwear"; and adapter of Robert Munsch's, *The Paperbag Princess and Other Stories.*

WORK IN PROGRESS: The New Babysitter, a picture book for preschoolers; "Ice Tales" and "The School Show" for children; *The Great Detective and Other Party Themes for Parents and Educators,* for Pembroke Books.

SIDELIGHTS: "My plays are designed to be performed *for* and by young people. I am particularly interested in the myths and stories of different cultures. I have been greatly influenced by travels in the Arctic, and by a year's residence on a prairie reservation.

"I like to work with children and find that their own writing is often highly dramatic. I have two suitcases full of children's work which is waiting to be put into another book! The title which a child offered in a letter 'I Am Living Now.'

"When my four children were young, we often played dramatic games, unfortunately they have 'outgrown' them—Julie works for the Royal Canadian Mounted Police; Tania is a doctor of biochemistry, Adam, a restaurant manager, and Vicki, a mother and an accountant. But I still play!

"When I was seven, my world changed a great deal. I escaped Nazi Germany to Great Britain. Theatre was a way of sorting out and accepting new life styles. It has remained the most rewarding and enriching part of my life.

"The family emigrated to Canada in 1968—none of us would live anywhere else."

HOBBIES AND OTHER INTERESTS: Matthew and Sarah, my two grandchildren; traveling, walking.

WHITCOMB, Jan   1906-1988

OBITUARY NOTICE—See sketch in *SATA* Volume 10: Born June 9, 1906, in Weatherford, Okla.; died of heart failure, April 27, 1988, in Menlo Park, Calif. Artist, illustrator, columnist, and author. Whitcomb, who was elected to the Society of Illustrators Hall of Fame in 1973, was best known for his portraits of beautiful women. He was a cover artist and columnist for *Cosmopolitan* and an illustrator for many other magazines, including *Collier's, Ladies' Home Journal,* and *McCall's.* After serving in the Navy as an artist during World War II, he helped found the Famous Artists Schools and was a member of the institution's faculty of portrait painting. Whitcomb began his artistic career in 1928 as a poster artist for Radio-Keith-Orpheum (RKO) Theaters in Chicago, Illinois, then worked as an advertising artist in Ohio. In 1935 he became vice-president of the Charles E. Cooper advertising art company in New York City. Whitcomb wrote and illustrated *How I Make a Picture, Pom-Pom's Christmas, All About Girls,* and *Coco, the Far-Out Poodle.*

FOR MORE INFORMATION SEE:

Who's Who in American Art, 15th edition, Bowker, 1982.

OBITUARIES

New York Times, April 29, 1988.

WIESEL, Elie(zer)   1928-

PERSONAL: Surname pronounced "Vie'-sel" or "Wie-sel." Born September 30, 1928, in Sighet, Romania; came to United States in 1956, naturalized in 1963; son of Shlomo (a grocer) and Sarah (Feig) Wiesel; married wife, Marion, 1969; children: Elisha (son). *Education:* Attended Sorbonne, University of Paris, 1948-51. *Religion:* Jewish. *Address:* University Professors, Boston University, 745 Commonwealth Ave., Boston, Mass. 02215. *Agent:* Georges Borchardt, 136 East 57th St., New York, N.Y. 10022.

CAREER: Foreign correspondent at various times for *Yedioth Ah'oronoth,* Tel Aviv, Israel, *L'Arche,* Paris, France, and *Jewish Daily Forward,* New York City, 1949-68; writer and lecturer, 1964—; City College of the City University of New York, New York City, Distinguished Professor of Judaic Studies, 1972-76; Boston University, Boston, Mass., professor of philosophy and religious studies and Andrew Mellon Professor in the Humanities, 1976—. Distinguished Visiting Professor of

ELIE WIESEL

Literature and Philosophy, Florida International University, 1982; Henry Luce Visiting Scholar in the Humanities and Social Thought, Whitney Humanities Center, Yale University, 1982-83. Member of board of overseers, Bar-Ilan University, 1970—; member of board of directors, American Associates of Ben-Gurion University of the Negev, 1973—, National Committee on American Foreign Policy, 1983—, International Rescue Committee, 1985—, Hebrew Arts School, and Humanitas; member of board of Governors, Tel-Aviv University, 1976—, Haifa University, 1977—, and Oxford Centre for Postgraduate Hebrew Studies, 1978—; member of board of trustees, Yeshiva University, 1977—, and American Jewish World Service, 1985—; chairman, U.S. President's Commission on the Holocaust, 1979-80, U.S. Holocaust Memorial Council, 1980-86; member of jury, 1984 Neustadt International Prize for Literature; chairman of advisory board, World Union of Jewish Students, 1985—; co-founder of the National Jewish Center for Learning and Leadership; advisor, Boston University Institute for Philosophy and Religion, National Institute against Prejudice and Violence, and the International Center in New York, Inc.

MEMBER: Authors League; Foreign Press Association (honorary life member); U.N. Correspondents Association; American Gathering of Jewish Holocaust Survivors (honorary president, 1985); Amnesty International; PEN; Writers Guild of America, East; Author's Guild; Writers and Artists for Peace in the Middle East; American Academy of Arts and Sciences (fellow); Royal Norwegian Society of Sciences and Letters; Jewish Academy of Arts and Sciences (fellow).

AWARDS, HONORS: Herzl Literary Award; David Ben-Gurion Award; International Kaplun Foundation Award from Hebrew University of Jerusalem; American-Israeli Friendship Award; Prix Rivarol, 1963, *The Town beyond the Wall;* two national Jewish book awards, 1965 and 1972, for *The Town beyond the Wall* and *Souls on Fire;* Ingram Merrill Award, 1964; International Remembrance Award from the World Federation of Bergen-Belsen Associations, 1965, for *The Town beyond the Wall* and all other writings.

Jewish Heritage Award, 1966, for excellence in literature; Litt.D. from Jewish Theological Seminary, 1967, Marquette University, 1975, Simmons College, 1976, Anna Maria College, 1980, Yale University, 1981, Wake Forest University, and Haverford College, both 1985, Capital University, and Long Island University, both 1986, Universite de Paris, Sorbonne, 1987; D.H.L. from Hebrew Union College, 1968, Manhattanville College, 1972, Yeshiva University, 1973, Boston University, 1974, College of St. Scholastica, 1978, Wesleyan University, 1979, Notre Dame University, and Brandeis University, both 1980, Kenyon College, and Hobart and William Smith College, both 1982, Emory University, Florida International University, Fairfield University, Dropsie College, Moravian College, and Siena Heights College, all 1983, Colgate University, 1984, State University of New York at Binghamton, and Lehigh University, both 1985, College of New Rochelle, Georgetown University, Hamilton College, Rockford College, and Tufts University, all 1986, and College of St. Thomas, and Villanova University, both 1987; Prix Medicis (France), 1968, for *Le Mendiant de Jerusalem.*

Prix Bordin from the French Academy, 1972, and Frank and Ethel S. Cohen Award from the Jewish Book Council, 1973, both for *Souls on Fire;* Eleanor Roosevelt Memorial Award, and American Liberties Medallion from the American Jewish Committee, both 1972, and Martin Luther King, Jr. Medallion from City College of the City University of New York, 1973, all for body of work; Literary Avodah Award from the Jewish Teachers' Association, 1972; Award for Distinguished Service

to American Jewry from the National Federation of Jewish Men's Clubs, 1973; Doctor of Hebrew Letters from Spertus College of Judaica, 1973; Doctor of Philosophy from Bar-Ilan University, 1973, and University of Haifa, 1986; Faculty Distinguished Scholar Award, 1974, and LL.D., 1975, both from Hofstra University; Scopus Award from the Hebrew University of Jerusalem, 1974; Rambam Award from the American Mizrachi Women, 1974.

Holocaust Memorial Award from the New York Society of Clinical Psychologists, 1975; Jewish Heritage Award from Haifa University, 1975; Spertus International Award, 1976; Myrtle Wreath Award from Hadassah, 1977; King Solomon Award, 1977; Humanitarian Award from B'rith Sholom, 1978; Joseph Prize for Human Rights from the Anti-Defamation League of B'nai B'rith, 1978; Presidential Citation from New York University, 1979; Inaugural Award for Literature from Israel Bonds Prime Minister's Committee, 1979; LL.D. from Talmudic University of Florida, 1979, and University of Notre Dame, 1980; Zalman Shazar Award from the State of Israel, 1979.

Prix Livre-International, and Bourse Goncourt, both 1980, and Prix des Bibliothecaires, 1981, (all France) all for *Le Testament d'un poete juif assassine;* S. Y. Agnon Gold Medal; Jabotinsky Medal from the State of Israel, 1980; Rabbanit Sarah Herzog Award from Emunah Women of America, 1981; Jordan Davidson Humanitarian Award from Florida International University, 1983; Literary Lions Award from New York Public Library, 1983; Fellow, Timothy Dwight College, Yale University, 1983; International Literary Prize for Peace from the Royal Academy of Belgium, 1983; Le Grand Prix de la Litterature de la ville de Paris, 1983, for *La Cinquieme fils;* Le Grand Prix Litteraire de Festival International de Deauville, 1983; Anatoly Shcharansky Humanitarian Award, 1983; Commander de la Legion d'Honneur, France, 1984; Congressional Gold Medal of Achievement, 1984; Distinguished Writers Award from Lincolnwood Library, 1984; Chancellor Joseph H. Lookstein Award from Bar-Ilan University, 1984.

Sam Levenson Memorial Award from the Jewish Community Relations Council, 1985; Comenius Award from Moravian College, 1985; Henrietta Szold Award from Hadassah, 1985; Anne Frank Award, 1985; International Holocaust Remembrance Award from the State of Israel Bonds, 1985; Voice of Conscience Award from the American Jewish Congress, 1985; Distinguished Community Service Award from Mutual of America, 1985; Covenant of Peace Award from the Synagogue Council of America, 1985; Freedom of Worship Medal from the Franklin D. Roosevelt Four Freedoms Foundation, 1985; Jacob Pat Award from the World Congress of Jewish Culture, 1985; Humanitarian Award from the International League of Human Rights, 1985; Doctor of Humanities, University of Hartford, 1985, and Lycoming College, 1987.

Nobel Peace Prize, 1986; Distinguished Foreign-Born American Award from the International Center, 1986; Freedom Cup Award from the Women's League for Israel, 1986; Jacob Javits Humanitarian Award of UJA Young Leadership, 1986; Medal of Liberty Award, 1986; Freedom Award from the International Rescue Committee, 1987; Achievement Award from the Artists and Writers for Peace in the Middle East, 1987; La Grande Medaille de Vermeil de la Ville de Paris, 1987; La Medaille l'Universite de Paris, 1987; La Medaille de la Chancellerie de l'Universite de Paris, 1987; Eitinger Prize from the University of Oslo, 1987; Lifetime Achievement Award from *Present Tense* magazine, 1987; Special Christopher Award, 1987; Profiles in Courage Award from B'nai B'rith, 1987; Achievement Award from the State of Israel, 1987; Seminary Medal from the Jewish Theological Seminary of America, 1987;

(Jacket illustration by Mark Podwal from *The Golem: The Story of a Legend as Told by Elie Wiesel*.)

Special Award from the National Committee on American Foreign Policy, 1987; Metcalf Cup and Prize for Excellence in Teaching from Boston University, 1987; Gra-Cruz da Ordem Nacional do Cruzeiro do Sul, Brazil, 1987; Centennial Medal from the University of Scranton, 1987; Golda Meir Senior Humanitarian Award, 1987; Hofstra University Presidential Medal, 1988; honorary fellow, Beth Hatefutsoth, 1988; Human Rights Law Award from the International Human Rights Law Group, 1988; Doctor of Humanities from the University of Miami, 1988; Doctor of Humane Letters from Ohio University, 1988; Doctor of Letters from the University of Connecticut and from the University of Central Florida, both 1988; Doctor of Laws from LaSalle University, 1988; Doctor of Philosophy from Ben-Gurion University of the Negev, 1988.

WRITINGS:

Un di velt hot geshvigen (memoir; in Yiddish; title means "And the World Has Remained Silent"), [Buenos Aires], 1956, abridged French translation published as *La Nuit* (also see below), foreword by Francois Mauriac, Editions de Minuit, 1958, translation by Stella Rodway published as *Night* (also see below), Hill & Wang, 1960.

L'Aube (novel; also see below), Editions du Seuil, 1960, translation by Anne Borchardt published as *Dawn* (also see below), Hill & Wang, 1961,

Le Jour (novel; also see below), Editions du Seuil, 1961, translation by A. Borchardt published as *The Accident* (also see below), Hill & Wang, 1962.

La Ville de la chance (novel), Editions du Seuil, 1962, translation by Stephen Becker published as *The Town beyond the Wall*, Atheneum, 1964, new edition, Holt, 1967.

Les Portes de la foret (novel), Editions du Seuil, 1964, translation by F. Frenaye published as *The Gates of the Forest*, Holt, 1966.

Le Chant des morts (essays and stories), Editions du Seuil, 1966, translation by Steven Donadio published as *Legends of Our Time*, Holt, 1968.

Les Juifs du silence (originally published in Hebrew as a series of articles for newspaper *Yedioth Ah'oronoth*), Editions du Seuil, 1966, translation and with an afterword by Neal Kozodoy published as *The Jews of Silence: A Personal Report on Soviet Jewry*, Holt, 1966.

Zalmen; ou, La folie de Dieu (play), Editions du Seuil, 1968, translation by Lily Edelman and Nathan Edelman published as *Zalmen; or, The Madness of God* (adapted for the stage by wife, Marion Wiesel; first produced as "The Madness of God," at Arena Stage Theatre, in Washington, D.C., 1974), Holt, 1968.

Le Mendiant de Jerusalem (novel), Editions du Seuil, 1968, translation by the author and L. Edelman published as *A Beggar in Jerusalem*, Random House, 1970.

La Nuit, L'Aube, [*and*] *Le Jour*, Editions du Seuil, 1969, published as *Night, Dawn,* [*and*] *The Accident: Three Tales*, Hill & Wang, 1972.

Entre deux soleils (essays and stories), Editions du Seuil, 1970, translation by the author and L. Edelman published as *One Generation After*, Random House, 1970.

Celebration hassidique: Portraits et legendes, Editions du Seuil, 1972, translation by M. Wiesel, published as *Souls on Fire: Portraits and Legends of Hasidic Masters*, Random House, 1972.

Le Serment de Kolvillag (novel), Editions du Seuil, 1973, translation by M. Wiesel published as *The Oath*, Random House, 1973.

Ani maamin: A Song Lost and Found Again (cantata; music composed by Darius Milhaud; first performed at Carnegie Hall, New York, 1973), translation by M. Wiesel, Random House, 1974.

(Cover illustration from *Night* by Elie Wiesel.)

(Cover illustration by Wendell Minor from *The Fifth Son* by Elie Wiesel.)

Celebration biblique: Portraits et legendes, Editions du Seuil, 1975, translation by M. Wiesel published as *Messengers of God: Biblical Portraits and Legends,* Random House, 1976.

Un Juif aujourd'hui: Recits, essais, dialogues, Editions du Seuil, 1977, translation by M. Wiesel published as *A Jew Today,* Random House, 1978.

Four Hasidic Masters and Their Struggle against Melancholy, University of Notre Dame Press, 1978.

(With others) *Dimensions of the Holocaust,* Indiana University Press, 1978.

Le proces de Shamgorod tel qu'il se deroula le 25 fevrier 1649: piece en trois actes (first produced in Paris, 1981), Editions du Seuil, 1979, translation by M. Wiesel published as *The Trial of God (as It Was Held on February 25, 1649, in Shamgorod): A Play in Three Acts,* Random House, 1979.

Images from the Bible (illustrated with paintings by Shalom of Safed), Overlook Press, 1980.

Le Testament d'un poete juif assassine (novel), Editions du Seuil, 1980, translation by M. Wiesel published as *The Testament,* Simon & Schuster, 1981.

Five Biblical Portraits, University of Notre Dame Press, 1981.

The Haggadah (cantata; music by Elizabeth Swados), S. French, 1982.

Somewhere a Master: Further Hasidic Portraits and Legends, Simon & Schuster, 1982.

Paroles d'etranger (essays, stories and dialogues), Editions du Seuil, 1982.

The Golem: The Story of a Legend as Told by Elie Wiesel, translated by A. Borchardt, Summit, 1983.

Le Cinquieme fils (novel), Editions Grasset, 1983, translated by M. Wiesel published as *The Fifth Son,* Warner, 1985.

Signes d'Exode (essays, stories, dialogues), Editions Grasset, 1985.

Against Silence: The Voice and Vision of Elie Wiesel (collection), 3 volumes, edited by Irving Abrahamson, Holocaust Library, 1985.

(With Josy Eisenberg) *Job ou Dieu dans la Tempete* (dialogue and commentary) Grasset et Fasquelle, 1986.

Le Crepuscule, au loin (novel), Grasset et Fasquelle, 1987.

Twilight, translated by M. Wiesel, Summit, 1988.

(With Albert Friedlander) *The Six Days of Destruction,* Paulist Press, 1988.

Member of editorial boards, *Midstream, Religion and Literature* (University of Notre Dame), *Sh'ma: Journal of Jewish Responsibility, Hadassah,* chairman of editorial board, *Holocaust and Genocide Studies: An International Journal.* Contributor to numerous periodicals.

WORK IN PROGRESS: A book on the Talmud similar to *Messengers of God.*

As a child he had been afraid of the forest, even in daytime. He had been told that it was inhabited by savage wolves. ■ (From *Gates of the Forest* by Elie Wiesel. Photograph by Naomi Savage.)

ADAPTATIONS:

"Night" (record or cassette), Caedmon, 1982.

SIDELIGHTS: Wiesel has taken one of the most remarkable journeys of the century. His life has brought him from the hills of Sighet, Romania to Auschwitz and Buchenwald prison camps and finally to Oslo, Norway where he received the Nobel Peace Prize on December 10, 1986.

He was born on September 20, 1928 in Sighet, Transylvania (now Romania), near the Czech border. The only son of middle-class parents (his father was a shopkeeper and involved in community affairs and his mother a teacher), Wiesel spent his early years as a serious and devoted student of the Talmud and the mystical teachings of Hasidism and the Kabala. "If someone had told me when I was a child that one day I would become a novelist, I would have turned away, convinced he was confusing me with someone else.

"For the pattern of my future had then seemed clear. I would pursue my studies in the same surroundings with the same zeal, probing the sacred texts and opening the gates to the secret knowledge that permits fulfillment by transcending self.

"Novels I thought childish, reading them a waste of time. You had to be a fool to love the fictitious universe made of words when there was the other, immense and boundless, made of truth and presence. I preferred God to His creation, silence to revelation.

"As for France—whose language I chose for my tales—its name evoked visions of a mythical country, real only because mentioned in Rashi and other commentaries on the Bible and Talmud.

"It took a war—and what a war—to make me change my road, if not my destiny."[1]

Young Wiesel was strongly influenced by his mother, a devout Jew and a "highly cultivated person." "It was she who brought me to *heder* to make me a good Jew, loving only the wisdom and truth to be drawn from the Torah. And it was she who sent me as often as possible to the Rebbe of Wizsnitz to ask his blessing or simply to expose me to his radiance."[2]

Other influences included his maternal grandfather, Dodye Feig, who gave Wiesel a love for stories and for storytelling. "A fabulous storyteller, he knew how to captivate an audience. He would say: 'Listen attentively, and above all, remember that true tales are meant to be transmitted—to keep them to oneself is to betray them.' He knew how intently I listened; he must have known that I would remember, but he had no way of knowing how closely I would follow his advice."[2]

Many years later, Wiesel would collect the legends that he heard from his grandfather and include them in a book, *Souls on Fire.*

His life in Sighet ended abruptly, when after Passover, 1944 the Nazis rounded up the entire Jewish community of Sighet, including the Wiesel family and shipped them to Auschwitz. Before the journey began, the inhabitants of the Romanian town (then under Hungarian rule) hastily buried their precious possessions to keep them from the Nazis. "In the early morning hours of that particular day, after a sleepless night, the ghetto was changed into a cemetery and its residents into gravediggers. We were digging feverishly in the courtyard, the garden, the cellar, consigning to the earth, temporarily we thought, whatever remained of the belongings accumulated by several generations, the sorrow and reward of long years of toil.

"My father took charge of the jewelry and valuable papers. His head bowed, he was silently digging near the barn. Not far away, my mother, crouched on the damp ground, was burying the silver candelabra she used only on Shabbat eve; she was moaning softly, and I avoided her eyes. My sisters burrowed near the cellar. The youngest, Tziporah, had chosen the garden, like me. Solemnly shoveling, she declined my help. What did she have to hide? Her toys? Her school notebooks? As for me, my only possession was my watch. It meant a lot to me. And so I decided to bury it in a dark, deep hole, three paces away from the fence, under a poplar tree whose thick, strong foliage seemed to provide a reasonably secure shelter.

"All of us expected to recover our treasures. On our return, the earth would give them back to us. Until then, until the end of the storm, they would be safe.

"Yes, we were naive. We could not foresee that the very same evening, before the last train had time to leave the station, an excited mob of well-informed friendly neighbors would be rushing through the ghetto's wide-open houses and courtyards, leaving not a stone or beam unturned, throwing themselves upon the loot."[1]

Fifteen-year-old Wiesel, his family and Jewish friends and neighbors were transported by train to their destination, Auschwitz-Birkenau. There his little sister and his mother were

He walked through the city's darkest streets. ■ (From *The Golem: The Story of a Legend as Told by Elie Wiesel*. Illustrated by Mark Podwal.)

The accident occurred on an evening in July, right in the heart of New York. . . . ■ (From *The Accident* by Elie Wiesel.)

taken from him and thrown—along with thousands of others—into the ovens. "An SS noncommissioned officer came to meet us, a truncheon in his hand. He gave the order:

"'Men to the left! Women to the right!'

"Eight words spoken quietly, indifferently, without emotion. Eight short, simple words. Yet that was the moment when I parted from my mother. I had not had time to think, but already I felt the pressure of my father's hand: we were alone. For a part of a second I glimpsed my mother and my sisters moving away to the right. Tzipora held Mother's hand. I saw them disappear into the distance; my mother was stroking my sister's fair hair, as though to protect her, while I walked on with my father and the other men. And I did not know that in that place, at that moment, I was parting from my mother and Tzipora forever. I went on walking. My father held onto my hand.

". . .Not far from us, flames were leaping up from a ditch, gigantic flames. They were burning something. A lorry drew up at the pit and delivered its load—little children. Babies! Yes, I saw it—saw it with my own eyes. . .those children in the flames. (Is it surprising that I could not sleep after that? Sleep had fled from my eyes.)

"So this was where we were going. A little farther on was another and larger ditch for adults.

"I pinched my face. Was I still alive? Was I awake? I could not believe it. How could it be possible for them to burn people, children, and for the world to keep silent? No, none of this could be true. It was a nightmare. . . .Soon I should wake with a start, my heart pounding and find myself back in the bedroom of my childhood, among my books. . . .

"We continued our march. We were gradually drawing closer to the ditch, from which an infernal heat was rising. Still twenty steps to go. If I wanted to bring about my own death, this was the moment. Our line had now only fifteen paces to cover. I bit my lips so that my father would not hear my teeth chattering. Ten steps still. Eight. Seven. We marched slowly on, as though following a hearse at our own funeral. Four steps more. Three steps. There it was now, right in front of us, the pit and its flames. I gathered all that was left of my strength, so that I could break from the ranks and throw myself upon the barbed wire. In the depths of my heart, I bade farewell to my father, to the whole universe; and, in spite of myself, the words formed themselves and issued in a whisper from my lips: *Yitgadal veyitkadach shme raba,. . . .*May His name be blessed and magnified. . . .My heart was bursting. The moment had come. I was face to face with the Angel of Death.

"No. Two steps from the pit we were ordered to turn to the left and made to go into a barracks.

"Never shall I forget that night, the first night in camp, which has turned my life into one long night, seven times cursed and seven times sealed. Never shall I forget that smoke. Never shall I forget the little faces of the children, whose bodies I saw turned into wreaths of smoke beneath a silent blue sky.

"Never shall I forget those flames which consumed my faith forever.

"Never shall I forget that nocturnal silence which deprived me, for all eternity, of the desire to live. Never shall I forget those moments which murdered my God and my soul and turned my dreams to dust. Never shall I forget these things, even if I am condemned to live as long as God Himself. Never."[3]

As the war came to a close, Wiesel and his father were moved to Buchenwald. The move caused the death of his father. ". . .I climbed into my bunk, above my father, who was still alive. It was January 28, 1945.

"I awoke on January 29 at dawn. In my father's place lay another invalid. They must have taken him away before dawn and carried him to the crematory. He may still have been breathing.

"There were no prayers at his grave. No candles were lit in his memory. . . .

"I did not weep, and it pained me that I could not weep. But I had no more tears. And, in the depths of my being, in the recesses of my weakened conscience, could I have searched it, I might perhaps have found something like—free at last!

"I had to stay at Buchenwald until April eleventh. I have nothing to say of my life during this period. It no longer mattered. After my father's death, nothing could touch me any more.

"I was transferred to the children's block, where there were six hundred of us.

"The front was drawing nearer.

I first met Grisha Paltielovich Kossover. . .one afternoon in July 1972. ■ (From *The Testament* by Elie Wiesel. Illustrated by Paul Bacon.)

"I spent my days in a state of total idleness. And I had but one desire—to eat. I no longer thought of my father or of my mother.

"From time to time I would dream of a drop of soup, of an extra ration of soup. . . ."[3]

When he was liberated in 1945 at the age of sixteen, Wiesel went to France, along with several hundred other children who had survived Buchenwald. It was there that he met his two older sisters, Batya and Hilda. "After the war I absorbed. I absorbed not only the suffering, which was not mine alone—suffering everywhere in the camps—but I absorbed, unwittingly, perhaps unconsciously, the obsession to tell the tale, to bear witness. . . .I knew that anyone who remained alive had to become a storyteller, a messenger, had to speak up."[2]

From 1948 to 1951 Wiesel mastered French and studied literature, psychology, and philosophy at the Sorbonne, earning money working as a tutor, choir director and translator. "All I wanted was to study in a very autodidactic manner."[2]

Today he continues to write in French, his adoptive language, and his wife Marion translates his work into English. "Why do I write in French? I write in French because it was the language I learned at sixteen, and it is valuable to me. Except for non-fiction, I don't try to write in English. A language is like a person, it doesn't like infidelity."[4]

In 1949 he went to Israel as a journalist for a French newspaper to report on Israel's independence. He stayed there for a few months. According to Wiesel, one of the major turning points of his life was his association with Francois Mauriac, a noted Roman Catholic writer, who encouraged the then young journalist to write about his experiences.

In 1956 Wiesel published in Yiddish *Un di velt hot Geshvigen* ("And the World Has Remained Silent"). In 1958 an abridged version, *La Nuit* ("Night") was published in Paris. An autobiographical account of his experiences, the book dealt with Wiesel's fears, guilt and questions concerning the Holocaust. "When I was in the camps. . .evil had attained such dimensions that they made it invincible. The fallout of that hate is still here, all around us. If we don't learn from what happened, if we remain indifferent, we are lost. I must—*we* must—bear witness. I must justify my survival.

"Every people, every human being is different. You have the same right, pride and authority as anyone else. The worst enemy to humankind is indifference."[5]

This memoir, adapted and translated into eighteen languages, became Wiesel's best-known work, and was the first of many books in which the author gives witness to the horrors of the Holocaust. "All my subsequent books are built around it."[6]

Wiesel also claims that "I have never spoken about the Holocaust except in one book, *Night*—the very first—where I tried to tell a tale directly, as though face to face with the experience."[6]

In 1956 Wiesel was sent on a journalistic assignment to New York to cover the United Nations. During his stay he was struck by a taxicab in Times Square. The accident necessitated a long convalescence which prevented him from making a required return to France to renew expired papers. As a "stateless person" he was persuaded to apply for United States citizenship, which he received in 1963.

In 1969 he married Marion Erster Rose, a native of Vienna and also a Holocaust survivor. Since their marriage the couple have made their home in New York City, although they spend time in Paris and Israel during the year. "I can't say today that I could be attached to anyplace, or anything. I can't own anything in gold. It's like I'm allergic to it. One night the German officers in camp ordered all valuables to be thrown in a pile. I saw a mountain of wedding rings and watches and jewelry. And it hit me. For this, my mother and father struggled all their lives.

"I work four hours a day on my books. I sleep four hours. I don't need any more. . . .I believe in small miracles—a good friendship, a good concert, a good surprise. Maybe a few people will be changed by my writings. I don't know. A gesture is never lost, although it may not attain its ultimate goal."[7]

Although known primarily as a Holocaust writer, Wiesel is also a writer whose work reflects his passionate relationship with all victims of prejudice. ". . .By struggling on behalf of Russian, Arab or Polish Jews, I fight for human rights everywhere. By calling for peace in the Middle East, I take a stand against every aggression, every war. By protesting the fanatical exhortations to 'holy wars' against my people, I protest against the stifling of freedom in Prague. By striving to keep alive the memory of the Holocaust, I denounce the massacres in Biafra and the nuclear menace. Only by drawing on his unique Jewish experience can the Jew help others. A Jew fulfills his role as man only from inside his Jewishness.

"That is why, in my writings, the Jewish theme predominates. It helps me approach and probe the theme of man.

"Of course, had there been no war, I would have sought self-realization in other ways. I would not, for example, have become a writer, or at least, I would have written something other than novels. And in the small yeshiva where I would have stayed, indefinitely poring over the same page of the same book, I would never have imagined one could justify one's existence except by strictly observing the 613 commandments of the Torah.

"Today I know this is not enough. The war turned everything upside down, changing the order and substance of priorities. For me, to be a Jew today means telling the story of this change.

"For whoever lives through a trial, or takes part in an event that weighs on man's destiny or frees him, is dutybound to transmit what he has seen, felt and feared. The Jew has always been obsessed by this obligation. He has always known that to live an experience or create a vision, and not transform it into link and promise, is to turn it into a gift to death.

"To be a Jew today, therefore, means: to testify. To bear witness to what is, and to what is no longer. One can testify with joy—a true and fervent joy, though tainted with sadness—by aiding Israel. Or with anger—restrained, harnessed anger, free of sterile bitterness—by raking over the ashes of

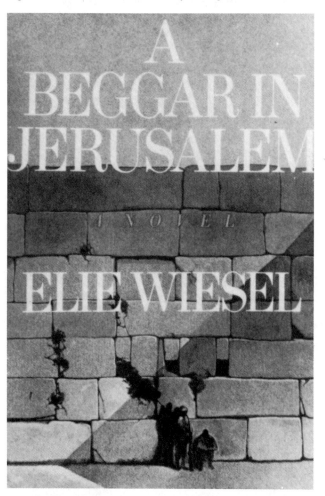

Dust jacket for the American edition of Wiesel's award-winning 1968 novel.

the holocaust. For the contemporary Jewish writer, there can be no theme more human, no project more universal."[1]

During President Carter's administration Wiesel was named chairman of the President's Commission on the Holocaust, then chairman of the U.S. Holocaust Memorial Council, a post he held until 1986. Now a permanent agency, it plans to establish a national museum as a monument to the Holocaust. During his tenure as chairman, he instituted National Days of Remembrance in the United States, and his leadership inspired the introduction of Holocaust curricula in numerous schools throughout the country. "Numerous committees devote countless days and weeks exploring various projects. The difficulties seem insurmountable: how can we *show* what must be remembered as an ontological event? How can we speak of the unspeakable? There *are* problems—there must be."

Wiesel, who also studies and occasionally teaches Hasidic texts and stories, was named Andrew W. Mellon Professor in the Humanities at Boston University in 1976, a post he continues to hold. He also enjoys writing for children and speaking to students. To one group of junior high school students in New York City, he advised: "You and you alone can justify my work. I write for children because I think adults may not understand. My writings are addressed to you. We are all the children of the same family."[5]

Keenly aware of the difficulties in trying to teach children about the horrors of the Holocaust, Wiesel, nevertheless, is dedicated to the task of bringing justice to all people and ensuring people's rights everywhere. He serves as writer, witness, teacher and moral activist. "After the event, we tried to teach, we felt we had to do something with our knowledge. We had to communicate, to share, but it was not easy. Behind every word we said, a hundred remained unsaid. For every tear, a thousand remained unshed. For every Jewish child we saw, a hundred remained unseen. . . .

"When I teach these matters, I teach of children. When one thinks of children or reads of them, one usually sees images of innocence, sunshine, happiness, play, laughter, teasing, dreaming, simple chants, so much promise. But not for us because to us childhood meant something else. It meant death, the death of childhood. . . .

"What can I tell you as a teacher who teaches young people? It is more than a matter of communicating knowledge. Whoever emerges in the field of teaching the Holocaust becomes a missionary, a messenger."[4]

In 1986, Wiesel won the Nobel Peace Prize. "Remembering is a noble and necessary act. . . .The rejection of memory becomes a divine curse, one that would doom us to repeat past disasters, past wars."[8]

He spoke for all the survivors when he invoked the spirit of those left behind. "No one may speak for the dead, no one may interpret their mutilated dreams and visions. And yet, I sense their presence. I always do—and at this moment more than ever. The presence of my parents, that of my little sister. . . ."[8]

In his acceptance speech, Wiesel urged mankind to remember the past and to work for universal peace. "None of us is in a position to eliminate war, but it is our obligation to denounce it and expose it in all its hideousness. War leaves no victors, only victims. . . .Mankind needs to remember more than ever.

Elie Wiesel (extreme right corner) in Buchenwald concentration camp, 1945. (Photograph by AP/Wide World.)

Mankind needs peace more than ever, for our entire planet, threatened by nuclear war, is in danger of total destruction. A destruction only man can provoke, only man can prevent.

"Mankind must remember that peace is not God's gift to his creatures, it is our gift to each other."[9]

FOOTNOTE SOURCES

[1] Elie Wiesel, *One Generation After*, Random House, 1970.
[2] Ted L. Esteas, *Elie Wiesel*, Ungar, 1980.
[3] E. Wiesel, *Night*, Hill & Wang, 1960.
[4] E. Wiesel, *Against Silence: The Voice and Vision of Elie Wiesel*, Holocaust Library, 1985.
[5] Jules Schwerin, "Can Prejudice Be Overcome?," *Parade*, February 23, 1986.
[6] "Elie Wiesel," *DLB Yearbook 1987*, Gale, 1988.
[7] David Richards, "Elie Wiesel," *Authors in the News*, Volume 1, Gale, 1976.
[8] Steve Fagin, "For Wiesel, Strochlitz, a Bond of Friendship, Love Steeped in Tragedy," *The Day* (New London, Conn.), December 14, 1986.
[9] "The 1986 Nobel Peace Prize," DLB Yearbook 1986, Gale, 1987.

FOR MORE INFORMATION SEE:

Elie Wiesel, *Night*, translated by Stella Rodway, Hill & Wang, 1960.
Times Literary Supplement, August 19, 1960, November 20, 1981.
Commonweal, December 9, 1960, January 6, 1961, March 13, 1964, October 14, 1966.
Saturday Review, December 17, 1960, July 8, 1961, July 25, 1964, May 28, 1966, October 19, 1968, January 31, 1970, November 21, 1970.
New York Herald Tribune Lively Arts, January 1, 1961, April 30, 1961.
Christian Century, January 18, 1961, June 17, 1970, June 3, 1981.
New Yorker, March 18, 1961, January 9, 1965, August 20, 1966, July 6, 1970, July 12, 1976.
New York Times Book Review, July 16, 1961, April 15, 1962, July 5, 1964, June 12, 1966, January 12, 1969, January 25, 1970, January 20, 1976, January 21, 1979, April 12, 1981, August 15, 1982.
Newsweek, May 25, 1964, February 9, 1970.
New Republic, July 5, 1965, December 14, 1968.
Book Week, May 29, 1966.

New York Review of Books, July 28, 1966, January 2, 1969, May 7, 1970.

Nation, October 17, 1966, February 24, 1969, March 16, 1970, January 5, 1974.

Washington Post Book World, October 20, 1968, January 18, 1970, August 8, 1976, October 29, 1978, April 12, 1981.

Washington Post, October 26, 1968, February 6, 1970.

Atlantic, November, 1968.

Christian Science Monitor, November 21, 1968, February 19, 1970, November 22, 1978.

New Leader, December 30, 1968, June 15, 1981.

TV Guide, February 15, 1969.

National Observer, February 2, 1970.

E. Wiesel, *One Generation After,* Random House, 1970.

Irving Halperin, *Messengers from the Dead,* Westminister Press (Philidelphia), 1970.

Best Sellers, March 15, 1970, May, 1981.

Time, March 16, 1970, May 8, 1972, July 12, 1976, December 25, 1978, April 20, 1981, March 18, 1985.

New York Times, December 15, 1970, March 10, 1972, April 3, 1981.

Thomas A. Idinopulos, "The Holocaust in the Stories of Elie Wiesel," *Soundings,* summer, 1972.

Byron L. Sherwin, "Elie Wiesel on Madness," *Central Conference of American Rabbis Journal,* number 19, 1972.

Lily Edelman, "A Conversation with Elie Wiesel," *National Jewish Monthly,* November, 1973.

Josephine Knopp, "Wiesel and the Absurd," *Contemporary Literature,* April, 1974.

Gene Koppel and Henry Kaufmann, *Elie Wiesel: A Small Measure of Victory,* University of Arizona, 1974.

Molly Abramowitz, *Elie Wiesel: A Bibliography,* Scarecrow, 1974.

Contemporary Literary Criticism, Gale, Volume III, 1975, Volume V, 1976, Volume XI, 1979.

Lawrence L. Langer, *The Holocaust and the Literary Imagination,* Yale University Press, 1975.

Harry James Cargas, *Conversations with Elie Wiesel,* Paulist Press, 1976.

Eric A. Kimmel, "Confronting the Ovens: The Holocaust and Juvenile Fiction," *Horn Book,* February, 1977.

Chicago Tribune Book World, October 29, 1978, March 29, 1981.

Robert McAfee Brown and H. J. Cargas, *Face to Face,* Anti-Defamation League, 1978.

People, October 22, 1979.

H. J. Cargas, *Responses to Elie Wiesel,* Persea, 1979.

Alvin Rosenfeld and Irving Greenberg, editors, *Confronting the Holocaust: The Impact of Elie Wiesel,* Indiana University Press, 1979.

John K. Roth, *A Consuming Fire: Encounters with Elie Wiesel and the Holocaust,* John Knox Press, 1979.

Michael G. Berenbaum, *The Vision of the Void: Theological Reflections on the Works of Elie Wiesel,* Wesleyan University Press, 1979.

National Review, June 12, 1981.

London Times, September 3, 1981.

Joe Friedemann, *Le Rire dans l'univers tragique d'Elie Wiesel,* Librairie A.G. Nizet (Paris), 1981.

Ellen S. Fine, *Legacy of Night: The Literary Universe of Elie Wiesel,* State University of New York Press, 1982.

Contemporary Issues Criticism, Volume I, Gale, 1982.

R. M. Brown, *Elie Wiesel: Messenger to All Humanity,* University of Notre Dame Press, 1983.

Christopher J. Frost, *Religious Melancholy or Psychological Depression? Some Issues Involved in Relating Psychology and Religion as Illustrated in a Study of Elie Wiesel,* University Press of America, 1985.

Et Mote, Bo & Harket (Oslo), 1986.

Carol Greene, *Elie Wiesel: Messenger from the Holocaust* (juvenile), Childrens Press, 1987.

WILKINSON, Sylvia J.   1940-

PERSONAL: Born April 3, 1940, in Durham, N.C.; daughter of Thomas Noell (a building contractor) and Peggy (an artist; maiden name, George) Wilkinson. *Education:* University of North Carolina at Greensboro, B.A., 1962; Hollins College, M.A., 1963; graduate study at Stanford University, 1965-66. *Politics:* Democrat. *Home:* 514 Arena St., El Segundo, Calif. 90245. *Agent:* Liz Darhansoff, 1220 Park Ave., New York, N.Y. 10028.

CAREER: Asheville-Biltmore College (now University of North Carolina at Asheville), instructor in English, art, and drama, 1963-64; College of William and Mary, Williamsburg, Va., instructor in English, 1966-67; University of North Carolina at Chapel Hill, lecturer in creative writing, 1967-70; University of Wisconsin, Milwaukee, associate professor of English, 1985; author. Visiting writer, Creative Writing Learning Institute of North Carolina, 1968-69. Writer-in-residence at Hollins College, 1969, Richmond Humanities Center, 1972-74, Sweet Briar College, 1973-75; visiting professor of writing, Washington University, 1984. *Member:* Authors League of America, Authors Guild, International Motor Sports Association, Sports Car Club of America, Sierra Club, Animal Protection Society. *Awards, honors:* Eugene Saxton Memorial Trust Grant, 1964, for *Moss on the North Side;* Wallace Stegner creative writing fellowship, 1965-66; *Mademoiselle* Merit Award, 1966; Sir Walter Raleigh Award, 1968, for *A Killing Frost,* and 1977, for *Shadow of the Mountain; Sports Car* magazine feature story award, 1972; National Endowment for

SYLVIA J. WILKINSON

the Arts creative writing fellowship, 1973-74; Guggenheim Fellowship, 1977-78, for fiction; Service Award from the University of North Carolina-Greensboro, 1978.

WRITINGS:

JUVENILE

The True Book of Automobiles, Childrens Press, 1982.
I Can Be a Race Car Driver, Childrens Press, 1986.

"WORLD OF RACING" SERIES; JUVENILE

Formula One, Childrens Press, 1981.
Formula Atlantic, Childrens Press, 1981.
Sprint Cars, Childrens Press, 1981.
Endurance Racing (illustrated with photographs by Jan Bigelow), Childrens Press, 1981.
Stock Cars (illustrated with photographs by J. Bigelow), Childrens Press, 1981.
Super Vee (illustrated with photographs by J. Bigelow), Childrens Press, 1981.
Can-Am (illustrated with photographs by J. Bigelow), Childrens Press, 1981.
Champ Cars, Childrens Press, 1982.
Trans-Am, Childrens Press, 1983.
Karts, Childrens Press, 1985.

OTHER

Moss on the North Side (adult novel), Houghton, 1966.
A Killing Frost (adult novel), Houghton, 1967.

Cale (adult novel), Houghton, 1970.
Change (teaching handbook), LINC Press, 1971.
The Stainless Steel Carrot: An Auto Racing Odyssey, Houghton, 1973.
Shadow of the Mountain (adult novel), Houghton, 1977.
Bone of My Bones (adult novel), Putnam, 1982.
Dirt Tracks to Glory, Algonquin, 1983.

Ghost writer for a boy's adventure mystery series. Contributor to anthologies. Also contributor of articles and reviews to periodicals, including *Writer, Ingenue, Sports Car, Sports Illustrated, Mademoiselle, Auto Week, Stock Car Racing, Southern Living,* and *American Scholar.*

WORK IN PROGRESS: Lying Dog, an adult novel for Algonquin Books.

SIDELIGHTS: "When I was six, I wrote a Santa Claus poem and won a contest. The prize was a talking doll. This is the doll that Ella Ruth gets for Christmas. Oscar-Roscoe sleeping in the hole in her belly is also true. Also Saint Nick was my doll and my daddy painted her a new face. I mention these incidents to show that I use incidents and objects as 'seeds'— but they must grow away from reality if they are to work well in fiction. An event in my life has to become a memory before my imagination can act on it. Then time can strip it down to the bare impulse and make it ready to work with in fiction.

"I had two things happen as I entered junior high that determined my future. Starrie was my other self when I was a child.

Elio de Angelis drove Colin Chapman's Lotus 81 at Long Beach. ■ (From *Formula One* by Sylvia Wilkinson. Photograph courtesy of Wayne Hartman Enterprises.)

At twelve I started putting down her stories in my Blue Horse notebook. I showed some of my writings to my seventh grade teacher who told me: 'You write what I tell you to write.' I held on to my manuscript then, secretly working at night in my attic room. The next person I showed my work to was Randall Jarrell, my creative writing teacher at the University of North Carolina-Greensboro when I was twenty. He read it and said, 'Miss Wilkinson, you have a gift.' That was the happiest day of my life. I finished the book in 1965 when I was twenty-five. I published it as *Moss on the North Side.* Starrie's name was changed to Cary, a name suggested by my graduate adviser and writing teacher at Hollins, Louis Rubin, Jr., who thought (rightly) that Starrie sounded like a dream name of a romantic child. In the thirteen years from twelve to twenty-five, I wrote eleven drafts, over 800 pages, and though the characters remained the same, most of the cowboys and Indians and melodrama disappeared in revisions. Without my editor, Shannon Ravennel, I would never have gotten it into publication shape.

"In addition to my unsympathetic teacher (whom I feel was put in my life to prepare me for the critics), the other crisis at twelve was a decision I made. Daddy told me I could have a horse or continue my dancing lessons; we couldn't afford both. I took the horse. It was on horseback that I planned all my fictional adventures, partly because I was alone except for my dog and horse and partly because it gave me the feeling of being in another place and another time—like a cowboy. My

But how do you study something that cannot be touched or seen? ■ (From *The Book of the Unknown* by Harold and Geraldine Woods. Illustrated by Joe Mathieu.)

parents have always respected my privacy. I missed the dancing lessons, but the decision was the right one in another way. When I was a teenage tennis champion (of a local nature), I fell during a match and tore the tendons loose in both ankles. A doctor told me I had been born with that weakness and it had been just a matter of time until it happened.

"A big part of my motivation to be a writer came from my mother's mother, Mama George. She was a farm woman with a third-grade education from Sunday School who listened to soap operas, read newspapers and comic books. But she was a storyteller with a natural sense of form and drama. She never repeated a story and never told a dull one. I became a writer out of an oral tradition, knowing I could never equal her standards. She would start rocking in her iron porch chair and start talking. She scratched her dog's back as she talked; they looked alike, both mongrel bulldogs with crooked legs. Mama George was the inspiration for Miss Liz in *A Killing Frost,* and for every grandmother I've ever written about. Eudora Welty once said the reason the South has so many writers is because it has so many porches. I was raised on these family stories and cowboy movies, not books."

Wilkinson writes magazine articles and books on auto racing in addition to her other writing. "Racing has been with me since I was a little kid. When I received my degree from grad school, my present to myself was a sports car."[1]

"Today I make half of my income at the race track as a timer and scorer for Indy and sports car teams including Bobby Rahal, the Indy winner in 1986, the Nissan team and Paul Newman.

"Writing is not a pleasant task for me. I find myself seeking for a thousand escapes from the hard chair in front of my typewriter—partly because it requires so much mental effort and no physical activity, tying me into a nervous knot like a ten-year-old in church." Even so, writing is a compulsion with her, "I could not stop writing if I tried."

FOOTNOTE SOURCES

[1]Fran Arman, "Her Writing Career Runs at Ovals," *Akron Beacon Journal* (Ohio), July 7, 1974.

FOR MORE INFORMATION SEE:

Durham Sun, July 23, 1966.
Fred Chappell, "Unpeacable Kingdoms: The Novels of Sylvia Wilkinson," *Hollins Critic,* April, 1971 (p.1).
Authors in the News, Volume 1, Gale, 1976 (biographical; p. 497).
Jane Vance, "An Interview with Sylvia Wilkinson," *Kentucky Review,* Volume II, number 2, 1981.
J. Vance, "Fat Like Mama/Mean Like Daddy: The Fiction of Sylvia Wilkinson," *Southern Literary Journal,* fall, 1982 (p. 22).
Frank N. Magill, editor, *Critical Survey of Long Fiction,* Salem Press, 1984 (p. 2889).

WOODS, Geraldine 1948-

PERSONAL: Born September 30, 1948, in New York, N.Y.; daughter of John (a clerk) and Frances (a secretary; maiden name, Derpich) Spicer; married Harold Woods (a writer), July 15, 1972; children: Thomas Merton. *Education:* College of Mount St. Vincent, B.A., 1970. *Religion:* Roman Catholic. *Home:* 307 East 78th St., New York, N.Y. 10021. *Agent:* Meredith G. Bernstein, Henry Morrison, Inc., Box 235, Bedford Hills, N.Y. 10507.

The casket of actor John Belushi is carried from the West Tisbury Congregational Church on Martha's Vineyard. . . . ■ (From *Cocaine* by Geraldine and Harold Woods. Photograph courtesy of AP/Wide World.)

CAREER: Teacher in New York City school systems, beginning 1970—. *Awards, honors: The United Nations* and *Equal Justice* were each chosen one of Child Study Association of America's Children's Books of the Year, 1986.

WRITINGS:

JUVENILE

Jim Henson: From Puppets to Muppets, Dillon, 1987.
Spain: A Shining New Democracy, Dillon, 1987.
Science in Ancient Egypt, F. Watts, 1988.

JUVENILE; ALL WITH HUSBAND, HAROLD WOODS

Saudi Arabia, F. Watts, 1978.
Drug Use and Drug Abuse, F. Watts, 1979, revised edition, 1986.
Real Scary Sea Monsters, Shelley Graphics, 1979.
Is There Life on Other Planets?, Shelley Graphics, 1979.
Is James Bond Dead? Great Spy Stories, Shelley Graphics, 1979.
Mazes and Other Puzzles (revised edition of Walter Sheperd's *Picture Puzzles*), Shelley Graphics, 1979.
Brainticklers (revised edition of the book by Charles Booth Jones), Shelley Graphics, 1979.
Mad Mind Benders (revised edition of C. B. Jones' *Brainticklers II*), Shelley Graphics, 1979.
Magical Beasts and Unbelievable Monsters, Shelley Graphics, 1980.
The Kids' Book of Pet Care, Waldman, 1980.
The Horn of Africa: Ethiopia, Sudan, Somalia and Djibouti, F. Watts, 1980.
The Book of the Unknown (illustrated by Joe Mathieu), Random House, 1982.
(Adapters) *Tarzan of the Apes* (illustrated by Tim Gaydos), Random House, 1982.
Bill Cosby: Making America Laugh and Learn, Dillon, 1983.
The South Central States, F. Watts, 1984.
Pollution, F. Watts, 1985.
The United Nations, F. Watts, 1985.
Cocaine, F. Watts, 1985.
Equal Justice: A Biography of Sandra Day O'Connor, Dillon, 1985.
The Right to Bear Arms, F. Watts, 1986.

Co-author with H. Woods of curriculum guides for Prentice-Hall. Contributor to magazines, including *Babytalk* and *Learning Disabilities Guide.*

WORK IN PROGRESS: Two adult mystery novels with husband, Harold Woods.

SIDELIGHTS: "[My husband and I] are most interested in mystery novels as art and pleasure. We are writing a series set in New York City. The hero is an 'emotional refugee from the sixties,' just like us."

WOODS, Harold 1945-

PERSONAL: Born September 4, 1945, in New York, N.Y.; son of Harold J. (a clerk) and Esther (a cashier; maiden name,

O'Brien) Woods; married Geraldine Spicer (a writer), July 15, 1972; children: Thomas Merton. *Education:* Marist College, B.A., 1968; Manhattan College, M.A., 1978. *Religion:* Roman Catholic. *Home:* 307 East 78th St., New York, N.Y. 10021. *Agent:* Meredith G. Bernstein, Henry Morrison, Inc., Box 235, Bedford Hills, N.Y. 10507.

CAREER: High school English teacher, Scotch Plains, N.J., 1968-70; *Catholic Worker,* assistant editor, 1969-72; teacher of religion and remedial reading at a Roman Catholic high school, New York City, 1972-74; Sacred Heart of Mary High School, Bronx, N.Y., teacher of remedial reading, 1974-78; writer, 1978—. *Awards, honors: The United Nations* and *Equal Justice* were each chosen one of Child Study Association of America's Children's Books of the Year, 1986.

WRITINGS:

ALL JUVENILE; ALL WITH WIFE, GERALDINE WOODS

Saudi Arabia, F. Watts, 1978.
Drug Use and Drug Abuse, F. Watts, 1979, revised edition, 1986.
Real Scary Sea Monsters, Shelley Graphics, 1979.
Is There Life on Other Planets?, Shelley Graphics, 1979.
Is James Bond Dead? Great Spy Stories, Shelley Graphics, 1979.
Mazes and Other Puzzles (revised edition of Walter Sheperd's *Picture Puzzles*), Shelley Graphics, 1979.
Brainticklers (revised edition of the book by Charles Booth Jones), Shelley Graphics, 1979.
Mad Mind Benders (revised edition of C. B. Jones' *Brainticklers II*), Shelley Graphics, 1979.
Magical Beasts and Unbelievable Monsters, Shelley Graphics, 1980.
The Kids' Book of Pet Care, Waldman, 1980.
The Horn of Africa: Ethiopia, Sudan, Somalia and Djibouti, F. Watts, 1980.
The Book of the Unknown (illustrated by Joe Mathieu), Random House, 1982.
(Adapters) *Tarzan of the Apes* (illustrated by Tim Gaydos), Random House, 1982.
Bill Cosby: Making America Laugh and Learn, Dillon, 1983.
The South Central States, F. Watts, 1984.
Equal Justice: A Biography of Sandra Day O'Connor, Dillon, 1985.
The United Nations, F. Watts, 1985.
Pollution, F. Watts, 1985.
Cocaine, F. Watts, 1985.
The Right to Bear Arms, F. Watts, 1986.

Co-author with G. Woods of curriculum guides for Prentice-Hall. Contributor to magazines, including *Babytalk* and *Learning Disabilities Guide.*

WORK IN PROGRESS: Two adult mystery novels with wife, Geraldine Woods.

Cumulative Indexes

Illustrations Index

(In the following index, the number of the volume in which an illustrator's work appears is given *before* the colon, and the page on which it appears is given *after* the colon. For example, a drawing by Adams, Adrienne appears in Volume 2 on page 6, another drawing by her appears in Volume 3 on page 80, another drawing in Volume 8 on page 1, and another drawing in Volume 15 on page 107.)

YABC

Index citations including this abbreviation refer to listings appearing in *Yesterday's Authors of Books for Children,* also published by the Gale Research Company, which covers authors who died prior to 1960.

Author Index

The following index gives the number of the volume in which an author's biographical sketch, Brief Entry, or Obituary appears.

This index includes references to all entries in the following series, which are also published by Gale Research Company.

YABC—*Yesterday's Authors of Books for Children: Facts and Pictures about Authors and Illustrators of Books for Young People from Early Times to 1960*, Volumes 1-2

CLR—*Children's Literature Review: Excerpts from Reviews, Criticism, and Commentary on Books for Children*, Volumes 1-16

SAAS—*Something about the Author Autobiography Series*, Volumes 1-8

Author Index